# Multinational Enterprises and Tort Liabilities

CORPORATIONS, GLOBALISATION AND THE LAW

**Series Editor**: Janet Dine, *Director, Centre for Commercial Law Studies, Queen Mary College, University of London, UK*

This new and uniquely positioned monograph series aims to draw together high quality research work from established and younger scholars on what is an intriguing and under-researched area of the law. The books will offer insights into a variety of legal issues that concern corporations operating on the global stage, including interaction with WTO, international financial institutions and nation states, in both developing and developed countries. Whilst the underlying foundation of the series will be that of company law, broadly-defined, authors are encouraged to take an approach that draws on the work of other social sciences, such as politics, economics and development studies and to offer an international or comparative perspective where appropriate. Specific topics to be considered will include corporate governance, corporate responsibility, taxation and criminal liability, amongst others. The series will undoubtedly offer an important contribution to legal thinking and to the wider globalisation debate.

Titles in the series include:

Human Rights and Capitalism
A Multidisciplinary Perspective on Globalisation
*Edited by Janet Dine and Andrew Fagan*

Company Law in the New Europe
The EU *Acquis*, Comparative Methodology and Model Law
*Janet Dine, Marios Koutsias and Michael Blecher*

EU Corporate Law and EU Company Tax Law
*Luca Cerioni*

Corporate Governance and China's H-Share Market
*Alice de Jonge*

Corporate Rescue Law – An Anglo-American Perspective
*Gerard McCormack*

Multinational Enterprises and Tort Liabilities
An Interdisciplinary and Comparative Examination
*Muzaffer Eroglu*

# Multinational Enterprises and Tort Liabilities

## An Interdisciplinary and Comparative Examination

Muzaffer Eroglu

*Queen Mary, University of London, UK*

CORPORATIONS, GLOBALISATION AND THE LAW

**Edward Elgar**
Cheltenham, UK • Northampton, MA, USA

Published by
Edward Elgar Publishing Limited
The Lypiatts
15 Lansdown Road
Cheltenham
Glos GL50 2JA
UK

Edward Elgar Publishing, Inc.
William Pratt House
9 Dewey Court
Northampton
Massachusetts 01060
USA

A catalogue record for this book
is available from the British library

Library of Congress Control Number: 2008932886

ISBN 978 1 84844 031 9

Typeset by Manton Typesetters, Louth, Lincolnshire, UK
Printed and bound in Great Britain by MPG Books Ltd, Bodmin, Cornwall

*To my mother*

*(Sevgili Anneme)*

# Contents

# Figures

# Preface

When I applied to open a bank account at a branch of HSBC Bank in Turkey with a view to using it during my visit to the UK, I was told that HSBC-Turkey and HSBC-UK are different companies and thus my account would not be valid in the UK. At that moment, my curiosity about multinational enterprises began. This interest led me to conduct research on the structure and liabilities of MNEs at Queen Mary College, University of London, which is the origin of this book.

The book examines problems related to tort liabilities of multinational enterprises (MNEs). The reason for the existence of the problems is that the legal theories and practice fail to take into account interdisciplinary features of MNEs. Thus there have been no satisfactory solutions to the problem of tort liability of MNEs.

In order to understand the questions of liability, there should be an examination of the concept of multinational enterprise using interdisciplinary methodology. Thus the book, in Part I, examines the social, economic, managerial and legal characteristics of MNEs and compares the findings of this examination to the current understanding of MNEs in the way that tort liability is applied to them. It concludes that there is a conflict between the legal understanding of the structure of MNEs and contemporary realities. First, a problem arises on the application of limited liability and separate legal personality principles to MNEs. Secondly, liability theories developed within the existing system misconceptualize the organizational characteristics of MNEs; while legal practice considers MNEs as simple vertically structured organizations, an interdisciplinary examination reveals more complex horizontal structures with unique characteristics. This conflict also creates problems of liability and prevents satisfactory solutions to problems of tort liability in the context of MNEs.

In Part II, the book examines the existing laws and principles related to liability of MNEs from a variety of jurisdictions. The aim of this examination is to assess whether these laws are adequate for the challenges that modern MNEs create. The book seeks, in each chapter, to understand how groups of companies are conceived by these laws and how tort liability rules would be different if modern understandings of MNEs are applied in these cases.

In Part III, the book identifies obstacles that should be tackled to solve the problems. Finally, the book proposes solutions to the problems of tort liability of MNEs based on the findings in the first and the second parts of the book.

In the process of preparing the book, I owe the biggest thanks to Professor Janet Dine, Queen Mary, University of London, for her invaluable support during the last four years. She was more than an adviser; she gave me many opportunities and inspired me with her immense knowledge and endless energy. I also thank Professor Peter Muchlinski, School of African and Oriental Studies, University of London for introducing me to the study of MNEs. I would like to thank my PhD examiners, Professor Paddy Ireland of University of Kent and Professor Mads Andenas of Institute of Advanced Legal Studies, for agreeing to examine my PhD and particularly for their encouragement to pursue this publication.

During the writing of the book I had the chance to discuss my ideas with many people. Amongst others, I particularly thank my friends Dr Stephen Turner, Dr Olga Martin-Ortega and Dr Linda Ceraso for their support, and dinner parties in Islington restaurants, which were a great incentive to keep me going. I also thank Dr Stavros Brekoulakis, Mr Andreas Themelis and Miss Kirsteen Shields for their valuable comments on some sections of the book. I also thank my students in Queen Mary College, University of London for their contribution to the discussions.

The Institute of Advanced Legal Studies Library was not only an excellent place to conduct academic research but also a perfect place to meet academics and students from all over the world. During the last four years, I met numerous people and discussed my ideas. It is difficult to count them all, thus I would like to thank them all. With this opportunity, I would like to thank IALS library staff for their help and kindness during my research.

I thank all the staff at Edward Elgar for their assistance during the preparation of the book.

I would like to express my deep gratitude towards my mother, Mukadder Eroglu, for her love and support. I would like to thank my sisters, Gulsum Akyurek and Rahime Balci and my brothers Mehmet Eroglu and Remzi Eroglu for their support throughout all my life.

Finally, I would like to thank the Ministry of Education of Turkey for their financial support during my research, without which I would not have been able to produce this book.

The data was last updated on 31 December 2007.

Muzaffer Eroglu
Centre for Commercial Law Studies, Queen Mary, University of London

# Abbreviations

| | |
|---|---|
| AATUHK | Amme Alacaklarinin Tahsili Usulu Hakkinda Kanun |
| ATCA | Alien Tort Claims Act |
| BITs | Bilateral Investment Treaties |
| BTC | Baku-Tbilisi-Ceyhan |
| CA | Companies Act |
| CERCLA | Comprehensive Environmental Response, Compensation and Liability Act |
| CEO | Chief Executive Officer |
| CSR | Corporate Social Responsibility |
| DFID | Department for International Development |
| DTI | Department of Trade and Industry |
| EC | European Commission |
| ECJ | European Court of Justice |
| EFTA | European Free Trade Association |
| EPZ | Export Processing Zones |
| EU | European Union |
| FDI | Foreign Direct Investment |
| GATT | General Agreement on Tariffs and Trade |
| GDP | Gross Domestic Product |
| HQ | Headquarters |
| IA | Insolvency Act |
| ICC | International Chamber of Commerce |
| ICSID | International Centre for the Settlement of Investment Disputes |
| ILO | International Labor Organization |
| IMF | International Monetary Fund |
| M-form | Multi-Divisional Form |
| MNE | Multinational Enterprise |
| NAFTA | North American Free Trade Agreement |
| NGO | Non Governmental Organization |
| OECD | Organisation for Economic Co-operation and Development |
| U-form | Unitary Form |
| UN | United Nations |
| UNCTAD | United Nations Conference on Trade and Developments |
| WIR | World Investment Report |
| WTO | World Trade Organization |

# Table of cases

## THE UK

## EUROPEAN UNION



## THE USA

## AUSTRALIA



## SWITZERLAND



## INDIA



## TURKEY



## GERMANY



## FRANCE



## OTHERS

# Table of statutes, other statutory and international instruments

## THE UK



## THE USA



## EUROPEAN UNION

## TURKEY



## GERMANY



## OTHERS

# Introduction

This book examines the tort liability of multinational enterprises (MNEs). Although the discussion of liability has increased in recent decades, the laws that apply to MNEs liability cases are not sufficiently developed to offer a satisfactory solution to MNEs' tort problems. The reason for the failure to find a solution to the tort liability problems can be found in the lack of understanding of the concept of MNEs in interdisciplinary studies. Accordingly, the statement of the book is that there is a conflict between the understandings of basic features of MNEs in legal studies and the realities of the modern concept of MNEs. Thus this book aims to provide interdisciplinary examination of MNEs and test the existing liability rules to see whether they are adequate to solve the problems and, as a result, it aims to propose solutions to the liability problems in the context of MNEs. Overall, there is a quest to discover if legal theories applied to corporate groups' liability are applicable to modern MNEs and, if not, where potential solutions may lie.

## BACKGROUND TO THE CONCEPT OF MNE

The recent movement in world trade is opening up domestic markets for investors from other countries. States are liberalizing their markets by offering generous and specific investment incentives designed to attract investors. International economic theory claims that overseas investment is good for MNEs for a number of profit-creating benefits while it is good for host countries as the capital and technology brought by MNEs is crucial for the economic development of countries and regions. Accordingly, there has been a progression to a more international economic world order, creating the concept of globalization.

Economic globalization, the linked process of trade and investment liberalization, privatization and deregulation, developed on the idea of open markets has brought huge increases in movements of capital, goods and services. MNEs are the vehicles for much of these globalized economic activities, and in turn, foreign direct investment (FDI) by MNEs accounts for an increasing proportion of global economic activity.

At a global level the world economy was in constant growth, with some intervals, in the 19th and 20th centuries. There were a number of factors and actors for this growth process. One of the main factors for international economic growth was the efficiency of considering companies as centres for capital creation. This practical usage of companies was one of the important reasons for the emergence and survival of economic capitalism. In the early stages of emergence of modern market economies, the clever use of companies as a capital creating tool was very efficient at the domestic level. Companies at a domestic level transformed themselves first into corporate groups with the help of rules allowing a trouble-free approach to the emergence of corporate groups. Corporate groups accumulated huge domestic savings with the ability to use it wherever possible and whenever profitable. Thus once the groups are comparatively large, they consider investing in foreign markets. While doing this they use every power they have accumulated in order to create more beneficial business environments for themselves. The key factor in determination of the relative efficiency of foreign incorporation derives from many internal and external factors. The most important reason for FDI is the ever-growing market pressure to increase their profits.

Since the first emergence of companies with modern company laws in the middle of the 19th century, there has been constant transformation of MNEs' investment strategies and organizational structure. An interesting point in this process was that neither political nor legal developments have been able to match this dynamic self-transformation in corporate groups' structure. Consequently, MNEs have acquired unique legal and political status in the world. Presently, despite the arguments, it is true that MNEs are one of the biggest actors in both developing and developed economies. In some situations, MNEs can even be in conflict with states, the most advanced social institutions created by humankind. This modern image of the corporations has been developed since the time companies first emerged. Hobbes, who found the rise of corporations threatening to the state's authority, noted 'the great number of corporations; which are as it were many lesser commonwealths in the bowels of a greater, like worms in the entrails of a man'.[1] The difference between that time and today is the greater internationalization of corporate activities and thus the emergence of bigger and more powerful corporate groups. Accordingly, MNEs are a phenomenon of the modern world and they raise some specific economic, financial, social legal and human rights problems. Their multinational nature, their economic and legal flexibility, their massive economic and financial power and their great political and social influence are important obstacles to any attempt to apply legal control to them.

[1] Hobbes, T., *Leviathan* (1651) cited in Hill, Jennifer, 'Changes in the Role of the Shareholder' in Ross Grantham and Charlie Rickett (eds), *Corporate Personality in the 20th Century* (Hart, Oxford 1998).

Since international policy-making works to the benefit of MNEs in many senses, the power of MNEs is not entirely self-built. International organizations are helping companies to operate on a large scale; the adherence to open market economies in international economic policy-making is expanding territories with open market economies in the world. Thus the current domestic and international policies of developed economies depend on supporting more corporate activities through any means at domestic or international levels. The fierce support of privatizations and market liberalization by the International Monetary Fund (IMF) and World Bank are important factors in the expansion process of MNEs' activities. Moreover the World Trade Organization (WTO), with ever-growing members, is changing the dimensions of international dispute settlement in trade matters, which gives MNEs more power to circumvent national court systems. Furthermore there has been an enormous increase in bilateral investment treaties (BITs) in the last two decades between developed countries and developing countries. The BITs grant power to MNEs to challenge host states according to dispute settlement provisions that mostly require international arbitration. MNEs have been given permission to use international dispute settlement tribunals such as the International Centre for the Settlement of Investment Disputes (ICSID). Regional and international trade agreements are designed to reduce the level of conflict related to MNEs' activities to a minimum. In many cases, human rights, environment and even public health are considered as obstacles to international trade since any conflicts under these concerns are considered a deterrent to MNEs. Thus this immense power of MNEs, the aid of some of the chief world powers and the complicity of many governments, have made it possible for them to interlink the basic norms that are contrary to the national and international public law in force, in the shape of BITs for the protection of foreign investments and regional agreements such as the North American Free Trade Agreement (NAFTA).[2]

The complex appearance of MNEs in the world economy provoked a good deal of criticism. MNEs are accused of causing serious harm to the people of the world and exploiting national economies and societies and even undermining democracy. In reaction to these problems, some people and countries demanded abandonment of MNEs' activities in their territories. On the other hand, most of the less-developed countries try to attract those companies to invest in their territories because MNEs are considered a basic source of technology, employment and capital and thus as main actors in economic development for their societies. This creates a dilemma, on the one hand, countries want to attract

2 Some UN reports point out these facts. See at UN, Economic and Social Council, 'Adverse Effects of the Illicit Movement and Dumping of Toxic and Dangerous Products and Wastes on the Enjoyment of Human Rights' (E/CN.4/2001/55, 19 January 2001).

more FDIs by giving economic and legal incentives but on the other hand, they have to protect their citizens against any breach of law and torts committed by MNEs.

It is not easy to attract MNEs to any territory; successful FDI attraction needs a very favourable scheme of economic and legal incentives. Sometimes exemption from liability for the breach of some basic human rights could be possible. In many countries, governments bend or remove their own labour and environmental legislation to allow MNEs a freer hand, or turn a blind eye to violations. States, such as Sri Lanka, have created export processing zones (EPZ), within which the state allows a separate system of law or waivers of national law. At worst MNEs and governments actively collude to operate profitable national sources; MNEs ignore abuses made by states in order to create better operating conditions, or even worse they demand any protest or civil activity be stopped at any cost. In many cases MNEs prefer less-developed countries as a primary place of investments to escape strict safety, labour and environmental regulations in developed countries. For example, San Diego based Sempra Energy decided to build its new natural gas-fired power plant just over the border in Mexico in order to avoid stringent air quality regulations in southern California and escape from completing detailed environmental impact statements.[3] As a result, MNEs have acquired strong economic power and they are one of the centres of policy-making in the world. The effects of MNEs are felt at every level of society from the bottom to the top, which makes examination of MNEs as international economic, social and legal institution a necessity.

In a legal examination one will see that, while all these developments are taking place in the world, the general principles of company law, which are applied to MNEs, have not changed since its first emergence. Companies were considered basic institutional forms to convince people to invest and to create a cumulative capital to make the necessary investment required for large-scale economic activities. For this reason shareholders were granted immunity of liability to convince them to invest their capital. This immunity later was also given to corporate shareholders, which altered the area of corporate law fundamentally and irrevocably.

Thus the broad ranges of economic incentives given by countries are just the tip of a huge iceberg. The real incentives lie under the structure of law of developed countries, which are transplanted by many developing and less-developed countries because MNEs and governments in developed countries as well as international financial organizations first demand a modern company law in a

---

[3] Ross, J.P., 'Sempra: Exporting Pollution, U.S.-Mexico Border Region to Pay the Price for California's Power' at http://www.corpwatch.org/article.php?id=2588 accessed 20 June 2006.

country eager to attract FDI. It is interesting for example in even such small and politically conflicted countries or territories, such as Kosovo, there is a push to legislate modern company laws, even though these communities have virtually no international trade yet. Moreover big economic powers, such as China and Russia, had to change their company laws to western style company laws to attract more investments in their territory. There are also ongoing efforts in Turkey to change company law, which is already western, to make it more modern and up to date.

In contrast to slow developments within the law, in the area of MNE in economics and management, there have been huge dynamics inside MNEs to change their own structures. While economic activity in the 19th century was growing at domestic and international levels, there was a need for better-organized institutions. This gap was filled by allowing corporations to have shares in other corporations. The result was the emergence of corporate groups in domestic business while MNEs took their place in the international business world. Accordingly the organization grew gradually while changing its structure over time to adopt better and more competitive business environments. There have been many attempts to understand basic operative and managerial structures of the MNEs. This has created a special area of studies in economic and managerial fields.

This complex structure gives grounds for more sophisticated problems in the area of MNEs, which is still mostly regulated by the rigid principles of company law settled in the 19th century. Thus there is always a claim that MNEs are primarily governed by the national legislation of the countries in which they operate. However, national legislations in developing countries are weak or they do not have the political will or technical know-how to enforce liability. Moreover, corporations' headquarters are increasingly located in one country, where they are registered, with sourcing or production networks linking them to subsidiaries in another country or countries, while they have share listing on several stock exchanges. They can move money around and within the enterprise, relocate their headquarters and subsidiaries in response to changing legal and social environments, and play one government off against another to obtain more favorable tax and regulatory treatment. Under these conditions, being regulated by host states does not increase the level of liability of MNEs but gives them power to manipulate the countries' fragile legal systems. As a result this complicated structure of the international economy puts MNEs in positions of extraordinary power and equally extraordinary lack of accountability to anyone or any authority except their shareholders. Accordingly the directors can always legitimate their decisions by claiming they have a duty to produce the best for the shareholders. Under these conditions, the only aim would be to maximize profit whatever it costs to outsiders of the company.

## MULTINATIONAL ENTERPRISE TORTS

While aiming at profit maximization, MNEs are not reluctant to use any possible incentives offered to them or any gap in the law. Current structures of company law offer many gaps in this sense; the businesses might use shell companies in order to escape from liability. Moreover at the international level, the corporation might divide up its assets to many locally operating subsidiaries while escaping overall group liability. Not surprisingly these problems of company laws' ability to regulate MNEs are not unknown at governmental and international organization levels.

One particular problem MNEs create is of the utmost importance and thus will be the centre of discussion in this book. With developments in the global economy and MNEs' transformation, other global common characteristics of the international economy have emerged, the globalization of corporate victims. In recent decades the world witnessed the global phenomenon of corporate torts. MNEs have been involved in mass tort actions in various parts of the world and mostly escaped justice easily. With the campaigns of non-governmental organizations (NGOs), the dark side of the global economic order has been revealed. It has become usual to witness a new example of corporate torts on a daily basis. These torts were more severe and common in less-developed countries. But it is also common to see the same level of corporate tort in developed countries. Some incidents have attracted worldwide publicity while many others were simply forgotten thanks to the difficulty in bringing a tort action against MNEs.

The cases for corporate torts vary from country to country according to their economic and social characteristics; in less-developed countries there is usually collusion between the state and MNEs. In severe cases MNEs are ignoring safety and environmental regulations causing many injuries and deaths. In developed countries, since the law is more developed, MNEs use the legal incentives given by company law statutes by dividing their entity into many sub-units to escape possible lawsuits. Yet despite this surge in interest in corporate tort responsibilities, there remain certain important countervailing factors. The most important among these is the disagreement between the objects and practice of globalization of tort victims, and that of economic globalization on the other. Certainly international trade law essentially grants numerous rights to MNEs and very few enforceable duties, and few if any significant rights in respect of tort victims.

What is interesting in this sense is the lack of action taken by states to create improvements in this situation. It is somehow understandable for less-developed countries to ignore most of the allegations in order not to lose investments but developed countries also take no action. There is hardly any effort by parliaments to change the current situation and courts do not try hard enough to create better regulations. Instead, with the efforts of NGOs, the existing laws, such as the Alien Tort Claims Act (ATCA), are usually stretched in an attempt to impose tort liability on MNEs.

Accordingly there are a number of obstacles that prevent justifiable solutions to MNEs' torts; from current legal systems to negative campaigns run by MNEs. There is a political unwillingness in less-developed countries not to scare MNEs. Moreover there might be collusion between MNEs and governments in less-developed countries so states are not willing to enforce existing laws and often pass laws which actively exempt MNEs from their national legal systems, often under pressure from their own economic needs. In developing countries the laws and models of the legal system, originating from the developed countries, where the companies have their centres, are weighting the system towards the already powerful. Thus both home and host countries' legal systems are not efficient enough to solve the problems.

Therefore MNEs escape from possible lawsuits with reverse forum-shopping, where the accused corporation fights to have a case refused in a country favourable to the complainants (usually the home country) and to get it returned to a location favourable to itself (usually the host country). This is the first strategy carried out by MNEs when faced with tort claims under home countries' laws. They use a number of gaps in private international law to reverse cases back to their origin where they are likely to remain unsolved. The cases that have overcome forum problems will have to struggle with the corporate veil and hidden ambiguities in the nationality of MNEs and the separation of identities of the parent company and the subsidiaries, created by MNEs to enable them to escape legal responsibility in any country where they operate.

There are a number of other factors that prevent liability; any small achievement at international level in creating better liability will be blocked by poor implementation mechanisms in most international regulatory instruments, if they are not already weakened by commitment to the voluntary regulations under corporate social responsibility (CSR) initiatives. Moreover internal codes of conduct allow corporations to claim to be good while not imposing any legal obligations on them, and so do not address the claims of MNEs' victims. Additionally the system of out of court settlement is giving rights to companies to avoid having an effective ruling on certain issues; in a number of recent cases even though MNEs argue that they are not liable, they settled cases so that substantial grounds for future claims have been prevented.[4] These problems are

---

[4] According to the report in the *Guardian* (www.guardian.co.uk/burma, and the *Guardian,* 15 December 2004) there was an out of court settlement between the energy MNE Unocal and Burmese villagers. The villagers claimed the company's Yadana pipeline has led to deaths, rapes and the disruption of their lives. The amount of compensation is not disclosed. The lawsuit was launched in 1996; the action was brought to California

not independent from each other and some of them are basic law problems while some of them are related mostly to the political preference of the countries.

## IDENTIFYING THE LEGAL PROBLEMS

In this book the discussion will concentrate on the core-law issues, mainly jurisdictional problems and company law problems. Leaving aside more social-political arguments, the focus of this book will be on the legal obstacles for creating MNEs' tort liability as the legal structure of corporate groups makes it possible for them to easily evade liability. This situation has been praised by many business and economic commentators for its success in raising capital through granting immunity from liability. This aspect was reflected very dramatically in a newspaper report. An American MNE, Halliburton, has settled asbestos claims for $5 billion. The interesting and important remark in this report is this part: 'Halliburton has won praise on Wall Street for the way it dealt with an issue that could have led to its demise. By separating the oil business from the other subsidiaries, it was able to protect itself from lawsuits and built up cash to pay a settlement.'[5]

Accordingly MNEs' gift of spreading power, their capacity to be present in several parts of the world and nowhere at the same time, allows them to avoid national jurisdictions. The unique characteristic of MNEs' structures together with private international law and company law makes access to justice in MNEs' tort situation very problematic. The treatment of foreign subsidiaries of MNEs as independent legal persons separate from a sophisticatedly structured group, results in a situation that victims of these subsidiaries might bring their legal actions only against torts committed by the subsidiary in its own jurisdiction.

Limited liability and separate legal personality, which first emerged as a capital-raising tool in the simple form of a company, is now used as a liability evading tool for corporate groups. Thus in a simple evaluation of limited liability, it will be seen that limited liability almost grants a company more rights than private property grants since private property owners are liable for the damage that is caused by the misuse of property. For example where a house or car causes damage to people, there is full liability of owners for compensation but if a company causes the same injury and goes bankrupt because of the

using the ATCA. There were US governmental fears that, if the action succeeded, it could lead to a flood of similar claims by indigenous people whose lands had been used for pipelines or oil drilling carried out by multinationals.

[5] The *Daily Telegraph* (London, 5 January 2005).

consequences, shareholders are liable for not more than they invested in the company. While all these negative sides of corporate law and private international law were being misused by MNEs to escape from liability, responses by law-makers to corporate groups' challenges were at a minimum level and in very specific circumstances. Both actors of law-making (courts and parliaments) have failed to give immediate and satisfactory responses to these unfair situations. Responses were mostly related to corporate groups' laws without a comprehensive examination of MNEs, thus they failed to create significant change in the current situation related to MNEs' tort liability.

Given the characteristics of MNEs, the expectations at international and national level of regulations are high but there have been different approaches to the issues. Regulators prefer to create CSR initiatives or guidelines, which do not have a clear enforcement mechanism.[6] While at a regional level, the EU, even though it was expected to be creative, considered the issues in a narrow sphere of company and group of companies' law.

Regulatory efforts have been concentrated on the issues mostly relevant to the practical operational environments of MNEs, rather than liability issues. Thus most of the efforts related to groups of companies were in favour of MNEs' activities or related to public law issues, such as tax law. At a global level, ideally, an international legal framework or convention is needed to discuss the activities of MNEs and to help encourage legislation at national level, but none has been drafted. However, it would be unfair to claim there have been no regulatory efforts for corporate tort liability; there have been some efforts, which tried to hold corporate groups directly liable for their torts by a different model of laws to create some sort of liability regime in the corporate groups' context. However, those efforts, either in statutory law or in case law, have been weak and inefficient.

## ORIGINS OF TORT LIABILITY PROBLEMS WITHIN CORPORATE GROUPS

Origins of the liability discussions lie within the main principles of company laws, which are based on the concept of separate legal personality of company and limited liability of shareholders. Under the theory of limited liability, shareholders have no obligations to the company or its creditors beyond their

[6] For example the EU considers voluntary corporate social responsibility initiatives as an effective tool to prevent human rights breaches of MNEs. See Green Paper 'Promoting a European Framework for Corporate Social Responsibility' COM (2001) 366 final, 18.7.2001.

obligations on the par value of their shares, or under their guarantee in the case of a company limited by guarantee. It is assumed that a company is a distinct economic unit, which enjoys economic and managerial independence, and therefore must be considered as a legal person separate from its members. The separate legal personality theory is applied to all companies regardless of their shareholders. Thus the theory covers sole trader companies and wholly owned subsidiaries of MNEs. Under this traditional rule of corporation, a subsidiary corporation's liability is also limited to the amount of its shareholders' investment, and the parent or any other company under the group cannot be held liable for the subsidiary's non-performed obligations.

In the beginning companies aimed to collect money from individuals since in early corporate history acquiring shares of another corporation was not approved by the courts. However, this rule changed dramatically after the acceptance of dropping all restrictions on acquiring shares in another company. The next stage then, with the emergence of corporate groups, was the discussion of whether limited liability protects the component companies of the new corporate groups in addition to the investors in the enterprise. *Salomon v Salomon & Co Ltd*[7] brought about the situation that incorporators of a company could structure its capital so as to minimize their risk of the company's failure. There is no requirement that the investment of the incorporators in a company must necessarily to a significant extent be in the form of equity. Hence separate legal personality meant just that, and it follows from this that a corporation is separate from its members and as such the latter not liable for its debts. This decision showed its effect for all corporations including corporate groups. Accordingly under traditional corporate law each component corporation of the group, whether parent, subsidiary or affiliate, for legal purposes was still separate and distinct from every other corporation in the group, and its rights and responsibilities were divorced from those of the other constituent companies of the group. For that reason, although the companies in the group, unlike its public shareholder-investors, were parts of the enterprise and engaged in the daily run of business, limited liability also insulated them from liability for the activities of its subsidiary companies because it was not discussed deeply and the simple logic determined the situation that limited liability protects shareholders, a corporation is a shareholder of the subsidiary, and therefore limited liability protects the shareholder corporation.[8]

---

7 [1897] AC 22 HL.

8 Blumberg argues that limited liability of corporate groups, one of the most important legal rules in modern economic systems, appears to have emerged as a 'historical accident'. See Blumberg, P.I., *The Multinational Challenge to Corporation Law* (OUP, Oxford 1993) p.57.

Accordingly, a typical group of companies constitutes an economic unit, which is divided into a great number of legal units, for purposes of exploiting any possible convenience and benefit. The limited liability company theory ignores contemporary economic realities because parent companies and their subsidiaries are collectively conducting a common enterprise. An MNE may have hundreds of subsidiaries around the world and each subsidiary may operate under its host country's regulatory arrangement, but in practical terms they operate in accordance with the main economic and managerial policies of the group. Therefore there is a compound multinational enterprise structure under which, according to law, companies are independent from each other, but, on the other hand, according to economic realties, they are entirely interrelated.

The attraction of a subsidiary is that the combination of legal personality and limited liability enables its controller to separate an area of activity, or particular assets, and to control the subsidiary's legal relationship with the wider organization because the law has given little recognition to the essential differences between subsidiaries and freestanding companies. There is an effective shifting of risk from the controllers and owners to the creditors of a subsidiary resulting from its separate legal personality. The control of shares by another company is not only control but also brings subsidiaries under common group management systems. Here the problems arise, as unlike the individual majority shareholders, the common management system may have a reason to direct the subsidiary to act contrary to its own interest and may even put its existence in danger. Thus there can be use of main corporate law theories to clearly further legitimate goals or possible abuse of corporate structure to avoid social conflict and corporate liability.

As a result of current case law, in order to make parent companies liable the plaintiffs would have to overcome the reluctance of the common law of tort to make one person responsible for the acts of another. English law offers virtually no prospect of success against parent companies on the basis of vicarious liability in the light of the Court of Appeal's approach to corporate personality in the *Adams v Cape Industries*[9] case by stating that 'each company in a group of companies … is a separate legal entity possessed of separate rights and liabilities'. Therefore it is logical to claim that adherence to limited liability in corporate groups is a common characteristic of modern laws.

9 [1990] 2 WLR 786.

## EXISTING LAWS REGARDING LIABILITY OF CORPORATE GROUPS AND BRIEF EXPOSITION OF UNDERSTANDINGS OF THE THEORY OF CONTROL

It is apparent that the unfair effects of limited liability in a corporate group context have forced courts to search for alternative ways to reduce these unjust effects. For this purpose, plaintiffs will be able to base their argument on theories for the liability of parent corporations and search for existing liability under tort law, corporate law and the existing case law, which are mainly based on the piercing the corporate veil (veil lifting) doctrine. The real function of the doctrine is to fill the gap in common law doctrines that statutory rules cannot resolve effectively.

The application of the veil piercing principles by the courts showed different features during the past century and it differs from one jurisdiction to another. Sometimes courts forced the boundaries of established rigid principles of company law; but mostly the result of the cases in which disregarding of the corporate veil was demanded was simply a repetition of *Salomon* principles. The courts have never taken an evolutionary step in creating alternatives as they did when establishing the principle of separate corporate personality in *Salomon*.

The main problem of veil piercing theory is its dependency on the control theory which makes its application very weak and rare. In order to establish liability on a group basis for certain behaviours, one needs to prove the existence of control of the parent over the subsidiary and intent of misuse of the relationship between subsidiary and other companies in the group. In practice, control is applied by powers of decision-making. The most striking conclusion from the liability principles created by courts for groups of companies is that generally the corporate veil will not be pierced unless the corporate shareholder dominates the corporate subsidiary and the corporate shareholder has engaged in a fraudulent or illegal conduct or other improper conduct, which has resulted in an injustice.

Therefore liability applied or suggested was based on a simplified formula, which considered corporate groups as vertically organized institutions, thus the control theory was one-way control applied by parent companies over subsidiaries. In cases of a horizontally structured MNEs group, the control theory is inapplicable. Thus the control theory is much more suited to vertically organized corporate groups under which the divisions between subsidiaries and the parent is more apparent and the parent exercises some level of control over its subsidiaries. Plaintiffs are required to prove the excessive control of parents over their subsidiaries. This requires a very detailed fact specific inquiry and thus is almost impossible to prove in the modern structure of corporate groups.

This misunderstanding has caused another negative result in that there have never been real discussions or applications of group liability; rather parent-subsidiary liability has been considered as the only possible way of establishing liability in corporate groups' context. Accordingly, there is a starting presumption of separateness between the parent and subsidiaries, which flows from basic legal doctrines of corporate law. On the other side of the conflict, the plaintiff has to try to overturn this presumption by showing complete control of the parent over subsidiaries. In this stage, there are other assumptions about the nature of control in corporate groups; veil lifted only where there's a clear single decision-making centre exercising complete control over subsidiaries, otherwise subsidiaries are held as a separate entity.

The reason for this failure could be found under the conception of MNEs in a legal world under which corporate groups have been traditionally considered as having one central decision-making body. Accordingly, in a group situation when one of the companies in the group has fallen under the control of the parent, the regulators incline to make the controller liable for the torts of the controlled company. Therefore the courts were never inventive beyond the theory of veil piercing, which has very strict conditions. Mostly theories related to veil piercing, developed for small companies, tried to be applied in the corporate group context. Eventually it was almost impossible to demonstrate and prove the strict requirements of veil piercing in corporate groups. Thus the efforts to extend veil piercing theory to corporate groups have failed.

In consideration of the piercing the corporate veil theory from a broader perspective, such an inadequately developed and complex structure of case law, even incapable of creating solutions for a private, one-man limited company, cannot be applied in modern times to corporate groups, particularly to MNEs with complex horizontal structure. Thus it is difficult to apply piercing the veil principles in subsidiaries' torts since there is no easy proof of control of one particular entity over another. This lack of modern and comprehensive understandings of groups of companies, especially from the perspective of MNEs, prevents scholars, practitioners, courts and parliaments from developing satisfactory regulations. This leads to the ensuing examination of the business management structure of MNEs.

## THE CENTRAL DISCUSSION OF THE BOOK

The book makes two major points. The first is that key elements of the existing law on MNE group structures are based upon a particular understanding of the nature of those structures. Particularly, the way in which central control is exercised is based on the system of vertical structures. This understanding is increasingly at odds with their real nature under which control is increasingly being exercised in a different, decentralized way. Hence there is a need for the law to take account of management literature which tracks changing nature and management of MNEs. In other words central authority and control in MNEs is not exercised in the way that the law implicitly assumes it is. Legal understandings of the nature of control based on the idea of a central command centre are simplistic and outdated.

The second point is a wider point about the disagreement there has always been between the legal structures of MNEs and their real nature. In legal theory, there is the idea of groups as made up of lots of formally separate entities. However, the economic business structure of MNEs reflects a different and more single enterprise structure for MNEs. In short the idea of separate corporate personality was not developed with either one-man companies or groups of companies in mind. Therefore this point reveals a wider problem which goes to the heart of company law, theory of separate corporate personality.

Accordingly these problems should be examined in detail and solutions should be suggested by considering the findings. The solution to the problem of misconception of control, from this perspective, is simply for the law to adopt a new and more appropriate conception of control. The second point seems to imply a much more fundamental legal reform, involving the questioning of the whole idea of a separate corporate personality as it applies to groups.

Interestingly academic discussions in the area of corporate groups' liability were somehow successful in pointing out the problems of the application of limited liability in corporate groups' context and thus evasion of liability against involuntary creditors. However, the solutions suggested were mostly short and unconvincing due to misinterpretation of economic and managerial characteristics of MNEs. Suggestions offered by academia have never been adequately creative to be considered as alternatives. The failure was due to lack of interdisciplinary examination in the area of MNEs' activities and thus misinterpretation of the way control by one entity over another in MNEs is used. There has always been a belief in the simple top to bottom control since they have never gone beyond the theory of a firm to develop a theory of a multinational enterprise.

Accordingly there is a requirement that MNEs must be examined from interdisciplinary perspectives in order to create better regimes of liability for MNEs' tort; there must be extensive efforts to discover what the basic theories behind the structure of MNEs are. This examination should cover economic, social, organizational and legal areas. When applying these requirements into the current book, the future of MNEs tort liability must be discussed from two perspectives, first there must be an examination of basic economic, managerial, social and legal characteristics of MNEs and, secondly, the existing regulations must be tested to see if they are efficient enough to meet the challenges. As a result, suggestions on MNEs' liability must be built on the results of extensive interdisciplinary and comparative methods.

This book aims to indicate the social, economic and organizational characteristics of MNEs. The purpose is to evaluate how different MNEs are conceived in other disciplines and how this perception of MNEs in legal discipline and practice has been absorbed. While doing this there will be indication of theories developed by legal practice in order to solve liability problems in the context of groups of companies. The concentration will be on the perception of MNEs' structure in legal theory and the liability theories developed on this perception, namely the theory of control in MNEs' management structure.

The idea of removal of separate legal personality in the corporate groups' context goes beyond the discussion of tort liability because it covers liabilities that arise from any activities of MNEs. Thus even though much of the analysis in this book can be interpreted as evidence to support the abolishment of separate legal personalities in the corporate groups' context, the central discussion is built on the quest to demonstrate problems regarding the tort liability of MNEs and to focus on the efficiency of existing law and principles.

## STRUCTURE OF THE BOOK

In order to bring modern interdisciplinary understandings of MNEs together with legal disciplines and to create modern proposals for MNEs' tort liability, the book is divided into three parts and eight chapters.

The first part of the book will be devoted to the examination of the basic social, economic, managerial and legal characteristics of MNEs under the title of 'Concept of Multinational Enterprise'. The aim of the part is to designate the basic feature of MNEs as unique institutions. The weakness of legal theory and regulations applied to MNEs will be better understood and this interdisciplinary examination will identify the basic theoretical problems in the area of tort liability of MNEs.

I wish to give some conceptual characteristics of MNEs in order to explain why they need special examination and draw conceptual limits of the MNEs for the present book. In a short explanation, the origin of contemporary conceptions of the MNEs lies in the belief that this modern, large-scale capitalist enterprise is a unique phenomenon, different in class from earlier business organizations such as the partnership and the small firm. Therefore this new phenomenon needs special examination in order to designate the differences from the patterns of small firms' limited models. These differences occur in economic, social, organizational and legal characteristics of MNEs. Economic, organizational and social differences, to the necessary extent, will be examined in order to create a better understanding of the legal regulations and proposed solutions to the liability problems of MNEs.

An MNE has two distinctive economic features. First it organizes and coordinates multiple value-adding activities across national boundaries and, secondly, it internalizes the cross-border markets for the intermediate products arising from these activities. Therefore it is different since no other institution engages in both cross-border production and transactions. Moreover MNEs are different from government and international organizations in that the management of MNEs is not concerned with the development targets of individual nation-states, regions or territories; in contrast, circumstances and country-specific economic policies of nations determine the outcome of relations with MNEs.

MNEs also distinguish themselves from other types of business enterprises by their main characteristic feature that, as parent companies, they exercise control over subsidiary firms that are scattered over several states. In other words although there are legally independent organizations under the group, the parent company exercises strict control over the subsidiaries. However, this excessive exercise of control and unique organization of MNEs have undergone changes in the last 30 years. The changes have taken place in the structure of MNEs towards less-hierarchically structured organizations under which the power of the parent companies has considerably reduced and the organizations have gone in the direction of decentralization. However, the fact of being a unique phenomenon under this new organizational structure still apparently exists, even making the phenomenon more interesting to conduct a study on.

The idea of what an MNE consists of is also a challenge for scholars so the limits of the study must be illustrated from this perspective. There is an overwhelming agreement in academia that minority joint ventures, co-operative alliances and networking relationships with other organizations should be considered as part of an MNE's sphere of influence because these kinds of relationships may give them some degree of control under an organizational structure or influence over the foreign companies associated with these organizations. There will be limited examination of networked enterprises in order to grasp the current discussion, and to prepare the ground for future MNEs' studies. However, leaving further research to another study, the present book covers the liability arising from the ownership relationships under groups of companies. In other words, the examination will be based on the legal bodies under the group that are tied to each other with ownership relationships (joint-stock MNEs); the ownership could be full, part or cross-ownership.

At this stage, I wish to draw attention to the fact that in the history of ideas, attempts have been made to conceptualize the phenomena that MNEs create. The phenomena were regarded as new without realizing that both the phenomena and their images themselves undergo changes in time. This applies evidently to the concept of the MNEs. Therefore one should bear in mind that MNEs are neither homogeneous in function nor consistent in character over time. This obliges researchers to undertake further studies over time considering new developments and adopting them into established theories in the area. Since it is the contemporary MNEs' organizations that are under critical examination, the present work claims to have special characteristics.

Chapter 1 will be an examination of social and economic characteristics of MNEs in parallel with the MNEs' emergence and maturing process from social and economic perspectives. There will be a search for where MNEs stand in current social-economic orders and how they operate. This examination will contribute to understanding the reasons for cross-border investments in the historical order. The process will be examined together with FDI movements and there will be a quest to discover the rationale behind the investment theory by simply asking why MNEs invest. Moreover the better understanding of FDI movement and growing direction of MNE developments will help to understand why there are liability problems related to the activities of MNEs. More importantly, this part of the study will enable better examination of the efficiency arguments of limited liability theory as it is considered to be the primary trigger for investment for companies. This examination will contribute to the discussion of tort liability by pointing out the basic social-economic characteristics of MNEs; the aim is to indicate that different social-economic characteristics need different laws and regulations.

The second chapter will be an examination of the organizational structures of MNEs under which there will be a close look at MNEs from the inside. The structural differences in organization of MNEs will be under historical, critical and explanatory examination. The basic features of managerial organizational structure of MNEs will be examined and later concentration will be on contemporary corporate structures. This examination will be vital for illustrating the need to move from the classical understanding of MNEs' structures in applicable law and proposed regulations. While doing this, some examples of structures of modern MNEs will be demonstrated. The main reason for examining the organizational structural developments lies behind the fact that as a social institution the regulation of liability of MNEs should be structured according to their organizational structure. MNEs shall be considered as an institution that has certain characteristics which define them and make them different from any other institution in society, such as company, trust or international economic organizations. In particular this book discusses the liability issues arising from MNEs' activities; in reality there have been many studies in the examination of multinational corporate groups and liability arising from their tortious actions. The past studies, in legal approach, have not taken horizontally structured MNEs into their main discussion. Therefore, this book will take these new developments as its main focus of research. In short, this managerial organizational examination has key importance for two reasons: first, the complex structure of MNEs prevents any liability theories and laws to be applied in MNEs torts. Secondly, the future law and theories must be built by considering the current characteristics of the structure of MNEs.

The third chapter of the book will be an examination of the legal theory behind MNEs' regulations and liabilities. This examination will be entirely devoted to understanding the legal evolution with the developments under the case and statutory law. Limited liability and corporate separate legal personality principles will be at the centre of the examination. The aim of this examination is to prove the inefficiency of current legal regulations, which are dependent on historical case and statutory law. Accordingly the efficiency of limited liability will be discussed under this chapter in order to indicate the conceptual differences between a limited liability company and a limited liability MNE. The examination will be historical; first the emergence of corporate groups and, secondly, an evaluation process of corporate personality and limited liability will be conducted. The difference between individual and corporate shareholders will be identified. The deficiencies in the legal structure will be identified in order to understand the origins of the legal problems and pave the way to offer efficient liability regimes.

As a result the combination of economical, social, organizational and, finally, legal examination, in the first part of the book, will provide a broader understanding of the concept of MNEs and provide a genuine and efficient background for regulatory efforts. With this examination, I aim to show that MNEs are representatives of the global economic order; their operational and organizational features are almost the same all over the world. The laws of national states differ as the social, cultural and traditional features of national states are different. However, it will be seen that in terms of MNEs' operations, the differences amongst national states are becoming increasingly insignificant.

In Part II of the book, I will examine the existing laws and principles that apply to tort liability of MNEs under the title of 'Exploring the Tort Liability of MNEs'. There will be examination of how the modern structure of MNEs creates obstacles to solving tort liability. Principles created by courts or parliaments or suggestions made by academics will be examined by asking if they match the demands to bring interdisciplinary approaches to MNEs' tort liability discussions or not.

Jurisdictional problems of imposing MNEs' liabilities will be examined in Chapter 4. Multi-jurisdictional characteristics of MNEs cause certain difficulties in establishing liability on MNEs. The importance of jurisdictional obstacles to imposing tort liability will be the beginning of the discussion. The so-called *forum non conveniens* theory and further obstacles will be examined by giving examples from English and American jurisdictions. Next, suggested solutions to the jurisdictional problems will be discussed. As it is presented, in recent years, as an important development in creating liability, the Alien Torts Claims Act will be examined in detail. As in other parts of the book, the examination of jurisdictional problems and suggested solutions will be comparative and interdisciplinary by questioning how current laws meet the challenges.

In Chapter 5, tort liabilities of MNEs in case law will be under critical examination. The problems in case law will be indicated by centralizing the arguments under the theory of piercing the corporate veil. The aim of the chapter will be to test the efficiency of the regulations and principles by asking whether they offer justified meaning of tort liability or not. The efficiency of the theory in application to modern MNEs will be tested and suggested solutions will be made.

In Chapter 6, comparative statutory and examples laws and principles regarding corporate groups' liability will be examined. Assessment will range from UK laws to some examples from the US, as well as approaches in EU law which will also be discussed. Moreover individual efforts from Germany and Turkey will be examined and further reference to laws from other jurisdictions will be made. The examination in this chapter will go beyond the tort liability discussions to groups' liability discussions in various branches of law in order to evaluate and compare the findings to theories developed for tort liabilities. The aim of this chapter is to discover the approaches of law-makers to the problem of groups of companies and MNEs liability and compatibility of these examples with interdisciplinary features of MNEs. These examinations are important for two reasons. First, it will demonstrate the efficiency of existing laws to create tort liabilities. Secondly, it will create a ground for suggestions that will be made in the third part of the book.

In Chapter 7, liability solutions beyond the corporate group liability discussion will be examined. There will be a quest to specify options to solve the liability problems in other areas of commercial law. However, I will put the self-regulation and corporate social responsibility discussions at the centre of the discussion. Particularly, voluntary regulatory options will be looked at from efficiency perspectives by testing their enforcement mechanism by centralizing the discussion on the issue of 'binding versus voluntary' regulation.

Part III of the book, Chapter 8, will examine how and on which criteria the future of MNEs' liability must be built. First, there will be a quest to find out what the obstacles to imposing better developed liability rules on MNEs are. The mistakes made during the history of regulations will be examined by comparing them to the findings of the previous parts of this book. Finally the book concludes by putting combined suggested solutions which are based on results of examinations made in the previous chapters.

# PART I

# Concept of multinational enterprise

# 1. Social and economic analysis of multinational enterprises

## INTRODUCTION

A multinational enterprise can be defined as an enterprise that has affiliates in more than one country. On the other hand, an MNE, in a strictly legal sense, can be defined as a collection of corporate entities, each having its own juridical identity and national origin, but each in some way connected by a system of centralized management and control, normally exercised from the seat of primary ownership.[1] This definition does not exist in any statute or in any official documents.

According to some researchers, MNEs have existed since ancient times.[2] They come to the conclusion, after researching ancient business history that MNEs were actively operating in the times of Roman, Greek, Mesopotamian and Anatolian civilizations. The first recorded MNEs appeared in the Old Assyrian Kingdom shortly after 2500 BC, when Sumerian merchants found in their foreign commerce that they needed men stationed abroad to receive, to store and to sell their goods. The researchers found that the MNEs of ancient times have some similar characteristics to contemporary MNEs. On the other hand, some other researchers find the forerunners of MNEs in medieval times in chartered trading colonizing enterprises.[3] For example the East India Company, chartered in London in 1600, established overseas branches. In the mid-17th century, English, French and Dutch merchant families sent relatives to America and to the West Indies to represent their firms. So too, in time, American colonists found in their own foreign trade that it was desirable to have correspondents, agents, and, on circumstance, branches in vital trading

---

1 Wallace, C.D., *The Multinational Enterprises and Legal Control Host State Sovereignty in an Era of Economic Globalisation* (Martinus Nijhoff, London 2002), p. 9.

2 Moore, Karl, *Birth of the Multinational: 2000 Years of Ancient Business History, from Ashur to Augustus* (Zed Books, London 1999).

3 Hertner, Peter and Jones, Geoffrey (eds), *Multinationals: Theory and History* (Gower, Aldershot 1986) p. 1.

centres to warehouse and to sell American exports.[4] These early-chartered companies can be regarded as symbolic predecessors of the modern MNEs.[5]

However, for the purpose of this book, there is not any practical reason to examine ancient business history; rather the focus must be on the modern MNEs and their historical development. Although earlier MNEs shared certain features with the modern MNEs, the evolution of the modern MNE dates back approximately to the last half, or more accurately the last quarter of the nineteenth century.[6] However, it must be stressed that the modern MNE is not a post World War Two phenomenon in contrast to common public belief.

## HISTORY OF FOREIGN DIRECT INVESTMENT AND EMERGENCE OF MNES

Firms from Europe and North America began to invest in overseas plantations, mines, factories, banking, sales and distribution amenities in large numbers in the first half of the 19th century.[7] This resulted in a significant growth in the size and number of firms, which can be considered early forerunners of modern MNEs, but these companies cannot be, in actual meaning, considered as an MNE since it is widely accepted fact that the emergence of modern multinationals started in the second half of the 19th century. This was due to the effect of the Industrial Revolution. Prior to the Industrial Revolution, most value added activities initiated by economic entities outside their national boundaries were provoked by three factors.[8] The first was the desire to promote trade and financial activities resulting from the needs of the state or that of individual producers or consumers. The second was to acquire new territories and new forms of wealth. The third was to discover new avenues for the use of domestic savings. Therefore the first MNEs were mainly resource-based investments with the aim of supplying the home country with food and raw materials; logically, the host countries were mostly colonial countries. However, this pattern changed at the

---

4 Wilkins, Mira, *Emergence of Multinational Enterprise* (Cambridge Mass, 1970), p. 1.

5 Carlos, A. and Nicholas, S.J., 'Theory and History of the Early Trading Companies' (1996) December, Journal of Economic History 56; Wallace, *The Multinational Enterprises*, p. 15.

6 Chandler, Alfred D., *Scale and Scope: The Dynamics of Industrial Capitalism* (Harvard University Press, Cambridge 1990); Wilkins, Mira, 'The History of Multinational Enterprise' in Rugman, A.M. and Brewer, T.L. (eds), *Oxford Handbook of International Business* (Oxford University Press, Oxford 2001), p. 4.

7 Dunning, J.H., *Multinational Enterprises and the Global Economy* (Addison-Wesley, Wokingham 1993), p. 99.

8 *Ibid.* p. 97.

beginning of the second half of the 19th century with the growth of large MNEs both in the United States and in Europe.

The effect of industrialization and improvements in technology and remarkable advances in domestic and international transport, communications and storage techniques created new market opportunities and led firms to reassess their location strategies. Firms started to search new territories for their economic well-being. These developments, together with the emergence of professionally trained managers and administrators, led both to a widening and deepening of value-added chains and to an expansion in the transactional division of the manufacturing economy.[9] As a result, combining mass production with mass distribution, they built up a harmonized system of goods flow from raw materials, via production, to the retailer and final consumers.[10] The implications of these later progresses were truly transnational and, consequently, many firms grew into multi-activity, multi-regional and multi-national organizations.

In the examination of American developments, one will see that, towards the end of the 19th century, American technology had already overtaken European technology in a wide range of metal using industries and in those utilizing mass production practices.[11] Consequently from the second half of the 19th century, MNEs with the power of these new technologies appeared in the United States with extraordinary speed and took their place in the economy in a radical way.[12] On the other side of the ocean, in Britain, the evaluation of multinationals came in a slower, more evolutionary manner.

US firms tried to capitalize on their advantages by stepping up their sales to the UK and thus the larger ones often moved overseas. They first set up branch offices and warehouses on foreign shores because frequently they found it difficult to export from their American plants; then as demand grew and local tariffs appeared or as shipping costs increased scheduling of flows across oceans became difficult.[13] In these conditions, the firms had two options;[14] one was concluding licensing arrangements with a foreign producer, the other was to set

---

9 Jones, G., 'The Performance of British Multinational Enterprise, 1890–1945' in Hertner, Peter and Jones, Geoffrey, *Multinationals: Theory and History* (Gower, Aldershot 1986); Wilkins, Mira, *Emergence of Multinational Enterprise* (Cambridge Mass, 1970); Dunning *Multinational...Global Economy*, p. 103.

10 Dunning, J.H., Cantwell, J.A. and Corley, T.A.B, 'The Theory of International Production: Some Historical Antecedents' in Hertner, Peter and Jones, Geoffrey, *Multinationals: Theory and History* (Gower, Aldershot 1986), p. 27.

11 Dunning, *Multinational...Global Economy*, p. 102.

12 Nicholas, S.J., 'The Growth of the Multinational Corporation' (1986 May) Corporate History Bulletin 396

13 *Ibid.*

14 Dunning, *Multinational...Global Economy*, p. 102.

up a foreign manufacturing affiliate. Some companies were not yet open to setting up production units abroad so they chose to contract with their foreign partners. However, some companies went further and set up factories in Britain to produce their products in the domestic territory. After some unsuccessful attempts, United States' Singer Sewing Machine can be given as an example of successful foreign direct investment in England.[15] By 1867 the Singer had established its first foreign manufacturing plant in Glasgow and was the first to produce and market a product at multinational level under basically the same form and trade name. This gives Singer perhaps the strongest claim to being considered the first true multinational.[16]

On the other hand, British economists regarded outward investment as an expansion of domestic activity, where the interests of investing countries and firms were assumed to match. Thus for British companies, the process of FDI was slow and it was only in the 1960s that they made the conversion to a more different range of experience across quite different countries and markets.[17] The main reason for the slow growth in FDI in Britain in the 19th century was that many firms which became multinational before 1914 preferred exporting to, rather than investing in, foreign markets. However this strategy was blocked by a variety of location specific factors. The spread of protectionism from the late 1870s was a major influence in this context. For that reason American MNEs and MNEs from some other countries preferred to locate subsidiaries in free trade areas. Britain was the principal free trade area at that time in contrast to the protectionist Continental Europe.[18] That explains why Britain was the first country that American companies chose to invest in.

Therefore some economists conclude that tariffs were the single most important trigger leading to foreign investment by market-seeking British and American MNEs before 1914; second was incentives offered by governments.[19] Another reason depended on competitive strategy to reduce freight and production costs for overseas investment. Moreover firms engaged in FDI to be near the market and to provide for the specific and special needs of local customers.

From that point one can reach a hypothesis that there were two different kinds of multinational investment before 1914, which were market-seeking investment and resource-based investment. But it should be borne in mind that

---

15 Tugendhat, Christopher, *The Multinationals* (Penguin, Harmondsworth 1973), p. 33.

16 Wallace, *The Multinational*, p. 9.

17 Dunning, Cantwell and Corley, p. 26.

18 Hertner and Jones, *Multinationals*, p. 10.

19 Jones, 'The Performance of British…'; Franko, L., *The European Multinationals* (London 1976); Dunning *Multinational…Global Economy*, p. 108.

the reason for investing overseas was prompted by the main principles of capitalism that growing in domestic markets led them to think about overseas options.[20] After companies decided to make cross-border investments, comes the time to think about entry strategies to other markets. Consequently by 1914, both resource-based and market-seeking investments were becoming strongly motivated by the desire to exploit sources of host countries as well as the desire to minimize the uncertainties of transitional product markets.[21] However, in general, there was little attempt by British or indeed European investors to exploit the benefits of using the main sources of countries; while US companies invested abroad to acquire intermediate products for their domestic factories, European MNEs primarily invested in the US to sell to the local market.[22]

In summary the 19th and the early 20th centuries witnessed the formation of MNEs from the United States and Great Britain, as well as from several European countries, to conduct large-scale trading operations or to exploit resources and raw materials in Latin America, Africa, Asia and Australia, or even to run public utilities such as tramways or gas and electric works. Beginning in the 1860s, the forerunners of the modern MNEs began to exceed their national boundaries in significant numbers and to establish actual production facilities beyond their own frontiers, and no longer only in the developing world, but also in strong consumer markets.[23]

## DEVELOPMENTS BETWEEN 1918 AND 1960

Both market-seeking and resource-based MNEs declined sharply in the immediate post World War One period. The reason for that was the movement of countries to more protectionist economies and associating foreign companies with their states of origin. As a result many firms considered other strategies of international expansion, such as licensing, participation in cartels and joint ventures; this was especially valid for German companies.[24] Although the number of new subsidiaries set up by MNEs continued to rise throughout the period, it was only in the 1930s that the value of the foreign direct capital stake

---

[20] Chandler, A.D., 'The Growth of Transnational Industrial Firms in the UK and US: A Comparative Analysis' (1980) 33 Economic History Review 396; Dunning, *Multinational...Global Economy*, p. 109.

[21] Dunning, *Multinational...Global Economy*, p. 118.

[22] Wilkins, M., *The Growth of Multinationals* (Edward Elgar, Aldershot 1991); Dunning, *Multinational...Global Economy*, p. 113.

[23] Wallace, *The Multinational*, p. 16.

[24] Hertner and Jones, *Multinationals*, p. 9.

exceeded its pre-war figure.[25] Only a slight recovery was on the way, especially for American companies.

The controversial development in that time was that although the United States was more resource-sufficient than the UK, she had built up a significant stock of FDI by 1914, and by 1939 the value of her foreign manufacturing subsidiaries' output was twice that of her export of manufactures.[26] This could be considered the time for the start of American domination because the American expansion was in fact relatively slow before World War One, whereas some very important positions had already been secured by European companies in America.[27]

The period between the two World Wars was not economically prosperous for companies, nor for the countries. In that time, companies established big trusts and monopolies. By the 1930s large-scale MNEs had become a crucially important institution in all industrially advanced market economies and contemporary MNEs had become a socio-political commonplace.[28] However, it must be pointed out that there were other important developments in the growing of some technologically developed and high consumer demand so the companies that were concentrated on such kinds of business expanded their development internationally, such as IBM, Unilever, Shell and Esso.[29]

The main idea for cross-border investment was still the same; European and American firms were prompted to establish branch plants mainly by their need to adjust goods to local supply capabilities and acquire power in the market to save on transatlantic transport costs and by the frequency of non-tariff barriers.[30] Therefore what was overwhelmingly important to the MNEs before 1945 was the idea of moving to other countries for basic marketing reasons and therefore it was limited to movements from developed economies to developed economies and usually between neighbour countries or countries which have close relationships for historical reasons. Investments (if we can call it investment) to less-developed countries were mainly investments in colonies. Thus it cannot be considered the same as the modern understanding of FDI and operating subsidiaries cannot be considered as similar to subsidiaries that exist in the 21st century; rather they had branch-like characteristics.

---

25 Dunning, *Multinational...Global Economy*, p. 120.

26 Dunning, Cantwell and Corley, p. 26.

27 Gurak, H., 'Multinational Enterprises and Foreign Direct Investments' available at http://129.3.20.41/eps/get/papers/0404/0404004.pdf.

28 Teichova, A., 'Multinationals in Perspective' in Teichova, Alice, Lévy-Leboyer, Maurice and Nussbaum, Helga (eds), *Multinational Enterprise in Historical Perspective* (Cambridge University Press, Cambridge 1986), p. 365.

29 Wallace, *The Multinational*, p. 22.

30 Nicholas, S.J., 'British Multinational Investment before 1939' (1982) Journal of European Economic History 605; Dunning, *Multinational...Global Economy*, p. 123.

The real expansion in American investment abroad began in the 1950s. America's more pragmatic evaluation than her European counterparts as well as her rising living standards, her governmental support of foreign investment and her competitive character were all contributory factors for this increase.[31] It is for this reason that those who centred in on the phenomenon of MNE only in the era of its late development tended to view the MNEs as an American phenomenon.[32]

## DEVELOPMENTS BETWEEN 1960 AND 1990

It must be accepted that production in more than one country under a common nationality of ownership or control had little importance in the world economy before the 1950s.[33] In explanation, MNE activities as a device for the transfer of resources between countries and as a means of controlling the use of these assets played a less important role in the world economic activities than it had since the mid 1950s and 1960s.[34]

The figure that before 1914 there were more European than American multinationals changed in favour of America after the First World War and especially after the Second World War, and consequently, there was American dominance in the world economy.[35] By 1960, the share provided by the US had jumped to 49 per cent, while that of Britain was down to 16 per cent.[36] The recipient areas had also changed markedly, with developed countries now accounting for two-thirds of global FDI, due largely to the substantial growth of US manufacturing investment in Canada and Western Europe in the 1950s.

There was European concern about growing American dominance in world economic activities. In 1968 when J.J. Servan-Schreiber published his book, *The American Challenge*, he warned Europeans of the increasing domination by US firms in high technology industries in Western Europe. The concern was less with the growing proportion of European production accounted for by US affiliates, and more with the implications of this phenomenon for the long-term competitiveness of the host economies.[37] The concern had its effect and the

---

[31] See further Muchlinski, P., *Multinational Enterprises and the Law* (OUP, Oxford 2007) p. 16; Tugendhat, *The Multinationals*, c.2; Hood, N. and Young, S., *The Economics of Multinational Enterprises* (Longman, London 1984), p. 12; Wallace, *The Multinational*, p. 22.

[32] Wallace, *The Multinational*, p. 22.

[33] Dunning, Cantwell and Corley, p. 19.

[34] Gurak, 'Multinational Enterprises…'.

[35] Franko, L, *The European*, p. 8.

[36] Dunning *Multinational…Global Economy*, p. 93.

[37] See Servan-Schreiber J.J., *The American Challenge* (Hamish Hamilton, London 1968).

post-war era of American multinational superiority was challenged after the 1960s. The rise of US FDI in the 1950s and 1960s was matched by an increase in FDI by West Germany and Japan and West Europeans in the 1970s.[38] More recently, in the 1980s and 1990s MNEs have emerged from some of the newly industrializing countries, eg South Korea, Hong Kong and Singapore and China. Related to the trend of FDI being largely between developed countries, cross-investment or intra-industry FDI has emerged. These new economic activities were a comparatively rare phenomenon before 1945.[39] As a result there was a shift from an American dominated era to a much more complex system of MNEs in which many nations increased their foreign investments and the United States became the world's leading host economy as well as home economy to MNEs.[40]

In that period, the increasingly accepted explanation for the foreign production of firms was based on the acceptance that it was a market replacing activity. The investment in production abroad would occur whenever and wherever firms supposed that the net benefits of using cross-border markets to establish new production units abroad.[41] Therefore in the 1970s and the 1980s MNEs preferred largely *Greenfield* investments.[42] However, affiliates were comparatively involved in little innovatory activities and thus they were less embedded in host countries and more importantly they were mainly under hierarchical structures and thus under the strict control of the parent companies.

## CONTEMPORARY DEVELOPMENTS: GLOBALIZATION OF THE WORLD TRADE

During the last half century and particularly in the last three decades, a new and separately individual vehicle of international economic activity has emerged as a result of the internationalization of productive activities of many enterprises, the modern MNE. Consequently the modern theory of international production has moved away from a reliance on country-oriented advantages in production

---

38 Hertner and Jones, *Multinationals*, p. 2.

39 Dunning, Cantwell and Corley, p. 36.

40 See UNCTAD, World Investment Reports, 1993–2003.

41 Dunning, J.H., 'The Key Literature on IB Activities: 1960–2000' in Rugman, A.M., Brewer, T.L. (eds), *Oxford Handbook of International Business* (Oxford University Press, Oxford 2001), p. 40.

42 Greenfield investment can be defined as direct investment in new facilities or expansion of existing facilities. However, Oxfam approached the definition of Greenfield investment as suspicious by defining FDI as a Greenfield investment 'when a foreign firm creates a new subsidiary'. See Oxfam America, 'Global Finance Hurts the Poor' (Oxfam America, 2002).

towards firm-specific advantages. Thus the emergence of the truly global enterprise and escalating of all forms of corporate structures is the most marked organizational development of the past three decades.[43]

This fast and nearly completed globalization of many enterprises is reducing the significance of the nationality of ownership as a feature influencing the contribution of such firms to national economic welfare. In some industrial sectors dominated by global producers, it is becoming increasingly difficult to distinguish between the nationalities of the ownership of value-added activities in any significant means.[44] This mobility, which is currently being dramatically enhanced by the advent of electronic commerce and money, is offering MNEs wider location options in respect of both the creation and use of these assets and products.[45] This makes differentiation of the FDI movement more difficult in the world, particularly between developed countries since exercise of manufacturing in more than one country has become the standard rather than the exception.[46]

Private direct investment by companies from industrialized countries, through legal corporate transactions in other industrialized and less-developed countries, has grown by overwhelming proportions in the period between 1946 and the present day; and it has entered the 21st century with all the signs of renewed strength. The networks of the MNEs have taken on global dimensions, and FDI has been recognized as an essential element in the economic well-being of both home and host country, as well as in the process of global economic integration.[47]

Widespread privatization and the deregulation and re-regulation of many service sectors have opened up huge opportunities for FDI in the utility, telecommunications and banking and finance sectors. Regional economic integration, especially in Europe, has also increased the ability of MNEs to internalize trade flows. Moreover one of the most distinguishing features of the new world economy is the easiness with kinds of assets and intermediate products that determine a nation's prosperity and growth are able to move across national boundaries.[48] From that aspect as well MNEs remain in a class of unique organization. And thus, the MNEs, with affiliates in many countries, have rapidly assured its place as 'the characteristic industrial organization of the age'.[49] It is already a common practice for a number of MNEs from developed countries to

---

43 Dunning, *Multinational...Global Economy*, p. 130.
44 *Ibid.* p. 11.
45 Dunning, 'The Key Literature...', p. 57.
46 Wallace, *The Multinational*, p. 30.
47 *Ibid.* p. 31.
48 Dunning, *Multinational...Global Economy*, p. 129.
49 Wallace, *The Multinational*, p. 30.

send raw materials or components to certain developing countries for labour-intensive assembling or processing. The products so manufactured are then re-imported into the industrialized countries or exported elsewhere for assembling, finishing or final sale.[50] Therefore profit-maximizing behaviour of the enterprises prerequisite the free flow of the factors of production, both capital or labour, in order to operate at the most favourable level with respect of global opportunities.[51]

One such alteration since the early investment period is that FDIs now rely less on removal, processing and transport of raw materials and look more to modern technological and scientific processes of diversifying production. The degree of openness in international trade has surpassed the pre World War One record levels in many countries with the consequence that growth in international trade is stronger than the growth in world production.[52] In particular the growth of foreign portfolio investment, mergers and acquisitions, strategic alliances and a host of network relationships have been particularly impressive over the last two decades.[53]

Multinational expansion in the field of financing production from pre-financing to credit-financing to self-financing of subsidiaries abroad, and finally, the progression in the sphere of finance from the old means of private banking to the new means of investment banking and to multinational banking created easily available funding for the companies who wanted to expand their operations in cross-border ventures. Consequently medium-sized enterprises have also internationalized and are being integrated into production and distribution networks in which the distribution and manufacturing of goods are globalized. The internalization of medium-sized enterprises is also challenging the borders of legal systems that regulate the area.

All these economic developments generated new movements in the world's economic order in the last two decades. The communist bloc has collapsed and countries from the bloc opened their public companies for privatization. Not only these countries but also most of the less-developed countries aim to attract more FDI. They try to reduce legal and economical barriers for MNEs in order to encourage them to invest in their territory.[54] They invent different kinds of incentives for MNEs and there is a battle to make the best offers for MNEs

50 Gurak, 'Multinational Enterprises'.

51 *Ibid.*

52 See further UNCTAD, World Investment Reports, 1993–2003.

53 *Ibid.*

54 See further Charlton, A., 'Incentive Bidding for Mobile Investment: Economic Consequences and Potential Responses (OECD Development Centre, Working Paper No 203, Paris 2003).

amongst less-developed countries.[55] The last two decades have witnessed the gradual reduction of trade barriers, which are welcomed by the MNEs.[56]

According to World Investment Report (WIR) 2006 of UNCTAD, the global stock of FDI in 2005 is $9 trillion which is owned by 77 000 transnational corporations and their 770 000 foreign affiliates.[57] FDI continues to be more important than trade in delivering goods and services abroad: global sales by MNEs reached $19 trillion in 2004, as compared with world exports of $8 trillion in 2002.[58] Companies are still continuing to invest abroad and FDI outflows increased in 2005 by 27 per cent to $916 billion and these MNEs are almost all from developed countries.[59] Firms from developing countries accounted only for $117 billion.[60] MNEs employed more than 62 million people abroad.[61] All these figures led to another definition for multinationals – that of 'foreign direct investment entity'.[62]

Also, interestingly, MNEs from the EU have become by far the largest owners of outward FDI stock, some $3.4 trillion in 2002, more than twice that of the United States with $1.5 trillion.[63] In developing countries, the inward FDI stock came to nearly one-third of Gross Domestic Product (GDP) in 2001.[64] The single market is expected significantly to affect investment flow into and within the EU.[65] These figures are expected to grow in number at the beginning of the 21st century.[66]

The globalization of FDI movement has not changed the fact that the most powerful MNEs are from developed countries since among the top 100 companies only five are from developing countries.[67] Another interesting statistic

---

55 *Ibid.*

56 UNCTAD, *Companies Without Borders: Transnational Corporations in the 1990s* (International Thomson Business Press, London 1996).

57 UNCTAD, World Investment Report 2006, p. 5.

58 UNCTAD, World Investment Report 2005, p. 4.

59 *Ibid.* p. 1.

60 *Ibid.* p. 2.

61 *Ibid.* p. 5.

62 Lipsey, Robert E, 'Foreign Direct Investment and the Operations of Multinational Firms: Concepts, History and Data' (National Bureau of Economic Research, Cambridge 2001).

63 UNCTAD, World Investment Report 2002.

64 UNCTAD, World Investment Report 2003, p. 14.

65 Muchlinski, *Multinational*, p. 24.

66 The figures from WIRs are given as examples to indicate the scale of global economic activities of MNEs. However there are criticisms that these figures are not reliable; for example the restructuring of Royal Dutch Shell in 2005 created a $74bn inward flow of investment from Netherlands to the UK without a significant change for the UK or Dutch economies. See *the Financial Times* (London, October 17 2006).

67 UNCTAD, 2006, p. 6.

relates to financial MNEs; financial MNEs from France, Germany, Japan, the UK and the US accounted for 74 per cent of the total assets of the top 50 financial MNEs in 2003.[68] Accordingly, less-developed countries continue to adopt new laws and regulations in order to attract more investment into their countries. There were 235 changes in laws alone in 2004 to open up borders to MNEs and introduce new promotional measures for MNEs.[69] In addition 20 countries lowered their corporate income tax.[70]

These figures indicate that the key to MNEs movement and behavioural policies is found in developed countries since developed countries host the biggest MNEs and also have significant financial resources. Thus the less-developed countries have to be involved in a bidding war to attract MNEs by introducing foreign investment laws as well as reducing their regulatory schemes.[71] In those conditions, it is not realistic to expect countries to increase regulations on MNEs; indeed it is often very difficult to keep existing regulations. Accordingly in these loose regulatory environments, MNEs are almost free to move from one jurisdiction to another one with little problem or little loss of profit.

The increasing effect of the global regulatory actors on international trade is another development in the world economy. The escalating volatility of financial and exchange markets, and the changing architecture of supranational institutions such as the World Trade Organization (WTO), World Bank and International Monetary Found (IMF) affect MNEs' ability to organize and move their products and capital across the globe. The aim of these institutions is always to open boundaries and reduce limitations so it is a common condition for countries who ask for credit or be accepted into memberships to open their boundaries to MNEs.

In the inner organizational structure of MNEs, the challenges of an innovation-driven economy and the emergence of new forms of international business activities, together with the increasing fluctuation of many cross-border transactions, led to new understanding of organizational structures for MNEs. It is forcing entities to rethink the roles played, and the relationships between the numerous decision-taking entities comprising MNEs. As a result there are methodical approaches to organization of MNE activities, alternative organizational forms often harmonize with each other and create more institutional pluralism. Considerable foreign-based innovatory activity with or without strategic alliances with foreign firms has been achieved.[72] As a result in MNE organization,

---

68 UNCTAD, 2005, p. 4.

69 *Ibid.* p. 8.

70 *Ibid.*

71 Charlton, 'Incentive Bidding'.

72 Bartlett, C.A. and Ghoshal, S., *Managing Across Borders—the Transnational Solution* (Harvard Business School Press, Boston 1989).

there are flattened pyramids; more heterarchical structures; more assignment of responsibilities to line subsidiary managers.[73] These new organizational models make MNEs' movements and organizations more challenging and more efficient allowing them to control world economic activities better and on a more global scale.[74]

## THEORIES OF MULTINATIONAL INVESTMENT

At this stage, a close look at the earlier determinants of MNE activities is necessary because the time of emergence of early MNEs and the acceptance of the long time debated limited liability[75] theory came at the same time. Thus the more we understand the drive behind investment decisions, the better proposals for regulations we can produce. The basic economic explanation for FDI lies in the natural evaluations of firms, which requires them to search for alternatives.[76] The firms run through opportunities in domestic markets before going for new adventures abroad in order to search for international opportunities for their value added activities.[77] Briefly once firms develop ownership advantages, international investment theory tells us that a particular combination of location, marketing and knowledge-transfer factors makes foreign production almost inevitable.[78]

Therefore after looking at the traditional explanations for the emergence of MNEs, one sees that investment theory connects the theory of the firm and location theory.[79] The enterprise, possessing certain firm-specific assets, finds some cost advantages in internalizing the use of these assets within the organization on a cross-border basis. Consequently the location incentives to establish operations abroad may derive from tariff or non-tariff barriers, lower unit labour costs, or host government policies such as offers of investments incentives or nationalistic regulatory policies which favour enterprises located within the market.[80]

The geographical differences can simply be explained by the fact that the supply of some goods is found in one location and demand for them in another.

---

[73] Dunning, 'The Key Literature', p. 48.

[74] See Chapter 2.

[75] See Chapter 3.

[76] Lall, Sanjaya, *The New Multinationals: The Spread of Third World Enterprises* (Wiley, Chichester 1983), p. 68.

[77] Caves, R.E., *Multinational Enterprises and Economic Analyses* (Cambridge University Press, Cambridge 2007), c.3.

[78] Lall, *New Multinationals*, p. 69.

[79] Caves, *Multinational...Economic Analyses*, c.3.

[80] Brewer, T. and Young, S., *The Multilateral Investment System and Multinational Enterprises* (Oxford University Press, Oxford 1998), p. 12.

However, geographic expansion of markets also allows more benefits for the firms; more productive division of labour, gains from specialization, exploitation of differences in resource contribution, and adaptation of skills can be mentioned as some examples for the locational benefits of investment.[81] Another locational influence on why companies see foreign countries as having better and more benefit-creating opportunities lies in the technological developments in home countries. Their power and technological superiority enables MNEs to suppress the destination market easily, rather than competing at home with other powerful companies and being exposed to severe price cuts and so on.[82] Furthermore the technological developments show their effect on management of companies since the growth due to the application of new technology and of management skills extends effective control and supervision of foreign subsidiaries to marketing, distribution, purchasing, facilities, personnel, production units and research and development encouraging companies to go for FDI with fewer risks.[83]

At the firm level, the size of firms has been found to have a strong and independent positive effect on internalization. Clearly while size reflects the influence of factors which create entry barriers at the industry level, it also acts as a powerful source of monopolistic advantage on its own providing privileged access to capital markets, to information, to production factors and government favours.[84] When natural power has emerged in the firm, how a firm reacts to the arbitrary opportunity for direct investment depends on a scale of economics and market knowledge. It also depends on how the opportunity is perceived in the hierarchy of the firm and the response by management.[85] This makes firm basis advantages less predictable and dependent on other conditions.

The inefficiency of exporting was also a reason to search for cross-border investment because one of the earlier actual physical expansions abroad, beyond mere export or licensing, was the realization that foreign markets' needs could perhaps be more effectively assessed and met by domestic managers, who could better understand the local consumer, than by a long-distance counterpart.[86] The

---

[81] Kobrin, S.J., 'The Architecture of Globalisation: State Sovereignty in a Networked Global Economy' in Dunning, J.H., *Governments, Globalisation, and International Business* (Oxford University Press, Oxford 1997) p. 149.

[82] Fieldhouse, D.K., 'The Multinational: a Critique of a Concept' in Teichova, Alice, Lévy-Leboyer, Maurice and Nussbaum, Helga (eds), *Multinational Enterprise in Historical Perspective* (Cambridge University Press, Cambridge 1986), p. 14.

[83] Teichova, 'Multinationals in Perspective', p. 366.

[84] *Ibid.*

[85] Nicholas, S, 'The Theory of Multinational Enterprise as a Transactional Mode' in Hertner, Peter and Jones, Geoffrey, *Multinationals: Theory and History* (Gower, Aldershot 1986), p. 76.

[86] Wallace, *The Multinational*, p. 18.

financial advantages of manufacturing in a foreign market closer to the target consumer were also discovered. [87]

Of course, during the history of FDI, the motivations for cross-border investments have shown various different characteristics. For example one of the earliest motivations was the desire to control sources of raw materials, which explains why historically multinational operations developed in the extractive colonized areas before becoming involved in manufacturing. Therefore Professor Dunning claims that it is not possible to produce everlasting certain theories for multinational investment.[88] He puts firm specific and location specific advantages together and explains investment theory under the name of 'eclectic theory' that is a combination of three inter-related factors:[89] first, the competitive (firm specific) advantages of existing or potential MNEs; secondly, the location advantages of particular countries in offering complementary assets, for these advantages to be exploited or amplified; and thirdly, the tendency of the firms possessing the ownership specific advantages to combine these with those of foreign based assets, by FDI, rather than by the market mechanism, or some kind of non-equity cooperative project.[90]

The specific conditions of country of origin of MNEs also had an important role for searching out overseas investment. At a time when Americans moved to internationalization, this movement was greatly stimulated by the Sherman Act of 1890. Although at home they were restricted by antitrust regulations, US companies were entitled to use whatever methods were necessary to conduct foreign trade.[91] Consequently the current analysis of MNEs argues that direct foreign investment is based upon certain monopolistic advantages possessed by firms.[92]

Indeed the early process of expansion of firms to national-market figures in the 19th century in the US economy was quite similar to their transformation to multinational status more recently.[93] There is evidence on the behaviour of early MNEs such as Singer Sewing Machine Company, which became foreign investors through a process of incremental problem solving, such as dealing with the unsatisfactory performances of foreign licensees or sales agents. The historical case studies also illustrate that the evolution of the decentralized multi-plant and multinational firm depended on the need for economic efficiency for the firms.[94]

---

[87] *Ibid.*

[88] Dunning, 'The Key Literature', p. 43.

[89] *Ibid.*

[90] See Buckley, P.J. and Casson, M., *The Economic Theory of Multinational Enterprise* (Macmillan, London 1985); Muchlinski, *Multinational Enterprises*, p. 33.

[91] Wallace, *The Multinational*, p. 20.

[92] Lall, *New Multinationals*, p. 1.

[93] Nicholas, 'Theory of Multinational', p. 64.

[94] Caves, *Multinational...Economic Analyses*, c. 3.

## CONCLUSION: MNES AS GLOBALIZED PROFIT SEEKING ORGANIZATIONS

Since their emergence, MNEs have been one of the few principal institutions affecting the formation and outcome of all kinds of economic relations; the other important institution has been the states. As Dunning states 'the powerful role of the MNE in the contemporary global economy reflects their capabilities and willingness to organize, for good or bad, cross-border production and transactions more effectively than any alternative institutional mechanism'.[95] In the last two decades, activities of MNEs have played an important role in the globalization processes of the world's economic activities.

As a result the 21st century can be described as the era of the emergence of truly globalized MNEs and the real and more effective freedom of movement of capital between countries, if it is not completely free. Moreover in economic characteristics, from a relatively simple vertical set of control procedures designed to support market transactions and resource seeking foreign investors, the MNE has evolved into a complex hierarchy of a network of vertical and horizontal intra and inter-firm connection aimed to carry on its global and regional objectives.[96] Thus these new types of MNEs, while investing, think about cost-effective structure of profit maximization, rather than market entry models of the 19th and early 20th centuries.

This movement from market orienting structuring of MNEs to cost-effective structuring of MNEs created more problems in the less-developed countries because of the inadequate laws of these countries and, in contrast, their need for FDI in order to develop. The MNEs have abused these weaknesses to secure many unjustifiable incentives from the governments. Also the competition for attracting more FDI in less-developed countries weakened the legal protection of their citizens against activities of MNEs. This makes already weak legal systems non-working. Since investments of MNEs are easily movable from one country to another, less-developed countries are afraid of deterring MNEs' investments in their countries. This situation creates severe competition amongst countries to attract more FDI and thus makes the country regulations very lenient, even worse, forces them to give judicial incentives to MNEs for their activities.[97] This situation is sometimes suggestive of the old colonial era.

---

[95] Dunning, *Multinational…Global Economy*, p. 133.

[96] *Ibid.* p. 232.

[97] For example, under the project of the Baku-Tbilisi-Ceyhan (BTC) Pipeline, some restrictions have been introduced for the governments not to change the law or make further changes to the law not applicable to the BTC consortium under which BP is the largest stakeholder and leading the design and construction process. For more details see Amnesty International 'Human Rights on the Line' available at http://www.amnestyusa.

On an economic basis, the very idea of a national market as an economic construct appears to have lost meaning in the post-modern world economy.[98] Given the emergence of globalization in every area of business, neither territoriality nor mutually exclusive geographic organization retains significance. The result has effects that raise questions about the meaning of sovereignty of national states in a global system that gives the MNEs the power to operate all over the world.

Currently, with the progressive reduction of tariff and non-tariff barriers through the GATT/WTO mechanism, one of the dominant factors influencing investments abroad, has simply come to be the need to gain and safeguard access to local and regional markets.[99] These new organizational and structural changes in world trade ease cross-border investment by creating more benefits, but making the competition for attracting FDI more severe for the host countries. Free trade zones like the European Union and NAFTA are also determinant bodies for the 21st century's international trade.[100]

Consequently nation states have contradictory interests and objectives in their relations with MNEs. Some states are powerful enough not to compromise the civil and social rights of their citizens, while others might be desperate for FDI and thus more open to compromise about the civil and social rights of their citizens so national boundaries, in this sense, still create significant differentials on the global economic surface.[101] The critical point, however, is that globalization implies that the national economy is no longer the unit of economic accounting or the frame of reference for economic strategies. The new structures and strategies in MNEs' governance operate in accordance with the rules of globalization. This leaves less-developed countries dealing with issues that they have no power to change.

The firm specific organization has changed the MNEs' social position. They are not simply groups of companies any more, they are one of the most impor-

---

org/business/humanrightsontheline.pdf accessed 22 June 2006. See also Lawson-Remer, T.E., 'A Role for the International Finance Corporation in Integrating Environmental and Human Rights Standards into Core Project Covenants: Case Study of the Baku-Tbilisi-Ceyhan Oil Pipeline Project' in DeSchutter, O. (ed.), *Transnational Corporations and Human Rights* (Hart Publishing, Oxford 2006).

[98] Kobrin, 'The Architecture of Globalisation', p. 159.

[99] See further WTO Secretariat, *From GATT to WTO: The Multilateral Trading System in the New Millennium* (Kluwer Law International, London 2000); Ruttley, P., MacVay, I. and Carol, G., *The WTO and International Trade Regulation* (Cameron May, London 1998); Thomas, J.S. and Meyer, M.A., *The New Rules of Global Trade* (Carswell, Ontario 1997).

[100] See further Weiler, J.H.H., *The EU, the WTO and the NAFTA; Towards a Common Law of International Trade Regulation* (Oxford University Press, Oxford 2000).

[101] Kobrin, 'The Architecture of Globalisation', p. 154.

tant economic and financial determinants of the world economy. They are known separately from their country of origin; they might be bargaining with the national states independently from their national state. It is almost impossible identifying them with a nationality as their assets and origins might be scattered all over the world. This indicates another misconception of the problems from social theory that MNEs are controlled and they operate under the control of the states.[102] Indeed states are becoming dependent on MNEs' control.

Accordingly the law-making bodies have failed to react to challenges in the modern theory of international investment from a reliance on country-oriented advantages towards firm-specific advantages. International private law still basically depends on the law of individual equal states, even though some bilateral harmonization has been achieved, especially under EU Law. These country-specific regulations show very limited characteristics under company and tort laws. On the other hand, international regulatory activities have concentrated on creating a more relaxed atmosphere for the MNEs, such as in tax and corporate governance. The improvements in the last two decades in international trade are impressive. The new and powerful transformation of GATT to WTO is progressing rapidly. The free-trade agreements are emerging everyday between developed countries and developing countries. The governments and international financial institutions seem to devote themselves heavily to easing the trade barriers across borders. All these mean a more powerful, bigger and wider spread of MNEs' influence. In contrast the liability for company groups is still regulated by 20th century's narrow understanding of company law based on a limited liability theory.[103]

At first sight, the main obstacle to the regulations seems to be limited liability rules. The examination of multinational investment theory and an historical approach has proved that the relation between limited liability and a company's investment decision is not certain. The examination of economic triggers for foreign investments coincides with the claimed benefits of limited liability.[104] In fact it is difficult to find any attempt to examine thoroughly the reasons why MNEs decided on different strategies once the decision to undertake FDI had been made. The reasons why some firms made *Greenfield* investments and others purchased existing firms, and why some firms established wholly owned subsidiaries and others joint ventures, remain vague.[105] Actually small and medium-sized enterprises choose joint ventures while big multinationals have chosen direct investment and therefore have established subsidiaries, mostly

---

[102] Birkinshaw, Julian and Hood, Neil (eds), *Multinational Corporate Evolution and Subsidiary Development* (Palgrave Macmillan, London 1998), p. 782.

[103] See Chapter 3.

[104] Muchlinski, *Multinational*, p. 35.

[105] Hertner and Jones, *Multinationals*, p. 10.

wholly owned.[106] This proves that establishing a subsidiary using company law for MNEs is due to the effects of economic and financial evaluation rather than incentives provided by the limited liability company.

While explaining the economic theories of multinational enterprise, the advantages of limited liability company are not mentioned. The studies that have examined some particular countries have proved that there is no certain relation between the decision of investment of the firms and the limited liability of corporate shareholders.[107] Even the modern investment theory provides little guidance on the factors influencing the allocation of resources when neither law nor custom prevails. Successful cross-border activity requires a combination of skills; the ability to identify profits opportunities, the judgement to evaluate them, and the tactical awareness to exploit them properly.[108] In other words, it depends on the practical reality of international business.[109] This proves that the understanding of the legal factors to the growth of MNEs is much less advanced than economic theory.[110]

---

106 Agarwal, S. and Ramaswami, S.N., 'Choice of Foreign Market Entry Mode, Impact of Ownership, Location and Internalisation Factors' (1992) 23 Journal International Business Studies 1.

107 See Jones, 'The Performance'; Hertner, P., 'German Multinational Enterprise before 1914: Some Case Studies' in Hertner, Peter and Jones, Geoffrey, *Multinationals: Theory and History* (Gower, Aldershot 1986); Fridenson, P., 'The Growth of Multinational Activities in the French Motor Industry, 1890–1979' in Hertner, Peter and Jones, Geoffrey, *Multinationals: Theory and History* (Gower, Aldershot 1986).

108 Casson, M., 'General Theories of Multinational Enterprise: Their Relevance to Business History' in Hertner, Peter and Jones, Geoffrey, *Multinationals: Theory and History* (Gower, Aldershot 1986), p. 55.

109 For example, it is still possible to establish an unlimited liability company in England. Moreover, German and Turkish laws have company forms with unlimited liability. See further Chapter 6.

110 Muchlinski, *Multinational*, p. 44.

# 2. Multinational enterprises as business organizations

## INTRODUCTION

There is a growing expectation in business and MNEs studies to examine the structural changes in MNEs because examination of the issues only on the basis of the simplified structure of MNEs is far from creating sound solutions to the problems examined in this book. Therefore this book includes examination of the modern structure of MNEs. This will provide a modern understanding of the concept of MNE in business management studies, which will create more efficient ways of thinking. The need to examine the organizational structure of business organizations lies in the fact that if we wish to develop an adequate economic as well as legal theory of the modern business enterprise and the contemporary economic activities of them, we must begin to build a sufficient business and economic understanding of business organizations and build new laws on these facts.[1] In other words, if one wonders at this stage why the structure of organizations has become the centre for discussions of legal theory, the answer lies in the realities of globalization that turned FDI and consequently international business activities towards a firm-based model rather than country of origin based model.[2]

Although the changes during the history of MNEs and its reflections have been, to some extent, observed and indicated in major economic, managerial and business studies, the history of the MNE studies from a legal perspective is based on the common misconception of business and economic analysis and its effect on law-making. It has stayed on the same assumption that economic analysis traditionally treated the MNE as a single decision-making centre, as if one mind were absorbing all relevant data and making all decisions on the basis of well-considered strategies. Accordingly the agency theory has been used in the parent-subsidiary relationship to develop and test a model of foreign subsidiary

1 Scott, John 'Corporate Groups and Network Structure' in McCahery, J., Picciotto, S. and Scott, S., *Corporate Control and Accountability* (OUP, Oxford 1993).

2 Randoy, Turquand Rule, 'Towards a Firm-based Model of Foreign Direct Investment' in Bjorkman, I. and Forsgren, M. (eds), *The Nature of the Transnational Firm* (Mumkgaard, Copenhagen 1997), p. 257.

control.[3] In fact, decision-making is decentralized within enterprises, and decisions can be highlighted by the structure of the internal organization chosen by the corporation and the incentives and the resources that it provides to its various groups of convenient specialties.[4]

For these reasons, there is a need to examine the modern structure of MNEs. This leads us to the aim of the chapter that is to examine the framework of progressed and differentiated organization forms and to link this framework to an elaborated theoretical analysis of the other historical fields of organization theory. This assessment will indicate how and to what extent business organizations have changed during the past century.[5] Next, I wish to create a theory of the modern structure of MNEs, with particular attention on decision-making processes within the enterprise.

The reason behind the emergence of a new organizational structure is the same as the reason for the emergence of MNEs: economic motivation and the economic background for the world business activities have changed.[6] The inspiration of groups of companies expanding overseas has increasingly shifted from one focused mainly on securing new markets or low-cost productive contribution, to a universal search for essential intelligence or limited competencies not readily available or very costly in the home market.[7] Bartlett and Ghoshal accurately point out that the need to secure key supplies of raw materials, to acquire new markets, to achieve further sales and to access low-cost factors of production such as cheap labour or low-cost capital comprised the earlier foreign investment inspiration.[8] At an early stage MNEs and foreign operations were regarded as organizational additions or as distant settlements to the domestic business and treated in an opportunistic rather than a strategic approach.[9]

---

3 O'Donnell, S.W., 'Managing Foreign Subsidiaries: Agent of Headquarters, or an Independent Network?' (2000) 21 Strategic Management Journal 525.

4 Caves, R.E., *Multinational Enterprises and Economic Analyses* (Cambridge University Press, Cambridge 2007), c.3.

5 Professor Dunning here explains on which conditions an MNE will structure itself. And, in general, the more numerous and complex the technologies required producing a particular product and the more products supplied by a firm, the more complex its organizational structure is likely to be. See Dunning, J.H., *Multinational Enterprises and the Global Economy* (Addison-Wesley, Wokingham 1993), p. 215.

6 Tavares, A.T., 'Strategic Management of Multinational Networks: A Subsidiary Evaluation Perspective' (University of Porto) available at http://www.ifm.eng.cam.ac.uk/cim/imnet/symposium2001/papers/tavares.pdf accessed 25 June 2006.

7 Bartlett, C.A. and Ghoshal, S., 'The Evaluation of Transnational' in Islam, I. and Shepherd, W. (eds), *Current Issues in International Business* (Edward Elgar, Cheltenham, UK, Northampton, MA, USA 1997), p. 110.

8 *Ibid.*

9 Gooderham, Paul N. and Ulset, Svein, 'Beyond the M-form: Towards a Critical Test of the New Form' (2002) 9 International Journal of the Economics of Business 117.

A common subject in all the discussions of organizational theory has been the remarkable changes in the competitive environment that have reduced the effectiveness of traditional MNEs' approaches, highlighting the need to move towards less-hierarchical structures because of their experience in the international operating environment. MNEs that do so, develop the best chance of existing and profiting.[10] Thus they search for the most efficient operating environments, which basically depend on aim of profit maximization. As a result, from an evolutionary perspective, there has been a shift in focus from measurement within traditional vertical models to movement towards the horizontally structured MNE models under which they can have the best chance of maximizing their profit.[11]

On this point Bartlett and Ghoshal have conducted the most important studies resulting in findings that large global corporations are creating a new organizational model in the 1990s. This model is significantly different from the multi-divisional form (M-form) and its previous shapes of organization that had dominated corporate structures over the last five decades and that had provided the background for much of present organization theory.[12] This movement in structure is not surprising because there had always been differences within the broader earlier vertical models as well.[13] There had been constant changes in structures of companies and groups of companies and MNEs since their first emergence. All these evolutionary developments have led to the claim that the modern theoretical perception of MNEs as differentiated networks of subsidiaries is the proper academic background to understand the global organizations of MNEs.[14]

However, one should bear in mind that each enterprise is, to some extent, unique and usually holds a combination of different organizational structures. No single existing paradigms can efficiently explain the multi-ingredient of a diversity of interactions shaping MNEs' structure.[15] Moreover the most favourable or supposed most profitable organizational structure of any particular MNE may change over time.[16] We will see these changes apparently in the assessment

---

[10] Bartlett and Ghoshal, The Evaluation of Transnational, p. 108.

[11] Malnight, T.W., 'The Transition from Decentralised to Network Based MNC Structures: An Evolutionary Perspective' (1996) (first quarter) Journal of International Business Studies 43.

[12] Ghoshal, S. and Bartlett, C.A., *The Individualized Corporation* (Harper Collins Publishers, New York 1997).

[13] Bartlett, C.A and Ghoshal, S., 'Beyond the M-form: Toward a Managerial Theory of the Firm' (1993) 14 Strategic Management Journal 23; Williamson, O.E, *Markets and Hierarchies: Analysis and Antitrust Implications* (Free Press, New York 1975).

[14] Tavares, 'Strategic Management'.

[15] *Ibid.*

[16] Dunning, *Multinational...Global Economy*, p. 215.

of structural changes of MNEs. The argument pursued in this chapter depends on the fact that evolution of the organizational structure of MNEs has changed over the last century from vertically structured organizations towards horizontally structured organizations. Therefore this work, in its overall perspective, will not exclude the examination of vertically structured MNEs; it will, to some extent, compare the different structural models and their reflections in law.

## THE HISTORICAL DEVELOPMENTS OF MNES' ORGANIZATIONAL STRUCTURES

In an historical perspective, one of the most significant factors in the rise of MNEs has been the development of concentration on organizational structure. The constant impact on the structure and organization of business became obvious from the last quarter of the 19th century and this led to the growth of large companies, which gradually increased their market shares at home and abroad, and later stood at the centre of considerable merger, acquisition and other strategically motivated movements.[17] In the early stages of the emergence of an enterprise, when an enterprise becomes an authority and director and controller of the actions of participating organizations, a plain hierarchy develops. The central position of the enterprise and the personal relations make the authority the most important co-ordination mechanism used in this form and creates a distinctive atmosphere that is simple and possible for a single centred enterprise to operate. When applied to groups of companies in their very earlier structural form, a simple hierarchical structure appears, as indicated in Figure 2.1. Accordingly the group consists of parent and wholly owned subsidiaries. The parent applies very strict hierarchical control over subsidiaries and is involved in every decision-making process. In this structure the role of subsidiaries is limited to very practical business duties. Thus they have similar characteristics to branches or agents of the corporation. This structure might be seen not only in earlier groups of companies but also in small-scale domestic corporate groups.

As the enterprise grows in an environment that is steady and thus projected, new forms may develop. This happened when MNEs were too big to be controlled by simple hierarchic structure and the unitary form (U-form) has been developed. The U-form adjusts the co-ordination by authority by introducing several levels of management and separates practical responsibilities among

[17] Teichova, A., 'Multinationals in Perspective' in Teichova, Alice, Lévy-Leboyer, Maurice and Nussbaum, Helga (eds), *Multinational Enterprise in Historical Perspective* (Cambridge University Press, Cambridge 1986) p. 365.

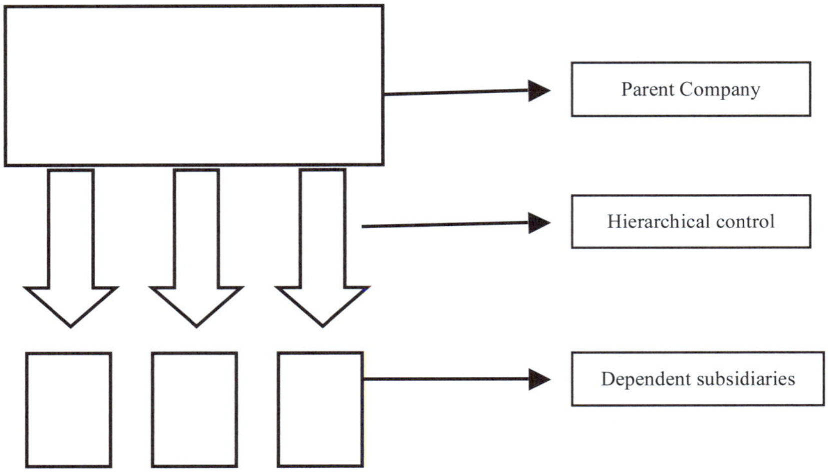


*Figure 2.1 Simple hierarchical structure*

managers at the same level. The U-form is also characterized by the introduction of a new important co-ordination mechanism, which can be defined as superior rules for the organization. This new form is co-ordinated by formalized procedures, by specific, written instructions for work performance and systems for planning and control. The U-form was a modernization that developed earlier forms, suitable for small and medium-sized companies and it reduced operation costs for co-ordination in large measurement, mass-production units by function, using a multilevel hierarchy with professional managers and relying on broad formalization for management.[18] In this form hierarchical control over subsidiaries was central while decision-making process had required strict involvement of the head of the organisation.

After passing through stages of measure expansion, geographic dispersal and vertical integration, enterprises finally grew by product diversification, experienced administrative problems within the functional structure of U- form and converted to the M-form, the multidivisional structure, in order to resume profitability.[19] The natural weakness in the U-form enterprises became significant only when the administrative load on the senior executives increased to such an

[18] See Williamson, O.E, *Markets and Hierarchies: Analysis and Antitrust Implications* (Free Press, New York 1975); Chandler, A.D., *Scale and Scope: The Dynamics of Industrial Capitalism* (Harvard University Press, Cambridge 1990).

[19] Alarik, B., 'From M-form to N-form: The Structure of Multinational Enterprises' (FE-rapport 2000-378) available at http://swoba.hhs.se/gunwba/papers/gunwba2000_378.pdf accessed 22 June 2006.

extent that they were incapable of handling their entrepreneurial responsibility efficiently.[20] This situation emerged when the operations of the enterprise became too complex and the problems of co-ordination, assessment and policy formulation too compound for a small number of top officers to handle long-term entrepreneurial, and short-term operational administrative activities. In order to overcome these challenges, the innovators built the multi-divisional structure with a general office whose management would focus on entrepreneurial activities and with autonomous, fairly self-contained operating divisions whose managers would handle operational ones.[21]

The M-form can be explained as a development from the U-form, as the U-form grew into differentiated businesses, new products and markets.[22] The M-form is characterized by a separation into semi-autonomous units with responsibilities for results, creating medium-sized corporations within the large enterprise.[23] Whereas the principal operating units in the U-form enterprise are the functional divisions, in the M-form enterprise,[24] these are half-autonomous operating divisions.[25] Another characteristic of the M-form is that the responsibilities are divided vertically in the hierarchy. The M-form separates top level from middle levels and gives the top level strategic responsibilities. The middle level is divided into divisions and each division is given responsibilities for certain front line units. There was a complex bureaucratic structure because the bureaucracy was the central element of western capitalism; in this way the bureaucratic organization was a product of its time and became the dominant form of organization discussed in the academic literature.[26] Divisions are given

---

20 Chandler, A.D., *Strategy and Structure* (MIT Press, Cambridge 1998), p. 299.

21 Gooderham and Ulset, 'Beyond the M-form'.

22 The M-form was characterized as multi-divisional, multi-product, multi-factory, multi-level, multi-hierarchical and multi-national.

23 Gooderham, Paul N. and Ulset, Svein 'Is the Governance of Transnational Really "Beyond the M-Form"? A critical Review of Barlett and Ghoshal's New Organisational Model' in Taggart, H., Berry, M. and McDermott, M. (eds), *Multinationals in a New Era* (Palgrave, London 2001).

24 Williamson explains the terms of M-form optimum divisionalisation involves; (1) the identification of separable economic activities within the firm; (2) according quasi-autonomous standing (usually a profit centre nature) to each; (3) monitoring the efficiency performance of each division and awarding incentives; (4) allocating cash flows to high-yield uses; (5) performing strategic planning in other respects. See Williamson, *Markets and Hierarchies*.

25 Gooderham and Ulset, 'Beyond the M-form'.

26 Therefore both U-form and M-form are based on hierarchy, and formalization, the division of labour, specialization and utilitarianism are the guiding organizational principles. See Pettigrew, A.M. and Fenton, E.M., 'Theoretical Perspectives on New Forms of Organizing' in Pettigrew, A.M. and Fenton, E.M. (eds) *The Innovating Organisation* (Sage Publications, London 2000), p. 11.

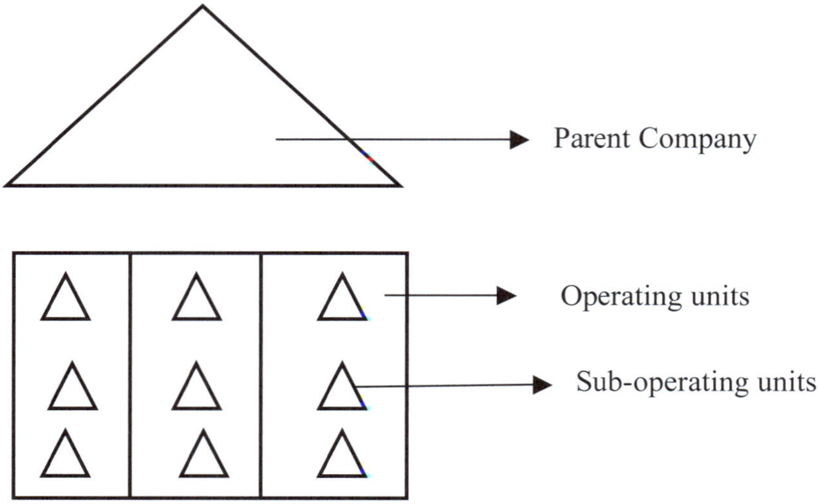


*Figure 2.2 M-form (vertical structure)*

decentralized responsibilities for their own operations while the overall strategic decisions are made at top level.[27]

The multi-divisional structure solved the overload and governance problems of the U-form by decomposing the larger enterprise into a number of half-independent divisions; profit centres, product, brand and geographical lines, and by separating strategic decision-making at the corporate level from operating decision-making at the divisional level that have responsibility for different markets or products, rather than functions. MNEs were transferred to M-form because, as Chandler's central discussion of strategy and structure claims, MNEs were being driven by market growth and technological change to develop greater diversity in their products and markets and were able to manage their new strategies efficiently only if they adopted a multidivisional organizational structure.[28] As noted by Williamson the M-form not only replaced the less efficient U-form structure but was also consequently extended to manage diversified assets – the conglomerate – and foreign direct investments – the multinational enterprises, that together made the M-form considered the genuine and standard models for MNEs.[29] This

27 See further Williamson, *Markets and Hierarchies*; Chandler, *Scale and Scope*.
28 Chandler, *Strategy and Structure*.
29 Williamson, *Markets and Hierarchies*; see also Gooderham and Ulset, 'Beyond the M-form'.

system was better suited to the activities of legally independent subsidiaries in various countries.

The more complex matrix structure of M-form was developed in order to meet expectation in business in the second half of 1970s. In the matrix structure two, or more, divisional structures are combined, for example divisions by products and division by geographical markets. This dual structure embraces the whole company and is stable over time.[30] In addition to the matrix, an alternative way of achieving the dual advantages of global standardization and national openness is the regional approach. By designing and implementing competitive strategies within a region, the MNE may overcome some of the very real staffing, communicational and motivational problems associated with the global approach.[31] The regional approaches to organization occurred in a way that MNEs set up regional centres that undertake some of the tasks of the centre so that there is a better communication amongst the units of the organization and more diverse and efficient allocation of staffing and financial sources. These organizational structures were developed because of the inadequacy of the alternatives to solve the problems that more globalized business environments raised. Moreover the matrix and regionally structured organizations have initiated examples of the first transformation to the horizontal structure.

In summary, before the final stage of developments in the last century, we can divide the organization of multinational enterprises into some stages.[32] First most MNEs go through an initial period with relatively autonomous foreign subsidiaries that are tied to the parent company by financial and managerial links in a way like in a branch or agency. Secondly, this unstructured system of subsidiaries was successful for some time, but if the subsidiaries grew rapidly and accumulated resources, pressures to increase control emerge at the headquarters as the international division increases in dimension. Top managers recognized a need for a worldwide perspective and thus a need for a global structure. This resulted in the development of the U-form and later evolved to the M-form. When both foreign sales and foreign product diversity are high, some companies adopted a new structure, the global matrix structure.

The structure indicated above was the general environment before the business was more complicated and more globalized. New information and communication technologies, the liberalization and globalization of markets, the integration of different products increased uncertainty in many industries and increased volatility in the last two centuries brought new way of designing

---

[30] Bartlett and Ghoshal, 'Beyond the M-form'.

[31] Marschan, Rebecca, *New Structural Forms and Inter-Unit Communication in Multinationals* (HSEBA Publications, Helsinki 1996), p. 6.

[32] Alarik, 'From M-form'.

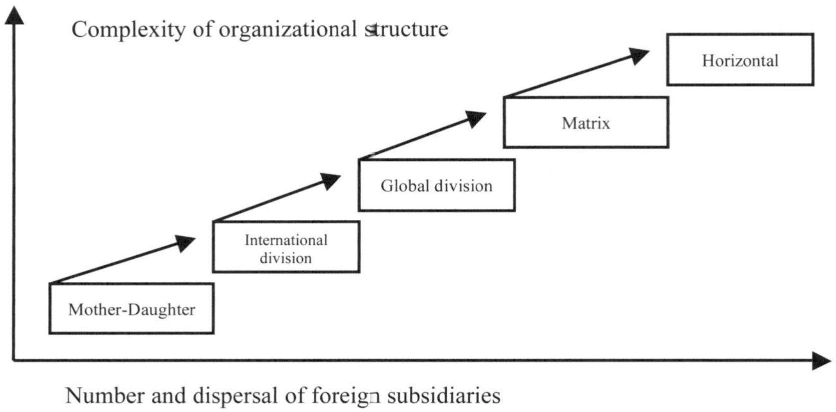


*Figure 2.3 The process towards less-hierarchical structure*[33]

organizational structure. The new structure was innovative and changed many basic characteristics of organizations of MNEs.

## HORIZONTALLY – LESS HIERARCHICALLY – STRUCTURED MULTINATIONAL ENTERPRISES

A new generation of scholars, the process school: Barlett, Ghoshal, Doz, Prahalad, Hendlund and others dominated the international business organization studies since the middle of the 1980s. They claimed that the organizational structure of MNEs was changing. They do not only claim to have discovered the emergence of a new organizational model but also claim to having contributed to a new concept and a new organizational theory of the MNE.[34] Accordingly they believe that the structural dimensions of MNEs are changing towards more flexible structure with characteristics of cultural control.[35]

A causative factor to the increasing use of new structural mechanisms in MNEs is that classic mechanisms – M-form and Matrix – alone are considered incapable of capturing the turbulence of today's competitive environment.[36] Therefore, the horizontally structured organization system is a creature of the information age, post-modern organizations held together by information tech-

33 Adapted from Marschan, *New Structural Forms*.
34 Alarik, 'From M-form'.
35 *Ibid.*
36 Marschan, *New Structural Forms*, p. 31.

nology.[37] The information era is a complete new challenge for humanity and human relations and, as happened in the past, new types of organizational structures have been developed to meet these new challenges.

The studies were from many different institutions in a short time. This proves that the changes were realized by many scholars. Different names are used to describe the new organization type: geocentric,[38] dynamic network,[39] heterarchy,[40] transnational,[41] integrated network,[42] horizontal,[43] multi-centre,[44] integrated players,[45] wired,[46] transcontinental,[47] multidimensional,[48] N-form,[49] integrated global, network-based,[50] metanational,[51] differentiated network,[52] individualized

---

37 Kobrin, S.J., 'The Architecture of Globalisation: State Sovereignty in a Networked Global Economy' in Dunning, J.H., *Governments, Globalisation, and International Business* (Oxford University Press, Oxford 1997), p. 153.

38 Perlmutter, H.V., 'The Tortuous Evolution of the Multinational Corporation' (1969) Jan–Feb, Columbia Journal of World Business 9.

39 Miles, R.E. and Snow, C.C., 'Designing Strategic Human Resources Systems' (1984) 13 Organizational Dynamics 36.

40 Hedlund, G., 'The Hypermodern MNC – A Heterarchy?' (1986) 25 International Studies of Management 9.

41 Bartlett, C.A., 'Building and Managing Transnational: The New Organisational Challenge In Competition' in Porter, M.E., *Global Industries* (Harvard Business School Press, 1986).

42 Bartlett and Ghoshal, 'Beyond the M-form'.

43 White, R. and Poynter, T.A., 'Organising for World-Wide Advantages' in Bartlett, C., Doz, Y. and Hedlund, G. (eds) *Managing the Global Firm* (Routledge, London 1996).

44 Forsgren, M., Holm, U. and Thilenius, P., 'Network Infusion in the Multinational Corporation' in Bjorkman, I., Forsgren, M., *The Nature of the Transnational Firm* (Handelshonjskolens Forlag, Copenhagen 1997).

45 Gupta, A.K and Govindarajan, V., 'Knowledge Flows and the Structure of Control Within Multinational Corporations' (1991) 16 The Academy of Management Review 768.

46 Hagstrom, P., 'The "Wired" Multinational Corporation: The Role of Information Systems for Structural Change in Complex Organizations' (Ph.D., Stockholm School of Economics, 1991).

47 Humes, S., *Managing the Multinational Confronting the Global-Local Dilemma* (Prentice Hall, New York 1993).

48 Johanson, J. and Mattson, L.G., 'Internationalisation in Industrial Systems: A Network Approach Compared with a Transaction Cost Approach' (1987) 17 International Studies of Management and Organisation 34.

49 Hedlund, G. and Ridderstrahle, J., 'Towards a Theory of the Self-Renewing MNC' in Toyre, B. and Night, D. (eds) *International Business: An Emerging Vision* (South Coralline Press Columbia SC University, 1997), p. 329.

50 Malnight, 'The Transition'.

51 Doz, Y., Santos, J. and Williamson, P., 'The Metanational: The Next Step in the Evolution of Multinationals' in Birkinshaw, J. (ed.), *The Future of Multinational Company* (Wiley, London 2004).

52 Nohria, N., *The Differentiated Network: Organising Multinational Corporations for Value Creation* (Jossey-Bass Publishers, San Francisco 1997).

enterprise,[53] embedded multinational[54] and less-hierarchical.[55] These names are separated on just very small differences in perceptions of the facts. I wish to name the new organizational type as horizontally structured multinationals and less-hierarchical multinationals.

For the purpose of this chapter, there is no need for detailed discussion of the definitions under each study; rather, leaving this ongoing study to the scholars in the management field, the book focuses on the common characteristics of horizontal structures and their reflections in practice. The researchers share a general view about the organizational evolution in MNEs; their structures are becoming less hierarchical. The fact that top management of several MNEs have had to reconsider the long-standing principle that 'the parent always knows the best' has required an essential change in the way the entire group is managed, turning it from a hierarchical pyramid into an integrated network of horizontally structured enterprises.[56]

The spreading of the sources, managerial capabilities, and strategic and operational decision-making throughout the organization in the new structure expanded the possibilities for foreign subsidiaries to both exploit and create firm-specific advantages, and thus play a greater and more active role in the success of MNEs. It also creates a more effective organization of knowledge, innovation and technological growth in international MNE organization.[57]

By decentralizing assets and resources into these specialized operating units, these enterprises are trying to generate an environment in which this limited knowledge can be developed and applied most properly. However this creates a greater need for a powerful horizontal integration process to ensure that the entire organization benefits from the specialized resources and expertise developed in its entrepreneurial units.[58] The transition between decentralized and network-based approaches must be considered as well. This involves the gradual linking and integrating of previously autonomous affiliates through a series of particular phases, each representing practical responses to existing external and internal challenges and opportunities.[59] The process of change is explained very well by Pettigrew and Fenton:[60]

---

53 Ghoshal, S. and Barlett, C.A., *The Individualized Corporation* (Harper Collins Publishers, New York 1997).

54 Forsgren, M., Holm, U. and Johanson, J., *Managing the Embedded Multinational* (Edward Elgar, Cheltenham, UK, Northampton, MA, USA 2005).

55 Marschan, *New Structural Forms*, p. 31.

56 Marschan, *New Structural Forms*, p. 5.

57 Tolentino, P.E., 'Hierarchical Pyramids and Heterarchical Networks: Organisational Structures of Multinational Corporations and Its Impact on World Development' (2002) 21 Contrib. Pol. Economy 69.

58 Bartlett and Ghoshal, 'Beyond the M-form'.

59 Malnight, 'The Transition'.

60 Pettigrew and Fenton, 'Theoretical Perspectives', p. 8.

> By depth we mean the flattening of hierarchies and the breaking down of barriers between functions in order to create the horizontal and vertical integration of knowledge. At the same time, the vertical integration of the value chain is being dismantled to allow the firm to concentrate on its core competencies. To this end, integration or interdependence becomes the necessities flexible organizational boundaries and requires greater cooperation and relational forms of organizing.

The main characteristics of horizontally structured MNEs are these:[61] first the enterprise consists of many centres as a result of shifting geographically and functionally the power of control from parent to subsidiary level. Secondly, subsidiaries are granted global or regional responsibilities for a particular function, or product line, or even whole business divisions. Such multi-centredness as opposed to the view of having one centre and the boundary is a major element in the new model.[62] Thirdly, the importance of culture control is stressed as a communication and decision-making mechanism.[63] Fourthly, the continuous flow of information across organizational and national boundaries is emphasized.

Accordingly a less-hierarchical structure comprises the following five dimensions:[64] (1) allocation of certain levels of decision-making authority to subsidiaries, which are considered capable for strategic decision-making; (2) de-layering of organizational levels; subsidiary units are given specialized roles in terms of functional and geographical operation.[65] Removing layers is a structural change which facilitates decentralized decision-making;[66] (3) geographical dispersion of key functions across units in different countries which can happen within the same jurisdiction as well; (4) de-bureaucratization of formal procedures, the formalized procedure of decision-taking abandoned in favour of independent decision-taking; (5) differentiations of work responsibility and authority among subsidiary units. This aims to facilitate more independent decision-taking by subsidiaries within well-defined responsibilities.

---

61 Marschan, *New Structural Forms*, p. 5.

62 Forsgren, Holm and Thilenius, 'Network Infusion'.

63 In a case study of a pharmaceutical company, Pettigrew and Fenton conclude that 'national firms were driven to cooperate via network cultural control, while the consultants and project teams were governed by cultural controls of both the network and pharmaceutical industry'. See Pettigrew, A.M. and Fenton, E.M., 'Integrating a Global Professional Services Organisation: The Case Of Ove Arup Partnership' in Pettigrew, A.M., Fenton, E.M. (eds) *The Innovating Organisation* (Sage Publications, London 2000).

64 Marschan, Rebecca, 'Dimensions of Less-Hierarchical Structures in Multinationals' in Bjorkman, I. and Forsgren, M (eds), *The Nature of the Transnational Firm* (Mumkgaard, Copenhagen 1997), p. 441.

65 Hedlund and Ridderstrahle, 'Towards a Theory'.

66 Marschan, 'Dimensions', p. 439.

In this modern form different dimensions are focused upon in a more flexible way, different for different parts of the company and different over time. The organization encourages managers to think in many dimensions, rather than imposing formalized vertical structures.[67] This is the dominant characteristic of these MNE forms, referred to as less-hierarchical structures in this book; they operate as integrated networks, rather than behaving as hierarchical control mechanisms.[68] Accordingly this new innovative structuring has led to more globalized MNEs placing less reliance on traditional hierarchical governance structures and dictating relationships, and moving towards a system of cross-networks based on multiple centres of heterarchical decision-taking.[69] The roles of subsidiaries are getting more important, subsidiaries are given roles as 'global innovators' and incorporated players.[70]

This new form decentralizes responsibilities for short-term profit and long-term developments to front-level units which combine with flexibility over the boundaries of divisions to assure demands, business relations and customers. Management at top and middle levels supports co-operation, by distributing specialized roles. The new model is grounded in a managerial perspective that is very different from that of existing economic and behavioral theories of the firm. Thus the new organization in MNEs also challenges management roles, implying that, rather than traditional top-down decision-making, decisions should be made through communication and collaboration between managers at different levels within different roles.[71]

Figure 2.4 indicates the main characteristics of horizontal organizations. Accordingly subsidiaries are characterized as specialized divisions. On the other hand, the role of the centre is defined as coordinator of decision-making. There is a complex exchange of components, products, people and information among independent subsidiary units. There should be no confusion, horizontal exchanges of information and other elements do not exclude headquarters but it does not necessarily permit headquarters to have a dominant position in decision-making.[72] In practice the process of moving towards a less-hierarchical structure is most commonly imposed from the top of the corporation through

---

67 Ghoshal and Barlett, *The Individualized Corporation*.

68 Forsgren, Holm and Thilenius, 'Network Infusion'; Hedlund and Ridderstrahle, 'Towards a Theory'.

69 Dunning, *Multinational…Global Economy*, p. 216.

70 Anderson, J.C., Hakansson, H. and Johanson, J., 'Dyadic Business Relationships Within a Business Network' (1994) 4 Journal of Marketing 1.

71 Ghoshal, S. and Barlett, C.A., 'The Multinational Corporations as an Inter Organizational Network' (1990) 15 Academy of Management Review 603.

72 White and Poynter, 'Organising for World-Wide'; Marschan, *New Structural Forms*, p. 3.

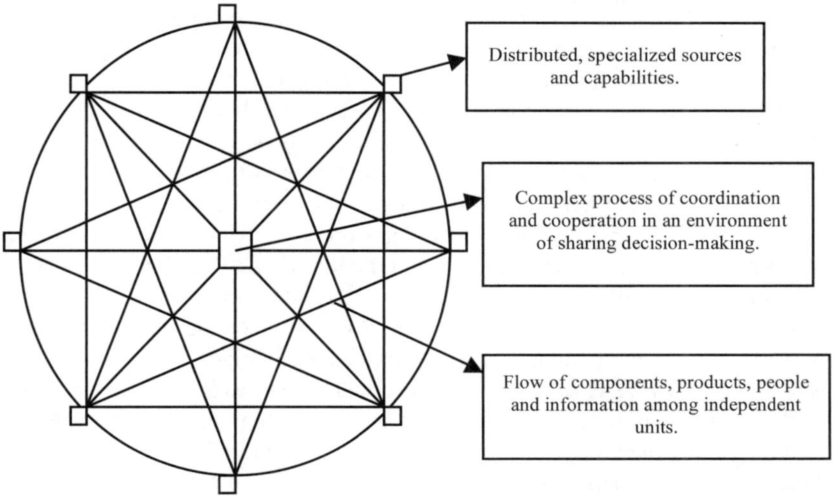


*Figure 2.4 The horizontal organization*[73]

an essentially centralized effort.[74] Thus the fact of the removal of hierarchy does not refer to complete removal of hierarchy. In contrast to the traditional hierarchical perspective, in which the centre controls all of the activities of MNEs and makes all strategic decisions, the horizontal perspective assumes multiple centres of expertise around the world, greater strategic rules for subsidiaries, and flexible governance structures.[75]

The first important case study[76] was conducted by Bartlett and Ghoshal[77] on ABB.[78] On ABB the middle managers' crucial horizontal linkage role is supported by a top management that creates a value-based perspective to support and reward collaborative behaviour, and by a front line management that exploits the personal networks such horizontal relationships facilitate. The managers had left their traditional roles of operational conductors of top-down decisions

---

[73] Adopted from Bartlett, C.A. and Ghoshal, S., 'Managing in a Transnational' in McKern, B. (ed.), *Managing Global Network Corporation* (Routledge, London 2003).

[74] Marschan, *New Structural Forms*, p. 1.

[75] Birkinshaw, J., 'How Multinational Subsidiary Mandates are Gained And Lost' (1996) 27 Journal of International Business Studies 467.

[76] Extensive case studies can be found at Pettigrew, A.M. and Fenton, E.M. (eds) *The Innovating Organisation* (Sage Publications, London 2000).

[77] Bartlett and Ghoshal, 'Beyond the M-form'.

[78] ABB is a Switzerland-based engineering company that operates around 100 countries and employs 108,000 people. Its total asset in 2006 is over $25bn. More information is available at http://www.abb.com.

and become the primary entrepreneurial actors of the enterprise. It is a very different process than the vertical planning and resource allocation process at the core classical model, but a vital one for a company competing in an increasingly knowledge-based economy.[79] Later, another study concluded that ABB has decentralized operational decision-making to its network of profit centres, whereas strategic decision-making is shared between the business areas and business segments, rather than concentrated entirely at the head office.[80]

Citibank's[81] European corporate banking structure in 1994 closely resembled network-based MNE models described in the literature.[82] The bank's structure incorporated centralized products and functional support centres – centres of excellence. Widespread straight horizontal flows between these units and local marketing units were similar to theories created by scholars. However, moving beyond this structure, research at Citibank could be used to develop a framework for the transition process in moving from decentralized towards network-based MNE organizational models.[83] For the better understanding of the structure we should examine the structure of Philips[84] as another example.

In Figure 2.5, it is seen that Philips has subsidiaries in multiple countries and each has managerial ties with the centre in Holland. Moreover there are regional centres and these centres also have ties with subsidiaries in the region. A more interesting finding in the chart is that regional centres have managerial ties with each other. This proves the decentralized nature of the management structure of the group. Moreover regional centres can make independent decisions from the centre in Holland.

The structure of Shell can be given as another example. The corporate governance chart on their website indicates that there is an advice and service relationship between service (function) companies and operating (business) companies. The operating companies have restricted relationship with parent companies because they receive these services from the service companies

---

79 ABB in 1997 had 39 business areas and over 1,000 subsidiaries with 5,000 profit centres in 140 countries. See further Ruigrok, W., Achtenhagen, L., Wagner, M. and Ruegg-Sturm, J., 'ABB: Beyond the Global Matrix towards the Network Multidivisional Organisation' in Pettigrew, A.M., Fenton, E.M. (eds) *The Innovating Organisation* (Sage Publications, London 2000), p. 117.

80 Ruigrok, Achtenhagen, Wagner and Ruegg-Sturm, p. 143.

81 Citibank is a US-based financial group and it is the leader in the world in banking sector. More information is available at www.citibank.com.

82 This is a result of Malnight's case study of Citibank. See Malnight, 'The Transition'.

83 Malnight, 'The Transition'.

84 Royal Philips Electronics of the Netherlands is one of the biggest MNEs in electronics industry. Philips employs 121,700 people in more than 60 countries. More information is available at www.philips.com.

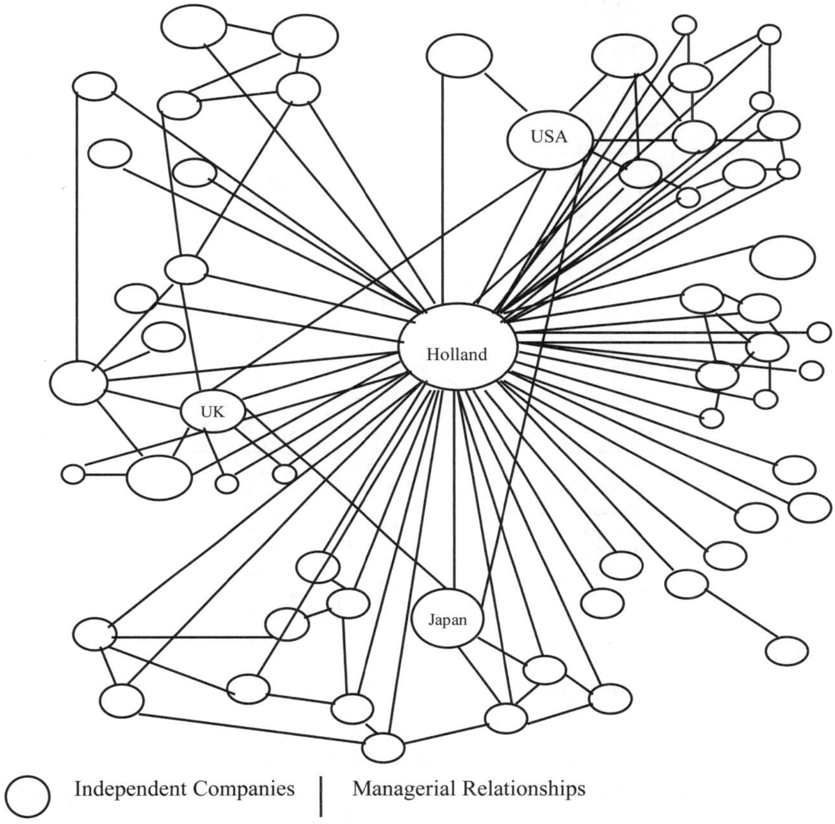


*Figure 2.5 Organizational structure of N.V. Philips*[85]

although there is no ownership relationship between those companies. The chart is also an indication of a power share between parent and subsidiaries. According to the earlier organizational chart, which indicates the ownership relationship of the Shell group before it was restructured in 2005, there was no ownership structure between the business and function companies in the groups.[86]

There are interesting similarities between the structure of Shell and the structure of Bayer. Similar to Shell, Bayer divides its main organizational structure

---

85 Adapted from Ghoshal and Barlett, 'The Multinational Corporations'.

86 It is available at http://www.shell.com/home/Framework?siteId=in-en&FC2=&FC3=/in-en/html/iwgen/about_shell/who_we_are/structure_of_shell_ga_1011.html accessed 31 December 2007.

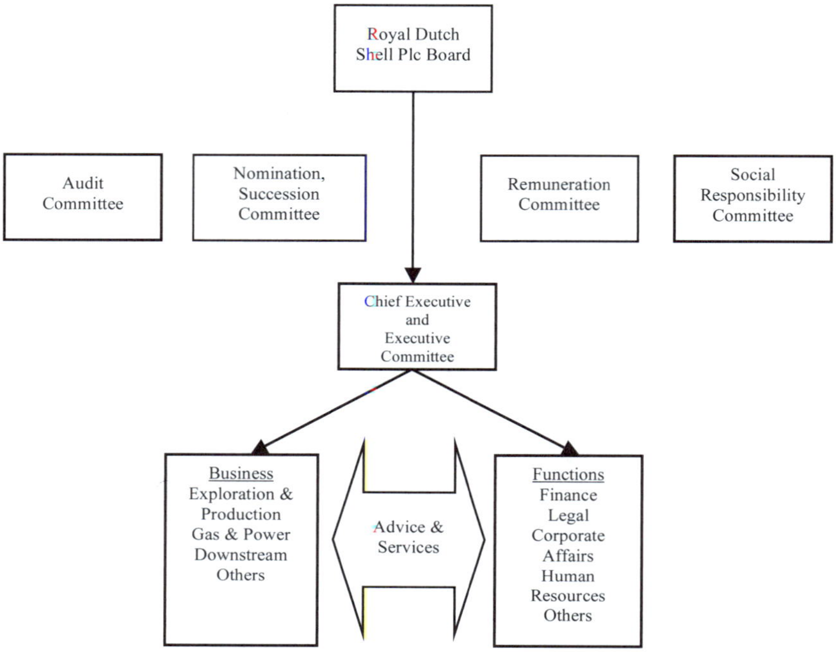


*Figure 2.6 Corporate governance structure of Shell in 2007*[87]

into three business operations companies and three central service companies. The main function of service companies is to develop better services for the group's business operating companies. Bayer has also a corporate centre whose function is not clearly stated on their website but, from the structure of the group, it can be claimed that it does not have a function like a parent company's function in a vertical organization. Rather its function is to create group principles that are applicable in operation of entities under the group and thus facilitate coordination amongst subsidiaries.

The most important conceptual difference between traditional vertical and less-hierarchical organizations is that traditional organizations are characterized by strong reliance on hierarchy and formal structure. In contrast less-hierarchical organizations are seen as not being constrained by formal organizational charts. Rather these forms of organization rely increasingly on informal control and

[87] Shell is a global group of energy and petrochemical companies, operating in more than 140 countries and territories, employing approximately 109,000 people. More information is available at http://www.shell.com.

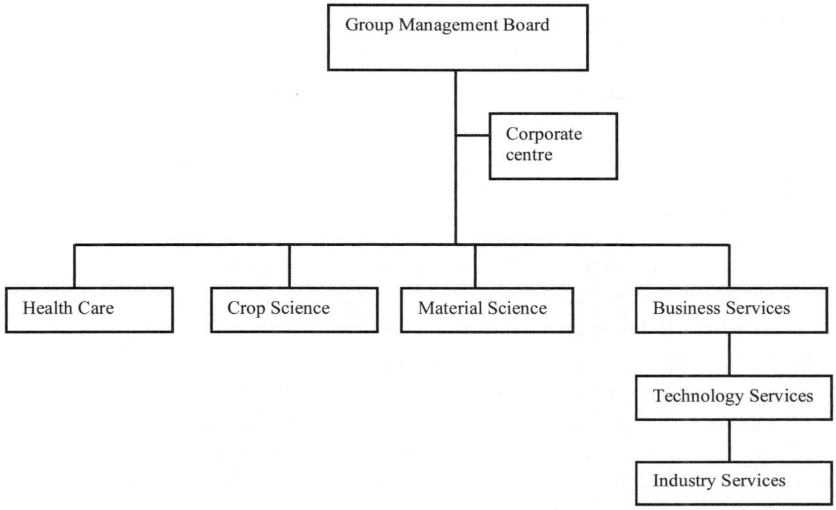


*Figure 2.7 The structure of Bayer*[88]

co-ordination mechanisms such as personal relationships and organizational culture to manage the dispersed subsidiary network.[89] The reduced degree of hierarchy reflects the increased influence of subsidiary units in relation to headquarters.[90] Horizontally structured MNE models have been associated with escalating horizontal linkages between scattered operating units through a collection of organizational mechanisms, whereas the earlier enterprises tended to emphasize an official organizational structure and their hierarchical operating mechanism.[91] Moreover the evolutionary structure developed in this chapter presents the direction of change being driven by steady adjustments in several aspects of operations of MNEs. Rather than swiftly moving towards horizontal structure, each stage represented a practical strategic response to then-existing challenges and opportunities.[92] Therefore some enterprises have completed their organizational evolution while some others have just started their process. We should also bear in mind that there is a dynamic changing process in any

---

[88] Bayer is a Germany-based pharmaceutical company. It operates worldwide through 350 subsidiaries and employs 110,200 people. More information is available at www.bayer.com.

[89] Ghoshal and Barlett, 'The Multinational Corporations'.

[90] Forsgren, Holm and Thilenius, 'Network Infusion'.

[91] Malnight, 'The Transition'.

[92] *Ibid.*

particular business enterprise. It is important to acknowledge the fact that MNEs are dynamic organizations with constant changing processes, rather than static organizational structures.

## REGIONALLY ORGANIZED MULTINATIONAL ENTERPRISES

Another way of operating MNEs is to divide an enterprise into area divisions; each is responsible for all operations in some overseas region. This solution is popular where the foreign subsidiaries supply one another with components or intermediate products. However, this requires close co-ordination.[93] Subsidiary units are granted highly specialized roles in terms of functional and geographical responsibilities. In order to increase the function of the new structure several companies have also created finance centres and regional research and development units to support activities of other subsidiaries.[94] Such a development movement shows the significance of global functional management and the need for the new structure.

What has happened, particularly within the EU, is that an MNE has transferred an organizational system to each group of its affiliates located in a particular region. The possible gains from internalized transactions between parents and subsidiaries were not sufficient to create the most efficient organizations, thus MNEs prefer regional horizontal structures in order to benefit from common governance of the value-added activities of affiliates.[95] Thus we cannot exclude relationships between sister units in regional organizations from the horizontally structured MNEs. Although there may be differences in what actors and relational magnitude influence the internal and the external parts of the organization, the subsidiary relations in an organizational context should be regarded as another system independent of the legal borders of the MNEs.[96]

There are no conceptual differences between regionally organized MNEs and horizontally organized MNEs. The regional divisions represent one of the functional, special expertise units of the enterprise and can co-exist with other units such as finance, research, marketing and production. Hence it is common to witness some enterprises that accommodate both regional divisions or specialized area divisions. The horizontal organizational structure is a requirement in

---

93 Caves, *Multinational…Economic Analyses*, p. 85.
94 Marschan, *New Structural Forms*, p. 22.
95 Dunning, *Multinational…Global Economy*, p. 130.
96 Forsgren, Holm and Thilenius, 'Network Infusion', p. 477.

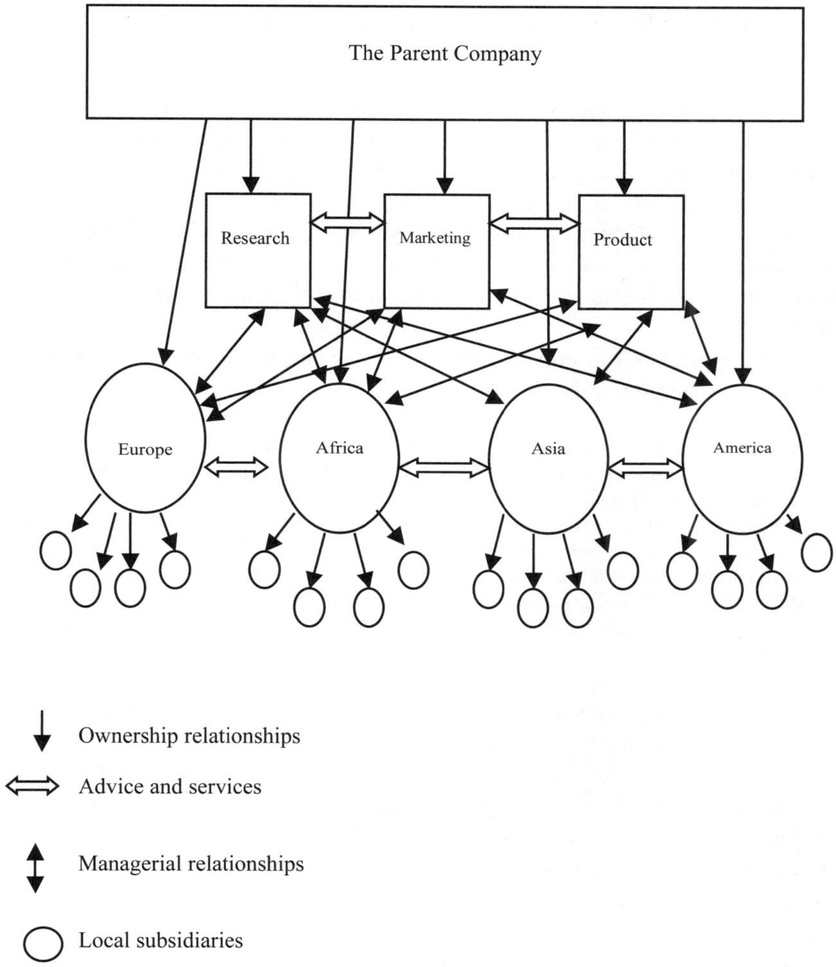


*Figure 2.8 The regionally and functionally divided horizontal organization*

order to reach maximum efficiency in these types of organizations. Therefore an organizational structure similar to that in Figure 2.8 is quite likely to exist in many enterprises.

## MANAGING ON GLOBAL CONCERN: COMMON GROUP POLICY

The horizontal structure occurs mainly in the internal relationships of companies and is very hard to display from outside. MNEs are reluctant to disclose their detailed data of organizational structure. Rather they prefer giving general information about the group as a whole without any particular reference to their structure. However, examining their annual financial and CSR reports reveals some indications that they are operating in a complex structure and the corporate centre is more policy determinant than direct controller of the subsidiaries.

For example, HSBC[97] emphasizes the global characteristic of the organization in their introduction to the group in their website:

> References to HSBC on this website refer to the HSBC Group of discrete legal entities, each of which is wholly or partly owned by HSBC Holdings plc. The entities, which form the HSBC Group, provide a comprehensive range of financial services to personal, commercial, corporate, institutional and investment, and private banking clients. To more easily promote the Group as a whole, HSBC was established as a uniform, international brand name in 1999. In 2002, HSBC launched a campaign to differentiate its brand from those of its competitors by describing the unique characteristics which distinguish HSBC, summarized by the words 'The world's local bank'.[98]

The important proposal derived from this introduction will be their natural acceptance of operating as a group and promoting this fact by creating an image at global level even though HSBC is made up of many legally independent companies incorporated in various jurisdictions around the world. Similar introduction and emphasis can be found on Shell's website. In their annual review, they give a brief explanation about what the group is comprised of and how they publicize their group:

> In this Review 'Group' is defined as Royal Dutch Shell together with all of its consolidated subsidiaries. The expressions 'Shell', 'Group', 'Shell Group' and 'Royal Dutch Shell' are sometimes used for convenience where references are made to the Group or Group companies in general. Likewise, the words 'we', 'us' and 'our' are

---

[97] HSBC Holdings is a public limited company incorporated in England and Wales. The HSBC group operates in five regions. HSBC's international network comprises around 10,000 offices in 82 countries and territories in Europe, the Asia-Pacific region, the Americas, the Middle East and Africa. HSBC Holdings plc is held by nearly 200,000 shareholders in some 100 countries and territories. More information is available at www.hsbc.com.

[98] Available at www.hsbc.com.

> also used to refer to Group companies in general or to those who work for them. These expressions are also used where no useful purpose is served by identifying the particular company or companies. The expression 'Group companies' as used in this Review refers to companies in which Royal Dutch Shell either directly or indirectly has control, by having either a majority of the voting rights or the right to exercise a controlling influence. The companies in which the Group has significant influence but not control are referred to as 'associated companies' or 'associates' and companies in which the Group has joint control are referred to as 'jointly controlled entities'. In this Review, associates and jointly controlled entities are also referred to as 'equity accounted investments'. The term 'Group interest' is used for convenience to indicate the direct and/or indirect equity interest held by the Group in a venture, partnership or company (i.e., after exclusion of all third-party interests).[99]

The selection of an MNE and examining its CSR reports will indicate similar facts regarding the integrated managerial structure. As a common theme in their CSR reports, MNEs are happy to create a report covering all entities in the group. Therefore it can be considered that having unified CSR is a reflection of modern structure. For example the CSR report of General Motors[100] takes a global approach:

> GM Corporate Responsibility reporting continues to evolve in order to present a global picture of its business. All specific regional and country/local activity can be found in the web report according to business unit structure: GMNA (US, Canada, Mexico), GME (Europe, UK, Sweden, etc.) GMAP (Asia Pacific Rim, including China, India and Australia) GMLAAM (Latin America, Africa and the Middle East).... The report is global in scope and highlights our key performance indicators for reporting year 2004/5.[101]

Accordingly in business theory MNEs operate in accordance with common group policy together with global management structure. They create a group image and try to promote group on this image. Therefore they are eager to use the terms of either brand name like Shell or HSBC or plural forms of expressing the corporate groups such as 'we, our group, us'. This is due to the fact that, from a business perspective, this new kind of enterprise is best understood as 'global' rather than 'multinational'.[102] The CEO of IBM states it very clearly as 'a reliance on hierarchies contained within one function, enterprise, or nation must be supplemented by new ways of establishing trust, based on shared values

---

99 Available at www.shell.com.

100 General Motors Corp. is the world's largest automaker. GM employs 280,000 people and manufactures its cars and trucks in 33 countries. More information is available at www.gm.com.

101 Available at http://www.gm.com/company/gmability/.

102 Palmisano S.J., 'The Globally Integrated Enterprise' (2006) 85 Foreign Affairs 127.

that cross borders and formal organizations … global corporate integration will involve significant changes in organizational culture'.[103]

Moreover, the groups include not only wholly owned subsidiaries but also controlled entities as well as associated entities. This is interesting because there is no limitation of percentage of ownership to claim the subsidiary belongs to the group; in a business sense, associated companies belong to MNEs.[104] In short MNEs operate as integrated groups and create a public image by promoting their enterprise as an integrated group with a group management board and global management structure and the common group policy. This situation may be best named as using Dunning's expression of 'global localization'.[105]

## NETWORKED ENTERPRISES: RELATIONSHIPS BETWEEN THE FIRMS UNDER DIFFERENT OWNERSHIP

In some cases of multinational business transactions, decisions are taken by not only the MNE but originate from the different firms that are connected to each other by contract rather than ownership.[106] This leads to claims that MNEs' definitions can be extended to include not only subsidiaries under common ownership and control but also networked companies that are connected to each other in some kind of contractual and strategic relationship. The basic structure of networked enterprises is examined here because they have shown that many relationships between firms and the network are both heterarchical and multidimensional and are similar to horizontally structured MNEs.[107]

Especially in the last two decades, inter-firm agreements have become an increasingly important form of cross-border economic involvement. There has been a huge increase in the number of international inter-firm agreements.[108] The network relationship is not only designed at the top level but also any subsidiary, as a characteristic of horizontal organization, tends to form a network relationship with multiple entities such as suppliers, customers, scientific bodies and investment agencies.[109] Accordingly in horizontally structured MNEs, each

---

103 *Ibid.*

104 Forsgren, Holm and Johanson, p. 93.

105 Dunning, *Multinational…Global Economy*, p. 133.

106 For historical evolution and extensive example case studies see Österle, H., Fleisch, E. and Alt, R., *Business Networking: Shaping Collaboration between Enterprises* (Springer, Berlin 2001); Forsgren, Holm and Johanson, *Managing*.

107 Dunning, *Multinational…Global Economy*, p. 258.

108 Goerzen, A., Beamish, P.W., 'The Effect of Alliance Network Diversity on Multinational Enterprise Performance' (2005) 26 Strategic Management Journal 333; see also UNCTAD, World Investment Report, 2000.

109 Tavares, 'Strategic Management'.

subsidiary is also embedded in a unique network of business relationship.[110] The coverage of network enterprises thus goes beyond the border of MNEs.[111] In a networked enterprise, the subsidiary has a dual role; one is inside the MNEs' organization as horizontally integrated players together with other subsidiaries; the other is an independent enterprise building outside networks.[112] These linkages might occur at various levels such as at domestic or multinational level. The increasing speed of technological complexity and the need for firms to respond ever more quickly to the actions of competitors have forced them to collaborate to maintain or advance their competitive position.[113] Moreover even the global integration of markets by a single enterprise, particularly in some industries, may no longer be sufficient to balance the huge costs and risks of technological development in a number of strategic industries. Thus there is a big increase in the number of technology-driven collaborative agreements or strategic alliances among leading MNEs from the major industrial countries; even the largest MNEs must cooperate to deal with the cost, risk and complexity of technology.[114] Alliances represent a transformation of the model of organization of international economic transactions from hierarchically structured MNEs to networked companies.[115]

Whereas most of the analysis of cooperative alliances has centred on the relationship between different groups but in international relationships, it is clear that modern MNEs are adopting a more pluralistic approach to their overseas activities. Consequently the form and structure of these networked groups will influence the model of the relationships between the firms under partnership.[116] A network relationship implies that there are some linked transactions of firms within the network.[117] There is a well-structured division of work amongst firms in the network. This change in corporate strategies often requires alterations at the level of important decision-making processes.[118] Thus networked enterprises can exercise some, but limited, control over each other; this control is not restricted to direct exchange information between the partners.[119] In short the activities are co-ordinated neither by the market nor by a central hierarchical plan but by the establishment of a set of relationships between the

110 Forsgren, Holm and Johanson, *Managing*, p. 6.
111 *Ibid.* p. 7.
112 *Ibid.* p. 103.
113 Kobrin, 'The Architecture of Globalisation', p. 151.
114 *Ibid.*
115 *Ibid.*
116 Dunning, *Multinational... Global Economy*, p. 92.
117 Goerzen and Beamish, 'The Effect of Alliance'.
118 Tavares, 'Strategic Management'.
119 Forsgren, Holm and Johanson, *Managing*, p. 20.

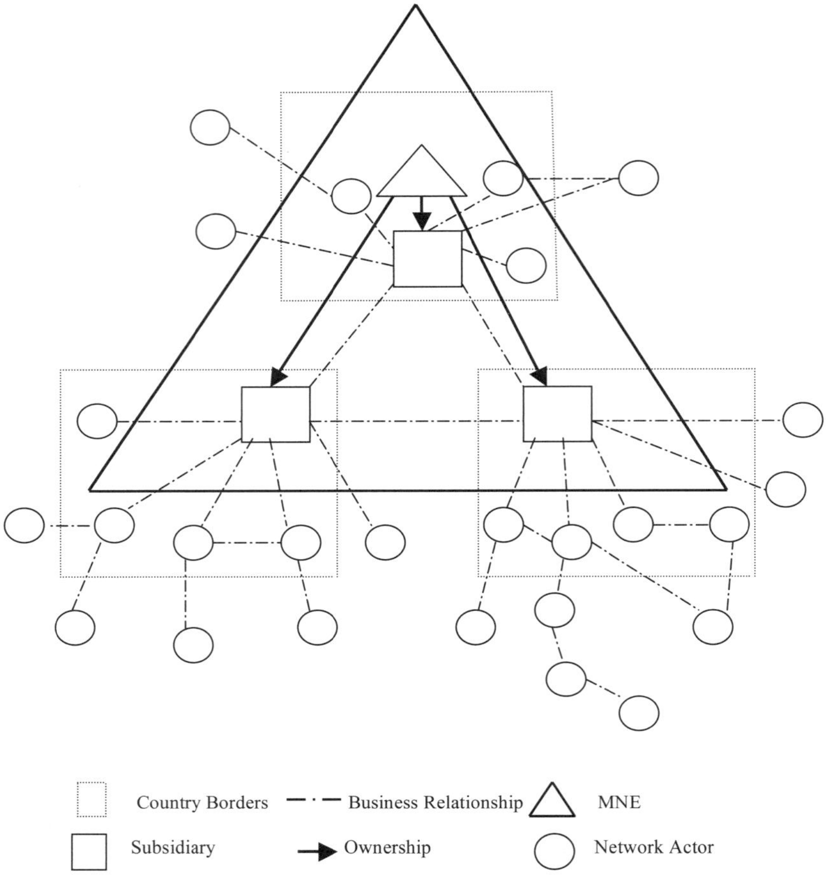


*Figure 2.9 The networked enterprise*[120]

members of the network.[121] As a result, these newly established relations create the network. From this perspective, the subsidiaries particularly play a central role as they are the units which work at the functioning frontier and handle day-to-day responsibilities through engaging in business relationships.[122]

It is a fact that cooperative alliances, brought about by the growth of inter-firm collaborative agreements, are reshaping of the boundaries of firms. This opens

120 Adopted from Forsgren, Holm and Johanson, *Managing*, p. 79.
121 Dunning, *Multinational...Global Economy*, p. 92.
122 Forsgren, Holm and Thilenius, 'Network Infusion'.

up new challenges to the researchers.[123] However, these strategic alliances represent a networked model of organization of international economic transactions, which can be distinguished from equity-based MNEs, which have different aims in their structure strategies. The relationship amongst the units in the network is limited and thus is not very advanced as in horizontal structures. Therefore it is very unlikely to see very sophisticated control mechanisms or intense exchanges of staff and components or broad financial assistance amongst the units in networked organizations. Accordingly one central question is relevant here, whether a networked enterprise organization is a separate organizational type employing distinctive control mechanisms.[124] We can conclude that although networked enterprises are a distinctive form of economic cooperation, they do not represent the same characteristics as horizontally structured MNEs due to lack of ownership relations amongst the firms. Therefore networks represent a type of arrangement with its own specific distinctive features, which hereafter must be considered separately.[125] As a result, as Professor Dunning points out, since they address somewhat different issues, it is unlikely that the network model of internalization will replace that of the structure under the MNEs' model.[126] I agree with this statement that networked enterprises have not reached, at least at the moment, a point of representation of a distinctive social economic institution. Thus the concentration of regulation, from binding regulatory perspective, should still be on equity-based MNEs.

At this stage it is necessary to mention other inter-firm agreements. The most popular inter-firm agreement is joint ventures,[127] which can be defined as a legal entity formed between two or more parties to undertake economic activity together. However, joint ventures represent one type of inter-firm agreement and this currently extends to networked or other more complex relationships. Some of the joint venture contracts are vertical contracts: technology-transfer agreements, franchise contracts and input-supply agreements. Some other relations are more heterarchical in these types of organizations. For the same reasons articulated under the networked companies, the main characteristics of the joint ventures are the same as networked enterprises structures;[128] joint ventures will not be examined in this book.

---

123 Dunning, *Multinational...Global Economy*, p. 92.

124 Kobrin, 'The Architecture of Globalisation', p. 151.

125 *Ibid.* p. 152.

126 Dunning, *Multinational...Global Economy*, p. 208.

127 See Muchlinski, P., *Multinational Enterprises and the Law* (OUP, Oxford 2007), p. 66–67.

128 Marschan, *New Structural Forms*, p. 4.

## CONCLUSION: MNES AS HORIZONTAL ORGANIZATIONS

All these evaluations of the MNE structures as a business organization conducted in this chapter indicate that the relationship between parent companies and national subsidiaries in an MNE is not identical to those among an interacting group of universities, or social service organizations or state regulatory bodies or international political and economic institutions.[129] MNEs distinguish themselves in their goal, which is maximizing the profits for their shareholders. Thus MNEs have undergone changes in order to adapt themselves to dynamics of the new world affected by globalization.[130] MNEs responded to the challenges (if we cannot say they created the challenges) first between the social and business organization and adopted new organizational and management structures. In particular the new structures of MNE organization are used to describe the emerging world economy: a shift from standardized mass production to flexible production, from vertically integrated, large-scale organizations to unification of the value chain and horizontally organized economic units.[131] In the business world, the structure of this organization is invisible from the position of any particular organization, and it has no legal status. More importantly, the horizontal organization as a system is independent of the legal borders of MNEs.[132] It is, nevertheless, a significantly important non-contractual aspect in setting the outline of limitation under which the structures of enterprises must operate.[133] Since it is a fact, the law must recognize these facts and should create an essential regulatory frame for the operation of these institutions.

The organizational system shows its effect on the governance of the organization by splitting the responsibilities between the managers on different levels. The new structure reveals its effect not only in management systems but also in the structure of subsidiary ownership since it has to create a suitable legal background for the new managerial system to operate. The reason for creating legally independent companies was to meet the needs that the M-form created by establishing semi-autonomous units in the enterprise. This autonomist management structure could be achieved best by creating legally independent units. Moreover the hierarchical characteristic of the M-form led to a simple legal structure, mostly fully owned subsidiaries and sub-subsidiaries with little cross-ownership.

---

129 Ghoshal and Barlett, 'The Multinational Corporations'.
130 Dunning, *Multinational...Global Economy*, p. 218.
131 Kobrin, 'The Architecture of Globalisation', p. 154.
132 Forsgren, Holm and Thilenius, 'Network Infusion'.
133 Scott John, 'Corporate Groups'.

The horizontal organization requires, on the other hand, more complex ownership structures for MNEs. This leads MNEs to consider ownership structures under the group since the risk and management roles are divided. Therefore in horizontal structures it is very likely to see very complicated structures of cross-ownership between the companies under the group. HSBC can be given as a very simple example for this. On their website they have published a very simplified scheme of their group ownership structure. According to the HSBC Group Structure of Principal Operating Companies at January 2004, HSBC Holdings plc is the main company. However, the more we go to a lower level the more cross-ownership we see. The subsidiary companies own shares of other subsidiaries ranking from 3 to 100 percent. This chart is only a simplified ownership structure, many of the lower units have been excluded.[134]

Consequently cross-ownership is a fact rather than an exception in MNEs' structures. The reason for cross-ownership is the need to create appropriate legal flexibility for horizontal managerial structures. The legal flexibility that limited liability of companies creates has been used to organize this flexible structure. Thus the new regulations of MNEs should consider the cross-ownership together with horizontal managerial structure.

In conclusion, the new organizational structure emphasizes two important characteristics of MNEs, which are very important for examination of the liability discussions made in this book. The first one is the emphasis on horizontal structure with complex ownership features and geographical and functional dispersal of subsidiaries at global level. The second important characteristic is the replacement of hierarchical control with more flat horizontal decision-making based on cultural control, which affects the decision-making procedures at the subsidiary level.

---

[134] Available at http://a248.e.akamai.net/7/248/3622/1453d3fea3a9f2/www.img.ghq.hsbc.com/public/groupsite/assets/about/hsbc_group_structure_chart.pdf accessed 25 June 2006.

# 3. The legal structure of multinational enterprises

## INTRODUCTION

Historically, both in civil and common law systems, company laws are based on the concept of separate legal personality. It is assumed that a company is a distinct economic unit, which enjoys economic and managerial independence, and therefore must be considered as a legal person separate from its members. Legal personality gives great flexibility to an organization in structuring its affairs and facilitates creative exploitation of property rights. It also gives representative rights; they can sue and be sued, represent themselves in a court and can undertake obligations independent from its shareholders. Consequently the English, American and even new emerging European Community company laws are still based on theory of the independence of companies. The independence theory covers all companies, including single-member companies and wholly owned subsidiaries of MNEs.

On the other hand, companies are creatures of national legal systems since they are incorporated in certain jurisdictions. They are tied to definite nationalities from different perspectives as well.[1] However, in transnational economic activities, a single and independent national company exists only in theory. Since the emergence of modern company laws in the second half of 19th century, there have been speeches, teachings, litigation and legislation about company law but the primary reality today is not only the company, it is also company groups that have dominated the business world.[2] Even small-scale economic activities might be structured to operate their business under a corporate group structure. The domination of corporate groups can apparently be seen in the case of cross-border business operations because the largest commercial and industrial enterprises of the world are typically organized as groups of companies. They have many subsidiaries scattered around the world and some of the MNEs are

---

[1] See Chapter 4.

[2] Nolan, A., 'The Position of Unsecured Creditors Of Corporate Groups: Towards A Group Responsibility Solution Which Gives Fairness And Equity A Role' (1993) 11 CSLJ 461.

bigger than national state economies.[3] However the legal status is still in a state of uncertainty as it depends on theories that are mainly based on a single private company. Thus although the group structured MNEs have symbolized the efficient modern business actor ever since its emergence, this new affiliated enterprise system has been viewed as a special problem for the balance between the majority and minority shareholders in the corporation, and as a potential danger for the creditors of a subsidiary.[4]

Groups of companies may, economically, be defined as a union of companies, which operate under an aim to ensure the profitability of the association as a whole.[5] Some common characteristics of the group enterprises are these: first, a typical group of companies constitutes an economic unit, which is divided into a great number of legal units, for purposes of exploiting any possible convenience and benefit. Secondly, a different and simpler functional group structure is applied in the complex legal structure of the group.[6] For more formal and general purposes, the OECD Guidelines for Multinational Enterprises provide the widest and the most accepted definition of MNEs in the international area.

> Multinational enterprises usually comprise companies or other entities established in more than one country and so linked that they may coordinate their operations in various ways. While one or more of these entities may be able to exercise a significant influence over the activities of others, their degree of autonomy within the enterprise may vary widely from one multinational enterprise to another, ownership may be private, state or mixed.[7]

Accordingly the characteristics of MNEs are these: first, they must be organized as more than one company, in a way that each and every company has its own legal personality, assuring that a subsidiary can have legal relations of its own, both within the organization and with outsiders.[8] Secondly, these companies must be related to each other through ownership and/or control and must operate as a commercial enterprise. Thirdly, the subsidiaries must perform in other countries rather than in home countries. According to these criteria, an MNE can be, in a practical approach, defined as a group of companies that

---

3 See Chapters 1 and 2.

4 Lutter, M., 'Enterprise Law Corp. vs. Entity Law Inc. – Philip Blumberg's Book from the Point of View of an European Lawyer (1990) 38 American Journal of Comparative Law 949.

5 Avgitidis, Dimitris K., *Group of Companies; The Liability of Parent Company for the Depths of its Subsidiary* (Sakkoulas, Athens-Komotini 1996), p. 71.

6 See Chapter 2.

7 OECD, Guidelines for Multinational Enterprises (27 June 2000), p. 18.

8 Griffiths, Andrew, *Corporate Governance and the Uses of Company* (University of Manchester, 1993).

through foreign direct investment organize subsidiaries under common ownership and management policy in a number of countries outside its home base.

The most outstanding feature of multinational company groups is their incredible complexity.[9] An MNE can have hundreds of subsidiaries all around the world with each subsidiary operating under its host country's regulatory arrangement, but practically they operate in accordance with the main economic and managerial policies of the group. Therefore there is a compound multinational enterprise structure under which, according to law, companies are independent from each other, but on the other hand, according to economic realties, they are completely interrelated. Thus even in a group of companies, it is sometimes difficult to distinguish between the legal personality of one member corporation and its wholly owned and controlled subsidiaries.[10] This complicated corporate structure is the main characteristic of both Civil law and Common law systems, which may be the most important common statement for the area of corporate affiliated enterprise system.[11]

The attraction of a subsidiary is that the combination of separate legal personality and limited liability enables its controller to separate an area of activity, or particular assets, and to control the subsidiary's legal relationship with the wider organization because the law has given little recognition to the essential differences between subsidiaries and freestanding companies. There is an effective shifting of risk from the controllers and owners to the creditors of a subsidiary resulting from the parent's limited liability.[12] Therefore the tendency in the UK as in the United States is for holding companies, other than pure investment companies, to hold the majority of the shares in all their subsidiaries, which will be sufficient to bring the subsidiaries under group structure.[13] This control of shares by another company is not only control but also brings subsidiaries under common group management systems. Here the liability problems arise, as unlike the individual majority shareholders, the common management system may have a reason to direct the subsidiary to act contrary to its own interest and may even put its existence in danger. Therefore being controlled and managed by a company shareholder and especially being open to be interfered with by other companies under a group structure could put corporate creditors at risk.

As a result modern enterprises largely comprise groups of corporations under common ownership and managerial structure. They present the possibility of

---

9 Hadden, T., 'Inside Corporate Groups' (1984) 12 Int'l J. Soc L. 271.

10 Nolan, 'The Position'.

11 Lutter, 'Enterprise Law Corp'.

12 Griffiths, *Corporate Governance.*

13 Hadden, Tom, 'Regulating Corporate Groups: International Perspective' in McCahery, J., Picciotto, S. and Scott, S. (eds), *Corporate Control and Accountability* (OUP, Oxford 1993), p. 347.

dividing an enterprise into smaller incorporated units to perform particular functions. The reasons for separate incorporations, other than economic reasons examined in the previous chapters, may range across a broad variety such as sheltering other units of the enterprise from subsidiary liability in specialized financial transactions and evading possible tort liability. Thus there can be use of corporateness to clearly further legitimate goals or possible abuse of corporate structure to avoid social conflict and corporate liability.[14] The main causes of the current problems in MNEs' tort liability concepts find their roots in two historical developments in the times of the emergence of capitalism and then powerful enterprises in the second half of the 19th century. The first one is the creation of a limited liability corporation and separate legal personality principles and the other one is allowing companies to have shares of another company. I wish to examine the second development first in order to reach a better understanding of the problems that groups of companies create.

## EMERGENCE OF GROUPS OF COMPANIES

In the early days, in America, the major restriction on corporate power, which is the lack of authority to acquire stock, was firmly established. Some states, such as New York and Illinois, went further and enacted statutes, expressly prohibiting corporations from acquiring and holding stock in another corporation.[15] As a result authorization for the ownership of shares of other corporations was very reluctantly granted and only to companies of a public character, such as railroad companies. In the absence of an express provision in the statute or the charter, it was held *ultra vires* or unlawful for a corporation to acquire shares in another corporation.[16] However this rule was changed dramatically after the acceptance of removing all restrictions and expressly authorizing businesses incorporated in New Jersey to acquire the stock of 'any other company that the directors might deem necessary'.[17] After New Jersey, other states followed and, eventually, the authority of corporations to own the shares of another corporation became universally recognized.[18]

---

14 Cashel, Thomas W., 'Multinational Challenge to Corporation Law: The Search for a New Corporate Personality' (1994) 9 JIBL 249.

15 Blumberg, P.I., *The Multinational Challenge to Corporation Law* (OUP, Oxford 1993), p.54.

16 Avgitidis, *Group of Companies*, p.69; Blumberg, P.I., *The Law of Corporate Groups: Tort, Contract, and Other Common Law Problems in the Substantive Law of Parent and Subsidiary Corporations* (Little Brown & Co, Boston, 1987), pp.56–60.

17 Blumberg, *The Multinational Challenge*, p.56.

18 Blumberg, *The Law... Tort, Contract*, p.59.

The first signs of softening in the legal position appeared in the railroads, whose exclusive operations led to the development of systems of bordering roads connecting important centres. Such provisions also appeared in charters of other railroads, bridge, steamship, and canal companies, but rarely appeared in the case of manufacturing companies.[19] Railroads thus comprised the first corporate groups in America. Subsequently the group structure has emerged as a usual business organizational structure and manufacturing companies followed the public sector companies and turned to be structured as a trust, similar to public trusts, like oil and sugar.

In 1890, the New York courts held the Sugar Trust to be unlawful and in 1892 the Ohio courts outlawed the Oil Trust.[20] Meanwhile the Sherman Antitrust Act was adopted in 1890. It became obvious that trust could no longer serve a mechanism for industry. Following the new legal situation, anxious corporate counsel recognized that the power to acquire shares of competitive corporations, if available, would serve as an alternative route to gain centralized control of competing firms and to achieve market concentration, perhaps even avoiding the Sherman Act.[21] New Jersey, being enthusiastic about enriching its treasury with licence fees from corporate promoters, enacted its ground-breaking statutes in 1888, 1889 and 1893. These new statutes provided an alternative route to industrial grouping, replacing the trust device that was then being outlawed.[22] The new law was the turning point for American business because a corporation no longer represented the whole enterprise; the enterprise became increasingly segregated between parent and subsidiary corporations. In contrast to the simple corporation with its clear line of distinction between the enterprise conducted by the corporation and the investors represented by the shareholders, the corporate group was rather different; the parent and shareholders combined made up the enterprise.

In Britain a company was able to purchase shares in another company only by virtue of a provision to this effect in the memorandum of association of the purchasing company. The English Companies Act 1862 provided for incorporation via the registration of companies. Under this system, the company powers were specified not only in the statute, but also in the company's memorandum of association. In England, therefore, corporate power to acquire and own the shares of another corporation could arise from provisions inserted in the memorandum by the promoters and their counsel.[23] Where the memorandum of

---

19 *Ibid.* p.57.

20 *People v North River Sugar Refining Co*, 121 N.Y. 582 (1890); *State ex rel. v Standard Oil Co*, 49 Ohio St. 137 (1892).

21 Blumberg, *The Multinational Challenge*, p.56.

22 *Ibid.*

23 Blumberg, *The Law… Tort, Contract*, p.61.

association was silent, the English court held that it was *ultra vires* for a company to purchase shares of another company. In *re Barned's Banking Co* and in *re Asiatic Banking Corp.*[24] it was held the power existed; neither the Common Law nor the 1862 Act invalidated the provision in the memorandum of association. With these cases pointing the way, the power to acquire and own shares of another corporation was thereafter simply achieved by drafting the memorandum of association accordingly.[25]

In summary, groups of companies first emerged more than 100 years ago, and met weak resistance from courts and in scholarly literature because they were not on the international level but rather mainly in the United States, and performing predominately in big business industries.[26] However, with use of the right to acquire shares in other companies as the main strategy to perform business, the group of companies became the basic company type in the developed industries. In England, corporate groups emerged at the beginning of the 20th century, especially after the completion of introduction of limited liability principles.[27] At this point it must be stressed that, at the time when limited liability was established, groups of companies were virtually unknown.[28] Thus examination of principles of limited liability and separate legal personality principles are necessary.

## LIMITED LIABILITY: DEFINITION OF THE CONCEPT AND HISTORICAL EVOLUTION

The economic and legal history of the concept of company depends on the nameless inventors of the principle of limited liability, as applied to trading corporations that were pioneers of the Industrial Revolution. The intelligence of these men produced the principle by which the productivity and power of modern companies reached its top. In 1911 the president of Columbia University moved to claim that: 'I weigh my words when I say that in my judgement the limited liability corporation is the greatest single discovery of modern times ... even steam and electricity are far less important than the limited liability

[24] *Re Barned's Banking Co, ex parte Contract Corporation* (1867) LR 3 Ch App 105; *Re Asiatic Banking Corp* (1869) 4 LR-Ch 252; *Great Eastern Railway v Turner* (1872) LR 8 Ch App 149.

[25] Blumberg, *The Law... Tort, Contract*, p.61.

[26] Lutter, 'Enterprise Law Corp'.

[27] Ireland, Paddy, 'Rentier Investment and Corporate Irresponsibility: A Brief History of Limited Liability' (forthcoming in Cambridge Journal of Economics, 2008).

[28] Avgitidis, *Group of Companies*, p.69.

corporation, and they would be reduced to comparative importance without it.'[29]

Limited liability, under the Companies Act,[30] means that shareholders have no obligations to the company or its creditors beyond their obligations on the par value of their shares, or under their guarantee in the case of a company limited by guarantee.[31] Limited liability restricts shareholders' liability to the company to the amount of money they invest, which means that, in case of insolvency and under payment to creditors, shareholders cannot be made to pay more than they invest. Under this traditional corporate rule, liability arising from a subsidiary corporation's activities is also limited to the amount of its shareholders' investment, and the parent or any other company under the group cannot be held liable for the subsidiary's non-performed obligations.[32] However, concepts should not be confused; it is not the company that enjoys limited liability, it is the shareholders of the company whose liability is limited.[33] The

---

[29] Cited at Lowry, John, 'In Defence of Salomon: Promoting The Corporate Veil' in Rider, Barry A.K. and Andenas, Mads (eds), *Developments in European Company Law, Vol 2/1997: The Quest for an Ideal Legal Form for Small Businesses* (Kluwer Law International, London 1999).

[30] Section 3 (Limited and Unlimited Companies) of Companies Act, 2006 states that: '(1) A company is a "limited company" if the liability of its members is limited by its constitution. It may be limited by shares or limited by guarantee. (2) If their liability is limited to the amount, if any, unpaid on the shares held by them, the company is "limited by shares". (3) If their liability is limited to such amount as the members undertake to contribute to the assets of the company in the event of its being wound up, the company is "limited by guarantee". (4) If there is no limit on the liability of its members, the company is an "unlimited company".'

[31] Farrar defines limited liability as 'it [limited liability] is a fundamental principle of corporate law that shareholders in a corporation are not liable for the obligations of the enterprise beyond the capital that they contribute in exchange for their shares' at Farrar, John H., *Company Law* (Butterworths, London 1998), p. 82; Thompson defines limited liability as 'a presumptive of law that facilitates the development of public markets for securities, permits the allocation of risk or benefits between parties and supports the certainty of planning by those who have organized the corporation' at Thompson, Robert B., 'Unpacking Limited Liability: Direct and Vicarious Liability of Corporate Participants for Torts of the Enterprise' (1994) 47 Vand. L. Rev. 1; Farmer gives another definition as that 'limited liability means that the investing shareholder is liable for the debts of the corporation only to the extent of its original investment in the entity, the stock purchase money' at Farmer, Richard S., 'Parent Corporation Responsibility for the Environmental Liabilities of the Subsidiary: A Search for the Appropriate Standard' (1994) 19 Journal of Corporation Law 770.

[32] Bakst, David S., 'Piercing the Corporate Veil for Environmental Torts in the United States and the European Union: The Case for the Proposed Civil Liability Directive' (1996) 19 B. C. Int'l & Comp. L. Rev. 323.

[33] Magaisa, Alex, 'Corporate Groups and Victims of Corporate Torts – Towards a new Architecture of Corporate Law in a Dynamic Marketplace Law' (2002) 1 Social Justice & Global Development Journal 1.

company, as a legal person, is liable for its torts and obligations arising from any source, but the limited liability theory is applied in order to protect shareholders in case the company's assets are not adequate to meet the obligations.

Limited liability was an entirely innovative doctrine, which was devised as a result of the pressures put on growing corporations during the first half of the 19th century to raise the capital required to take advantage of the emerging technology of the times.[34] Accordingly in the UK, the Limited Liability Act 1855 was quickly replaced by the Joint Stock Companies Act 1856 which was the Act that introduced the rule into English law that such companies would have to add 'Limited' or 'Ltd' to their name.

In the beginning companies aimed to collect money from individuals since in the early corporate history acquiring shares of another corporation was not approved by the courts.[35] However this rule changed dramatically after the acceptance of dropping all restrictions on acquiring shares in another company. This means that limited liability had become the established rule long before corporate subsidiaries, basically groups of companies, were common or even, in general, legal. The new situation, with the emergence of corporate groups, is the discussion of the question of whether limited liability protects the constituent companies of the new corporate groups in addition to the investors in the enterprise. To be able to answer this question the separate personality of companies from its shareholder must be clarified under the examination of two famous English cases, *Salomon v Salomon & Co Ltd*[36] and *Lee v Lee's Air Farming Ltd.*[37]

The facts of the *Salomon* case are as follows. Mr Salomon created a company whose shareholders were himself, his wife, his daughter and four of his sons. At that time there was a requirement of a minimum seven shareholders in order to set up a limited liability company. Mr Salomon then sold his business to the company and received a further 20000 shares and a £10000 debenture from the company as the purchase price. Mr Salomon continued to run the business as managing director and, as he also had 20001 of the 20007 shares, was very much in control. The company soon encountered financial difficulties, with Mr Salomon selling his debenture to raise further money for the business, but despite this it was eventually wound up. The assets of the company were sufficient to pay the debenture holder but not the company's unsecured creditors. The liquidator claimed that the company was a scheme designed to defraud creditors and thus that the debenture should be saved, or alternatively that it was merely

34 Hansmann, Henry and Kraakman, Reiner, 'Toward Unlimited Shareholder Liability for Corporate Torts' (1990-1991) 100 Yale L.J. 1879.

35 Blumberg, *The Multinational Challenge*, p.54.

36 [1897] AC 22 HL.

37 [1961] AC 12 PC.

the alias or agent of Mr Salomon. These arguments were accepted by the Court of Appeal.

Consequently in 1897 this issue of limited liability and separate corporate personality was finally settled by the highest judicial body in the UK; the House of Lords ruled that individuals could organize their affairs as they wanted and that if they choose to do so via incorporation they were entitled to the protection of limited liability as long as the incorporation was in accordance with the formal rules of the relevant legislation.[38] Thus *Salomon* brought about the situation that incorporators of a company could structure its capital so as to minimize the risk to them of the company's failure by taking some form of secured debenture; there is no requirement that the investment of the incorporators in a company must necessarily to a significant extent be in the form of equity.[39] Hence separate legal personality meant just that, and it follows from this that a corporation is separate from its members and as such the latter is not liable for its debts.[40] After the decision, in very short time all important business enterprises converted to limited liability companies.[41]

These decisions on these two cases showed their effect for all corporations including corporate groups. Accordingly under traditional corporate law each component corporation of the group, whether parent or subsidiary, for legal purposes was still separate and distinct from every other corporation in the group, and its rights and responsibilities were divorced from those of the other constituent companies of the group.[42] For that reason although the companies in the group, unlike its public shareholder-investors, were parts of the enterprise and engaged in the daily running of business, limited liability also insulated them from liability for the activities of its subsidiary companies because it was not discussed deeply and the simple logic determined the situation that limited liability protects shareholders, a corporation is a shareholder of the subsidiary, and therefore, limited liability protects the shareholder corporation.[43] This

---

38 Bowmer, Simon, 'Company Law to Pierce or not to Pierce the Corporate Veil – Why Substantive Consolidation is not an Issue Under English Law' (2000) 15(8) JIBL 193.

39 Prentice, D.D., 'Group Indebtedness' in Wooldridge, F. and Schmitthoff, C.M. (eds), *Groups of Companies* (Sweet & Maxwell, London 1991), p. 57.

40 In *Lee v Lee's Air Farming*, the Privy Council held that Lee, as a separate and distinct entity from the company which he controlled, could be an employee of that company so that Lee's wife could claim workers' compensation following her husband's death. Separateness of personality enabled him to be an employee as the pilot and thus his widow was entitled to compensation under the scheme.

41 Ireland, 'Rentier Investment'.

42 Collins, Hugh, 'Ascription of Legal Responsibility to Groups in Complex Patterns of Economic Integration' (1990) 53 Modern Law Review 731.

43 *Ibid.*

situation can briefly be defined as follows: under limited liability the group collects the full reward if the subsidiary is successful, but does not bear the full loss in case of disaster.[44] Therefore limited liability rules are usually acknowledged to create incentives for excessive risk-taking by permitting corporations to avoid the full costs of their activities.[45] In statutory developments, there have been several Companies Acts since 1897, the latest one being the Companies Act 2006, and changes to the incorporation formalities have been made; yet no attempt has ever been made to legislate against the rule in *Salomon*. Some attempts have been made to avoid or exempt certain areas from the general rule but with the exception of specific statutory Acts, little has been achieved.[46]

In conclusion, under the economic circumstances of the time when the limited liability doctrine was accepted, economic analysis assumed that a society with greater wealth, measured in terms of profit maximization, was necessarily better off than a society with less.[47] Therefore limited liability permitted parties to allocate the risk of an enterprise to a more efficient risk-bearer in particular circumstances, namely the voluntary or involuntary creditors of corporations.[48] Nevertheless the full effects of application of limited liability were not clear at the time of its emergence, or even in recent times because the emergence of limited liability was not an essential characteristic of corporate law.[49] In reality because of the escalation of industrialization, limited liability finally emerged as a political pressure, not as a usual consequence of the concept of a corporate body.[50] Thus in England and America, the adoption of limited liability was problematic and followed political debate state by state. It must be stressed that it was only during the first quarter of the 20th century, half a century after the acceptance of limited liability, that this power was universally recognized.[51] For example, California insisted on unlimited liability companies until almost the middle of last century.[52]

---

44 See Dine, Janet, *The Governance of Corporate Groups* (Cambridge University Press, Cambridge 2000); Blumberg, *The Multinational Challenge.*

45 Note, 'Liability of Parent Corporations for Hazardous Waste Cleanup and Damages' (1985–1986) 99 Harv. L. Rev. 986.

46 Griffin, Stephen, '(Case Comment) Holding Companies and Subsidiaries – The Corporate Veil' (1991) 12 Comp Law 16; see Chapters 5 and 6.

47 Freedman, Judith, 'Limited Liability: Large Company Theory and Small Firms' (2000) 63 M.L.R. 317.

48 Thompson, Robert B., 'Piercing the Corporate Veil: An Empirical Study' (1990–1991) 76 Cornell L. Rev. 1036.

49 See Chapter 1.

50 Ireland, 'Rentier Investment'.

51 Avgitidis, *Group of Companies*, p. 69.

52 See Leebron, David W., 'Limited Liability, Tort Victims, and Creditors' (1991) 91 Colum. L. Rev. 1565.

## Reasons for Limited Liability

The origins behind limited liability is to encourage people to invest money in corporations and therefore it has been viewed as an essential element in free-market economies by allowing investors to contribute capital to an enterprise without risking their personal wealth.[53] Thus the argument of mainstream law and economics analysis in favour of limited liability is based on the use of incorporation to raise capital from outsiders.[54] This puts the limited liability into an invention central to the creation of a modern capitalist economy.[55] The limitation of risk functions is an incentive to investment and, therefore, it is a factor contributing to economic development. There are three main economic functions of limited liability: stimulating investments, minimizing cost and shifting risk.[56]

Stimulating investments is considered as the primary economic function of limited liability. Since shareholders are not liable for more than they invest, it is believed that companies will attract more money for their shares. Accordingly, the most important economic need for the limited liability company is that it encourages investment by absent investors, because investments under a limited liability regime have greater expected value and are less risky to investors than investments under unlimited liability.[57] Even today there is a strong belief that limited liability plays an effective role for enterprises on the consideration of stimulating investments.

The cost-minimizing function of limited liability manifests itself in four different ways. First, limited liability reduces the costs involved in the separation between management and ownership. Secondly, limited liability reduces the information costs that a shareholder has incurred in order to be constantly aware of the real value of his investments.[58] This creates an advantage in that it decreases the investors' need to monitor the management of the company because they are responsible for just the amount they invest.[59] Thirdly, limited liability reduces the costs involved in the operation of securities markets. Limited liability relieves a company's shareholders of the usual risks and responsibilities of ownership and therefore reduces their need to be involved in management or to

---

53 Farmer, 'Parent Corporation'.

54 Freedman, 'Limited Liability'.

55 Easterbrook, Frank H. and Fischel, D.R., 'Limited Liability and the Corporation' (1985) 52 U. Chi. L. Rev. 89.

56 *Ibid.*

57 Leebron, 'Limited Liability'.

58 Presser, Stephen B., 'Thwarting the Killing of the Corporation: Limited Liability, Democracy, and Economics' (1992–1993) 87 Nw. U. L. Rev. 148.

59 Easterbrook and Fischel, 'Limited Liability'.

be more than mere investors.[60] Finally, limited liability reduces the company's cost of raising capital; it enables a company to be financed on the most favourable terms. From the market economy perspective, since limited liability allows for the free transfer of shares, it promotes market economies and creates a competitive atmosphere for companies while facilitating diversification of portfolios, which is considered very important for development of economies.[61]

Easterbrook and Fischel stress the importance of limited liability to the corporate structure; only in such an environment can the critical features of centralized management and investor willingness to bear the risk exist.[62] Limited liability makes investors willing to give management functions to a centralized corporate group and to undertake risky projects. The claim is that limited liability company principles encourage involvement in economic activities which are necessary for the economic well-being of the society. Thus not only shareholders but also creditors benefit from these rules. As to involuntary creditors, their loss from limitations on liability is moderated by economic incentives that benefit through being a member of the society, which adequately substitutes for the personal liability of shareholders.[63]

Therefore the discussion and problems are collected on the fact that limited liability removes the risk of the company's failure from shareholders and shifts it to creditors. On this characteristic of limited liability, there is a conflict between economic principles that are based on the aim of reaching profit maximization and legal principles that are based on reaching basic justice. The economic theory accepts the injustice for creditors but it claims limited liability creates incentives for society as whole and, thus, it is justifiable and must be sustainable. Moreover the economic theory assumes that creditors can alter the terms by negotiating with the company. However, shifting the risk causes unsolved problems in the case of international mass torts since tort victims involuntarily involve in corporations. As a result, shifting the risk gives very important incentives to company groups to structure themselves as a group of limited liability entities. Thus the efficiency of economic analysis for limited liability must be discussed, particularly from groups of companies' perspective.

## Economic Analysis of Limited Liability

Supporters of the limited liability company theory have structured their arguments on the hypothesis of the absence of limited liability and they mainly claim

---

[60] Griffiths, *Corporate Governance.*
[61] Freedman, Limited Liability.
[62] Easterbrook and Fischel, 'Limited Liability'.
[63] Easterbrook and Fischel, 'Limited Liability'.

that in the case of unlimited liability the efficiency of capital markets will be seriously damaged.[64] Therefore the standard arguments for limited liability are based on the empirical claim that, on balance, corporations create more wealth than they destroy. Whereas it is regrettable that third party creditors must sometimes suffer, the benefits outweigh these unfortunately distributed costs.[65] The argument of creating more wealth for society has turned out to be the main problem of the globalized economic world. The calculation of benefits is based on the simple methodology that if economic activities of companies with limited liability create in total more wealth than it loses, that is benefiting the whole of society and, thus, should be promoted and supported. However this calculation of benefits of limited liability ignores the distribution of the loss, which is mainly loaded onto involuntary creditors. Therefore the theory must be reconsidered as it is unjustifiable to impose the burden of risk on the people with no consent.

Supporters of limited liability company theory introduce their arguments against the assumption of unlimited liability for companies under three titles. First, unlimited liability is dangerous for shareholder and capital economies. Secondly, making shareholders unlimitedly liable puts them in danger of being suddenly and unexpectedly thrown into personal bankruptcy and shareholders would have the difficulty of assessing and monitoring a company's management because many shareholders do not have sufficient knowledge to monitor and evaluate a company's operations. Consequently it might make shareholder diversification costly or impossible. Another important problem that could arise in the case of unlimited liability is conflict of law and enforcement problems.[66]

As a result the most important question in assessing the justification of limited liability is whether limited liability allocates risk to those most capable of bearing it. At the time the limited liability company first appeared the main concern was not fair allocation of risk but the distribution of resources between people according to political and economic criteria.[67] However this still seems to be a common defence for limited liability even though business, law and companies themselves have undergone fundamental changes.[68]

According to the risk shifting argument, in order to determine the most efficient allocation of risk between corporate groups and involuntary creditors, two criteria should be examined: the ability of the parties to avoid risk and their

64 Alexander, Janet Cooper, 'Unlimited Shareholder Liability through a Procedural Lens' (1992–1993) 106 Harv. L. Rev. 387.

65 Dent, George W., 'Limited Liability In Environmental Law' (1991) 26 Wake Forest Law Review 151.

66 Alexander, 'Unlimited Shareholder'.

67 Booth, Richard A., 'Limited Liability and the Efficient Allocation of Resources' (1994–1995) 89 Nw. U. L. Rev. 140.

68 Presser, 'Thwarting the Killing'.

ability to bear the risk. It is obvious that groups of corporations can apparently bear and avoid risks better than involuntary creditors.[69] Therefore limited liability does not provide a fair allocation of risk between corporate shareholders and creditors, especially in the case of immunity of shareholders from liability to involuntary creditors.[70] This injustice will be severe when putting MNEs into the centre of the arguments, with their immense economic power and complex structure. The economic explanations of limited liability are usually based on the consideration of individual shareholders rather than company shareholders. Thus limited liability reflects a desire to help out smaller investors, those more typical of the people, thus reflecting justice as much as economics. Then limited liability should be most welcomed for smaller enterprises that are dependent on individual contributions and not those possessing great economic wealth.[71] Accordingly the realities related to economic and business structures of MNEs have proved that it is unfair to sustain the current legal structure. In other words the conceptual structure of company law has become ever more divorced from the economic and social realities to which it applies and has taken on a life of its own.[72] Actually there has always been a disagreement between the legal structures of MNEs, which is based on the idea of groups as made up of lots of formally separate entities and their real nature, as reflected in their managerial structures in Chapter 2, which are very different. In brief, the idea of separate corporate personality was not developed with either single-member companies or groups of companies in mind. Much of the discussion made in this part of the book confirms the claims of Kahn-Freund that the Salomon decision was 'calamitous'.[73]

The argument of promoting capital market efficiency via limited liability is not exactly convincing either, because before the adoption of limited liability there was a developed capital market industry in England and in other western countries; for example, California kept its unlimited *pro rata* liability system until the middle of the 20th century.[74] There was no evidence that limited liability for corporate groups was making much difference in economic development since MNEs already have the resources to invest in third countries.[75] Moreover

---

[69] Note, 'Liability of Parent'.

[70] Farrar, John H., *Company Law* (Butterworths, London 1998), p. 83.

[71] Presser, 'Thwarting the Killing'.

[72] See Ireland, P., 'Company Law and the Myth of Shareholder Ownership' (1999) 62 Modern Law Review 32.

[73] Kahn-Freund, O., 'Some Reflection on Company Law Reform' (1943–1944) 7 Modern Law Review 54.

[74] Weinstein, Mark I., 'Limited liability in California' (2005) 7 American Law and Economics Review 439.

[75] See Chapter 1.

the MNEs are always given immense incentives by countries to invest in their territory so they are already in a good bargaining position. Giving them extra protection, especially through limited liability, is making them untouchable by the law.

The relative monitoring cost for alternative risk bearers argument cannot be justified if the alternative bearer is an MNE that can have assets bigger than many less-developed countries' economic power. Experience has already proved that monitoring of another company under a group is part of conducting business,[76] thus it cannot be claimed that if company shareholders are unlimitedly liable, the group will apply detailed and costly monitoring processes. Moreover the disclosure requirements[77] for groups of companies are increasing; MNEs are required to disclose most of their economic and financial relations as a group, which makes the monitoring argument less valid.

The supporters of limited liability explain the fairness of limited liability on the basis that it is swallowing liability rather than shifting it and under unlimited liability regimes creditors may be left uncompensated after the resources of shareholders have been exhausted.[78] Subsequently involuntary creditors can mostly find enough compensation in case of tort; if they cannot, it is the unfairness of social life. However incidents like Bhopal,[79] Shell in Nigeria[80] or use of asbestos by Cape Industries in South Africa,[81] have demonstrated that the damage is not swallowed; it is fiercely felt by the people who are exposed to disaster.

All the ideas in support of limited liability meet at the middle point that despite its difficulties and unfairness, limited liability may be a necessary evil.[82] Consequently there is an agreement on the need for criticism of limited liability, but also on the fact that unlimited liability is neither a practical nor a theoretically superior alternative to limited liability companies. It can be concluded that limited liability may well be a necessary consequence of trading in modern

---

76 See Chapter 2.

77 See further Villiers, C., *Corporate Reporting and Company Law* (CUP, Cambridge 2007).

78 Freedman, 'Limited Liability'.

79 See for the detail of the case at www.bhopal.net. For legal discussions see Muchlinski, P.T., 'The Bhopal Case Controlling Ultra-hazardous Industrial Activities Undertaken by Foreign Investors' (1987) 50 Modern Law Review 545.

80 See further Human Rights Watch, 'The Price of Oil; Corporate Responsibility and Human Rights Violations in Nigeria's Oil Producing Communities' at http://www.hrw.org/reports/1999/nigeria/ accessed 25 June 2006.

81 See Magaisa, A.T., 'Suing Multinational Corporate Groups for Torts in Wake of the Lubbe Case' (2001) 2 Law, Social Justice and Global Development 1.

82 Grundfest, Joseph A., 'Limited Future of Unlimited Liability: A Capital Markets Perspective' (1992–1993) 102 Yale L.J. 387.

capital markets rather than an optional rule that can be abandoned by the legal system if some other doctrine seems preferable.

Moreover the difficulty in finding an alternative and the relative importance of limited liability for settled market economies might lead to the claims that even if limited liability were not introduced by law-makers or in case of abandonment of it, the business practice could have invented limited liability in the liberal markets through the principles of freedom of contract. This argument has valid points from the perspective of voluntary creditors since the relationship between voluntary creditors and companies is established on the basis of mutual consent with the full knowledge of dangers and benefits of limited liability. Thus in contractual liability, even if unlimited liability is introduced, it is very likely that companies will have clauses that prevent shareholders from unlimited liability. However, because of the complex and unexpected characteristics of corporate torts, it is not possible to agree with this argument in respect of involuntarily creditors. Companies cannot introduce limited liability for shareholders in tort claims. The argument carried out in this book is to establish liability for corporate torts, particularly MNEs' liability for subsidiaries' tort. The nature of corporate tort makes it impossible to do some prearrangements with victims to accept limited liability for shareholders. There is a legal impossibility since the parties are not identifiable in advance. As a result the arguments that limited liability would have been introduced in any situation are not valid in the context of MNEs' tort.

Finally the justice argument must be considered. Modern states are constantly trying to improve economic, social and legal systems in order to create better living conditions for their people. Thus legal principles and regulations for the future must be built on the aim of achieving justice. Consequently the regulations must be justifiable covering every part of society. It is a fact that the economic development is definitely good for humanity but wealth achieved at the cost of another's disaster cannot be defended and thus cannot be claimed justifiable. The economic analysis, with justice theory, demonstrates that the limited liability company for corporate shareholders is no longer justifiable, especially not in the case of MNEs, which are professionally, legally and economically organized to be able to plan and insure possible liabilities so it is inconsistent to provide them with the same protection as individual shareholders. Hence the possible risk of application of limited liability in corporate groups' context must be discussed.

## Evaluation of Risks and Problems in Limited Liability Corporate Groups

For many years corporations have benefited from the same protection via limited liability as have individuals even in the situation of holding the entire equity interest.[83] Thus economic units of MNEs enjoy great freedom to define their identities by dividing their activities between several distinct legal persons so that they ensure liabilities attaching to any one person will not also attach to the others in the group.[84] Consequently the key question, in the case of tort, which person committed the wrong, is likely to receive an artificial answer when the wrongdoer has made use of the doctrine of separate corporate personality to structure its business. Obviously it is also unsatisfactory for plaintiffs if the artificial person claimed to have committed the wrong has inadequate funds to meet any compensation.[85]

The problem of liability of corporate groups occurs because, according to existing common practice, a parent corporation could always choose to split the enterprise up into separate corporations, making sure that those subsidiaries dealing with risky activities held the minimum assets possible because MNEs always try to ensure effective ways of profit transfer when they are negotiating FDI agreements.[86] A plaintiff would then only be able to obtain a successful recovery of damages if he could establish a chain of primary duties leading back from a subsidiary to those in the group of companies with sufficient assets to satisfy any judgment. After the *Adams v Cape Industries*[87] and *Multinational Gas*[88] cases such an approach is, for the moment, extremely unlikely because it was held that the courts are not free to disregard the principles of *Salomon* merely because they consider that justice requires it.[89] More importantly it was not fraudulent for a group of companies to use the doctrine of separate corporate personality in such a way as to minimize its group exposure to future liabilities.[90]

No courts, since *Salomon*, in any case involving the legal responsibility of a parent corporation for the acts of its subsidiary, has examined as a matter of first

---

83 On the other hand, the problems of limited liability are not restricted to the problem of involuntary creditors. In many areas of practice, problems might arise: shareholders might manipulate their control holdings, the accounts of the group or an affiliate in the group may be misled, they might dominate the minority interest very easily, and finally they can avoid taxation, anti-trust, monopoly and other regulations.

84 Anderson Michael, 'Transnational Corporations and Environmental Damage: Is Tort Law the Answer' (2002) 41 Wasburn Law Journal 399.

85 Baughen, S., 'Multinationals and the Export of Hazard' (1995) 58 MLR 54.

86 See Muchlinski, P., *Multinational Enterprises and the Law* (OUP, Oxford 2007), Chapter 15.

87 [1990] 2 WLR 786.

88 *Multinational Gas and Petrochemical Co v Multinational Gas and Petrochemical Services Ltd and Others* [1983] 2 All ER 563.

89 See Chapter 5.

90 Baughen, 'Multinationals'; Meeran, R., 'The Unveiling of Transnational Corporations: A Direct Approach' in Addo, M.K. (ed.), *Human Rights Standards and the Responsibility of Transnational Corporations* (Kluwer Law International, The Hague 1999).

consideration whether the doctrine of limited liability shielded the other companies in the group from liability for the debts of a subsidiary in the typical multi-tiered MNEs in the modern economy. This has resulted in three, four or even more separate layers of limited liability. Acceptance of this wide interpretation of limited liability allows for an illegitimate shifting of risk from a subsidiary to the involuntary creditors of the MNEs.[91] Therefore in mass tort cases, the assets and personality of the entire group may be needed to ensure a sufficient capital fund from which to satisfy claims. This is very justifiable where it is a fact that the group acts as an integrated economic entity, which together creates the prosperity of the enterprise.[92]

Where injuries are severe and tort victims are not fully insured, social justice requires that shareholders would be better risk-bearers than tort victims, particularly in respect of MNEs.[93] Especially after mass tort actions of small and undercapitalized entities, the problem was considered critical.[94] Therefore in order to evaluate group liability for subsidiaries' tort actions, one needs an appropriate model because traditional legal principles are not sufficient. This leads to claims that the concept perhaps accurately reflected the era in which it was developed – when individual shareholders were investors and were not active in the operation of the corporation – and a question arises whether it does so today.[95] Blumberg answers to the question; this development occurred without much critical analysis of the issue of limited liability of corporate groups and thus he argues that limited liability of corporate groups, one of the most important legal rules in modern economic systems, appears to have emerged as an 'historical accident'.[96]

In another approach the problem of liability in MNE tort creates a conflict between economic realities and legal principles. In particular, legal regulations have failed to reflect the economic challenges in practice where the limited liability of companies under a group for the debts of its subsidiary does not provide social benefits. Contemporarily the nature of the challenge is that legal systems of the world are confronted by revolutionary changes in corporate structure and operation caused by the emergence of corporate groups, particularly MNEs. The legal system that could largely resolve the legal problems presented by the early period of the Industrial Revolution is incompetent in its

---

[91] Muchlinski, P., 'Holding Multinationals to Account: Recent Developments in English Litigation and the Company Law Review' (2002) 23 Company Lawyer 168.

[92] Muchlinski, 'Holding Multinationals'.

[93] Leebron, 'Limited Liability'.

[94] Cheffins, Brain R., 'Company Law: Theory, Structure and Operation (Clarendon Press, Oxford 1997), p. 507.

[95] Cashel, 'Multinational Challenge'.

[96] Blumberg, *The Multinational Challenge*, p. 57.

established form of dealing effectively with the problems of the multi-tiered MNEs functioning with a parent corporation, sub-holding companies and hundreds of subsidiary corporations organized under the laws of countries around the world.[97] Particularly the social cost-benefit evaluation is questionable where companies own all the stock or have complete control of their subsidiary corporations or operate as a complex group under which the separation is barely noticeable.[98]

It would be unfair to claim there is no discussion of the liability problems in legal regulatory environments since the problems have triggered some discussions in different branches of legal professionals as well as in parliaments. Although finding its legitimacy in economic theory, in legal theory limited liability has only been criticized and all the attempts have been concentrated on reducing its negative effects instead of elimination. Therefore the issue of limited liability within corporate groups' context has not received a sufficient degree of legislative attention. Accordingly the case law has touched the problem very delicately under the principle of veil piercing.[99] In legislative attempts, the last Company Law Review in the UK failed to break out of that cast, concluding in their report that there is no problem relating to liability of corporate groups. Thus the Companies Act 2006 has no regulation on this matter.[100] This disappointing development has turned all eyes on the regulations at European Community level that group specific laws, which are needed to protect creditors, will receive detailed debate in the light of developments.[101] However, the EU Action Plan[102] does not offer any solutions for groups of companies relating to liability issues, even worse, they do not see any problem relating to liability issues under groups of companies.[103] Moreover it must be stressed that the problem is not that there is a lack of laws and regulations relating to corporate groups but, although there are a great quantity of laws in the area, these laws often do not address the issue of groups as such, but rather deal with some of the relevant regulatory problems of company law and in the process also covering the issue of groups.

---

97 *Ibid.* p. IX.

98 Hofstetter, K., 'Parent Responsibility for Subsidiary Corporations: Evaluating European Trends' (1990) 39 ICLQ 576.

99 See Chapter 5.

100 See Chapter 6.

101 Davies, Paul L., *Gower and Davies' Principles of Modern Company Law* (Sweet & Maxwell, London 2003), p. 210.

102 Communication from the Commission to the Council and the European Parliament 'Modernising Company Law and Enhancing Corporate Governance in the European Union – A plan to Move Forward' COM (2003) 284 final. See Chapter 6 for details.

103 See Chapter 6.

The final issue that should be addressed under this topic will be the evaluation of creditors' classification. In accordance with liability clauses, it is highly possible that firms with limited liability will undertake projects with too much risk. Enterprises will capture the benefits from such activities while bearing only some of the costs, while shifting other costs to creditors; this is a real cost of limited liability.[104] The main argument put in terms of economic analysis is that it externalizes the loss through uncompensated transfers of risk to creditors; the objection was met by pointing out that the risk transfer was in fact fully compensated by other economic benefits to the society or creditors. With a tort creditor, the economic analysis produces a problem since it is clear that the loss ineffectively externalized; the tort victim is not in a position to bargain for a compensating benefit or to avoid or monitor the risk to which the company is exposing them.[105] Therefore legal systems must distinguish contractual creditors who choose to maintain a relationship with the company and non-contractual creditors that are in the position of acquiring creditor status without any intentional relationship with the corporation.[106] It is appropriate to claim that, in liability discussions, voluntary and involuntary creditors must be treated separately.

## CONCLUSION: LIMITED LIABILITY MULTINATIONAL ENTERPRISES

Professor Schmitthoff's claim that the question of limited liability of the parent company for the torts of a subsidiary under certain well-defined conditions is one of the great unsolved problems of modern company law.[107] The historical overview amply demonstrates that limited liability did not emerge as a necessary attribute of corporate personality but as a legal means of achieving a major economic and social purpose, which was encouraging more people to participate as members of companies in economic activity.[108] This means the legal rule of limited liability emerged in order to serve economic social necessities of the times. The applicability of limited liability has not changed since its emergence

---

104 Easterbrook, Frank H. and Fischel, Daniel R., *The Economic Structure of Corporate Law* (Harvard University Press, London 1991), p. 53.

105 Pettet, B., 'Limited Liability – A Principle for the 21st Century' (1995) 48 CLP 124.

106 Haar, Brigitte, 'Piercing Veil And Shareholder's Product And Environmental Liability in American Law as Remedies for Capital Market Failures – New Developments and Implications for European and German Law After *Centros*' (2000) EBOR 317.

107 Schmitthoff, C.M. and Wooldridge, F. (eds), *Groups of Companies* (Sweet & Maxwell, London 1991).

108 Ireland, 'Rentier Investment'.

but its area of application has extended to company shareholders and thus to groups of companies.

However the limited liability company theory ignores contemporary economic realities because parent companies and their subsidiaries are collectively conducting a common enterprise so the limited liability doctrine, which is designed to protect shareholders not enterprises themselves, has lost the support of economic efficiency in the case of corporate groups.[109] Therefore application of economic theory for limited liability to the groups of companies has no impact on the investment decision of shareholders of the group.[110] Also, in economic arguments for companies, any economic goal that can be achieved by the creation of a wholly owned subsidiary could equally be achieved by the formation of a division within a single corporate entity.[111]

It is obvious that when the responsible party is a subsidiary of a larger corporation, the plaintiffs may forcefully argue in the courts that the corporations under common and cross-ownership should be held legally responsible for the tortious acts of its subsidiary.[112] For this purpose, plaintiffs will be able to base their argument on theories for the liability of parent corporations and search for existing liability under tort law, corporate law and the existing case law, which is mainly based on the piercing the corporate veil doctrine.

In brief, the application of limited liability was not an obligatory characteristic of company law, but rather a political decision of states and countries to make investment in companies more attractive for individuals. Thus supporters of limited liability do not base their arguments on the idea of necessity of limited liability for corporate law, but rather support economic and practical efficiency and the unavoidability of limited liability for capital markets and companies. Thus it can easily be claimed that using economically efficient systems for limited liability is a somewhat overworked term, particularly in cases of its application to corporate groups.[113] This means a limited liability company does not represent anything more than the economic and political preferences of states. And the increasing use of the corporate form for businesses, together with the recent arrival of potentially massive tort liability, suggests that the issue should be reconsidered.[114]

---

109 Blumberg, *The Multinational Challenge*, p.59.

110 Note, 'Liability of Parent'.

111 Austin, Robert P., 'Corporate Groups' in Grantham, Ross and Rickett, Charlie (eds), *Corporate Personality in the 20th Century* (Hart, Oxford 1998).

112 Farmer, 'Parent Corporation Responsibility'.

113 Fridman, S., 'Removal of the Corporate Veil: Suggestions for Law Reform in *Quintex Australia Finance Ltd v Schroders Australia Ltd*' (1991) 19 ABLR 211.

114 Hansmann, Henry and Kraakman, Reiner, 'The Essential Role of Organizational Law' (2000) 110 Yale LJ 387.

Since the origins of states several thousand years ago, the law-makers have regularly created rules for economic activity, responding to citizen demands and seeking to create a wealthier society. The modern nation state following this long tradition has created rules to increase wealth in its society. On the other hand, citizens increasingly demanded new and stronger rules to protect them in the era of nationally based capitalism. Rules that would restrict investors and companies in order to prohibit child labour, assure healthy foods and drugs, guarantee the safety of transportation, and support the stability of financial markets can be given as examples.[115] Now the demand to protect society against limited liability corporate groups is increasing. The national democratic state, which represents the most effective system, cannot ignore this demand any more.

## CONCLUSION OF PART I: MNES: LIMITED LIABILITY, HORIZONTALLY ORGANIZED, PROFIT SEEKING, GLOBAL INSTITUTIONS

The basic legal systems in the world consider companies as economically and managerially independent units, which leads to the recognition of this independence and granting companies with legal personality. In this situation, if one questions the separate corporate legal personality theory and its origins, independence theory must be the centre of the examination. Economic scholars have already started to question separate corporate personality in the case of corporate groups. Economic and managerial organizations of subsidiaries are built in concert with another company, in some cases with no common ownership except for being under the same MNE group. However in law, the theory and practice have been built on the separate legal personality and, instead of changing it, developments in the case and statutory laws have just strengthened its applicability since its emergence in the 19th century. The economic activities of companies have been globalized; the MNEs have gained social characteristics, and become one of the phenomena for the new world order. The international economic institutions and, in some cases, states recognize MNEs as international economic actors. Thus the recognition of MNEs has been settled socially and economically. What the law should reflect is the social and economic developments in the society. However, corporate law has failed to reflect the

[115] James, A.P. and Jason, G., 'Making Corporations Accountable, A Background Paper for the United Nations Financing for Development Process' (Global Policy Forum, December, 2000), http://www.globalpolicy.org/socecon/ffd/2000papr.htm accessed 25 June 2006.

developments; instead it still follows the principles of a case which was decided more than 100 years ago.

The law has failed to absorb the new circumstances permitting companies to hold shares of another company. It showed almost no attempt to regulate the new situation. This failure can be mentioned as the source of many of the problems I am discussing in this book. The law has failed to recognize the fact that enterprises organize themselves as a group when they are operating cross-border as well as in a domestic market. Although this fact is clear, the law still insists on the theory of separate corporate personality. Therefore the law has failed to respond to the challenges that MNEs, one of the greatest modern time institutions created. The law has even failed to reach a legal definition of MNEs. Even though the investment theory of MNEs suggests different realities than efficiency arguments of limited liability rules suggest, there has been no action to change the law that grants limited liability protection to the groups of companies, as it did to individual shareholders. Thus the examination of MNEs' economic history and current economical social characteristics indicates that limited liability is not a necessary element of the existence and operation of MNEs. Thus the law failed to understand these realities, which cause problems in practice when there are claims for tort liability of MNEs.

The law has failed to react to the developments of new structural organizations of MNEs. The practice and the theory still consider MNEs as vertically integrated companies that have one top and many equal sub-divisions. However the structure, first, changed to be multi-divisional; the law hardly responded to these changes. And then matrix and regional integration came; the law demonstrated no alterations in its approach. With the emergence of horizontally structured MNEs, the law seems to have lost control over regulation of MNEs. These changes in structure prove that an enterprise operates as a single economic unit and, thus, the divisions between the units of the enterprises cannot be distinguished in the way that separate legal personality suggests. Thus the new structural organizational realities must be considered when dealing with any rules of liability in the MNEs context.

Accordingly the complex social, economic, managerial and legal structures not only make reaching liability difficult but also cause MNEs to commit torts. The pressure applied by the group's central management over subsidiaries to be cost-efficient and profitable is excessive. Managers of subsidiaries work under the pressure of high expectations set by groups as whole. Their efforts have always concentrated on maximizing profit and success in business. Therefore it is not abnormal for subsidiaries to use the social and economic power of the group and exploit any legal ambiguity. The wider examination and better legal regulation of MNEs will have positive effects on preventing the corporate tort.

Under these conditions the questions that must be answered are these: to what extent we can claim separate corporate personality? What is the end for separate company theory under a group structure? How could the new and complicated horizontal structures and cross-ownerships affect the current principles? Can modern legal systems still pretend that existing law is fair and needs no revision? Or is it time to go for real and effective solutions? The author thinks the time has already come for reconsideration of legal principles that determine the area of company law and tort liability. Law-makers at national and international level should take immediate steps to create solutions based on these new findings of interdisciplinary characteristics of MNEs.

Furthermore the examination should focus on the modern definition of MNEs. First, a comprehensive definition of the concept of MNEs must be produced in law. The MNEs proudly identify themselves as a group and even give facts about their group activities. We can give Bayer as an example. The following is taken directly from its website:

> Bayer is represented by some 350 companies (as of December 31, 2003). The cornerstones of its business activities are in Europe, North America and the Far East. In 2003, Bayer employed some 115,400 people and had sales of EUR 28.6 billion. The capital expenditure budget for the current year is EUR 1.8 billion, the R&D budget EUR 2.3 billion.[116]

It is interesting that even though MNEs name themselves as a group and arrange all their activities accordingly, the law still insists on regulating them as separate and independent companies. This increases the need to make a comprehensive examination of MNEs; the present part of the book is devoted to producing a definition and basic characteristics of MNEs. After indicating the interdisciplinary basics of MNEs, the next step must be building comprehensive legal responsibilities for MNEs. The companies are given legal personality because they are considered economically and managerially independent units. Now not only companies but also MNEs are economically and managerially independent units. The MNEs have a management board for the group; they provide financial reports for the group; they have disclosure requirements for the group. They are also keen to develop common CSR for the group. These new aspects of MNEs have different characteristics from a single company's basic characteristics. For this reason, the new regulations must be built on the facts of new social, economical and organizational structure. As already mentioned, the new structure, evolved from vertical structure to the horizontal structure, can provide an adequate regulatory framework for all differently structured MNEs. With this new conception of MNEs, there must be reconsideration of legal principles that prevent the achievement of MNEs' liability for their torts.

---

116 Available at http://www.bayer.com/ accessed 25 November 2005.

In conclusion the present part of the book has aimed to indicate the interdisciplinary characteristics of MNEs from social, economic, managerial and legal perspectives. The findings indicate that the developments in social and economic and managerial studies have not been met by developments in legal studies. This situation creates problems because the basic legal principles are outdated and the same principles, when applied in practice, cause problems in the area of tort liability of MNEs. This forces us to examine applicable laws in practice and proposals to liability of MNEs by questioning how they are suited to the contemporary understandings.

Part II will examine applicable laws to tort liabilities of MNEs. Even though this part of the book concludes that limited liability and separate legal personality principles do not regulate MNEs and thus create problems of liability, it is clearly seen that there have been no efforts to remove the limited liability and separate legal personality principles in the corporate groups' context. Part II concentrates on another problem in existing laws; while developing liability principles within the limit of separate legal personality theory, the law-makers have made a fundamental mistake by ignoring contemporary characteristics of MNEs. Thus the discussion in Part II focuses on the liability principles developed within the framework that preserve the main principles of company laws.

# PART II

# Exploring the tort liability of multinational enterprises

# 4. Jurisdictional problems

## INTRODUCTION

Reaching the justified liability of MNEs' tort is blocked not only by problems of substantive company law but also many procedural and jurisdictional problems create huge hurdles. In other words the complex design of international private law presents significant obstacles to suing MNEs in the venues in which they can be held liable. Therefore in transnational litigation, past experiences have illustrated the complex interplay between principles of substantive corporate law and procedural rules of international civil litigation.[1] Even though litigation is supposed to be the last resort as a means of ensuring that MNE groups comply with standards and duties of care in relation to their operations, it plays a very important role because the choice of law issues and interpretations of law are determined usually according to the law of the forum states.[2] Moreover the power of MNEs and the inefficient legal structure of host countries prevent plaintiffs reaching satisfactory compensation.

Generally, people who have been injured as a consequence of the tortious activities of MNEs sue the companies in the forum of the parent company's state to benefit from its legal systems' advantageous structure. However, many of the cases brought in the forum of the UK and the US have been dismissed on the ground of the principles of *forum non conveniens* under which the American and English courts considered the host states' forums distinctly and clearly more appropriate to hear the cases.

When there is a tort committed by a subsidiary of an MNE, plaintiffs have a number of options for starting legal actions. The first option is to sue the subsidiary in the host country. However there is very little possibility of success if there is an inadequate and unfair justice system or insufficient capital sources of subsidiaries or the basic problem of company law principles. The second possible action is to sue the parent corporation in their country of domicile. This seems the only logical option for plaintiffs to be awarded

---

1 Magaisa, A.T., 'Suing Multinational Corporate Groups for Torts in Wake of the Lubbe Case' (2001) 2 Law, Social Justice and Global Development 1.

2 Muchlinski, P., 'Holding Multinationals to Account: Recent Developments in English Litigation and the Company Law Review' (2002) 23 Company Lawyer 168.

satisfactory compensation. However the problem of independency theory and limited liability theory creates procedural and substantial problems for the plaintiffs, lawyers and judges. This makes the possible establishment of tort liability for accused companies very difficult. The other possible way is to sue other companies under the group, which may be domiciled in the same jurisdiction or a different jurisdiction. Even though it could bring a different perspective to the examination of liability of MNE groups, this option has not been tried yet because it is a breakthrough departure from existing rules. However the possible acceptance of jurisdiction over other subsidiaries for each other's tort requires establishment of group liability based on the modern structure of MNEs.

Even when jurisdiction has been achieved over the corporations in home states, courts have the discretionary authority to decline to hear the case under the doctrine of *forum non conveniens*. Under the principle, US courts are very committed to the application of the principle[3] while in the UK courts are comparatively more flexible, especially after the recent *Lubbe v Cape Industries* case. On the other hand, civil law countries have solved the problems by not employing the *forum non conveniens* doctrine. The question of jurisdiction in courts in civil law jurisdictions is not problematic when the defendant is based in the countries where they have been sued. Both under Civil law and under the EC Convention on Jurisdiction and Enforcement of Judgments in Civil and Commercial Matters[4] (the Brussels Convention), the rule of the so-called *forum rei* applies; jurisdiction of the court of the defendant's domicile. This is the main rule on jurisdiction in Article 2 of the Brussels Convention. Thus in normal civil proceedings before civil law courts any consideration of *forum non conveniens* does not apply.[5] Moreover the principles of the Brussels Convention and decisions of the European Court of Justice have brought the application of *forum non conveniens* doctrine in the UK closer to the application in other EU countries.

Consequently the jurisdiction problems are the first problems that plaintiffs will face on the way to suing an MNE and thus they have an important effect

---

3 Blumberg, P.I., 'Accountability of Multinational Corporations: The Barriers Presented by Concepts of the Corporate Juridical Entity' (2000–2001) 24 Hastings Int'l & Comp. L. Rev. 297.

4 Council Regulation (EC) No 44/2001, of 22 December 2000 on Jurisdiction and the Recognition and Enforcement of Judgments in Civil and Commercial Matters (Official Journal L 12 of 16.01.2001).

5 Betlem, Gerrit, 'Transnational Litigation against Multinational Corporations Before Dutch Civil Courts' in Kamminga, Menno T. and Zia-Zarifi, Saman (eds), *Liability of Multinational Corporations Under International Law* (Kluwer Law International, The Hague 2000).

on the provisions of MNEs' liability. Accordingly in this chapter, general jurisdiction rules on companies and the common law approach to the problem of jurisdiction in litigations concerning MNEs will be explained. The *forum non conveniens* doctrine will be at the centre of the discussions and the applicability of current principles will be discussed in accordance with the general characteristics of MNEs established in the previous part of the book. There is a test of existing jurisdiction whether they have the capacity to solve the problems that modern structure of MNEs creates. The possible ways of elimination of jurisdictional obstacles will be discussed later. Particular attention will be given to the Alien Tort Claims Act. There is some doubt whether the Act is an efficient model to solve the problems.

## JURISDICTIONAL RULES FOR COMPANIES AND MNES

According to the Civil Jurisdiction and Judgments Act 1982, which incorporates the Brussels Convention into UK law, the jurisdiction rules for companies can be summarized as follows; a corporation may be sued in the courts of the state where: (1) it has its statutory seat or is incorporated, or under whose law it is formed; (2) it has its central administration; or (3) its business, or other professional activity is principally carried out.[6] Accordingly the seat of a company shall be treated as its domicile and, in order to determine that seat, the court is to apply its rule of internal law.[7] In the UK the statutory seats means the registered office, or if there is no such office, the place of incorporation or, if there is no such place, the place under the law of which the company formation took place.[8]

On the other hand, there are specific jurisdiction rules: (1) a corporation may also be sued in the courts of a state where it has a branch, agency or other establishment, in respect of a dispute arising out of its operations in that state;[9] (2) where a corporation operates in a state through a subsidiary or other related corporation in circumstances where that second corporation has no independent existence in fact, since the first corporation takes all material decisions as to the conduct of the business of the second corporation, the second corporation shall be treated as a branch of the first corporation for the purposes of the preceding

[6] Brussels Convention Article 60(1); See Collins, L, *Dicey and Morris on the Conflicts of Laws* (Sweet & Maxwell, London 2000), p. 284.

[7] The Civil Jurisdiction and Judgments Act 1982 article 53(1); See Collins, *Dicey and Morris*, p. 287.

[8] The Brussels Conventions article 60(2); See Clarkson, C.M.V. and Hill, J., *Jaffey on the Conflicts of Laws* (Butterworths, London 2002).

[9] The Civil Jurisdiction and Judgments Act 1982 article 5(4).

rule;[10] (3) a corporation may also be sued in the courts of a state in respect of a claim arising directly out of an activity carried out by that corporation in that state.[11]

In common law countries the establishment of a local branch or the provision of a local address for service has traditionally led to general jurisdiction.[12] Thus the key question may arise in what circumstances a local subsidiary may be treated as a branch of the parent company. This issue is of particular importance in cases where a group of corporations operates as a unified economic enterprise especially under horizontal organization.[13] However as regard the meaning of the word 'branch', it has been agreed that a subsidiary is not a branch. Therefore any other corporations cannot be sued for the activities of subsidiaries if plaintiffs do not claim any particular tort against them, or there exists another exemption by the statutory or case law.[14] The matter has been considered in the Brussels Convention. Article 5(5) creates special jurisdiction over companies 'as regards a dispute arising out of the operations of a branch, agency or other establishment'. Thus companies can be sued in 'the courts of the place in which the branch, agency or other establishment is situated'. If the branch is not an independent legal person it could not be sued at all and the result of this provision is that the legal entity constituting the corporation may be sued not only at its own seat but at the place where the branch is domiciled.[15] As it is clear from the phrasing of the Convention, subsidiaries are not considered as a branch or agency. The practice in international civil litigation and domestic litigation has apparently shown that subsidiaries cannot be classified under the 'other establishments' because company law principles treat subsidiaries as independent legal personalities.

## DOMICILE

The Civil Jurisdiction and Judgments Act enacted distinct rules governing jurisdiction in cases concerning such matters where the defendant is domiciled in a member state of the EU, as well as rules governing jurisdiction over defendants domiciled in other parts of the UK. The Civil Jurisdiction and Judgments

---

10 Collins, *Dicey and Morris*, p. 299.

11 The Civil Jurisdiction and Judgments Act 1982 article 5(3); See Collins, *Dicey and Morris*, p. 328.

12 The Civil Jurisdiction and Judgments Act 1982 article 5(4).

13 See Chapter 2.

14 North, P. and Fawcett, J.J., *Cheshire and North's Private International Law* (Butterworths, London 1999), p. 295

15 Betlem, 'Transnational Litigation'.

Act 1991 enacted the parallel Convention of 1989 (the Lugano Convention) signed with countries of members of the European Free Trade Area (EFTA) into UK law. There are thus four sets of rules respecting domiciles of companies: (1) EU domiciliary; (2) EFTA domiciliary; (3) domiciliary of the UK; and (4) the rest of the world population.[16]

Determining domicile for defendants is a jurisdiction issue so it is not related to parent companies' liability for subsidiaries' tort. Actually there is no real legal problem in determining the domicile of English parent corporations. The Civil Jurisdiction and Judgments Act 1982[17] provides that a corporation or association has its seat in the United Kingdom, if and only if: (a) it was incorporated or formed under the law of a part of the United Kingdom and has its registered office or some other official address in the United Kingdom; or (b) its central management and control is exercised in the United Kingdom. This Act was made law in accordance with the Brussels Convention Article 53.[18] The article provides that 'in order to determine that seat, the court shall apply its rules of private international law'.[19] Additionally the European Court of Justice (ECJ) decided in a case that the Brussels Convention is applicable where the defendant has its domicile or seat in a contracting state, even if the plaintiff is domiciled in a non-contracting country.[20]

The seat of a company constitutes its domicile and must be determined by the court's private international law in which the UK refers to the doctrine of incorporation. Actually the concept of seat of corporation has no precise equivalent in UK law and it was necessary to provide expressly in the 1982 Act for the determination of corporations. Therefore section 42 of 1982 Act provides that a corporation has its seat in the UK if and only if '(a) it was incorporated or formed under the law of a part of the UK and has its registered office or some other official addresses in the UK or (b) its central management and control is exercised in the UK'.[21]

There is a difference between the common law understanding and that of the Convention; there is no question of the need for a permanent home under the 1982 Act. Thus under the 1982 Act it will be possible for a person to have more than one domicile, whereas in common law only one domicile is possible.[22]

---

16 Collier, J.G., *Conflict of Law* (Oxford University Press, Oxford 2001), p. 72.

17 Civil Jurisdiction and Judgments Act 1982 s. 42.

18 Darcy, L.C. and Murray, B., *Cleave Schmitthoff's Export Trade* (Sweet & Maxwell, London 2000), p. 442.

19 Civil Jurisdiction and Judgments Act 1982 article 52(1).

20 Société *Group Josi Reinsurance Company v Compagnie d'Assurances Universal General Insurance Company* Case 412/98 (ECJ 13 Jul 2000).

21 Collins, *Dicey and Morris*, p. 288.

22 *Ibid.* p. 287.

Therefore in determining the seat of a Panamanian company with its central management and control in Germany, it will have its seat for the purpose of the 1982 Act both in Panama and in Germany.[23]

The important problem with domicile is the issue of presence of the defendant company. The company has to be present in the jurisdiction at the time the proceedings are started. In *Adams v Cape Industries Plc*,[24] the Court of Appeal confirmed that such 'presence' would not be established merely through the presence in the foreign jurisdiction of either a subsidiary company or a company.[25] In order to establish jurisdiction in case of subsidiary involvement there is a necessity for an investigation of all aspects of the relationship between the subsidiary and the parent because the current law in the UK still relies on traditional notions of agency.[26] Under the rule, the relationship between the parent and subsidiary must be similar to the one between agent and principal.[27] In the United States courts look at the economic realities of the situation; if the parent and subsidiary form an economic unit it should be possible to establish jurisdiction on the basis of presence of its subsidiary or indeed against a foreign subsidiary on the basis of the presence of the parent in the US.[28] This is a more logical approach and would be very helpful to create better jurisdiction coverage for MNEs. However the establishment of economic unity in the MNEs context is not totally different from establishment of agency relationships. Both require a substantial degree of examination of intra-group relationship, which is a very difficult task to do.[29]

On the lack of a legal institution called MNE, determining domiciles of companies which operate under MNEs' structure is a very complicated task. Thus each company is considered as independent legal units and in each case the domiciles of companies is examined independently. Mere existence of ownership relationships between the subsidiary and the parent does not necessarily create jurisdiction over the parent by the forum of the subsidiary nor does it create jurisdiction over the subsidiary by the forum of the parent company. As a result, as with establishing liability over MNEs, establishing domicile and thus jurisdiction over all components of MNEs is not possible. Establishing domicile and jurisdiction over parent or subsidiary outside of their incorporation state needs to be decided after a detailed examination of general

---

23 *The Diechland* (1990) 1 QB 361; See Collins, *Dicey and Morris*, p. 288.

24 [1990] 2 WLR 786.

25 Baughen, S., 'Multinationals and the Export of Hazard' (1995) 58 MLR 54.

26 Collins, *Dicey and Morris*, p. 299; North and Fawcett, *Cheshire and North's*, p. 295.

27 See Chapter 5.

28 North and Fawcett, *Cheshire and North's*, p. 295.

29 See Chapter 2.

and specific jurisdiction rules created by the complex rules of private international law. Accordingly under this adopted Common Law rule, English courts have jurisdiction for each company that is domiciled in the UK courts. This means that the plaintiff is entitled to choose the jurisdiction of the court, but on this point the doctrine of *forum non conveniens* provides an interpretation gap for the case not to be heard in the UK and the US legal system has similar characteristics.[30]

Therefore the question of jurisdiction rules for MNEs is apparently too compound because it depends largely on the laws of a mixture of states. In many circumstances the issue is left with apparent difficulty in the international system which emerges in a number of situations; any state where a parent of an MNE is based lacks the territorial jurisdiction to regulate the activities of subsidiaries located abroad, while the host states in which the subsidiaries are located lack jurisdiction over any other components with whom they constitute integrated economic enterprise.[31] In these circumstances, 'MNEs enjoy a degree of independence from national jurisdictions that is unique in the global legal order'.[32] As a result there is, in theory, no court in the world that exercises jurisdiction over all the components of an MNE.[33] For this reason the plaintiffs have to sue corporations according to tort law principles in the home countries or host countries. They cannot sue parent corporations in the host states where they are not domiciled unless there are exemptions. Consequently they have to choose home countries' forums to sue the parent companies. Here lies another obstacle, the common law doctrine of *forum non conveniens*.

## *FORUM NON CONVENIENS*

*Forum non conveniens* is a common law doctrine that allows a court to dismiss a case, although personal jurisdiction and venue are correct, for the reason that there is another forum which is more appropriate.[34] It is a creature of equity and

---

30 Anderson, Michael, 'Transnational Corporations and Environmental Damage: Is Tort Law the Answer?' (2002) Wasburn Law Journal 399.

31 Lutter, M., 'Enterprise Law Corp. vs. Entity Law Inc. – Philip Blumberg's Book from the Point of View of an European Lawyer' (1990) 38 American Journal of Comparative Law 949.

32 Anderson, 'Transnational Corporations'; Ward Halina, 'Corporate Accountability In Search Of a Treaty? Some Insight From Foreign Direct Liability' (Briefing Paper of the Royal Institute of International Affairs No 4, May 2002).

33 Anderson, 'Transnational Corporations'.

34 Duval-Major, J., 'One-Way Ticket Home: The Federal Doctrine of Forum Non Conveniens and the International Plaintiff' (1991–1992) 77 Cornell Law Review 650.

only defendants can claim *forum non conveniens* because plaintiffs are entitled to original choice of forum.[35] *Forum non conveniens* was originally invoked to protect the defendant from being harassed by a plaintiff choosing a genuinely inconvenient or inappropriate forum. Despite this intent, it has in many instances become a device for MNEs to escape liability for tortious acts committed abroad by its subsidiaries.[36]

In the cases that *forum non conveniens* is applied by UK and US courts it is frequently MNEs that are defendants in actions brought by foreign plaintiffs for injuries that have occurred in a foreign country. The implications of the *forum non conveniens* doctrine are quite different in the voluntary creditors context as opposed to the involuntary creditors context. In the former cases, the commercial parties are usually contesting a forum because they wish to secure the best deal for themselves. Moreover dismissing the case or transferring it to another country has little effect on the final solution because of the certain commercial characteristics of disputes.[37] Under the latter cases foreign plaintiffs are in a weaker position since they have been exposed to tort involuntarily. They have no chance to negotiate for the choice of forum. In contractual disputes, plaintiffs might have a clause to determine the forum where disputes will be settled. However in the disputes where there are no prearranged forum clauses, there is still space for the application of *forum non conveniens*. That is why it is not unusual to see the application of *forum non conveniens* in contractual disputes. However the emphasis in this section will be on the application of *forum non conveniens* in the context of tort victims.

Tort victims of MNEs choose the UK and the US courts because they find the courts attractive for obtaining better punitive awards. On the other hand, defendants consider *forum non conveniens* as a part of litigation strategy as cases are usually moved to distinct forums where they end with a little punitive award or sometimes with no award. For example in the *Bhopal*[38] case, the conflict was settled for far less than what would have been a jury's award in the US.[39]

The *forum non conveniens* doctrine gives too much discretion to courts but there is very little clarity in its application. There are two kinds of applicable version of *forum non conveniens*: the abuse of process version and the most

---

35 Folsom, M.W., Gordon, J. and Spanogle, A., *International Business Transaction* (West Group, St. Paul. Minn. 2001), p 347.

36 Anderson, 'Transnational Corporations'.

37 Duval-Major, 'One-Way Ticket Home'.

38 See Bhopal case, Union Carbide Corp. Gas Plant Disaster at Bhopal, India in December 1984 F. Supp. 8 42.

39 Birnbaum, S.L. and Dunham, D.W., 'Foreign Plaintiff and Forum Non Conveniens' (1990) 16 Brook. J. Int'l. L. 241.

suitable forum version.[40] The *forum non conveniens* doctrine was substantially based on abuse of process by the plaintiff until the mid-1970s and the courts generally applied the abuse of process version, thus if they think there is another appropriate forum they dismiss the case on the ground of forum shopping rules. The defendants' first objection to plaintiffs' writs is usually that plaintiffs abuse the process since they have made the claim in the UK or the US although there is a more appropriate forum. Dismissal for abuse of process was practised by the courts before the 1980s in the US and it was also in common use in the UK.[41] Later the US courts changed their approach because it was obvious that everybody has a right to sue companies in their home states under the rules of general jurisdiction. In the UK in *Lubbe v Cape Plc*, at all stages, the judges refused the claim for abuse of process. They agreed on the basis that battling to establish a forum in a more appropriate forum must be considered as basic rights of plaintiffs. With the evaluation of the decision under the *Lubbe* case, it can be concluded that every plaintiff can try to establish a forum in a more appropriate venue. This should not be interpreted as an abuse of process, but instead be considered the fundamental right of plaintiffs as access to justice and the justice system is considered one of the basic human rights. Thus if plaintiffs believe the English court should have jurisdiction over a dispute arising from activities of MNEs, it must be considered as legitimate rights of individuals on their attempt to access to the justice systems.

In the UK, *forum non conveniens* principles were clarified and made common principle under the *Spiliada Maritime Corporation v Consulex Ltd*[42] case.[43] The principles can briefly be explained in that a stay will be granted if the defendant shows that there is another available forum, which is clearly and distinctly more appropriate than the UK forum. The plaintiff can only prevent the dismissal of the case if he can prove that justice cannot be obtained in the new forum. After the *Spiliada* case with the establishment of most suitable forum criteria, the approach of US and English courts towards *forum non conveniens* became very similar.[44]

Accordingly there is a two-limbed test. In the first limb, the burden rests on the defendant to show not only that England is not the natural or appropriate forum for the trial, but also that there is another available forum, which is clearly

---

40 Robertson, D.W., 'Forum Non Conveniens in America and England: A Rather Fantastic Fiction' (1987) 103 Law Quarterly Review 398.

41 Meeran, R., 'The Unveiling of Transnational Corporations: A Direct Approach' in Addo, M.K. (ed.), *Human Rights Standards and the Responsibility of Transnational Corporations* (Kluwer Law International, The Hague 1999).

42 [1987] AC 460.

43 See further Collier, *Conflict of Law*, p. 88.

44 Robertson, 'Forum Non Conveniens'.

and distinctly more appropriate than the English forum. Hence it is not sufficient for the defendant to establish a mere balance of convenience in favour of the foreign forum. The defendant has to show that there is a 'clearly and distinctly' more appropriate forum elsewhere. Then the court will grant the stay 'unless there are circumstances by reason of which justice requires that a stay should nevertheless not be granted'. In the second limb, the burden of proof shifts to the plaintiff to show that substantive justice cannot be achieved in the alternative forum.[45]

Based on the second limb of *forum non conveniens*, it can be claimed that the English courts' approach towards to the doctrine has changed after the two decisions of *Connelly v RTZ* [46] and *Lubbe v Cape Plc.*[47] The *Cape Plc* cases concerned the claims made by employees of South African subsidiaries and other claimants who lived near the mining area. The plaintiffs claimed that they were exposed to asbestos during the period of time that the subsidiaries were active in the mining area. In 1997 two writs were issued by the plaintiffs' solicitors. The first action was on behalf of Rachel Lubbe and four others.[48] The judge ordered a stay of the Lubbe action. Lubbe appealed the decision and the Court of Appeal lifted the stay. The defendant's petition was refused by the House of Lords. After the House of Lords' decision the same law firm issued a writ on behalf of Hedrick Afrika and 1538 others. The defendant applied and reapplied to stay the Afrika and Lubbe actions on the ground of *forum non conveniens* and/or abuse of process. The defendant submitted that the English court must not carry on with the case because, under the *Spiliada* principles, the South African forum is distinctly and clearly more appropriate for the trial of action.[49]

---

45 Magaisa, 'Suing Multinational'.

46 [1998] AC 854, In *Connelly* the plaintiff had been employed in Namibia for a subsidiary of an English parent company. He was a Scotsman who worked in Namibia for some time and came back to England. After returning, he was diagnosed with cancer of the throat. He sued the parent company in the UK because he thought that the justice was not achieved in Namibia for practical reasons. Legal aid was not available there and medical witnesses were usually in England.

47 [2000] 1 WLR 1545.

48 Second action was on behalf of Vicenzina Gisondi and three others. These plaintiffs were Italian citizens so they had the right to bring a case against an English domicile company in the UK in accordance with the Article 2 of the Brussels Convention.

49 The Court of Appeal granted a stay on the ground that the alternative forum was available after the defendants' submission. In addition, it was obvious that the action must proceed as a group action and in group concept, the South African forum was distinctly and clearly more appropriate. The private interest factors point to the South African forum because essential documents are in South Africa, nearly all witnesses are there and medical evidence is reachable there. For legal aid problems, the decision was that it might not be possible to get legal aid in South Africa but it does not make it necessary to set up a forum in the UK. In addition, the judge thought that if the case is kept

Although the Court of Appeal granted a stay, the House of Lords removed the stay.

The reasons for the removal of the stay by the House of Lords in the *Cape Plc* cases were similar to those of *Connelly.*[50] There was no legal aid and contingency fee available to lawyers in South Africa and, additionally, South African courts were not experienced enough to handle a group action. These two recent decisions point out that after evaluating private interest factors, if there is a possibility that justice may not to be achieved, courts should decide that the cases must be tried in England. Additionally the *Thor chemical*[51] litigations opened the way for English parent corporations to be sued in the UK. However it remains to be seen whether the *Cape* and *Thor* litigation open the way to further cases against UK-based MNEs.[52]

On this level the influence of the ECJ on UK law must be discussed. The UK enacted the Civil Jurisdiction and Judgments Act 1982, which is based on the Brussels Convention. The Act was prepared under characteristics of the Civil Law, and came into effect in 1987. Consequently there has been no dispute in the UK about the appropriate forum in relation to plaintiffs who are from other European member countries. In the *Cape Industries* case, for the Italian plaintiffs the defendant did not appeal against the decision of the court because they were from a member state of the EU. The situation of plaintiffs from other member states was determined in an earlier case of *Re Harrods (Buenos Aires) Ltd.*[53] Although English courts were reluctant to abandon the *forum non conveniens* doctrine the ECJ reinforced invalidity of *forum non conveniens* against European plaintiffs in the *Group Josi Reinsurance Company SA v Universal General Insurance Company* judgment in July 2000.[54] The ECJ has extended the general principle established by the Brussels Convention that defendants

---

in the UK, there may be some procedural problems related to examining evidence in South Africa.

50 See further Collier, *Conflict of Law*, p. 93.

51 *Sithole and Others v Thor Chemicals* (LTL 2/3/1999). In this case, the plaintiffs claimed damages for personal injury or loss of support arising from the death of breadwinners and also looked to a parent company, this time of a mercury processing plant. It was alleged that the parent company had been advised by the health and safety authorities in the UK that the process adopted in the UK company was potentially injurious to employees' health. Notwithstanding that, the parent company exported the process, in a substantially unchanged form, to an operation in Cato Ridge, KwaZulu-Natal. In that matter, the defence of *forum non conveniens* was also raised but dismissed by the House of Lords.

52 Ward, 'Corporate Accountability'.

53 *Re Harrods (Buenos Aires) Ltd* [1991] 4 All ER 334.

54 *Société Group Josi Reinsurance Company v Compagnie d'Assurances Universal General Insurance Company* Case 412/98 (ECJ 13 Jul 2000).

can be sued in the courts of the EU member state in which they are domiciled. However the English courts refused to accept the principle in cases where the alternative court was located in a non-EU country.[55]

The Brussels Convention has been superseded by the Council Regulation on the Jurisdiction and Recognition and Enforcement of Judgments in Civil and Commercial Matters[56] (the Brussels Regulations). As far as Article 2 is concerned the Regulations are materially the same as the Brussels Convention. The English court is required to apply the rules set out in the Brussels Regulations. Therefore the recent *Owusu v Jackson*[57] decision has continued that trend by curtailing the ability of the English court to invoke the doctrine of *forum non conveniens*.

Mr Owusu, the claimant, a British national domiciled in the UK, suffered serious injuries in Mambee Bay, Jamaica, when he struck his head when swimming against a submerged sandbank. Mr Jackson, the first defendant, also domiciled in the UK, had let the holiday villa to Mr Owusu. Mr Owusu sued Mr Jackson in the English courts for breach of an implied term that the private beach where the accident occurred would be reasonably safe or free from hidden dangers. Mr Owusu also sued several Jamaican companies in the same action. Mr Owusu commenced his claim in the English High Court in October 2000. Mr Jackson and Jamaican defendants challenged the jurisdiction of the English court on the grounds of private interest factors of *forum non conveniens*. The judge refused to stay the proceedings. The judge referred to the decision of the ECJ in *Group Josi Reinsurance*, which held that whether the jurisdictional rules in the Brussels Regulations applied depended upon whether the defendant had its domicile in a contracting state, and the rules applied to a dispute between a defendant domiciled in a contracting state and a claimant domiciled in a non-contracting state. He concluded that on the basis of the ECJ ruling in *Group Josi*, the decision of the English Court of Appeal in *Re Harrods* was bad law.

The ECJ went on to hold that the *forum non conveniens* doctrine was incompatible with the Brussels Regulations. The Regulations and the ECJ's interpretation of it have impacted significantly on the common law rules in relation to jurisdiction by favouring certainty over the flexibility which was built

---

[55] In *Re Harrods (Buenos Aires) Ltd*, the Court decided that the domicile principle in the Brussels Convention has no application to cases where there is a choice of jurisdiction between the English forum and the courts of a non-Convention country. In such a case, the *forum non conveniens* doctrine will apply by virtue of Article 49 of the Brussels Convention.

[56] Council Regulation (EC) No 44/2001, of 22 December 2000 on Jurisdiction and the Recognition and Enforcement of Judgments in Civil and Commercial Matters (Official Journal L 12 of 16.01.2001).

[57] Case-128/01 (ECJ 1 March 2005) [2005] 2 WLR 942.

into the common law rules. However the ECJ declined to answer a second question referred to it, namely whether the application of *forum non conveniens* is ruled out in all circumstances. This leaves open the possibility of the doctrine of *forum non conveniens* still having application in certain circumstances. Cases to which the Brussels Convention or the Brussels Regulations do not apply might be unaffected by the decisions in this case.

In comparing the UK approach to the US one, the UK approach to *forum non conveniens* has never precisely mirrored the US approach, because US courts have granted *forum non conveniens* dismissals whenever, on balance, forum connections were more strongly in favour of a foreign forum, while recent English cases have emphasized the importance of substantive justice for the plaintiff, taking into account the importance of legal aid as well as the general need to ensure that *forum non conveniens* does not result in a denial of access to justice.[58]

In the US, *forum non conveniens* principles were established under the case of *Gulf Oil Corporation v Gilbert.*[59] In that case the Supreme Court established a two-step procedure for deciding whether to dismiss a case on *forum non conveniens* grounds.[60] First, a federal court must determine whether an adequate alternative forum exists. If it does, the court must then decide in which forum the litigation would best serve the private interests of the litigants and the public interest of the forum. In international issues, relying on *Piper Aircraft Co v Reyno*,[61] the court noted that, in answering a *forum non conveniens* question, a district court must first determine whether or not the proposed alternative forum is adequate. The court stated that it must then consider the relevant private interests of the parties and public interest factors relating to the current and alternative forum.[62]

The position of the US courts did not change in the *Bhopal* litigations[63] and the case was dismissed on the ground of *forum non conveniens*. The judge decided that the Indian court was more suitable because private interest factors supported the efficiency of the Indian court. The Indian government and public

---

58 Anderson, 'Transnational Corporations'.

59 330 US 501 [1947].

60 See Robertson, 'Forum Non Conveniens'; Duval-Major, 'One-Way Ticket Home'.

61 454 US 235 [1981].

62 Chinen, M.A., 'Jurisdiction: Foreign Plaintiffs, Forum Non Conveniens and Litigation Against Multinational Corporations' (1987) 28 Harvard International Law Journal 209.

63 The case was brought by Indian victims of the gas leak disaster of December 1984 at Union Carbide's pesticides plant in Bhopal. The Indian plaintiffs, with the government of India, argued for US jurisdictions against Union Carbide Corporation, parent Company of Union Carbide of India.

were very interested in the problem so public interest factors were pointing to an Indian venue. Additionally the judge was convinced the Indian court could handle the case. Thus the *Bhopal* decision, like *Piper* before it, indicates that US courts are very reluctant to entertain claims brought by foreign plaintiffs against an American firm.[64] Indeed the US approach openly discriminates in favour of local litigants, placing unfair obstacles in the way of foreign plaintiffs wishing to sue US companies in the United States.[65] Actually discussing the public interest in the case, international society has been used ironically to promote prejudiced outcomes because the US approach basically depends on the idea that the injuries done by an American business to foreign people abroad are not America's problem. The legal policy problem under the *forum non conveniens* principle which is valid for both English and American courts is that US and UK courts are in fear of there might be a flood of cases to their courts and it would make them more congested. By allowing transnational business to choose legal systems imposing a lower regulatory burden than the United States, the US courts have effectively lowered regulatory standards. By refusing to exercise jurisdiction in a case like *Bhopal*, a court effectively allows a US enterprise to avoid US tort liability and encourages other manufacturers to locate plants abroad.[66]

## Assessment Criteria of *Forum Non Conveniens* Doctrine

The criteria are classified in two segments: private interest factors and public interest factors. Public interest factors are American-based criteria and rejected by the House of Lords in England. This examination is important for assessing the suitability of the doctrine of *forum non conveniens* to address conflicts arising from the activities of modern MNEs.

### Private interest factors

Private interest factors can be classified as factors related to procedural problems in litigations and issues directly related to the case. In the evaluation of private interest issues, the courts have often concentrated on the location of evidence and witnesses, enforceability of witness summons, and where the respective

---

[64] Muchlinski, P.T., 'The Bhopal Case Controlling Ultra-hazardous Industrial Activities Undertaken By Foreign Investors' (1987) 50 Modern Law Review 545.

[65] Prince, Peter, 'Bhopal, Bougainville and OK Tedi: Why Australia's Approach to Forum Non Conveniens is Better' (1998) 47 International and Comparative Law Quarterly 573.

[66] See Robertson, 'Forum Non Conveniens'; Dunham, D.F and Gladbach, E.F 'Forum Non Conveniens and the Foreign Plaintiffs in the 1990s' (1998-1999) 24 Brook. J. Int'l. L. 665; Prince, Bhopal.

parties reside. American courts also consider the possibility of enforcing a judgment.[67] Moreover English courts have given weight to practical considerations that are important for proper judgments such as the availability of legal aid, contingency fee agreements and language barrier problems, which question the adequacy of the foreign forum.[68] Briefly, the courts ask if substantive justice could be achieved in an alternative forum by questioning the adequacy of the foreign forum and diversity of proceedings.

## Evidences and Witnesses

In tort cases against MNEs, evidence and witnesses are usually found in the host countries where the subsidiaries perform their activities. So overseas witnesses are likely to be more common in these cases, which causes the forum to weigh against the home country. If documents in the possession of the overseas subsidiary are likely to be relevant, the parent company will usually have power to require their production. This argument can, however, be advanced in a defendant's favour where documents are in the possession of some other overseas parties (such as a government body), which are unlikely to volunteer the documents. In those circumstances a court order will be necessary, but an order from an English court would probably be unenforceable; this is therefore a factor in favour of the court declining jurisdiction.[69] However many issues are likely to be resolved by means of expert evidence, and this will reduce the need to call witnesses of fact and lift the balance back in favour of the English forum. Under the problem of the enforceability of witness summons, it is important to consider whether or not the foreign country is a party to the 1970 Hague Convention on the Taking of Evidence Abroad in Civil and Commercial Matters.[70] If so, subpoenas issued out of the English court will be enforceable in that jurisdiction and this will minimize the impact of any evidence advanced by the defendants as to the existence of relevant witnesses in the foreign jurisdiction. Even if the Hague Convention cannot be relied upon, there is also the possibility of obtaining depositions from foreign witnesses by means of letters of request.[71]

It should not be ignored that the actions are against groups of companies for tort of subsidiaries so courts have to check all possible decision-taking procedures or transactions in the group and listen to managers and other workers of

---

67 Dunham and Gladbach, 'Forum Non Conveniens'.

68 *Ibid.*

69 Meeran, Richard, 'Process Liability of Multinationals: Overcoming the Forum Hurdle' (1995) Nov. JPIL 170.

70 Convention on the Taking of Evidence Abroad in Civil or Commercial Matters (The Hague, 18.3.1970 Treaty Series 020/1977 Cmnd 6727).

71 Meeran, 'Process Liability'.

the companies. Under new developments in technology and communication of the operating companies, the documents or all the information that is needed can be easily produced in any jurisdiction because there are already very well-developed flows of information amongst companies in the group.[72] Thus the horizontal structure makes it impossible to point another jurisdiction as more appropriate in terms of evidence and witnesses. Therefore it is really difficult to decide that host countries are more suitable due to availability of evidence, and even if they are, this suitability cannot be distinct and clear any more. Additionally the consideration of the likelihood of finding expert witnesses makes the forum of developed countries more appropriate. In brief, it can be claimed that in MNEs' tort, the balance of the available forums will be in the midpoint to declare one of them as more appropriate.

## Enforcement

Courts might consider the enforcement rules as a significant factor.[73] If there is no possibility of enforcing a judgment against the defendant company, a stay should not be granted. In *Adams v Cape Industries* the English Court of Appeal held that the Texas judgment was not enforceable against *Cape Industries* because the parent company had not been present in Texas at the relevant time and the presence of its subsidiary could not constitute the necessary presence by the parent itself. Therefore because of the risk of non-enforcement in application of *forum non conveniens*, the defendant parent at least should be forced to guarantee to obey the foreign forum court's decision and pay the awards, as applied in the *Bhopal* case. This solution may not be as effective as hearing the case in the parent companies forum but at least it can prevent the plaintiffs giving up the case because of enforcement problems.

In cases brought in home countries under which *forum non conveniens* is applied, there will be problems of reverse enforcement. According to general principles only subsidiaries are domiciled in host countries so if there is a finding against parent companies, the enforcement problem will occur because of the non-domicile status of the parent companies in host states. This will create a problem that when the proceeding is finalized in host states, the plaintiffs will have to look for possible enforcement mechanisms in home countries. If there is any enforcement agreement between the involved states, the enforcement must not be considered as criteria for assessing the application of *forum non conveniens* because both rulings will be treated in the same way. On the lack of enforcement agreement, the enforcement problem will be two sided. Moreover

[72] See Chapter 2.
[73] Dunham and Gladbach, 'Forum Non Conveniens'.

under a horizontal organizational structure, involvement of more than one entity in MNEs' tort actions is very likely. In a modern complex structure, entities are most likely to be domiciled in various jurisdictions. In this situation, in whichever jurisdiction the case is pursued, there will be a question of enforcement against other entities. This makes the application of *forum non conveniens* more problematic in tort cases brought against modern MNEs. Accordingly enforcement problems do not only occur in home countries but also occur in host countries. This makes consideration of enforcement as an assessment criterion for *forum non conveniens* incompetent.

## Efficiency of the Alternative Forum

American and English courts, in the decision-making process, in addition to other elements, evaluate the efficiency of alternative courts. If they come to the conclusion that the alternative courts are efficient enough to hear the case they grant a stay. They do not have specific criteria for the evaluation as the assessment criteria used in the past cases are vague. Some issues concerning the adequacy of the Indian forum were raised by the plaintiffs in the *Bhopal* case. First, the plaintiffs argued that the Indian forum was inadequate because it lacked the innovation necessary to deal with litigation as complex as the *Bhopal* case. In dismissing this argument, the New York court relied on the testimony of the defendant's expert to show that the Indian judiciary had responded in the past by creating complex legal problems. Secondly, the plaintiffs argued that the Indian forum was subject to widespread delays. The court responded that this could happen in the US as well. Thirdly, the court were not persuaded by the plaintiffs' further argument that substantive Indian law is incapable of handling the complexity of the *Bhopal* litigation. The plaintiffs' fourth argument focused on whether Indian procedural law would prevent the litigants from receiving an adequate trial. The court responded with concerns that India's discovery procedures would not be as expansive as those of the US but finally decided that it was efficient enough to handle the case.

In the UK, in the *Cape Industries* case, the House of Lords did not find South African courts experienced enough to handle a group action case. These discretionary evaluation criteria make the future of cases dependent on the characteristics of the state of the alternative forum; if the country has a developed legal system they grant the stay, if not, they do not. One of the specific findings of Sir John Wood in the *Connelly* case was that 'whilst the plaintiff had obtained legal aid to sue RTZ in England, the chances of him securing funding to litigate in Namibia were remote'. Additionally the legal aid problem was one of the main arguments in the *Cape Industries* case and it was discussed widely by the parties. Even though it was proven that there was no legal aid available in South Africa for personal injuries, the Court of Appeal decided that unavailability of legal aid is not sufficient to remove the stay. Nevertheless the House of Lords revised the decision as they considered that legal aid was very important for the future of the case and therefore, together with the absence of any contingency fee agreement, it might prevent justice being achieved. This makes MNEs' tort liability cases dependent on where the tort action occurs and thus it is impossible to predict the outcome of future cases.

Under these harsh conditions of *forum non conveniens*, in the UK, the plaintiffs' last argument against the theory is human rights issues under which they claim they cannot obtain substantive justice in the alternative forum. Hence it is argued that the dismissal of a case under *forum non conveniens* violates Article 6 of the European Convention on Human Rights,[74] which regulates entitlement to a fair hearing. These claims regarding *forum non conveniens* dismissal have not been taken to the European Court Human Rights. In a possible situation where the issue is brought to the European Court of Human Rights, I do not think the court will decide in favour of the plaintiffs because in *forum non conveniens* dismissals the courts claim that they are not rejecting the cases because the alternative forum is available to reach a substantive judgment. However the effect of European human rights laws will limit the application of *forum non conveniens* further in the UK.[75] Moreover the recent *Owusu v Jackson* decision of the ECJ will reduce possible success in this matter.

Under the private interest factors each practical argument might be raised in any case. The claims that American and English courts' arguments can be evaluated to prove that English and American forums are appropriate as well because MNEs perform their business under very complicated business structures.[76] Thus all private interest factors may point to a home countries forum in addition to that of host countries. Under the complicated economic and managerial structure of business it is impossible to prove any particular forum is distinctly and clearly more appropriate. Most of the documents can easily be obtainable in any country under which any component of the MNEs is domiciled. The system of information exchange is also applicable for courts; in case of requirements any witness or any documents can be contacted in any state. More importantly in tort claims, while evaluating the decision-making process and the roles of subsidiaries of MNEs, multi-jurisdictional examination is a requirement. The modern structure shows that MNEs are not single decision-making centres; rather each entity is involved in the decision-making process by following common group policies. Thus any tort committed by one subsidiary

---

74 Convention for the Protection of Human Rights and Fundamental Freedoms (Rome 4.XI.1950).

75 Anderson, 'Transnational Corporations'.

76 See Chapter 2.

under a group will have complex roots in the process that led to the incident. Wherever the case is heard, a complex examination of the facts is inevitable. Thus dismissing the case on the ground of *forum non conveniens* does not create a convenience. If the aim is to achieve substantive judgment, as claimed by the courts, *forum non conveniens* is definitely not a tool to do so.

**Public interest factors**

Public interest factors are applied by American courts to prevent flows of cases to the United States. American courts examine the public interest factor in three topics: the public policy aspect of the dispute, the choice of law issue and the administrative burden issues. The main justification for the application of public interest factors is that courts should not require American citizens to bear the cost of jury service and court expenses when they had little connection to the subject-matter of the case.[77] In the *Bhopal* case the American courts decided that Indian courts are more interested in the problem and thus are more appropriate to hear the case. Moreover the nature of law also pointed at Indian law. During the case, for example, the district court focused on the Indian government's extensive regulation of its country's chemical industry as evidence indicating that the Indian government had a strong interest in the dispute, and therefore supporting a *forum non conveniens* dismissal on the basis of public interest factors. Most important public interest factors in the court's decisions were the local interest factors in the action and application of foreign law.[78] However the Indian government itself initially sued in the US District Court for the Southern District of New York on behalf of all individual victims, suggesting that the government was not opposed to the US judicial system crafting a solution to a problem that arose in India.[79] The Chief Justice of the Supreme Court of India stated: 'in my opinion that these cases must be pursued in the United States ... it is the only hope these unfortunate people have'.[80]

Therefore assessing public policy issues is very complex. It may be true that the Indian government and public were interested in the problem but the American public was also interested in the problem because problems of chemical industry plants are an important public issue in the US. In addition the same enterprise had similar kinds of plants and chemical foundations in the US that

77 Birnbaum and Dunham, 'Foreign Plaintiff'.

78 Dunham and Gladbach, 'Forum Non Conveniens'.

79 Muchlinski, 'The Bhopal Case'; Miller Laurel E., 'Forum Non Conveniens and State Control of Foreign Plaintiff Access to U.S. Courts in International Tort Actions' (1991) 58 U. Chi. L. Rev. 1369.

80 Cited at Robertson, D., 'The Federal Doctrine of Forum Non Conveniens' (1994) 29 Texas ILJ 353.

needed to be strictly regulated. This means that the interest of the public is always two sided, citizens' interest and public administrative bodies' interest.

In the light of global developments and globalized activities of MNEs, movements and actions of MNEs are discussed at a worldwide level. For example recent asbestos-related liability claims and pharmaceutical liability cases attract attention from all over the world at an administrative and public level. In the *Bhopal* case as well, the worldwide public attention has been significant. Persons from the UK were never part of the Bhopal disaster but the involvement of NGOs, media and even at an administrative level was very high.[81] Moreover the globalization of MNEs as well as economic institutions in the world brings more globalized media coverage. People all over the world have a chance to follow news worldwide. Even small accidents can be viewed by millions of people. The easy use of the Internet makes information exchanges very fast and wide. People are organized according to their concerns and campaigners create public policy not only at the domestic but also at a global level. The issue of the liability of MNEs is definitely one of the most discussed global problems. Consequently many people either from a developed country or a developing country have an interest in the issues. Thus there are many NGOs contributing to the formation of public policies at a local and global level. Moreover the governments, neither in developed countries nor in developing countries, have the luxury to ignore these discussions. This makes the issues of corporate torts a matter of public policy in any country, from different perspectives.

Therefore the interpretation of American courts' decisions on the basis of these arguments proves that the basic reason for dismissing cases on the ground of *forum non conveniens* is to keep disputes against American MNEs out of American courts. However in *Lubbe v Cape*,[82] the House of Lords did not find it suitable to apply public interest factors. It is a correct interpretation of the public policy issues because public policy is not a legal issue, so determining the future of cases on the ground of public interest factors could make the courts involved in policy-making discussion that would have a very negative effect on their credibility.

---

81 For example the BBC has a whole section on the Bhopal tragedy available at http://news.bbc.co.uk/1/hi/programmes/bhopal/default.stm. Moreover, the UK government's Health and Safety Commission applies its control of major accident hazards by giving the Bhopal tragedy as an example. Available at http://www.hse.gov.uk/comah/sragtech/caseuncarbide84.htm.

82 *Lubbe v Cape Plc* [2000] 1 WLR 1545.

## Criticism of *Forum Non Conveniens* Doctrine

In tort liability cases, on one side, there is a big MNE and on the other side there are people from less-developed countries, who cannot even pay the court expenses without legal aid. These unfortunate people choose the forum of the parent company's country because in their own country the punitive awards are very small, the quality of judgment is poor and they cannot even find lawyers to represent them. On the other side, there are powerful MNEs some of which have bigger assets than most of the less-developed countries have.[83] This power may give them a chance to interfere in the courts in the plaintiffs' countries.

These legal barriers may prevent plaintiffs from recovery in their home country.[84] Thus after the dismissal of cases, many plaintiffs lose their wish to follow the cases because they have lost their lawyers, money and courage. Most of the cases are abandoned, and those that are not are mostly settled for less than their estimated value.[85] MNEs try hard to shift cases to the plaintiffs' forum in order to stay away from high punitive awards.[86] Furthermore even if the plaintiffs win the cases they will become engaged with enforcement problems; the decisions by courts where plaintiffs are resident may not be enforced, which may make all their efforts useless. This criticism sometimes finds support from the judiciary, Justice Doggett in the case of *Dow Chemical Company v Castro Alfaro*[87] stated that:

> The doctrine of forum non conveniens is obsolete in a world in which markets are global and in which ecologists have documented the delicate balance of all life on this planet.... [It] enables corporations to evade legal control merely because they are transnational.... In the absence of meaningful tort liability in the United States for their actions, some multinational corporations will continue to operate without adequate regard for the human and environmental costs of their actions. This result cannot be allowed to repeat itself for decades to come. As a matter of law and of public policy, the doctrine of forum non conveniens should be abolished.

Accordingly the *forum non conveniens* is a complete waste of time and plaintiffs' resources and both the *Bhopal* and the *Cape Industries* cases amply demonstrate how the *forum non conveniens* can hold back speedy resolution of disputes by keeping claimants locked into a process that focuses on determining

---

83 See Dine, J., *Companies, International Trade and Human Rights* (CUP, Cambridge 2005), Chapter 1.

84 Sahni, B.P., *Transnational Corporate Liability: Accountability for Human Injury* (Cameron May, London 2006), p. 140.

85 Robertson, 'Forum Non Conveniens'.

86 Ward, 'Corporate Accountability'.

87 *Dow Chemical Company v Castro Alfaro* 786 S.W.2d 674 (Supreme Court of Texas 1990).

the proper forum for the action.[88] Plaintiffs and defendants just apply to court to, in the words of Professor Robertson, 'litigate in order to determine where they shall litigate'.[89]

In both the English and American law systems the principle of *forum non conveniens* is very broad and vaguely interpreted and gives judges nearly unlimited discretion rights. Although there have been attempts to establish basic principles, they cannot embrace all possible situations. Consequently this unclear situation just helps MNEs escape from liability. The adoption of the most suitable forum version of the *forum non conveniens* doctrine has made it impossible to predict the outcome of a jurisdictional issue that would have been easy to forecast without the principle.[90]

The multinational business, as it is obvious by its name, considers every business relationship at the same level.[91] For them the classification of people on the basis of citizenship is over. They make profit from their activities from all over the world and distribute these profits to their company's shareholders mostly resident in home countries. However the judges know that courts are supported by taxpayers so English and American courts act in a way that since their citizens pay tax for a better quality jurisdiction, courts must not be busy with claims of non-citizens. It is true that citizens pay taxes but a good sum of this income comes from the overseas activities of MNEs. The Shell Company declared a profit of more than £12.5 billion in 2006[92] and it is not difficult to guess where this money came from: Nigeria, Indonesia, the Middle East and Africa, basically from all over the world. This profit is distributed to shareholders resident in the UK and these shareholders pay taxes. Courts also claim that they do not dismiss the cases but transfer them to another forum. However, in practice, obtaining rights after the stay is almost impossible. More importantly as Professor Robertson explains, a court in New York cannot transfer a case to India, it can only dismiss:

> These astonishing references to transfer in the international forum non conveniens context are part of a disguised vocabulary whereby the true effects of forum non conveniens dismissal are masked … in the real world, everyone knows that international plaintiffs who suffer forum non conveniens dismissals in the United States are typically unable to go forward in the hypothesized foreign forum.[93]

Moreover since many advances in technology and transportation have taken place, the modern context of convenience cannot be interpreted in the same

---

88 Ward, 'Corporate Accountability'.
89 Robertson, 'Forum Non Conveniens'.
90 *Ibid.*
91 See Chapter 1.
92 See Shell Financial Report, 2006; available at www.shell.com.
93 Robertson, 'Forum Non Conveniens'.

way as that of decades ago.[94] The modern characteristics of the organizational structure can never point out any particular jurisdiction clearly. It is a fact that a jurisdiction can be convenient in some aspects but none of the alternative jurisdictions for MNEs' tort liability litigation will be clearly and distinctly more appropriate. The characteristics of the modern managerial and organizational structure of MNEs suggest that the distinction between member organizations is not as clear as it used to be. This fact plays an important role when deciding the convenient forum in MNEs' torts because under complex horizontal organizations it is almost impossible to declare one single forum as more appropriate. The decision-making process is now complicated as it includes parent, subsidiary and other operational subsidiaries, while considering common group policy.[95]

For example in a hypothetical tort committed by a subsidiary of a petroleum MNE in a less-developed country, more particularly where there was a problem in their exploring plant and, as consequence, the leak polluted rivers and caused huge environmental damage and impact on the life of local people. In this case the tort is committed in the subsidiary's forum. However the process of building and operating the plant involves the parent as a policy determinant as well as a negotiation body before establishing the local subsidiary. It also involves research and technology subsidiaries in the group as basic determinants of operational technology. It may also involve the construction department which will be the one responsible for building the pipeline and further infrastructure. Another important aspect of such projects, financing, is usually dealt with by the financing department. In short the process of building a plant and operating involves many different divisions and companies in an MNE under which each subsidiary has diverse responsibility in special time periods.

If defendants argue that the forum of the subsidiary is more convenient, the private interest factors will point out many different forums as evidence can be found in various jurisdictions. For example the original decisions of investments are taken in headquarters, and the corporations responsible for the technology might be in other jurisdictions. Witnesses and responsible people on the process will be scattered around various forums as well. Expert witnesses will be available mostly in the forum of the parent. In brief, the concept of convenience does not apply to the modern structure of MNEs under which it is almost impossible to determine a more suitable forum. Thus the *forum non conveniens* doctrine has no practical applicability. More importantly, the issue of searching for convenience must not prevent the search for justice as pointed out by the courts in the *Cape* and *Connolly* cases.

---

94 Dunham and Gladbach, 'Forum Non Conveniens'.

95 See Chapter 2.

All these explanations prove that, as an empirical matter, *forum non conveniens* decisions invariably determine the outcomes of international tort cases and thus have an effect on substantive law.[96] Consequently the doctrine prevents the common law from reaching a substantive conclusion in determining tort liability of MNEs. Considering these realities together with the non-suitability of the *forum non conveniens* principle to the modern concept of MNE, we should discuss the alternatives and suggested solutions.

## Suggested Solutions to *Forum Non Conveniens*

If courts, in cases of torts committed by MNEs, discriminate against people living in the jurisdictions of subsidiary companies, a quest to search for an appropriate solution must start. One straightforward answer is to amend the rules of private international law that discriminate against foreign litigants. The movement towards a global judgment convention in The Hague Conference on Private International Law may provide part of the answer here,[97] but even if that effort results in a viable treaty that is widely ratified by states, it may still contain room for the application of the *forum non conveniens* doctrine.[98] Under these conditions, other solutions could be achieved in common law, because the *forum non conveniens* doctrine is a creature of equity, and might be abolished.

### Conditional *forum non conveniens*

In the *Bhopal* case, Judge Keenan decided that India had an adequate forum and the capability to deal with the case, but imposed some conditions for the defendant. The subsequent conditions were laid down: (1) Union Carbide must consent to submit to the jurisdiction of the courts of India and continue to waive defences based upon the statute of limitations; (2) Union Carbide must agree to satisfy judgment rendered by an Indian court, and if applicable, upheld by an appellate court in that country, where such judgment conforms with the minimal requirements of due process; (3) Union Carbide must be subject to discovery under the model of the US Federal Rules of Civil Procedure after an appropriate demand by plaintiffs.[99] The American court tried to seem fair when imposing conditions for the defendant. However imposing conditions for the defendants cannot provide consistent solutions for the problems because each case has its own specific conditions. As it has been apparently shown in the *Bhopal* case, the

96 Miller, 'Forum Non Conveniens'

97 Muchlinski, P., *Multinational Enterprises and the Law* (OUP, Oxford 2007), p. 176.

98 Anderson, 'Transnational Corporations'.

99 Abraham, C.M. and Abraham, S., 'The Bhopal Case and the Development of Environmental Law in India' (1991) 40 ICLQ 334.

dispute has not yet been solved in a satisfactory way for victims.[100] More importantly these conditions cannot bring the expected level of protection for the plaintiffs and thus cannot help to establish MNEs' tort liability. The conditions were imposed because the court wanted to relieve public concern and protest in the US. However the facts seem to contradict the American courts' professed belief that conditional dismissal for *forum non conveniens* is not a decision going to the character and result of the controversy; as Professor Robertson states 'pretending that such dismissals are not outcome-determinative is a rather fantastic fiction'.[101]

**Judiciary and Judicial Procedure Act in the USA (28 USC § 1404(A))**

When there is a problem of imposing conditions in *forum non conveniens* dismissal and the impossibility of transferring a case from one forum to another, principles of American federal law can be considered as an alternative to *forum non conveniens* dismissal. After enactment of the procedural law of 28 USC 1404 (A) in 1948, *forum non conveniens* problems amongst American district courts lost their applicability. The law provides that 'for the convenience of parties and witnesses, in the interests of justice, a district court may transfer any civil action to any other district or division where it might have been brought'.[102] Courts have been given more discretion to transfer under the Act than they had to dismiss on grounds of *forum non conveniens*. Moreover the change of venue does not influence the law applied to the case and is therefore only a procedural decision that will not alter the outcome of disputes.[103] It is a good solution for domestic forum problems in the United States but application of the same rules could be too utopian at the international level. Judge Marshall's opinion for the majority in *Piper* noted that the development of the section 1404(A) transfer rules were drafted in accordance with the doctrine of *forum non conveniens*, but that the district court's discretion to dismiss is in fact more substantial under the transfer statute than under the common law doctrine.[104] Thus the relocation of a case within the federal system is more flexible than its dismissal for purposes of litigation outside the United States.

At least in theory, transferring a case from one federal court to another does not need to seriously disrupt its progress because the case does not have to be refiled; there will be no problem with the relevant statute of limitations having expired while the case was pending in the first court.[105] However in transnational

---

100 For more information see www.bhopal.net.
101 Robertson, 'Forum Non Conveniens'.
102 *Ibid.*
103 Miller, 'Forum Non Conveniens'.
104 Dunham and Gladbach, 'Forum Non Conveniens'.
105 Robertson, 'Forum Non Conveniens'.

civil litigation, it is not possible to transfer cases to another state. The courts can only dismiss the cases on the basis of *forum non conveniens*. Moreover the aim of plaintiffs for starting their legal actions in America is to escape the inefficiency of legal procedural systems in the forum state of the subsidiary. Thus even a successful transfer of the case to an alternative forum does not provide justifiable solutions.

**Australian approach to *forum non conveniens***

In the UK and the United States the courts apply the most suitable forum approach in *forum non conveniens* discussions. Accordingly in the UK the courts dismiss the case whenever there is an alternative forum clearly and distinctly more appropriate and, similarly, in the United States whenever the balance of convenience points to the alternative forum. However Australian case law takes a different approach, which is clearly in favour of tort victims in comparison to English and American approaches. The key element in Australia's approach is its maintenance of the notion that a *forum non conveniens* stay should not be granted unless the choice of forum is clearly oppressive or difficult for the defendant. In *Voth v Manildra Flour Mills*,[106] the High Court affirmed a test, declaring that an Australian court would need to be 'clearly inappropriate' before a stay on *forum non conveniens* grounds could be granted.[107] This sets a specific standard against which requests for such stays can be measured, which is rightly difficult for a local defendant to meet.[108] The Australian doctrine has retained the aim of protecting the defendant from harassment caused by a clearly inappropriate choice of forum by the plaintiff. Instead it uses the very reason foreign plaintiffs would have for taking a matter to court which is their great interest in the case as the main ground for rejecting a hearing.[109] The great benefit of such an approach is its avoidance of the US's balance of foreign forum and UK's most suitable forum doctrine, under which a foreign plaintiff is at an immediate disadvantage. On the basis of the *Bhopal* case, adoption of the Australian *forum non conveniens* approach by American courts would have been more in keeping with US global responsibilities, both in terms of foreign citizens being able to recover proper compensation from MNEs, and in terms of the legal standards that US corporations should be required to observe in their overseas

---

106 (1990) 171 CLR 538. It has been decided that a 'local court in which the particular proceeding have been instituted that is so inappropriate a forum for their determination that their continuation would be oppressive or vexatious to him'. See further Sahni, *Transnational Corporate*, p. 131.

107 Prince, 'Bhopal'.

108 Joseph, Sarah, *Corporations and Transnational Human Rights Litigation* (Hart Publishing, Oxford 2004), p. 122.

109 Prince, 'Bhopal'.

operations.[110] Therefore the Australian approach represents a more acceptable solution to the *forum non conveniens* doctrine but the risk of dismissal is always present under this approach as well. Moreover, lengthy time losses might occur in Australia before reaching a final decision about jurisdictional claims.

**Brussels and Lugano conventions**

In the EU, a co-ordinated system for deciding issues of jurisdiction already exist under the Brussels Convention on Jurisdiction and Enforcement of Judgments in Civil and Commercial Matters.[111] It establishes (Article 2) a general principle that defendants can be sued in the courts of the EU member state where they are domiciled. The result of an interpretation of the article will be that, between member states, plaintiffs can sue defendants in the defendants' domiciles ignoring other probable domiciles. Consequently courts cannot apply the *forum non conveniens* doctrine for plaintiffs from member states because under the Brussels Convention there is no place for broad jurisdiction-declining discretion and it seems to operate quite well without it. The Lugano Convention[112] is not different from the Brussels Convention in the principles applied; it just made the applicability of Brussels Convention principles broader by including EFTA countries.[113] Therefore the more countries sign these Conventions, the narrower the applicability of *forum non conveniens* will be.

In brief, the Brussels and Lugano Conventions provide the most justified jurisdiction regulation. Both Conventions prohibit the dismissal of the cases on the ground of the *forum non conveniens* doctrine, so they have created safe and predictable solutions to jurisdictional problems for plaintiffs exposed to tort actions by MNEs. However the countries in which the Conventions are applied are limited and basically developed countries. Thus there are still problems in application of the doctrine and even though its application is fundamentally narrowed in the UK by ECJ decisions,[114] American courts still widely apply the doctrine of *forum non conveniens*.

---

110 *Ibid.*

111 Council Regulation (EC) No 44/2001, of 22 December 2000 on jurisdiction and the recognition and enforcement of judgments in civil and commercial matters (Official Journal L 12 of 16.01.2001).

112 Lugano Convention of 16 September 1988 on Jurisdiction and the Enforcement of Judgments in Civil and Commercial Matters.

113 O'Brien, J., *Conflict of Law* (Cambridge University Press, Cambridge 2001).

114 *Owusu v Jackson*; See Muchlinski, *Multinational*, p. 158.

## THE ALIEN TORT CLAIMS ACT

The Alien Tort Claims Act[115] (ATCA) allows foreigners to bring a civil suit in a US District level court for a crime committed anywhere in the world by an individual, government or corporation that violates the law of nations or a treaty of the United States.[116] This Act grants the district courts competence to hear tort claims from non-Americans who have been a victim of a violation of a norm of 'the law of nations' or a treaty to which the US is party, no matter where the violation has occurred.[117] Therefore the ATCA litigation has drawn considerable attention from academics and public interest NGOs,[118] and is seen as an attractive option to solve jurisdictional problems in MNE torts because it provides access to US courts.

The ATCA was originally created for use against pirates, but it was left inactive and forgotten until 1980 when it was rediscovered and put to use by lawyers in the landmark case of *Filartiga v Pena-Irala*.[119] Using the ATCA, two Paraguayan family members brought a suit against a former Paraguayan state official who had committed acts of torture against a member of their family. They won a guilty verdict and were rewarded a significant monetary amount. Later the Act gained a new importance when the Second Circuit held

---

115 28 USC § 1350.

116 See further Zia-Zarifi, Saman, 'Suing Multinational Corporations in the U.S. for Violating International Law' (1999–2000) 4 UCLA J. Int'l L. & Foreign Aff. 81; Londis L., 'The Corporate Face of the Alien Tort Claims Act: How an Old Statute Mandates a New Understanding of Global Interdependence' (2005) 57 Me. L. Rev. 141; Wouters, Jan, DeSmet, Leen and Ryngaert, Cedric, 'Tort Claims Against Multinational Companies For Foreign Human Rights Violations Committed Abroad: Lessons From The Alien Torts Claim Act' (Institute for International Law, Working Paper 46, November, 2003) at http://www.law.kuleuven.ac.be/iir/nl/wp/WP/WP46e.pdf; Bornstein, H.R., 'The Alien Tort Claims Act in 2007: Revolving the Delicate Balance Between Judicial and Legislative Authority' (2007) 82 Ind. L.J. 1077; Deye, K., 'Can Corporations be Held Liable under the Alien Tort Claims Act?' (2005–2006) 94 KY. L.J. 649; Slawotsku, J., 'Doing Business Around the World: Corporate Liability under the Alien Tort Claims Act' (2005) Mich. St. L. Rev. 1065; Rivera, F., 'A Response to the Corporate Campaign against the Alien Tort Claims Act' (2003–2004) 14 Ind. Int'l & Comp. L. Rev. 251; Olah, F.C., 'MNC Liability for International Human Rights Violations under the Alien Tort Claims Act: A Review and Analysis of the Fundamental Jurisprudence and a Look at Aiding and Abetting Liability Under the Act' (2006–2007) 25 QLR 751.

117 Wouters, DeSmet and Ryngaert, 'Tort Claims'.

118 For example, the settlement in *Doe I v Unocal Corp* is presented as historical achievement by NGOs. See the Center for Constitutional Rights 'Historic Advance for Universal Human Rights: Unocal to Compensate Burmese Villagers' available at http://ccrjustice.org/newsroom/press-releases/historic-advance-universal-human-rights:-unocal-compensate-burmese-villagers.

119 630 F.2d 876 (2d Cir. 1980).

in *Kadic v Karadzic*[120] that the ATCA could be used against private individuals.[121] *Karadzic*'s clear expansion of the capacity of human rights claims under the ATCA to cover private non-state actors facilitated applying the same reasoning to private non-state actors in a corporate structure. In the cases that so far apply the *Karadzic* rationale directly against corporate defendants, the results indicate that American courts are willing to consider claims based on violations of international human rights laws against MNEs.[122] This standing was confirmed by *Doe I v. Unocal Corp*[123] which clarified that the ATCA cannot only be invoked against state actors, state officials and private actors for acts of state but also against private actors for purely private acts.[124]

Accordingly corporations can be held liable for violations committed 'in concert with' government officials. This principle of private corporate liability under the ATCA has been upheld in a handful of preliminary decisions, although some have been dismissed on other grounds and none has yet resulted in a final judgment.[125] In *Doe I v Unocal Corp* for example, the district court found that a corporation can be held liable for private acts of slavery and forced labour because the international law prohibitions apply to all actors. Furthermore for MNEs tracking the development of the *Unocal* case, the use of an 'aiding and abetting' test in comparison with one of 'state action' to define private liability under the ATCA, is important because it potentially lowers the bar significantly for aliens to sue MNEs in US courts.[126] Similarly in *Beanal v Freeport-McMoRan*,[127] the district court found that a private corporation could be held liable for genocide, which by definition is barred whether committed by 'public officials or private individuals'.[128]

According to the case law, which has settled some criteria, a successful claim under ATCA must present three elements: (1) an alien sues; (2) for a tort; (3) committed in violation of the law of nations.[129] The third presents the most ana-

---

[120] 70 F. 3d 232 (2d Cir. 1995).

[121] Zia-Zarifi, 'Suing Multinational'.

[122] *Ibid.*

[123] 110 F. Supp. 2d 1294 (C.D. Ca. 2000).

[124] Wouters, DeSmet and Ryngaert, 'Tort Claims'.

[125] There are confusing reports of the cases in the media and the internet as if some cases reached to final conclusion. Actually many of these cases have survived the dismissal on the basis of jurisdiction.

[126] Khalil, S.A., 'The Alien Tort Claims Act And Section 1983: The Improper Use Of Domestic Laws to "Create" and "Define" International Liability for Multinational Corporations' (2002) 31 Hofstra Law Review 207.

[127] 969 F.Supp. 362 (EDLa. 1997).

[128] Stephens, Beth, 'Corporate Liability: Enforcing Human Rights Through Domestic Litigation' (2000–2001) 24 Hastings Int'l & Comp. L. Rev. 401.

[129] See *Filartiga v Pena-Irala*.

lytical difficulties because it forces American courts to identify customary international law and treaties.[130] Thus only a limited number of recognized, serious human rights crimes such as torture or genocide can, in practice, serve as the basis of an ATCA suit rather than catching all civil liability claims of aliens.

The provision of a violation of the law of nations is unusual in that it requires plaintiffs to find their cause of action in international law rather than the national law of either the US or the state where the injury occurred. In practice this means that the grounds for bringing a tort claim under ATCA are very narrow, and have been restricted mainly to serious violations of human rights.[131] The latter form of individual liability that exists in the lack of state action is strictly limited to 'offences recognized by the community of nations as of universal concern'.[132] Moreover the international law rules must be specific, universal and obligatory.[133] Consequently there is a huge limitation burden on plaintiffs to establish jurisdiction over companies. This heavy burden is the result of the more complex early legal analysis required in establishing subject-matter jurisdiction in ATCA cases, because plaintiffs relying on the ATCA must identify enforceable and universal international norms and properly claim their violation by the defendant.[134]

Moreover there are significant procedural hurdles to be overcome in bringing ATCA cases, including not only *forum non conveniens*, but also arguments regarding the act of state doctrine and sovereign immunity. Similar problems may arise in other jurisdictions, such as the UK, which do not have an equivalent of the ATCA, but may apply the act of state doctrine and sovereign immunity.[135] In summary the possible obstacles in ATCA litigation can be examined under the following titles.

(1) As discussed earlier, the category of torts that can be brought under the ATCA is limited within the scope of international law. An examination of MNEs' torts will show that most of the torts committed by MNEs never meet the criteria of being against international law. Thus they will never be able to be taken to court under ATCA claims. For example, the tort committed in the *Bhopal* case, or asbestos-related claims may never fall under the scope of ATCA

---

[130] Zia-Zarifi, 'Suing Multinational'.

[131] Stephens, Beth, 'Corporate Accountability: International Human Rights Litigation Against Corporations in US Courts' in Kamminga, Menno T. and Zia-Zarifi, Saman (eds), *Liability of Multinational Corporations under International Law* (Kluwer Law International, The Hague 2000).

[132] Khalil, 'The Alien Tort Claims Act'.

[133] Wouters, DeSmet and Ryngaert 'Tort Claims Against'.

[134] Zia-Zarifi, 'Suing Multinational'.

[135] Anderson, 'Transnational Corporations'.

litigation. Even the cases that have international aspects have been dismissed – in litigation against *Freeport*, plaintiffs claimed that the defendant violated at least three international environmental law principles: (a) polluter pays; (b) the precautionary principle; (c) the proximity principle.[136] However the court held that even if it is true, it did not amount to a violation of the law of nations because the three norms were not universally binding and not sufficiently definable.[137] These cases show that American courts do not believe international environmental law has achieved the level of universality and specificity necessary for supporting the ATCA jurisdiction.[138] Therefore these interpretations of international law only protect negative human rights, which do not cover most of the tort claims because torts are determined according to national laws. Thus most tort actions will never be brought under the ATCA. Moreover a successful ATCA litigation requires state action in the tort process. In many ways international law analysis affirmed in *Kadic* matches the parent-subsidiary joint action analysis in that it involves assigning unlawful actions to an entity (the state) that only indirectly caused the harm. The joint action test requires either a conspiracy or wilful participation with the state actor, or a substantial degree of cooperative action between the state and private actors.[139] Accordingly it is not surprising that cases brought under the ATCA litigation are very limited. The future of the Act depends on its analysis of the tort. In order to be considered an efficient piece of legislation, the Act should be amended in a way to change 'the law of nation' to any tort action.[140]

(2) ATCA requires that the corporations must have 'sufficient contact' in the US for an American court to have jurisdiction to judge them. The defendant must have minimum contact and the contact must be systematic and continuous.[141] This might prevent most of MNEs from other jurisdictions being brought into the US courts. It is argued that where a parent company is not US-based, US courts had no jurisdiction. For instance with Total, a French company which is a partner in the same joint venture as Unocal in Burma, the court did not

---

136 In the same way, the court in *Flores v S. Peru Copper Corp* 343 F. 3d 140 (2d Cir. 2003) held that it lacked subject-matter jurisdiction over the Peruvians' environmental claims styled as claims for life and health. Similarly, in a recent case, *Sosa v Alvarez Machain* (124 S. Ct. 2739, 2766 n.20 (2004), the court confirmed that the door for ATCA claims is still ajar subject to vigilant door-keeping, and thus open to narrow class of international laws today.

137 Zia-Zarifi, 'Suing Multinational'.

138 *Ibid.*

139 Londis, 'The Corporate'.

140 Bornstein, 'The Alien Tort Claims Act'.

141 Mattei, Ugo and Jeffrey, L., 'U.S. Jurisdiction over Conflicts Arising Outside of the United States: Some Hegemonic Implications' (2000–2001) 24 Hastings Int'l & Comp. L. Rev. 381.

establish jurisdiction because the company lacked sufficient contact with the US[142] because there was no agency relationship between Total and its US subsidiaries.[143] This argument was raised in the case of the murder of Nigerian activist Ken Saro-Wiwa and others brought in New York by their families against Shell. Shell's argument was that it bears no responsibility on the grounds that it does not exist in the US. The court's response to this argument was interesting, foreign corporations are subject to a suit when doing business in the United States, even if such contacts are a small part of their worldwide operations. As a result, US courts upheld personal jurisdiction over Royal Dutch Petroleum Company and Shell Transport and Trading Company,[144] two foreign corporations, based on the operations of their investor relations' offices in New York.[145] Indeed corporate liability greatly expands the practical sweep of ATCA litigation, as it is less likely to be limited by practical questions of personal jurisdiction. MNEs are more likely to be present in the United States for personal jurisdiction purposes than are individual performers.[146] This is very important because it establishes jurisdiction over companies even though they are not domiciled in the US. More importantly, this decision should be interpreted in a way that the existence of a subsidiary in the US must be sufficient to establish jurisdiction over all components of MNEs. Of course, there is always a risk to require establishment of agency relationship between the parent and US subsidiary.

(3) The issue of whether the ATCA abolishes the obstacles that current law creates must be examined as well. The structure of company law and the organization of MNEs still prevent most of the cases being tried in home countries. In ATCA cases in accordance with practice, plaintiffs aim at parent corporations.[147] Thus in order to assert jurisdiction over a foreign parent corporation, plaintiffs must show that the parent either directly conducted business within the jurisdiction, or that the parent conducted business indirectly through subsidiaries that acted as the parent's *alter ego* or agent, and that these business contacts were continuous and systematic enough to make the court's assertion of jurisdiction reasonable under constitutional and international standards.[148]

---

142 See *Doe v Unocal Corp.*

143 Udwadia, S., 'Corporate Responsibility for International Human Rights Violations' (2003–2004) 13 Cal. Interdisc. L.J. 359.

144 *Wiwa v Royal Dutch Petrolium Co* 226 F 3d 88 2d Cir. 2000.

145 See further Stephens, 'Corporate Liability'.

146 Ramsey, Michael D., 'Multinational Corporate Liability under the Alien Tort Claims Act: Some Structural Concerns' (2000–2001) 24 Hastings Int'l & Comp. L. Rev. 361.

147 Londis, 'The Corporate Face'.

148 Zia-Zarifi, 'Suing Multinational'.

This means the parent must be directly connected to a tort claim in order to be held liable, which leads us to situations which have very similar conditions to veil piercing.[149] For example in the *Bowoto v Chevron* case the court held that the plaintiffs had supplied sufficient evidence that ChevronTexaco could be found responsible for the actions of its subsidiary. Therefore, the case could go forward to trial to determine if plaintiffs may produce evidence to pierce the corporate veil.[150] Here plaintiffs are only permitted to go further with their argument, it is not a final decision of making the parent liable under ATCA.

(4) In litigations under the ATCA, plaintiffs must be aliens in order to bring a suit, and will usually be a foreigner, thus being subject to a *forum non conveniens* application is always possible because the ATCA does not abolish the applicability of the principle. In *Wiwa v Shell*, the American court dismissed the case on the ground of available English jurisdiction although plaintiffs claim they cannot bring the case under English law.[151] The application of doctrine of *forum non conveniens* under the ATCA suggests that only a very few cases might appear in the American courts.[152] In the earlier cases *forum non conveniens* was consistently rejected in most ATCA litigations but it was applied in the case of *Texaco v Aguinda.*[153] The case was ultimately dismissed on *forum non conveniens* grounds. This case involved environmental claims against Texaco for its operations in Ecuador.[154] Thus the risk of being dismissed in ATCA cases still exists so the encouraging effect of ATCA cases has been turned into ineffective litigation that cannot bring another option for the most common situations.[155] Accordingly *forum non conveniens* has become more effective as a defence given that human rights liability in the wake of *Flartiga* has expanded beyond violations of fundamental human rights by government officials, to violations by corporate entities and private individuals who conspire with or act as agents of oppressive governments.[156] Some example cases which were rejected on

---

149 See Chapters 5.

150 *Bowoto v Chevron Texaco Corp.*, 312 F. Supp. 2d 1229 (N.D. Cal. 2004); for earlier developments see *Bowoto, et al. v Chevron, et al.*, No. C99-2506 (N.D. Cal. filed 27 May 1999).

151 Zia-Zarifi, 'Suing Multinational'.

152 *Ibid.*

153 *Aguinda v Texaco* No. 93 Civ. 7527, 200 U.S. Dist. See further Shaw, Courtney, 'Uncertain Justice: Liability of Multinationals under the Alien Tort Claims Act' (2001–2002) 54 Stan. L. Rev. 1359; Zia-Zarifi, 'Suing Multinational'. Additionally, for information about the impact of the company on nature see http://www.texacorainforest.com.

154 Shaw, 'Uncertain Justice'.

155 Zia-Zarifi, 'Suing Multinational'.

156 Boyd, Kathryn Lee, 'Inconvenience of Victims: Abolishing Forum Non Conveniens in U.S. Human Rights Litigation' (1998–1999) 39 Va. J. Int'l L. 41.

*forum non conveniens* principles include: *Bowoto v Chevron Texaco*, *Saro-Wiwa v Shell*, *Torres v S. Peru Copper Corp*,[157] *Aguinda v Texaco*.[158]

(5) In the case of a final judgment under ATCA litigations, the question arises why a foreign court should enforce the decisions of American courts to punish their corporations and citizens. They will not be very eager to enforce the decisions especially if these decisions involve discussion of foreign state sovereignty. For example, in the case of *Sarei v Rio Tinto*[159] the US Department of State warned that adjudication of the Bougainville claims in US courts posed a 'very grave' threat to the 'conduct of our foreign relations'. This concern was backed by declarations from the Papua New Guinea government that litigation in US courts had 'potentially very serious ... implications', 'especially its relations with the United States'.

In conclusion MNEs, unlike the other defendants in ATCA lawsuits, have the motivation, money and experience to litigate fully all jurisdictional limits and advantages of corporate structure available to them to avoid litigation on the merits.[160] The pressure has resulted in the situation that many ATCA cases that have been brought against corporations; only few have survived,[161] with many more facing a motion to dismiss because the courts thought the claims failed to adequately assert a violation of international law or because the courts believe

---

157 *Torres v S. Peru Copper Corp.* 113 F. 3d 540 (5th Cir. 1997).

158 See for other examples Bruno K., 'De-Globalisation Justice, The Corporate Campaign to Foreign Victims of Corporate-Induced Human Rights Violations of the Right to Sue in US Courts' 24 (2003) Multinational Monitor n. 3.

159 *Sarei v Rio Tinto plc*, 221 F. Supp. 2d 1116, 1121–27 (C.D. Cal. 2002). Residents of the island of Bougainville in Papua New Guinea filed a suit against Rio Tinto under the Alien Tort Claims Act in the US federal court in 2000. The plaintiffs allege that: Rio Tinto was complicit in war crimes and crimes against humanity committed by the Papua New Guinean army during a secessionist conflict on Bougainville; environmental impacts from Rio Tinto's Panguna mine on Bougainville harmed their health in violation of international law; and Rio Tinto engaged in racial discrimination against its black workers at Panguna.

160 See further Zia-Zarifi, 'Suing Multinational'; for examples of negative campaigning see Griswold, Daniel T., 'Abuse of 18th Century Law Threatens U.S. Economic and Security Interests' (Cato Institute, 25 January 2003) at http://www.cato.org/dailys/01-25-03.html accessed 27 June 2006. See also Commentary by the ICC Chairmanship, Extra-territorial Application of National Laws (Department of Policy and Business Practices, December 2002) available at http://www.iccwbo.org/id506/index.html?cookies=no accessed 27 June 2006.

161 Recent examples of cases which escaped the dismissal are: *Bowoto v Chevron Corp.*, No. C99-02506SI, 2007 WL 800940 (N.D. Cal. Mar. 14, 2007); *Bowoto v Chevron Texaco Corp.*, 312 F. Supp. 2d 1229 (N.D. Cal. 2004); *Khulumani v Barclays National Bank Ltd No. 052141p – 10/12/2007* U.S. 2nd Circuit Court. These cases are presented as success for just having escaped the dismissal on the basis of jurisdiction, even though there is no final judgement yet.

that an adequate forum existed in the nation in which the abuses occurred. The *Unocal* case was one of the most advanced, despite a brief from the US Justice Department arguing against the plaintiffs' use of the statute.[162]

Accordingly in its current form the ATCA does not offer solutions to MNEs' tort litigation. The design of the litigations is very complex and time-consuming; plaintiffs have to overcome multiple barriers even before discussing the substantial liability of the corporations. ATCA litigations are still subjected to a very narrow sphere of the law of nation test. Unless it is amended by Congress, it will stay as a very popular Act that attracts media and NGOs' attention even though it produces exceptional jurisdiction over MNEs in the United States. The important issue that should be kept in mind is that the ATCA only establishes jurisdiction over companies. It does not establish direct liability which requires establishment of certain criteria which will be discussed in following chapters. In conclusion, the ATCA is a tiny step on the way to make MNEs liable for their tort action and thus should not be presented as a solution.

## CHOICE OF LAW PROBLEMS IN MNES' TORT LITIGATION

Even if the hurdles of jurisdiction are surmounted, the potential plaintiff who is up against a parent company in its home state is faced with the task of establishing the applicable law. Here a question will arise: which national law should govern the activities of an enterprise doing business in many different nation states? It has a formalistic response, which holds that each of the individual corporations that make up the MNE group is subject to the law of its own domicile, but this answer is not sufficient to respond to all practical issues.[163] Where the tortious act is deemed to have taken place in the same jurisdiction as the injury, a single *locus delicti* can be identified. For this reason, foreign plaintiffs are almost certain to find themselves subject to the laws of the state in which the injury occurred, even if that law is applied by a court of the parent state. With transnational corporate fault, however, it may be impossible to recognize a single place of the wrong because multinational group liability cases can involve many events, persons, and impacts in several countries.[164] This is due to modern characteristics of MNEs under which it is difficult to trace the elements of actions

---

162 See Birchall, Jonathan, 'The Questions Over Aiding and Abetting: Alien Tort Statute an Oil Company's Fight with the Human Rights Lobby Tests an 18th Century Law' The *Financial Times* (London, 5 August 2004).

163 Anderson, 'Transnational Corporations'.

164 *Ibid.*

taken by the groups.[165] On this subject, where a tort is committed partly at home and partly in a foreign jurisdiction, the law to be applied will be that of the country with which the acts constituting the tort have the most real and substantial connection. In case of the fault of a multinational subsidiary, a probability that foreign law will be applied to an action tends to weigh against the English jurisdiction. In order to determine the law likely to be applied, the court will consider where each element of the tort (breach of duty and damage) arose.[166] As a result, since there is no apparent consent, it seems that the applicable law must be determined case by case by the competent forum courts.[167]

It is of course possible that the parties may decide an applicable law in tort conflicts, on the basis of mutual agreement, but this is unlikely due to opposing interests. In most cases involving MNEs, the MNE will persistently seek to apply the law of the more favourable state, which will most likely be host countries' law.[168] As a result the choice would appear to lie between the laws of the forum, the law governing the parent corporation, the law governing the subsidiary corporation and the law governing tortious liability.[169] In the cases of doubt and conflicting situations, courts should prefer the forum that is most favorable to the plaintiffs.[170]

## CONCLUSION: OVERCOMING THE JURISDICTIONAL PROBLEMS

Procedural problems create many obstacles to achieving justifiable solutions against MNEs for their torts, and are thus preventing plaintiffs finding justice against MNEs' torts. The cases that have been dismissed under *forum non conveniens* are often the end of the matter in the sense that when a case is dismissed on that ground the plaintiffs may not pursue the claims no matter how legitimate their claims are. Similarly it is possible that when the defence of *forum non conveniens* fails the defendant may admit to the substantive claim and settle.[171] Discussion of the jurisdiction in many important cases took years

---

165 See Chapter 2.

166 Meeran, 'Process Liability'; Chinen, 'Jurisdiction'.

167 Nygh, Peter, 'The Liability of Multi-National Corporations for their Subsidiaries' (2002) EBOR 27.

168 Anderson, 'Transnational Corporations'.

169 Nygh, 'The Liability of Multi-National'.

170 Lowenfeld, A., 'National Jurisdiction and the Multinational Enterprise' in Lowenfeld, A. (ed.), *International Litigation and the Quest For Reasonableness* (Clarendon, Oxford 1996), p. 88.

171 Magaisa, 'Suing Multinational'.

before any consideration of substantial liability. In this sense even though the ATCA is presented as a solution to jurisdictional problems, many cases brought under the Act took years to overcome dismissal on the base of jurisdiction and only very few survived the dismissal.

In the UK in recent years the ECJ's decisions play a very important role in the resolution of jurisdiction problems in MNEs' tort liability cases. There has been very strict application of Article 2 of the Brussels Regulations, which briefly regulates that companies can be sued wherever they are domiciled and courts cannot decide the opposite. Accordingly the recent *Owusu* case of ECJ will significantly reduce (if not completely remove) application of the *forum non conveniens* doctrine by the English courts. However American courts still widely apply *forum non conveniens*. In consideration of alternatives to jurisdictional problems discussed in the chapter, each one still has a particular disadvantage. Thus none of the alternatives discussed above seem to remove jurisdictional problems entirely.

More importantly, overcoming jurisdictional barriers does not necessarily solve the substantial liability problems which are the product of applicable principles of modern company law.[172] Therefore the discussion must focus on whether, in abolishing substantive obstacles to the MNEs' liability, procedural problems will need special regulation or they will disappear without any further action. For example some courts have reasoned that in providing specific statutory protections in areas such as antitrust, securities regulation, environmental, or employment laws, the legislature must have indented to override the common law *forum non conveniens* doctrine.[173] However as the ATCA litigation abundantly demonstrates the discussion of jurisdiction will have certain space in future tort claims.

Moreover the horizontal organization of MNEs makes the determination of the proper venue nearly impossible from the perspective of where tort action is committed.[174] Decisions and actions, which caused the tort, may be spread over many jurisdictions not necessarily making any of them clearly more convenient. Thus the courts have to involve substantial discussion about the structure of the group even when they are determining the jurisdiction problem. For example in the *Bowoto v Chevron* case the court held that the plaintiffs had supplied sufficient evidence that ChevronTexaco could be found responsible for the actions of its subsidiary.[175] The court had to involve a fact-specific inquiry in order to allow the jury to discuss substantial matters.[176] As a result, the issue should

---

172 *Ibid.*

173 Boyd, 'Inconvenience of Victims'.

174 See Chapter 2.

175 *Bowoto v Chevron Texaco.*

176 The judge decided that the parent was actively involved in the conduct of the subsidiarys' security, and very high levels of communication and large numbers of the

be discussion of substantial liability because in jurisdictional problems the relationship between the parent and subsidiary has to be discussed in order to establish jurisdiction on the parent for the subsidiarys' acts.

In the near future discussions of jurisdictional matters in MNEs groups context, it seems quite likely that the jurisdiction discussion will be more in connection with the discussion of substantial liability in the corporate groups context. Jurisdictional barriers have been reduced with the decisions of *Lubbe* and *Connelly* by English courts in recent years and more with the ECJ's effort. However these will not completely remove discussions of jurisdictions in MNEs' tort. Thus the jurisdictional problems should be addressed by lawmakers.

Thus the best solution for the problem could be developed from the American courts' interpretation in ATCA litigation. The courts of any country where MNEs have subsidiaries can be entitled to hear the case with the requirement of minimum contact to the forum of the state where the subsidiary is domiciled. Thus the minimum contacts theory introduced by American courts should include subsidiaries as the presence of a subsidiary is an important element on the activities of MNEs. There could be broader jurisdiction over MNEs through their subsidiaries and it would reduce the claims that there is no court in the world that has jurisdiction over all components of MNEs. The minimum contact theory is also suitable for the modern structure of MNEs. The modern horizontal structure supports the idea that the presence of any subsidiary can be considered as the presence of the group. Thus a jurisdiction over all components of MNEs can be established by the forum where a subsidiary is domiciled and open a way to further establishment of group liability over MNEs. This approach will abolish the application of *forum non conveniens* in MNEs' tort context and will give great flexibility to plaintiffs to choose where to progress their civil liability actions. As a result, in a horizontal structure, any jurisdiction that is resident to any components of an MNE might be the venue to hear the cases.

parent's employees were working on the subsidiary. The judge concluded that there was an excessive degree of control, and thus there is an agency relationship between the subsidiary and parent. See Muchlinski, P., 'Multinational Enterprises and the Law' (OUP, Oxford 2007), p. 312.

# 5. Tort liability of multinational enterprises in case law

## INTRODUCTION

For decades a call for the home countries to accept increased responsibility for regulating the unjust impacts of MNEs has been expressed through transnational and local litigation demanding fundamental action by the courts. These claims aim at holding MNEs legally accountable for the negative environmental, health and safety, labour or human rights problems generated by their operations.[1] In contrast to demands for more advanced tort liability regimes, almost every legal system provides the direct liability for groups of companies for the acts of their subsidiaries only under special circumstances.[2] Similarly, in case law, the situations in which the courts will ignore separate corporate personality and trace responsibility back to the underlying economic reality of groups of companies and MNEs are very rare and unsatisfactory.[3]

In this chapter, I will examine case law approaches to the problems of tort liabilities of MNEs. The English case law approach is examined as the main jurisdiction together with an examination of American and other jurisdictions for comparative purposes. The case law will be examined to find out whether they have created efficient theories and principles to solve the liability problems in the MNEs context. There will be a search to discover whether the case law has been sufficiently developed to meet the changes and challenges that MNEs' business, managerial, social and economical features create.

The apparent unfair effects of limited liability and corporate separate legal personality in a corporate group context have forced courts to search for alternative ways to reduce these unjust effects. While doing this, they have adopted principles that have been used in similar legal situations. The liability created

---

[1] Ward, Halina, 'Governing Multinationals: The Role Of Foreign Direct Liability' (Briefing Paper of the Royal Institute of International Affairs, Energy and Environment Programme, No 18, February 2001).

[2] Muchlinski, P., *Multinational Enterprises and the Law* (OUP, Oxford 2007), p. 317.

[3] Gallagher, Lynn and Peter Ziegler 'Lifting the Corporate Veil in the Pursuit of Justice' (1990) July J.B.L. 292.

by case law for corporate groups could find its rationale in the characteristics of various principles of law such as fraud, agency, single enterprise liability or simply a requirement of justice. Alternatively liability could be imposed on a parent by reason of its failure to exercise proper control and management over its subsidiary.

The case law examination will lead us first to the theory of piercing the corporate veil (veil piercing). It can be claimed that piercing the corporate veil is the most litigated but slightest appreciated subject in corporate law. The real function of the doctrine is to fill the gap in common law doctrines that statutory rules cannot resolve effectively.[4] Piercing the corporate veil is not, however, the only response to possible misuse of the entity form in corporate group context. There are also various legal theories imposing liability on parent companies based on tort, agency, or statutory standards introduced under certain purpose built laws.[5] Consequently the veil-piercing doctrine here is used in a broad meaning that covers most situations under which courts interfere with separate legal personality in corporate law. The court intervention with the corporate law principles will be discussed broadly here; not only groups of corporations but also general situations where the veil piercing doctrine has been applied will be discussed, such as single person companies. However the basic emphasis will be on the courts' practice regarding groups of companies, particularly MNEs.

The application of the veil piercing principles by the courts revealed diverse features during the past century and it differs from one jurisdiction to another. Sometimes courts forced the boundaries of established rigid principles of company law; but mostly the result of the cases in which disregarding of the corporate veil was demanded was simply a repetition of *Salomon* principles. The courts have never taken an evolutionary step in creating alternatives as they did when establishing the principle of separate corporate personality in *Salomon*. This strong adherence to the *Salomon* principles has prevented the courts from creating sound reasoning for interventions where the corporate structure was ignored. Thus when the courts are asked to justify the principles behind the intervention, the general response seems to be 'the situation demands' or 'justice requires'. This state of affairs creates many difficulties in such a developed legal system. First of all it creates arbitrary justice, rather than the sound application of logical legal rules to difficult factual circumstances. The present complicated

---

4 See Cohen, David L., 'Theories of the Corporation and the Limited Liability Company: How Should Courts and Legislatures Articulate Rules for Piercing the Veil, Fiduciary Responsibility and Securities Regulation for the Limited Liability Company' (1998) 51 Okla. L. Rev. 427; Thompson, R.B., 'Piercing the Veil within Corporate Groups: Corporate Shareholders as Mere Investors' (1999) 13 Connecticut Journal of International Law 379.

5 Thompson, 'Piercing the Veil'.

approach cannot satisfy those who believe that a legal system should be built, as far as possible, on a foundation of principles and certainty. Hence the applicable principle of court interference is not clear and most importantly it has never been an alternative to limited liability company and separate legal personality theories.[6]

In particular, the most advanced case of group liability for an MNE was established in *Amoco Cadiz*[7] in the United States in a tort claim which is found in the decision of the US district court for the Northern District of Illinois for an oil spill by the *Amoco Cadiz* off the coast of France on 16 March 1978, where the parent company was held liable for the defaults of its subsidiary on the grounds of its close control over the operating subsidiary. In this case, the parent was also held liable as a joint tortfeasor for its own active involvement in the alleged negligence. In *Amoco Cadiz*, the court found that the vessel-owning subsidiary, its parent company and the ultimate parent of the corporate group were all individually liable. Despite some conclusions that argue that this is a case of enterprise liability, it is submitted that the decision is a piercing approach to the extent that it deals with intra-group liability.[8] The court described the parent company as an integrated multinational enterprise, which is engaged through a system of subsidiaries in the exploration, production, refining, transportation and sale of petroleum products throughout the world. The parent itself was initially involved and controlled the design, construction, operation and management of the *Amoco Cadiz*.[9] Therefore parent and subsidiaries were liable on the grounds that: (1) this was an integrated multinational corporation; (2) the parent exercised such control over its subsidiaries that they could be considered mere instrumentalities of the parent; (3) the parent was liable on the grounds of its own active involvement in the conduct said to be negligence and through its close control over the operating subsidiaries.

Another example of advanced liability for corporate groups could be found in India. The Indian Supreme Court decision in *Mehta v Union of India AIR*[10]

---

6 Neyers, Jason W., 'Canadian Corporate Law, Veil-Piercing, and the Private Law Model Corporation' (2000) 50 U. Toronto L.J. 173.

7 [1984] 2 Lloyd's Reports 304.

8 Cashel, T.W. 'Groups of Companies – some US Aspects' in Wooldridge, F. and Schmitthoff, C.M. (eds), *Groups of Companies* (Sweet & Maxwell, London 1991), p. 43.

9 See further Rosenthal, Linda and Raper, Carol, 'Amoco Cadiz and Limitation of Liability for Oil Spill Pollution: Domestic and International Solutions' (1985–1986) 5 Va. J. Nat. Resources L. 259; Kipp, Matthew 'Piercing the Veil of the Amoco Cadiz Decision: Judge Posner's Jurisdictional Analysis Runs A Ground' (1988–1989) 38 DePaul Law. Rev. 703; Eskenazi, Nancy J., 'Forum Non Conveniens and Choice of Law in Re: The Amoco Cadiz Oil Spill' (1993) 24 J. Mar. L. & Com. 371.

10 [1987] SC 965 1086.

was binding authority for a principle of complete liability for enterprises engaged in a hazardous or naturally dangerous industry. It was therefore acceptable to lift the corporate veil between Union Carbide and its Indian subsidiary, in the *Bhopal* case, in order to hold the former liable for the tort. Thus in the *Bhopal* case, where the Indian authorities and the plaintiffs tried to base liability on the unity of enterprises, the idea has been repeated.[11]

In the UK, as early as 1969 Lord Denning had promoted veil lifting in the corporate groups' context. Consequently there were some important decisions such as *DHN Food Industries*[12] under which the House of Lords argued that a group of companies was in reality a single economic entity and should be treated as one. However, the improved standard of liability was always rejected immediately after the positive decisions. The most important return to the original occurred in *Adams v Cape Industries Plc*[13]. *Adams* apparently indicated that there are no fundamental principles of group or single economic liability for a group of companies under English Law. The facts of the case were quite complex but we can summarize that what the court had ultimately to determine was whether judgments obtained in the United States against Cape Industries, an English registered company whose business was mining asbestos in South Africa and marketing it globally, would be recognized and enforced by the English courts. In the absence of agreement to the foreign jurisdiction, this depended on whether Cape could be considered to have been present in the United States. On a detailed examination of the facts, the answer depended on whether Cape could be presumed to be present in the United States through its wholly owned subsidiaries or through a company with which it had close business links. The court rejected all the arguments by which it was sought to make Cape liable.

The *Adams v Cape Industries* case is interesting for this chapter since it combines arguments of veil piercing accumulated during previous cases. Originally plaintiffs structured their arguments on different principles to establish liability on Cape Industries; these arguments were built on the past experiments under which the courts pierced the corporate veil. These principles are vague as they can be claimed in any situation that groups of companies are involved.

First, the most used and least controversial argument for piercing the corporate veil is, at least in logic, fraud, façade or sham arguments. This exemption today is basically expressed as permitting disregard of the corporate veil when the corporate structure is a mere façade hiding the true facts. The theory has

---

[11] Muchlinski, *Multinational,* p 318.

[12] *DHN Food Distribution Ltd v London Borough of Tower Hamlets* [1976] 1 WLR 852.

[13] *Adams v Cape Industries* [1990] 2 WLR 786.

been exercised in the previous judgment in a variety of names. The fraud argument of plaintiffs in *Adams* was rejected stating that dividing the company and establishing independent subsidiaries is not a sham. Secondly, the single economic unit principle suggests that groups of companies are operating as a part of the same mind and logic so they must be considered as a single economic unit. However, the *Adams* judgment suggested that there is no general principle that all companies in a group of companies are to be regarded as one. On the contrary, the fundamental principle stated in the case is unquestionably that 'each company in a group of companies ... is a separate legal entity possessed of separate rights and liabilities'. Thirdly, the plaintiffs argued that a company having the power to act as an agent might do so as an agent for its parent company or indeed for all or any of its individual members if it or they authorize it to do so. However, being a subsidiary of a parent company does not necessarily mean that subsidiary companies are agents of the parent. Finally, when there is a difficulty in proving the above-mentioned arguments, plaintiffs argue that the interests of justice require corporate veils to be pierced. There is no apparent judgment, which has been concluded on the dependence of the interest of justice arguments. So the interest of justice has represented simply a way of referring to the grounds mentioned above in which the veil of incorporation has been pierced.

Consequently the interpretation of the judgment in *Adams* leaves us only with three conditions in which the veil of incorporation can be lifted. First, if the court is interpreting a statute that allows the court to look beyond the corporate veil. Secondly, where special circumstances exist indicating that the corporate veil is a mere facade concealing the true facts, the court may lift the veil of incorporation. The third exception is the establishment of an agency relationship between the parent and subsidiaries.

The court in *Adams* directly rejected the concept of a group as constituting a single economic entity and also declined to pierce the corporate veil where the subsidiary, although in many aspects wholly dependent for its survival on its parent, had been set up to shield the parent from potential liability in connection with its activities.[14] In brief, the courts have been reluctant to develop a concept of single enterprise law. They seem to a greater extent to refuse to tolerate the single economic unit theory and confine the examples in which they are likely to interfere with the *Salomon* principle to subjective fraud by the controllers.[15] Therefore *Adams* presents a mainly harsh example of the application of the

---

[14] Prentice, Daniel D., 'Some Aspects of the Law Relating to Corporate Groups in the United Kingdom' (1998–1999) 13 Conn. J. Int'l L. 305.

[15] Dine, Janet, *The Governance of Corporate Groups* (Cambridge University Press, Cambridge 2000), p. 45.

*Salomon* principle of strict separate corporate personality into corporate groups.

Similar to *Cape Industries*, the *Thor Chemicals*[16] case has effectively been based on an argument that the parent company's involvement in the day-to-day management of the relevant overseas facility was such that it should be directly responsible for injuries sustained as a consequence of operations technically carried out by another company in the group.[17] However, the problem of proving the existence of a duty of care, and of its breach, must be kept separate from the wider issue relating to the extent to which groups of companies could benefit from the principle of limited liability as a means of protecting themselves against tort claims arising out of the actions of their subsidiaries.[18] Therefore it is important to examine whether excessive control *per se* will result in certain legal consequences, in particular the collapse of the limitation of liability between the parent corporation and its subsidiary, or whether additional elements are needed.[19]

Next the book will provide a brief discussion of the current situation in terms of vicarious liability of MNEs. Later there will be a deeper examination of the situations where courts possibly pierce the corporate veil; the aim is to evaluate compatibility of these principles to the current realities of contemporary operations and structures of MNEs. To be able to evaluate the basic principles of case law and future developments in this area, one has to look to the essential facts of each situation. Additionally, a cross-border comparative examination is helpful. Accordingly there will be discussion of the basic principles of piercing the corporate veil, namely fraud, agency and single economic unit.

## VICARIOUS LIABILITY IN GROUPS OF COMPANIES

Vicarious liability becomes justifiable in those cases where the liability arising from company law principles is doubtful in the light of recognized legal rules, but where it is necessary for parent companies to meet the losses of corporate creditors.[20] However, the extent of a parent corporation's liability for the acts of its subsidiaries will depend on the applicable principles of law concerning

[16] *Sithole and Others v Thor Chemicals* (LTL 2/3/1999).

[17] Ward, 'Governing Multinationals'.

[18] Muchlinski, P., 'Holding Multinationals to Account: Recent Developments in English Litigation and the Company Law Review' (2002) 23 Company Lawyer 168.

[19] Lutter, M., 'Enterprise Law Corp. vs. Entity Law Inc. Philip Blumberg's Book from the Point of View of an European Lawyer' (1990) 38 American Journal of Comparative Law 949.

[20] See Muchlinski, *Multinationals*, pp. 309–313.

corporate group liability.[21] Under English law, plaintiffs would have some likelihood of succeeding in a claim against the parent corporation based on its breach of a principal duty owed to them. However, any claim based on vicarious liability would have virtually no chance of success because the English law of tort is reluctant to make one person responsible for the acts of another outside the master-servant, the principal-agent or the employer and independent contractor sphere of vicarious liability.[22] Therefore the idea of vicarious liability based on the natural structure of the group has not yet been accepted by the courts.

In order to establish vicarious liability one has to prove a strict relationship between parties. However, under the existing corporate law (statutory and case law) which is based on the limited liability principles and separate corporate personality, the chance of establishing vicarious liability for corporate groups is slight. That is why courts search for alternatives to impose liability on parent companies, namely veil-piercing principles and its derivatives.

In reality the courts must engage in a fact-specific inquiry into the relationship between the parent corporation and its subsidiary.[23] To be able to impose liability on parent corporations, it must have broken some of its general duties. For example, in *Amoco Cadiz*, the parent company was held liable because all the important decisions, including those relating to the design, construction, operation and management of *Amoco Cadiz*, were taken by the parent company or with its authorization. However, even the parent liability in *Amoco Cadiz* was not direct. Liability was established because of the close control of the parent over the subsidiary.

On the other hand the recent developments in English litigation have created some expectations. The *Cape Industries v Lubbe* and *Connolly* cases[24] might be interpreted in a way that holds that English courts are willing to establish duties on parent companies on the basis of vicarious tort liability. However, the outcome of cases on the substantial legal principles are not clear as they have been settled out of court. More importantly the main reason for granting jurisdiction against those companies was not the substantial issue of law but the non-availability of efficient judicial systems, particularly a shortage of legal aid, in the host countries where the original case should have been brought. As a result, these cases were just concerned with jurisdiction issues and in the final outcome, the courts allowed hearing the cases in the UK; there was no decision on group liability of MNEs. For that reason, interpreting these cases as an

---

21 Muchlinski, 'Holding Multinationals'.

22 Baughen, Simon, *Corporate Accountability and the Law of Tort: The Inclusive Verdict of Bhopal* (University of Manchester, 1993).

23 Meeran, Richard, 'Process Liability of Multinationals: Overcoming the Forum Hurdle' (1995) Nov. JPIL 170.

24 See Chapter 4.

improvement in MNEs' liability is not credible and is misleading. Similarly, some cases brought under the ATCA in the US, established jurisdiction over companies to continue to discuss substantial issues. These cases are also presented as if they establish liability over parent companies. However, they only established jurisdiction and have not produced final judgments on substantial liability.[25]

Even if there is a wish to establish vicarious liability, it is very difficult to determine the duties of parent companies. Some basic duties of parent corporations can be summarized under the following categories.[26] On the lack of a clearly established principle under company law, one has to look to similar characteristics of other legal relationships, the agency-principal and the master-servant principles to determine the duties of parent corporations.[27] The basic duty then will be acting dutifully and in good faith. There are other duties, which are mostly derivatives of the general duties. We can first mention choosing of skilled directors; if this choice is negligently made, the carelessness will be identifiably linked with any damage that subsequently results from the negligence of the directors.[28] Thus the corporation might be held liable for not performing its primary duties. The second duty is a duty to warn; the work may be hazardous to third parties unless specific information held by the employer is revealed to the subsidiary. Finally, there is a duty to supervise[29] within the specific sphere of the contracts of employment, but there is no general duty to supervise the activities of a subsidiary as an independent company.[30]

The discussion of determining the basic duties of MNEs has been going for decades. There are several attempts at different levels to determine these duties. One of the recent and most important attempts has been under the UN Economic and Social Council.[31] The UN norms determine basic duties for MNEs under different titles. Accordingly they have duties for human rights, labour, consumer and environmental issues. However similar to other corporate social responsibility and international instruments on this matter, these norms do not have strong enforcement mechanisms since they are non-binding instruments and are un-

---

25 See Chapter 4.

26 Baughen, S., 'Multinationals and the Export of Hazard' (1995) 58 MLR 54.

27 Baughen, *Corporate Accountability*.

28 Ibid.

29 Nygh, Peter., 'The Liability of Multi-National Corporations for their Subsidiaries' (2002) EBOR 27.

30 Baughen, *Corporate Accountability*.

31 UN. Econ. & Soc. Council (ECOSOC), Sub-Comm'n on Promotion and Prot. of Human Rights, *Norms on the Responsibilities of Transnational Corporations and Other Business Enterprises with Regard to Human Rights*, UN Doc. E/CN.4/Sub.2/2003/12/Rev.2 (26 Aug 2003).

likely to become the subject of a binding treaty in the near future.[32] Therefore it is not possible to claim that parent companies have the same duties under vicarious liability rules since there is no court mechanism or national law to enforce these duties on MNEs.[33] Thus it is difficult to claim that these norms are part of the legal systems and should be considered as binding legal rules. Similar to the UN Norms, other international instruments cannot be considered as binding in determination of the duties of MNEs. However, these initiatives might be considered as main justification sources in the determination of the basic duties of parent companies and groups of companies in cases where vicarious liability is applied. Alternatively, it can be assumed that these norms are the basic responsibility of MNEs and, therefore, legal systems should introduce vicarious liability of MNEs in breaches of these norms.

These facts lead us to the question of whether vicarious liability serves as an effective means of enforcing group liability standards in a cross-border context of MNE activities. One is forced to admit that it plays no role, at least for the moment. The closest example of established liability, the case of *Amoco Cadiz* does not meet the criteria of vicarious liability. Even when courts establish legal rulings based on the ideas mentioned in the previous paragraphs, these rules create very partial and rare liability since there has to be a connection between parent companies' fraudulent acts and the damage, which makes establishment of liability very difficult.[34] A parent company might always avoid liability by proving it has performed its duties at a required level. In cases where the parent has failed in its duties, the connection must be proven between its act and the damage. Even if all the conditions have been established, it is very difficult to establish that this is a group liability because rather than ignoring separate legal personality, this situation might be defined as another person being found liable for its participation in a tortious act.

This brings us to the discussion of modern structures of MNEs. The vicarious liability discussed above could be applied to parent companies for their mis-

---

[32] See Wallace, R.M.M. and Martin-Ortega, Olga, 'The UN Norms: A First Step to Universal Regulation of Transnational Corporations' Responsibilities for Human Rights?' (2004) 26 Dublin ULJ 304; Weisbrodt, D. and Kruger, M., 'Current Developments: Norms on the Responsibilities of Transnational Corporations and Other Business Enterprises with Regard to Human Rights' (2003) 97 American Journal of International Law 901; Sorell, T., 'The UN Norms' in Dine, J. and Fagan, A. (eds) *Human Rights and Capitalism* (Edward Elgar, Cheltenham, UK, Northampton, MA, USA 2006); Gelfand, Jacop, 'The Lack of Enforcement in the United Nations Draft Norms: Benefit or Disadvantage?' in DeSchutter, O. (ed.), *Transnational Corporations and Human Rights* (Hart Publishing, Oxford 2006).

[33] See Chapter 7.

[34] Anderson, Michael, 'Transnational Corporations and Environmental Damage: Is Tort Law the Answer' (2002) 41 Washburn Law Journal 399.

control or for not taking necessary control to prevent a tort. Accordingly there has to be a strict relationship between the parent and the subsidiary. However, the control relationship in a modern structure has been differentiated and there is a more horizontal (cultural) control rather than strict control and day-to-day involvement of the parent suggested by vertical structure.[35] Any claim of vicarious liability against a parent in a horizontal structure therefore has little chance of success because it aims to make one person liable for the other under certain conditions. Thus the theory of vicarious liability based on entity liability has a better chance of success in application to smaller and vertically structured groups of companies rather than to bigger and more complexly structured MNEs.

## PIERCING THE CORPORATE VEIL

The corporate veil is based on the distinction between the personalities of each company within groups of companies. It follows that a person who decides on the actions of another may take advantage himself of a series of legal devices in order not to be responsible for the consequences.[36] Accordingly the basic principle behind the veil piercing is that where a company is used for an illegal or improper purpose or where there is a 'necessity to achieve justice', the corporate veil must be pierced.[37] Hence in relation to the liability of groups of companies, the common law doctrine of piercing the corporate veil might offer a means of justifying liability in circumstances where the subsidiary has inadequate assets to meet the claims against it, but where the case for compensation of the claimants is harsh to oppose on justifiable grounds.[38]

The general rule, under both English and US law, is that if the parent had a certain level of control over the subsidiary, the court may lift the corporate veil and hold the parent liable if additional conditions are met.[39] Therefore the parent corporation may be held liable for the torts of its subsidiary where the nature of their corporate relationship suggests that the subsidiary has become a mere instrumentality or alter ego of the parent corporation.[40] However these piercing

---

35 See Chapter 2.

36 Scovazzi, T., 'Industrial Accidents and the Veil of Transnational Corporations' in Francioni, F. and Scovazzi, T. (eds) *International Responsibility for Environmental Harm* (Graham & Trotman, London 1991).

37 Bowmer, Simon, 'Company Law to Pierce or not to Pierce the Corporate Veil – Why Substantive Consolidation is Not an Issue Under English Law' (2000) 15(8) JIBL 193.

38 Muchlinski, *Multinational*, p. 314.

39 Lutter, 'Enterprise Law Corp'.

40 A survey of the veil piercing in Belgium, England, Germany and the Netherlands found that the doctrine is applied only in clear-cut cases of 'abuse of limited liability'.

the veil situations, outside the areas justified by statutory interpretation, have occurred only in very specific circumstances throughout the 20th century. For example in the United States the courts have never lifted the veil so as to remove limited liability in the case of a public company and will not do so as a matter of routine in private companies.[41]

In Anglo-American jurisprudence, the piercing the veil doctrine can be applied to both contract and tort liability. The simple logical thinking asserts that courts should pierce the corporate veil more often in tort cases than in contract cases because tort victims do not choose their association with a corporate entity, while plaintiffs with contractual relationships have the opportunity to evaluate the risks of doing business with the corporation and voluntarily disregard these risks.[42] However Professor Thompson's empirical study of piercing the corporate veil cases in the US pointed out that courts pierced more often in the contract context than in the tort context and that this difference is statistically significant.[43] Moreover there is a lower percentage of piercing within corporate groups than those applied to individual shareholders.[44] There is no trend over time that courts appear to be moving towards permitting piercing in more and more situations.[45] The Thompson studies for American veil piercing jurisprudence demonstrate general confusion of this area of law in the finding that factors listed were less objective and contained a total of 85 factual reasons for piercing the veil and a sampling of the cases in the data set for deciding whether to pierce. Furthermore it was necessary to classify the factors into 12 different areas in attempt to demonstrate the standards of the court.[46]

An empirical study in England indicates that the courts in particular have been likelier to lift the veil between a closely controlled company and its subsidiary. They have been likelier both to lift the veil and to keep the veil in place

See Berkamp, L. and Pak, Wan-Q, 'Piercing the Corporate Veil: Shareholder Liability for Corporate Torts' (2001) 8 Maastricht J. of European and Comparative Law 167.

41 Davies, Paul L., *Gower and Davies' Principles of Modern Company Law* (Sweet & Maxwell, London 2003), p. 190.

42 Farmer, Richard S., 'Parent Corporation Responsibility for the Environmental Liabilities of the Subsidiary: A Search for the Appropriate Standard' (1994) 19 Journal of Corporation Law 770.

43 Thompson, 'Piercing the Veil'.

44 *Ibid.*

45 *Ibid.*

46 These areas are: undercapitalisation; failing to follow corporate formalities; overlap of corporate records; functions of personnel; misrepresentation; shareholder domination; intertwining and lack of substantive separation; use of the conclusory terms 'alter ago' and 'instrumentality'; general ground of fairness; assumption of risk; refusal to let a corporation pierce itself; and statutory policy. See Thompson, Robert B., 'Piercing the Corporate Veil: An Empirical Study' (1990–1991) 76 Cornell L. Rev. 1036.

when asked to do so by a governmental body than when asked to do so by a company or its shareholders. More importantly they have shown themselves consistently unwilling to lift the veil to enable the victims of a company's tort to recover from its shareholders.[47]

In another study that examines the 55 Australian cases involving insolvency and demanding piercing the veil, the researcher came to a conclusion that the percentage of piercing the veil is 24 per cent. In recent years there is an increasing demand for piercing the veil and most of the demands are dependent on contract or statutory basis. Piercing the veil demand for tort actions were just five and in two of them the court decided to pierce the corporate veil.[48] The study also reveals the basis for justifying piercing the veil; plaintiffs have argued mostly on the basis of agency, 34 cases, and then they argued on the basis of group enterprises, fraud and unfairness. The study indicates that the percentage of piercing the veil on the group enterprise basis is the lowest.[49] As a result the Australian approach almost mirrors the American and English approaches. Australian courts have pierced the veil for the same reasons, as do American and English courts: agency, fraud, sham or façade, group enterprises, unfairness and injustice.[50] The courts pierce the corporate veil less frequently when the controller is a parent company than when the controller is one or more individual shareholders. And the group enterprises argument is the least likely basis to pierce the veil.[51] Courts pierce more frequently in a contract context than in a tort context.[52]

There is another confusing characteristic of the veil-piercing doctrine that the practical application of the veil-piercing doctrine might reveal situations under which the courts based their explanation for piercing the veil. The most common reasons for piercing the corporate veil are,[53] first, the discovery that the corporation is merely an alter ago of the shareholders; a subsidiary corporation is owned and controlled by the parent and the subsidiary has been relegated to the status of an alter ago of the parent and the recognition of them as separate entities

---

47 Mitchell, Charles, 'Lifting the Corporate Veil in the English Courts: An Empirical Study' (1999) 3 Company, Financial and Insolvency Law Review 15.

48 Ramsay, I.M., 'Models of Corporate Regulation: The Mandatory/Enabling Debate' in Grantham, Ross and Rickett, Charlie (eds) *Corporate Personality in the 20th Century* (Hart, Oxford 1998).

49 *Ibid.*

50 Ramsay, I.M. and Noakes, D.B., 'Piercing The Corporate Veil In Australia' (2001) 19 Company and Securities Law Journal 250.

51 *Ibid.*

52 *Ibid.*

53 Bakst, David S., 'Piercing the Corporate Veil for Environmental Torts in the United States and the European Union: The Case for the Proposed Civil Liability Directive' (1996) 19 B. C. Int'l & Comp. L. Rev. 323.

would lead to an inadequate or fraudulent result. The second reason is fraud and misrepresentation; when a corporation misrepresents the nature of its activities, its ability to perform, its financial condition, or its financial structure. The third reason is under-capitalization. The list grows by moving towards a detailed examination but it is unnecessary to discuss every mentioned veil-lifting reason since it depends on the interpretation of cases by the courts at the time.[54]

Moreover the degree of piercing and reasons for piercing are very different in many cases. Establishing group-based liability is not the only reason for veil-piercing in the corporate group concept; rather the veil-piercing doctrine pursues many other legal objectives.[55] Thus the application of lifting the veil is not always disadvantageous to corporate groups. In some situations the veil-piercing doctrine is applied in favour of corporate groups. In this sense, Ottolenghi divides the reasons behind the veil piercing into at least four categories. The first one is 'peeping behind the veil'; the veil is lifted only to get information involving the person who controlled the company.[56] The second one is 'penetrating the veil'; the aim is to impose upon the shareholders responsibility for the company's act or to establish their direct interest in the company's assets. The third one is 'extending the veil'; the veil of each one of the components is lifted only to draw it again over a large number of components.[57] The last one is 'ignoring the veil'; this is the most extreme one and applied if the court thinks the company is not established in the commercial ground.[58] The examples are provided in order to illustrate the point that the application of the doctrine, with its complexity, can produce results that contradict the reasonable policy considerations that lay behind the doctrine.[59]

Based on these practical facts mentioned earlier, the courts concentrate on three main doctrines to apply the reasons for piercing. It will be useful to examine the principles behind the veil piercing in order to test their efficiency regarding their application to MNEs' tort liability cases.

---

[54] Dobson, J.M., 'Lifting the Veil in Four Countries: The Law of Argentina, England, France and the US' (1986) 35 ICLQ 839.

[55] Ottolenghi, S., 'From Peeping Behind the Corporate Veil to Ignoring It Completely' (1990) 53 MLR 338.

[56] See for example *Daimler v Continental Tyre Co* (1916) 2 AC 217.

[57] Piercing the veil on the basis of single enterprise argument falls under this section. See below.

[58] Fraudulent trading clauses in Insolvency Act fall in this category. See Chapter 6.

[59] Thompson, 'Piercing...Empirical Study'.

## Fraud Doctrine

Fraud consideration for veil piercing can lead to disregarding the legal entity doctrine in the Anglo-Saxon law and the concept of fraud is contained in most of the English decisions. Fraud in English and American law can be found as a remedy both at common law and equity.[60] The fraud approach to veil piercing is a sanction to which the courts turn when they think that the company was not founded for commercial or other sound grounds, but only as a means to defraud creditors or to circumvent laws.[61]

In fraud cases the court will look directly at the realities of the situation and reference must be made to further matters, which the courts consider. Some examples of references are: [62] the type of company – a closely held company, subsidiary or holding company; the motives for the formation of the company – commercial ones as opposed to fraudulent purposes, defeating creditors, evading laws; the type of legal action – a claim in tort, contract, bankruptcy; the identity of the person seeking the lifting of the veil – a distressed third party or the controlling shareholder himself is also important. In *Gilford Motor Company Ltd v Horne,*[63] Mr Horne was an ex-employee of the Gilford motor company and his employment contract provided that he could not solicit the customers of the company. In order to defeat this, he incorporated a limited company in his wife's name and solicited the customers of the company. The company brought an action against him.[64] The Court of Appeal was clear that the company was formed as a device, in order to mask the effective carrying on of business by Mr Horne. In view of this sham, the Court of Appeal declined to recognize the separate legal personality of the limited company.[65] *Jones v Lipman*[66] has strengthened the decision in *Gilford*. The relatively recent case of *Trustor AB v Smallbone*[67] also confirmed the power of the courts to pierce the veil in the case of fraud.

---

60 Dobson, 'Lifting the Veil'.

61 Ottolenghi, 'From Peeping'.

62 *Ibid.*

63 [1933] Ch. 935.

64 Payne, J., 'Lifting the Corporate Veil: A Reassessment of the Fraud Exception' (1997) 56 CLJ 284.

65 *Ibid.*

66 [1962] 1 WLR 832. Under the case a man contracted to sell his land and thereafter changed his mind in order to avoid an order of specific performance he transferred his property to a company. Judge Russell specifically referred to the judgments in *Gilford v Horne* and held that the company here was 'a mask which (Mr Lipman) holds before his face in an attempt to avoid recognition by the eye of equity' he awarded specific performance both against Mr Lipman and the company.

67 [2001] 3 All ER 987.

In *Re a Company*,[68] Cumming-Bruce LJ stated that the court would use its powers to pierce the corporate veil if it is necessary to achieve justice irrespective of the legal efficiency of the corporate structure.[69] In another decision, *Creasy v Breachwood Motors Limited*,[70] the company had been used for an illegal or improper purpose, the court pierced the corporate veil where the business of a defendant company in litigation was transferred to an associated company so as to leave the defendant company without assets.

In fraud cases, not only dishonesty is examined but also fraudulent purpose is required in order to pierce the veil. This means that it is not sufficient just to prove that the company was established dishonestly but also it must be proven that the transaction which caused the damage has been conducted for fraudulent purposes. Accordingly under the fraud doctrine, three elements must generally be shown by a plaintiff before the two entities will be treated as one for legal purposes:[71] (1) the parent company must control the subsidiary, not just through stock ownership but through a complete domination of the policy; (2) the control must be used to commit a fraud or wrong by the parent through the subsidiary, to avoid legal obligations or statutory duties or to unjustly limit the plaintiff's rights; (3) the above-mentioned control and breach of duty must cause the injury or loss complained of.[72]

The first requirement is that the subsidiary lacks a separate independent identity of its own. Not having a separate identity may arise in two ways: excessive control by the parent, and the lack of real separate existence.[73] In the classic doctrinal formulation, control must extend to the extreme where the subsidiary has no mind, willpower or existence of its own.[74] In other words there must be excessive domination over the subsidiary by the parent. In order to establish the domination criteria, it should be first mentioned that the issue is not simply the power to control but it is the exercise of control; total control or equally the absence of any independent judgment. Shortly the subsidiary should exist only

---

68 *Re a Company Ltd* [1985] BCLC 333.

69 Lowry, John, 'In Defence of Salomon: Promoting the Corporate Veil' in Rider, B.A.K. and Andenas, Mads (eds) *Developments in European Company Law, Vol 2/1997: The Quest for an Ideal Legal Form for Small Businesses* (Kluwer Law International, London 1999).

70 *Creasy v Breachwood Motors Limited* [1992] 2 BCC 638.

71 *Lowendahl v Baltimore & ORR* 247 App. Div. 144, 154 (1st Dept 1936). These requirements are established in this American case but also accepted in some form in the UK.

72 Payne, 'Lifting the Corporate Veil'; Cashel, 'Groups of Companies', p. 28.

73 Blumberg, Phillip I., 'Accountability of Multinational Corporations: The Barriers Presented by Concepts of the Corporate Juridical Entity' (2000–2001) 24 Hastings Int'l & Comp. L. Rev. 297.

74 *Ibid.*

in name.[75] In the case of *Lowendahl v Baltimore & ORR* the required level of control has been described as 'control, not merely majority or complete stock control, but complete domination, not only of finances, but of policy and business practices in respect to the transactions attacked so that the corporate entity had at the time no separate mind, will or existence of its own'.[76] How these factors are balanced in practice, and when alter ego liability will be found once control is established, is subject to a fact-specific inquiry in each case.[77]

The second prerequisite to applying the piercing the veil under fraud doctrine is that the control must be used to commit a fraud or wrong by the parent through a subsidiary. It must be shown that the subsidiary has been used as a shield to complete some fraudulent or unjust or inequitable conduct for the benefit of the parent or controlling shareholder. The conduct must be morally declarable or primarily unfair.[78] A final requisite is that the defendant's conduct has to have caused injury to the plaintiff. It is obvious that if there is no harm to the creditors, there is no need to pierce the corporate veil.

It is very difficult to congregate these three conditions in a single case. Therefore the fraud-based piercing the veil cases disclose no very obvious pattern, and it remains hard to predict when the courts will lift the veil in practice.[79] Moreover in *Adams v Cape Industries*, it was decided that there was no fraud for a group of companies for choosing to use the doctrine of separate corporate personality in such a way as to minimize its group exposure to future liabilities. The logic behind this is that, under the English perspective, parent corporations are no more than a shareholder.[80] A company exists for the benefit of shareholders so they can manage their affairs as they wish, provided they acted in good faith and the desire to limit liability by using legal rules is not a fraud.[81]

In the US case *Pepper v Litton*,[82] the judgment explicitly recognizes that the law's primary duty is to protect the citizen against sharp practice and, particularly, which is brought about by abuse of the legal principles in question.[83]

---

75 Whincup, Michael, 'Inequitable Incorporation – the Abuse of a Privilege' (1981) 2 Company Lawyer 158.

76 See Hofstetter, Karl, 'The Ecological Liability of Corporate Groups: Comparing US and European Trends' in Teubner, G., Farmer, L. and Murphy, D., *Environmental Law and Ecological Responsibility: The Concept and Practice of Ecological Self-Organisation* (Wiley, Chichester 1994).

77 Farmer, 'Parent Corporation'.

78 Blumberg, 'Accountability of Multinational'.

79 Mitchell, 'Lifting the Corporate Veil'.

80 See also *Multinational Gas and Petrochemical Co v Multinational Gas and Petrochemical Services Ltd* [1983] 2 All ER 563.

81 *Adams v Cape Industries.*

82 308 US 295, 310, 313 (1939).

83 Whincup, 'Inequitable Incorporation'.

Accordingly fraud doctrine has been applied in a broader approach in the US. Professor Blumberg sets out three requirements for piercing the corporate veil.[84] The first one is a demonstration that the subsidiary lacks separate independent identity of its own. Such lack of separate identity may arise in two ways: excessive control by the parent, and lack of the forms of separate existence. Control is the most ambiguous element of the rule because at least 11 individual factors may be considered by a court in determining the degree of control exercised by the parent; the lack of independent action by the subsidiary's officers and directors, if directly proven, is conclusive.[85] The second traditional requirement for piercing is showing that the subsidiary has been used as a shelter to accomplish some fraudulent or unjust or inequitable behaviour for the benefit of the parent or controlling shareholder. The conduct must be ethically guilty or basically unfair. The final requisite is that the defendant's conduct has to have caused an injury to the plaintiff. In short, the conditions in America are not fundamentally different than those in England.

## Common Law Agency Doctrine

Agency is a 'legal relationship between a principal and natural and legal persons with permanent authority to prospect for and visit customers with a view to negotiating and when appropriate concluding agreement in the name and for account of the principals'.[86] Agency law is a varied and extended institution, based both on the law of torts and contract law. It centres on the notions of control and authority which are exerted by one person over another. Liability being imposed on the controller, principal, for the acts performed by the person subject to control, agent, with his authority.[87] Accordingly the separate corporate personalities of two different companies will also be ignored if one of them is held to have been acting as the agent for the other.[88] For an agency relationship, the common law requires not merely control but also a consensual transaction. The parties must agree that the subsidiary is acting for the parent – the principal with subsidiaries typically utilized to protect the parent corporation from liability.[89] In some cases, courts accept implied agency relationship and impose the same liabilities on parties for this relationship. However, this requires es-

---

84 Blumberg, 'Accountability of Multinational'.

85 Graham, Boyce L., 'Navigating the Mists of Metaphor: An Examination of the Doctrine of Piercing the Corporate Veil' (1990–1991) 56 J. Air L. & Com. 1135.

86 ICC, *Commercial Agency: Guide for the Drawing up of Contracts* (International Chamber of Commerce, Paris 1983) p. 5.

87 Dobson, 'Lifting the Veil'.

88 Gallagher and Ziegler, 'Lifting the Corporate Veil'.

89 Blumberg, 'Accountability of Multinational'; Dobson, 'Lifting the Veil'.

tablishment of many factual relationships between the parent and the subsidiary, which is very difficult to prove under the current structure of MNEs and groups of companies.[90] Therefore it should not be surprising that very few parent-subsidiary relationships satisfy the common law requirements for an agency relationship.[91]

The agency rules are illustrated in a number of English decisions.[92] In *Smith, Stone and Knight Ltd v Birmingham Corporation*,[93] Birmingham Corporation, a local government authority, compulsorily acquired premises occupied by The Birmingham Waste Co Ltd, a wholly owned subsidiary of Smith, Stone and Knight. In order to succeed in an action for compensation for loss of business, the parent company had to establish that the subsidiary was its agent in conducting business on the premises.[94] The judge found that in conducting business on the premises the subsidiary had acted as the parent's agent. In *Smith, Stone*, the subsidiary was described as the agent or employee or tool or simulacrum of the parent company because it was carrying on business on behalf of the parent. Therefore this particular feature of agency in English and US law has created an idea that is especially well adapted to cases of abuse of corporate personality.[95]

However, the current thinking on agency as a means of veil piercing is inadequate for the following four reasons. First, there is a disagreement over whether or not an agency, as currently applied, actually represents veil piercing. Secondly, there is a logical inconsistency of asserting that the corporation is a puppet, under the complete control of another, while simultaneously it is an independent legal actor who can enter into binding agency agreements. Thirdly, the majority of cases traditionally dealt with under agency are most likely to be mere instances of statutory interpretation.[96] Fourthly, it is very difficult to prove an agency relationship under the complex structure of groups of companies since veil piercing based on agency argument requires a clear indication of connection between the parent and the subsidiary, while the examination of structure of modern MNEs in the second chapter of this book suggests the opposite.

In the majority of the cases, the subsidiary was described, either expressly or impliedly, as the agent of its parent. However the description of the subsidiary

---

90 See Chapter 2.

91 Blumberg, 'Accountability of Multinational'.

92 See also *Ebbw Vale UDC v South Wales Traffic Licensing Authority* [1951] 2 KB 266.

93 [1939] 4 All ER 116.

94 Gallagher and Ziegler, 'Lifting The Corporate Veil'.

95 Avgitidis, Dimitris K., *Group of Companies; The Liability of Parent Company for the Depths of Its Subsidiary* (Sakkoulas, Athens-Komotini 1996), p. 164.

96 Neyers, 'Canadian Corporate Law'.

as an agent of the parent was not based on the typical elements of an agency relationship but on a number of facts suggesting that the subsidiary was closely controlled by its parent. The term agent was merely used as a description, interchangeably with other labels, such as tool, simulacrum, façade, alter ago and creature, in order to emphasize the substantial degree of the parent's domination over the affairs of the subsidiary.[97]

In the case where the court attempted to examine whether the relationship between the parent and the subsidiary was that of a principal and an agent in the strict legal sense, it was pointed out that it is necessary to bear in mind the fundamental principle that the relationship of principal and agent can only be established by the consent (actual or implied) of the principal and the agent.[98] And in the absence of such consent, the supposition of an agency relationship was rejected by the English courts.[99] Therefore it is not surprising that in *Adams v Cape Industries* on the agency issue for the acts of the subsidiary on the part of the parent corporation, the court did not give any credit to the agency claims.[100] The explanation was simple – that there is no real or expressed agency agreement.

Examining the characteristics of the agency relationship, one sees no inaccuracy in coming to the conclusion that the agency argument is a variation of fraud doctrine. It is just better suited to the complexity of corporate groups since two separate personalities are involved in the case. Where the fraud doctrine was not enough to establish liability, the agency was created on the same basic necessity of the parent applying excessive control over the subsidiary. Thus similar to the fraud doctrine, agency theory sees the liability as liability of controller for its unlawful control over its subsidiary. Thus it can be claimed that agency argument is not functional enough to be applied to tort committed by subsidiaries of MNEs that operate under complex structure.

## Single Economic Unit Doctrine

In *DHN Food Distribution Ltd v London Borough of Tower Hamlets*,[101] Lord Denning MR decided on the treatment of a parent company-subsidiary relationship as a single economic unit commenting that there is evidence of a general tendency to ignore the separate legal entities of various companies within a group and to look instead at the economic entity of the entire group.[102]

97 Avgitidis, *Group of Companies*, p. 170.
98 See *Atlas Maritime Co SA v Avalon Maritime Ltd* [1991] 1 WLR 917.
99 Avgitidis, *Group of Companies*, p. 170.
100 Baughen, *Corporate Accountability*.
101 [1976] 1 WLR 852.
102 Gallagher and Ziegler, 'Lifting The Corporate Veil'.

And it was decided when a parent company owns all the shares of the subsidiaries 'these subsidiaries are bound hand and foot to the parent company and must do just what the parent company says ... the three companies should, for present purposes, be treated as one'.[103] *DHN* is probably the strongest case, in England, in the tort victims' favour because it was strongly arguable that the court there did not base itself on the particular statutory provisions but on a more general approach founded on the idea of single economic entity.[104] Thus the development somehow was fundamental for corporate law. After the decision of the Court of Appeal in *DHN*, it has been said that the courts may disregard *Salomon* principles for corporate groups wherever it is just and equitable to do so.[105] However, the rejection of these claims came immediately by the House of Lords in *Woolfson v Strathclyde Regional Council*.[106] The court indicated some doubt about whether the Court of Appeal in the *DHN* case had properly applied the principle that it is appropriate to pierce the corporate veil only where special circumstances exist indicating that it is a mere façade concealing the true facts.[107] Moreover the subsequent views expressed by the Court of Appeal in *Multinational Gas and Petrochemical Co v Multinational Gas and Petrochemical Services Ltd and Ors*[108] claimed that the *DHN* decision was an abnormality. It is suggested that the decision in *Multinational Gas* can be considered in the same light as that of *Salomon*, in that no injustice would have been caused to any party by upholding the separate entity principle.[109]

Consequently, the judgments in *Woolfson*, *Multinational Gas* and *Industrial Equity Ltd v Blackburn*[110] distinctly indicate that the decision of the Court of Appeal in *DHN* was abnormal and that the principle that each company in a group of companies is a separate legal entity possessed of separate legal rights and liabilities is now unchallengeable by judicial decision.[111] More recently in *Polly Peck International Plc (in administration)*[112] Robert Walker J emphasized that 'it was not open to the court to disregard the principle of separate corporate personality and treat a closely integrated group of companies as a single economic unit on the basis merely of perceived injustice, particularly in cases where

[103] Ottolenghi, 'From Peeping'.
[104] Davies, *Gower and Davies*, p. 185.
[105] Rixon, F.G., 'Lifting the Veil Between Holding and Subsidiary Companies' (1986) 102 LQR 415.
[106] [1978] SLT 159.
[107] Avgitidis, *Group of Companies*, p. 174.
[108] [1983] 2 All ER 563.
[109] Gallagher and Ziegler, 'Lifting The Corporate Veil'.
[110] [1977] 137 CLR 567.
[111] Nakajima, Chizu, 'Lifting the Veil' (1996) 17(6) Comp. Law. 187.
[112] [1996] 2 All E.R (Ch D).

the separate legal existence of these companies assumed greater importance once they became insolvent'.

In the application of the single economic unit theory, parent and subsidiary were treated as a single economic unit when there was evidence indicating that the parent could make any arrangements which they pleased in regard to the management of the business of the subsidiary, or that every step taken by the subsidiary was determined by the policy of the parent, or that the subsidiaries were bound hand and foot to the parent company and must do just what the parent says or that the parent controlled the purse strings, on an item-by-item basis.[113] Similarly, courts in the US and in the EU use some form of economic unity theory to pierce the corporate veil.[114] As with the English doctrine, under the theory, the main factor in piercing the corporate veil is the level of control by the parent over the subsidiary.[115]

In simple evaluation, the agency and the single economic unit approaches provide more reliable principles in establishing liability on parent corporations because two separate personalities are confirmed but the use of close control principles tend to lead to the conclusion that there is only one person involved.[116] That is why it is a fact that in some American cases fraud and agency principles have been brought together to govern the particular situation of abuse of control.[117] However, it may be concluded that there is no substantial difference between the English interpretation of the agency, the single economic unit and the fraud doctrine. In reality the agency principles applied in *Smith* may be used as a test for inferring that the subsidiary is the instrument of the parent. Both the English and the American doctrines have the influence of treating parent and subsidiary companies otherwise than the independent legal entities and they deeply trust in facts which may vary from case to case but they all resemble each other in the idea that a substantial degree of managerial control is exercised by the parent company. The only difference is that the American courts have imposed liability on the parent company on the ground of such control more often than the English courts have generally done.[118] Consequently the development of agency and single economic unit theories finds its logic on excessive control of the subsidiary. Therefore the applications of agency and single enterprise principles have been easily shielded by the *Salomon* and later *Adams*, principles.[119] Thus Blumberg claims that liability principles that rest on agency

---

113 Avgitidis, *Group of Companies*, p. 182.
114 Bakst, 'Piercing the Corporate Veil'.
115 *Ibid.*
116 Dobson, 'Lifting the Veil'.
117 *Ibid.*
118 Avgitidis, *Group of Companies*, p. 189.
119 Baughen, *Corporate Accountability*.

and single economic unit became no more than vague, symbolic variations of the piercing the veil jurisprudence on the principle of fraud.[120]

## CONCLUSION: ABANDONING THE VEIL PIERCING

The first striking conclusion from the case law of liability of a group of companies is that generally the corporate veil will not be pierced unless the corporate shareholder dominates the corporate subsidiary and the corporate shareholder has engaged in a fraudulent or illegal or other improper conduct, which has generated an injustice. Thus the doctrine of lifting the veil plays a small role in liability discussions in English law, except for the area of particular contracts or statutes. Even where the cases for applying the doctrine may appear very logical, such as an under-capitalized, single-member company, which might or might not be an element of a corporate group, the courts are unlikely to pierce the corporate veil.[121] In their legitimacy effort, the courts always refer to lack of legislative effort on the issue claiming that even though the legislature has intervened to deal with various issues relating to corporate groups, they have not acted on this particular matter. As a result the English courts consider that their function in formulating any overreaching principle of fundamental changes in corporate group liability is greatly circumscribed. The courts, even the House of Lords, are reluctant to intervene in a matter that requires strong legislative attention.[122] Accordingly it is logical to claim that the devotion to limited liability in corporate groups is a common characteristic of modern laws as one American court decided:

> The doctrine of limited liability is intended precisely to protect a parent corporation whose subsidiary goes broke. That is the whole purpose of the doctrine, and those who have the right to decide such questions, that is, legislatures, believe that the doctrine, on the whole, is socially reasonable and useful. We think that the doctrine would largely be destroyed if a parent corporation could be held liable simply on the basis of errors in business judgment.[123]

However, referring the MNE liability problems only to parliaments is not very convincing since the same judicial system created the current inflexible regime of liability under the principles of limited liability and veil piercing. It

---

[120] Blumberg, P.I., *The Multinational Challenge to Corporation Law* (OUP, Oxford, 1993) p. 143.

[121] Davies, *Gower and Davies*, p. 189.

[122] Prentice, Dan D., 'Veil Piercing and Successor Liability in the United Kingdom' (1995–1996) 10 Fla. J. Int'l L. 469.

[123] *Radaszewski v Telecom Corp.* [1981] F.2d 305.

is also interesting that there has been little criticism of the *Salomon* principles and little demand for its modification either judicially or legislatively. Thus Professor Prentice went further to claim that, on current form, the *Salomon* principles may endure for another 100 years.[124]

Under these current rigid principles, the court created system of liability in common law is not well developed. There is no clear set of principles for any emerging doctrines for liability and it is difficult to predict when and under which conditions courts will disregard the separate entity principle. The need for English courts to choose such symbolic terms as mere fraud, sham, dummy or alter ego in their judgments indicates their difficulties. In America as well, one of the most serious limitations of US law in dealing with group liability has been the arbitrary piercing the veil jurisprudence since the symbolic use of piercing law has prevented US courts from developing a clear general concept of group responsibility.[125] Piercing the veil for a parent corporation with a subsidiary facing tort claims is uncertain, which makes a settlement difficult and litigation costs high.[126]

In consideration of the piercing the veil theory from a broader perspective, such an inadequately developed and complex structure of case law, even incapable of creating solutions for private, sole trader limited companies, cannot be applied in modern times to corporate groups, particularly to MNEs with complex horizontal structures. All the basics of the veil-piercing doctrine have been built on excessive control by parent corporations over subsidiaries. However, under the modern complicated horizontally structured corporate groups, the control has been spread over subsidiaries, which appears in two ways. There are more self-dependent and self-operated subsidiaries and there are changing components of control and influence over others operating in the group.[127] Consequently in this new and complicated structure, it is almost impossible to establish a simplified method of control under which excessive control of one entity over another is established. Since there is no easy proof of control of one particular entity over another, it is difficult to apply piercing the veil principles in subsidiaries' torts.

One can claim that the single economic principle was, in a way, an attempt to adopt the new structure to the case law. I would rather consider the single economic unit as a first reaction to the liability problems in corporate groups, particularly in vertically integrated groups. The problems of court created liability stem from the fact that efforts to create liability theories were inefficient and

---

[124] Prentice, 'Veil Piercing and Successor'.

[125] Hofstetter, Karl, 'Parent Responsibility for Subsidiary Corporations: Evaluating European Trends' (1990) 39 ICLQ 576.

[126] Thompson, 'Piercing...Empirical Study'.

[127] See Chapter 2.

apparently fruitless and at the time of the decisions, they were completely outdated because the complexity of MNE structure was already at the next level that the case law could not predict.[128] That is why the bigger and more complicated corporate groups get, the less likely they are to be subjected to piercing the veil principles. Referring back to examination of corporate structure and complicated ownership and managerial structure of the given examples in the second chapter of this book, there are multi-veil corporate groups. In those groups there are much more complex ownership structures than the veil piercing theory suggests. Moreover these complex ownership structures require much more complex horizontal managerial control and operation.

In conclusion the main problem of veil-piercing theory is its dependency on the control theory which makes its application very weak and rare. In the case of a horizontally structured MNEs group, the control theory is inapplicable. However, the piercing the corporate veil theory still depends on control theory under which excessive control of the parent over its subsidiaries is a requirement. Thus the control theory is much more suited to vertically organized corporate groups under which the divisions between subsidiaries and parent is more apparent and the parent exercises some certain level of control over its subsidiaries. Consequently, piercing the veil theory is now obsolete and must be abandoned in favour of liability theories, which should be based on modern structures of MNEs.

[128] See Chapter 2.

# 6. Comparative laws and principles regarding corporate group liability

## INTRODUCTION

One of the most important problems for regulation of groups of companies and MNEs is that only a few legal systems propose a unified approach towards groups of companies[1] and none of them regulate liability issues in tort. Therefore national courts, with the lack of statutory provisions to trust in, use general legal principles of civil and commercial laws to obtain justice in a particular case. More importantly in contrast to expectations, there are new laws to extend limited liability to other business forms.[2] For example, the UK recently enacted the Limited Liability Partnership Act 2000, which has extended the imperfections of limited liability to partnerships.

On the international level, the more difficult question remains, how MNEs can be put under harmonized regulations: whether MNEs might be subject to one uniform regulatory structure or different regulations covering their various activities in different countries. The voluntary regulation of MNEs also appears as a part of the liability discussions.[3] It may be argued, in the light of previous chapters, that an MNE should be subject to a single regulatory scheme because it has a private managerial structure capable of integrated global management over all its components. On the other hand, this type of uniform regulation, even if it could be achieved, would be problematic with regard to the sovereignty of independent states.[4]

However the fact that corporate groups have not been regulated in a way that is equivalent to that of other organizational forms, such as joint stock companies, should not prevent us from emphasizing their importance as institutions and the connected requirement to provide legal answers to the questions they

---

1 Germany, Portugal and Brazil are examples.

2 Griffin, S., 'Limited Liability: A Necessary Revolution' (2004) 25(4) Comp. Law. 99.

3 See Chapter 7.

4 Anderson, Michael, 'Transnational Corporations and Environmental Damage: Is Tort Law the Answer' (2002) 41 Washburn Law Journal 399.

present.[5] It will be unfair to claim that the phenomenon of liability in the MNE context has not received any attention from regulators. Conducting a more careful examination, it will appear that even though they are commonly made outside the field of limited liability and tort liability issues, legal references to corporate groups are quite frequent in most legal systems. Thus it is not extraordinary to find rules related to groups of companies in tax law, labour law, competition law and commercial law. Consequently liability of groups of companies as a discussion appears in the context of many legislative references to corporate groups in company law and/or other abundant legislative divisions of law. It does not appear to be rational to consider corporate groups as an illegitimate institution when they are in reality regulated in many different contexts.[6] This regulatory approach has already been quite a widespread reality for years but the need for comprehensive regulation including liability issues has only recently been widely discussed and understood.[7]

This brings us to the purpose of this chapter, which is to provide and elaborate on the discussion of different approaches to the problems of liability of groups of companies. The discussion will have natural limitations in that only those developments, which will have relevance to group liability discussion, will be covered here. Comparative legislative examples will be given from a number of jurisdictions. It should be kept in mind that the book does not aim to cover every jurisdiction, nor all the regulations in the examined jurisdictions. Rather there will be an examination of specific legislative efforts that are important for the purpose of the book, which is to discuss the tort liabilities of MNEs. The examples will be tested to discover whether they have created efficient theories and principles to solve the liability problems in the MNEs context. There will be a search to discover whether any of these examples has been adequately developed to meet the changes and challenges MNEs' business, managerial, social and economical features put in law.

Even though there are some regulations, which directly or indirectly require lifting the corporate veil, it is obvious that these regulations cannot create a situation under which corporate groups liability is achieved because the protection provided by such measures is invoked very rarely. For the purpose of this book, the importance of these regulations lies in the fact that as the laws indicate, in case of need, alternatives to the limited liability doctrine and piercing the corporate veil theory could be created. Moreover examination of statutes and interpretations of these statutes by the courts will provide an answer to the

5 Irujo, José Miguel Embid, 'Trends and Realities in the Law of Corporate Groups' (2005) 6 EBOR 65.

6 *Ibid.*

7 *Ibid.*

question of whether regulators have adapted to the modern characteristics of MNEs or the regulations are still based on vertical structure because one of the reasons of failure of the statutory law is that it cannot fully embrace the current realities of groups of companies.

With this aim, this chapter examines the current situation and discussions in the UK and developments in the European Union as central to the research. Moreover there will be an examination of some interesting legislation, with references to case law, from various jurisdictions. The German Stock Corporation Act has attracted lots of interest from scholars for being a unique regulation of corporate groups. For this it deserves an examination. The American legislation of Comprehensive Environmental Response, Compensation and Liability Act (CERCLA) will be very broadly discussed and questioned as to whether it serves as an example of efficient liability regime for corporate groups. There will be an examination of an interesting legislation from Turkey, under which the shareholders of a private limited liability company are proportionally liable for the companys' debt owed to the state. Again there is an effort in Turkey to regulate corporate groups under the draft commercial code; as it refers to many regulations regarding groups of companies, it is important to test the efficiency of an up-to-date draft bill, which combines principles regarding corporate groups' regulations in Europe. Moreover as an alternative to case law, the approach of growing international commercial arbitration institutions to the issue of corporate groups' liability under the lights of arbitral awards and reactions of the national courts will be examined. The examples are chosen as indications of interpretations of liabilities of groups of companies within various branches of law and from diverse legal systems.

## LAWS RELATED TO CORPORATE GROUPS' LIABILITY IN ENGLAND

In England, most regulations in relation to corporate groups have been introduced on an ad hoc basis in response to a specific problem or abuse, rather than in pursuit of any coherent legislative or regulatory strategy.[8] In English company law, there are some provisions relating to groups of companies but there is no section devoted to groups of companies, neither is there a particular group of companies' law.

A number of Companies Act 2006 (CA) provisions require related corporations to be treated as if they are one with the parent company. Part 15, Chapter

---

[8] Hadden, Tom, 'Regulating Corporate Groups: International Perspective' in McCahery J., Picciotto S. and Scott S. (eds) *Corporate Control and Accountability* (OUP, Oxford 1993).

4 of the CA requires the presentation of group accounts as consolidated statements in order to provide a true and fair view of group activities. There are different duties on the parent on the basis of whether the parent is qualified as small or big. The requirement of providing a consolidated statement necessitates treatment of all the enterprises within a group as though they were one. Moreover, CA, s. 409 provides that a parent company has to disclose details of subsidiaries' names, country of activity and the shares it holds in the subsidiary. Part 16 of the CA, titled 'Audit', requires parent companies to provide certain information about their subsidiaries.[9] Some tax and employment legislations also follow the approach of considering groups of companies as single enterprises. For example the Employment Rights Act 1986 protects employees' statutory rights when transferred from one country to another within a group.

Insolvency Act 1986 (IA) provisions make the most significant impact on corporate personality and limited liability in England. Where the business of the company has been carried out to defraud creditors, the courts, on a winding-up, are entitled to look behind the veil of incorporation to find parties that know about the carrying-on of the fraudulent behaviour and thus are personally liable for the debts of the company. There are two principal devices that could be used to impose such liability: liability for fraudulent trading and liability for wrongful trading under ss 213 and 214 of the IA.[10] The application of the provisions on fraudulent and wrongful trading in the context of the parent-subsidiary relationship relies upon evidence demonstrating that the parent company exercises some degree of managerial control over its subsidiary. The limited liability of the parent is lifted either where the parent was knowingly party to the carrying on of its subsidiary's business with intent to defraud creditors (IA, s. 213 on fraudulent trading) or where the parent was the director or the shadow director of its insolvent subsidiary (IA, s. 214 on wrongful trading).[11] Although s. 213 on fraudulent trading covers almost all the circumstances in which a parent is engaged in the management of its subsidiary, it is subject to the very strict requirement of establishing intent to defraud. On the other hand, although s. 214 on wrongful trading is free from the evidential difficulties of s. 213 it applies

---

[9] CA, s. 500 'Auditor's Right to Information from Overseas Subsidiaries' regulates that '(1) Where a parent company has a subsidiary undertaking that is not a body corporate incorporated in the United Kingdom, the auditor of the parent company may require it to obtain from any of the following persons such information or explanations as he may reasonably require for the purposes of his duties as auditor. … (3) If so required, the parent company must take all such steps as are reasonably open to it to obtain the information or explanations from the person concerned.'

[10] See further Prentice, D.D., 'Group Indebtedness' in Wooldridge F. and Schmitthoff C.M., *Groups of Companies* (Sweet & Maxwell, London 1991), p. 57.

[11] Avgitidis, Dimitris K., *Group of Companies; The Liability of Parent Company for the Depths of Its Subsidiary* (Sakkoulas, Athens-Komotini 1996), p. 224.

only in circumstances where the parent company is found to be the shadow director[12] of its subsidiary and its independency might be removed by the interior organization of the group.[13] The sections operate only when a company has gone to insolvent liquidation and declaration can be made only against a person who, at some time before the beginning of the winding up, was a director or shadow director of the company and knew, or should have decided, at that time, that there was no rational outlook that the company would keep from going into insolvent liquidation.

Although the IA provisions require very strict conditions similar to those required for veil piercing, they still constitute, as Professor Davies states, probably the most extreme departure from the rule in *Salomon*'s case yet achieved in the UK.[14] However, the requirements for a successful establishment of liability on parent corporations indicate that ss 213 and 214 of IA can be considered just an enacted equivalent of the veil-piercing principles in the case law. Therefore it cannot be claimed as a successful piece of legislation to remove negative effects of limited liability principles in groups of companies' context.[15] Consequently the criticism made of piercing the veil doctrine for being out of date and thus not practically functional can be repeated in evaluation of wrongful and fraudulent trading principles in the IA. The Act considers a group of companies as simple vertical organizations symbolized as one entity applying control over another. Therefore it has failed to bring any advanced liability regime and it is impossible to bring one unless the statute adopts the modern structures and characteristics of group of companies.

## DEVELOPMENT IN ENGLISH COMPANY LAW

This lack of breakthrough in statutes for a group of companies leads us to search for what the new Companies Act 2006 offers. The new Companies Act should be examined through its preparation process, which has three stages; the first is a consultation report from the Company Law Steering Group in 2001, the second is the Draft Company Law Reform Bill in 2005 and final stage is the Companies Act 2006.

---

12 According to s. 251 of the CA a shadow director is 'in relation to a company, means a person in accordance with whose directions or instructions the directors of the company are accustomed to act'.

13 Avgitidis, *Group of Companies,* p. 225.

14 Davies, Paul L., *Gower and Davies' Principles of Modern Company Law* (Sweet & Maxwell, London 2003) p. 196.

15 Griffin, 'Limited Liability'.

## Company Law Review Steering Group, Modern Company Law for a Competitive Economy

With a close look at the Steering Group's proposal[16] one can observe that the Steering Group saw no advantage in imposing a fundamental regime on groups of companies. They simply believe, in their own words, that '[having a groups of companies' law] would take away flexibility in the way businesses organise themselves and would strike at the limited liability basis for company law'.

As an alternative to a developed group of companies' law, the Steering Group offered a view on the question of group liability in tort and also considered the question of accountability, in particular by suggesting some new methods of group governance based on the concept of an 'elective regime' for groups. They believe that the most productive way for reform is to adopt an 'elective regime' under which, in exchange for a guarantee by the parent company of the liabilities of a subsidiary and satisfaction of certain publicity requirements, the subsidiary should be exempted from the requirements (under the Companies Act) relating to an annual account and audit. An elective subsidiary must fall within the definition of a wholly owned subsidiary under the Companies Act. The Steering Group see little point in requiring all wholly owned subsidiaries to be included in this regime. This gives great flexibility to corporate groups to join the elective regime or not.

The Steering Group discussed the various options for the nature of the guarantee by the parent. But their initial view was that there should be no requirement for a reciprocal guarantee whereby the elective subsidiary would also guarantee the liabilities of the parent, nor is there a requirement of a cross-guarantee from one elective subsidiary to another. Either of these would have the effect of a form of pooling of assets and liabilities across the elective group. This might create a relatively efficient regime of liability for the group. However, the Steering Group rejected a pooling of liability across the group as a whole by supporting the system of simple bilateral guarantees. The reason was that the system of bilateral guarantees is likely to prove simpler in practice and would avoid the possibility that the creditors of an elective subsidiary could be at risk because of liabilities arising in a sister elective subsidiary. The approach of the Steering Group apparently indicates that they consider groups of companies as vertical organizations. The proposed guarantee should work as a normal guarantee in that an unsatisfied creditor would take action against the elective subsidiary, joining the elective parent in the action. The Steering Group find joint and several liability of a parent inappropriate because of the fact that this

16 The Company Law Review Steering Group, Modern Company Law for a Competitive Economy Final Report (DTI, London 2001).

would enable the creditor to sue the parent without suing the subsidiary, which is considered unacceptable. Thus this system is definitely not efficient to solve the jurisdictional problems arising from the activities of MNEs.[17]

In brief, the most important problem of a group of companies has been left with no solution in the Steering Group's proposal. They regard it as entirely proper for a holding company to separate an activity, by using a subsidiary, in order to avoid the risk of liability, including tort liability, because the Group claims many torts are closely linked with contractual liabilities, such as liability for professional services and misrepresentation and product liability. More interestingly, the Group founded the legitimacy of their findings on the fact that they are not aware of any jurisdiction providing for parent companies to be automatically liable for the torts of their subsidiaries. Thus they claimed that defining the circumstances in which the use of limited liability in this way is regarded as abusive would be difficult. Nor are they aware of cases where parent companies have engaged in such abuse. They find the easiest excuse and refer the problems to the insolvency law stating that the undercapitalization of subsidiaries, and their operation in a way which creates undue risks of insolvency, are matters best dealt with by the insolvency law. They concluded the proposal by saying that 'we do not therefore propose any reform in this regard'.

In particular the proposal did not offer any fundamental or innovative regime. It simply stated that there is no regime offering those kinds of regulations in the world. However, their elective regime even falls short of the types of regime established 40 years ago by the German Stock Corporation Act of 1965.[18] The only significance of the Steering Group's proposal is that, for the first time, reflection is being given to the question of whether English law should have a dedicated regime for groups of companies.[19]

The regime in the Steering Group's proposal was just a reflection of pressure that currently businesses apply on regulators. Thus it contained many weak suggestions.[20] First, there is no obligation for the parent to make an election. Moreover it is applicable for only wholly owned subsidiaries. Secondly, the proposal is silent on whether election could extend to any subsidiary. This is completely in contradiction to the modern characteristics of the MNEs. The horizontal structure indicates that the groups of companies might include many wholly owned subsidiaries together with many partly owned subsidiaries. Moreover there is a complex cross-ownership in corporate groups, which might

---

[17] See Chapter 4.

[18] See below.

[19] Muchlinski, P., 'Holding Multinationals to Account: Recent Developments in English Litigation and the Company Law Review' (2002) 23 Company Lawyer 168.

[20] *Ibid.*

result in many sub-corporate groups within a group.[21] Thus it is unreasonable to expect success for the elective regime that covers only wholly owned subsidiaries without requiring the parent to extend the regime to other subsidiaries. Allowing parents to make the choice will result in a situation that is similar to the current law under which the corporate groups are not considered as single enterprises but they are represented by many legal entities without necessarily creating any group liability.

The jurisdictional problems have been left completely untouched. The elective regime would apply only to EU-based parent companies, but not to groups whose parent company is outside the EU. Failing to cover parents from outside the EU means failing to regulate MNEs originated in different jurisdictions. The parent might easily insulate itself by removing their assets to countries out of the EU. This is already common practice. For example in *Multinational Gas* the assets of the joint venture company in question were located in Liberia, while the main business operations were carried out in England through services-only companies.[22]

The rejection of a pooling approach to the definition of the limits of assets available to claimants ignores a basic problem in mass tort litigation, where the economic activity of the group as a whole is involved in the hazardous processes that lead to the harm. It is common in commercial practice to ask for reciprocal guarantees when dealing with groups of companies. Thus sometimes contractors with the group ask for guarantees from different companies under the group to secure their credit. However, the proposals refuse to create a reciprocal guarantee between the parent and subsidiary. The reason for this depends again on misunderstanding of the structure of corporate groups in business practice. The one-way guarantee is typical of the vertical understanding that was used in past experiences in case and statutory law and failed to create a satisfactory liability regime. The horizontal structure suggests that not only should there be reciprocal guarantee but also there should be a group guarantee for creditors of any subsidiary because even in the selection of the elective regime there is no guarantee that the parent will be asset rich. Thus successful proposals in this sense should have included pooling of assets, at least for the claims of involuntary creditors.

In conclusion the proposal of an elective regime is frustrating for those who expected a regime at least better than the German Stock Corporation Act. It is disappointing because it would definitely tempt manipulative corporate planning by groups of companies by leaving them to decide whether to elect or

---

[21] See Chapter 2.

[22] See *Multinational Gas and Petrochemical Co v Multinational Gas and Petrochemical Services Ltd and Others* [1983] 2 All ER 563.

not.[23] Thus the Steering Group's approach to corporate groups' liability may fairly be described as a major inadequate treatment of an issue of key importance in the reform of any system of company law because dismissing the problem of subsidiaries' liabilities by diverting it into the uncertain future of insolvency law reform is deeply unsatisfactory.[24] These kinds of proposals are the production of understandings of groups of companies which lack proper examination of modern corporate groups.

## COMPANY LAW REFORM BILL, THE 2005 WHITE PAPER AND THE COMPANIES ACT 2006

As the Steering Group unreservedly admits, its proposals are 'not a radical recasting of company law', but it considers that these proposals are 'a sensible reduction of burdens in groups without weakening their existing position'. Therefore it is not surprising that the Company Law Reform Bill, the 2005 White Paper[25] prepared by the Department of Trade and Industry (DTI) mostly depends on the suggestions and reports of the Steering Group and has the preamble:

> The DTI derives our working ambition of 'prosperity for all' by working to create the best environment for business success in the UK. We help people and companies become more productive by promoting enterprise, innovation and creativity…We champion UK business at home and abroad. We invest heavily in world-class science and technology. We protect the rights of working people and consumers. And we stand up for fair and open markets in the UK, Europe and the world.

With the proposal all positive expectations have vanished, even the little ones that the Steering Group's handling of the group of companies as at least a matter of consideration seem to have fallen on deaf ears. The objective of the DTI proposal is to maintain the UK's position as one of the most attractive places in the world to set up and run a business. The Draft Bill thus even did not mention the group liability problem so as not to scare the MNEs, which happily operate in the UK.

Accordingly there is a huge contradiction in both the Steering Group Report and the government's White Paper, by claiming they aim to create future company law for the country but they just ignore the phenomenon of MNEs that is

---

23 Boyle, T., 'The Company Law, Review and Group Reform' (2002) 23 Company Lawyer 35.

24 *Ibid.*

25 DTI, Company Law Reform Bill, the White Paper (CM 6456, March 2005).

one of the most important features of the current and future issues of company laws. The DTI proudly announced that they are innovative but in terms of creating pioneering law they refer to the non-existence of laws in other jurisdictions. Thus it can easily be claimed that they are innovative in the fact that they can pretend there is no problem in a situation where the discussion of liability is intense and call for better regulation is more organized. As a result, the new Companies Act 2006 based on these principles does not offer any solution in this matter.

The purpose of this book is not only to indicate the liability problems of groups of companies and particularly MNEs but also, assuming that the existence of the problems is not in dispute, the book aims to test the suitability of the current laws and proposals or discussions on the issues to new economic and organizational realities of MNEs. Unfortunately the new Companies Act offers no changes in this matter, thus, with huge disappointment I wish to turn my attention to the developments in the EU regulations.

## DEVELOPMENTS IN EUROPEAN COMMUNITY LAW

European Company law recognizes that a corporation is a separate legal entity and thus must have a legal personality. This rule applies not only when the shareholders are natural persons, but also when the shareholders are corporations.[26] Accordingly, under traditional European company law, a member company in a group cannot be required to satisfy the obligations of another member company in the group.[27] Because of the settled rigid principles of limited liability in the member states and the EU company law itself, the EU has not achieved a comprehensive group liability regime.[28] The efforts to produce a fact-specific groups of companies' directive have collapsed. Consequently there is no basic principle for liability for corporate groups in the EU. The Community rather defines and uses several notions of the group enterprise to be applied in various domains for different regulatory purposes.[29] Starting from the Seventh Company Law Directive[30] and by various other legal provisions,

---

26 Bakst, David S., 'Piercing the Corporate Veil for Environmental Torts in the United States and the European Union: The Case for the Proposed Civil Liability Directive' (1996) 19 B. C. Int'l & Comp. L. Rev. 323.

27 *Ibid.*

28 Irujo, 'Trends and Realities'.

29 Adinolfi, A., 'The Legal Notion of the Group Enterprise: The EC Approach' in Sugarman, D. and Teubner, G. (eds) *Regulating Corporate Groups in Europe* (Baden-Baden, Nomos 1990).

30 Seventh Council Directive 83/349/EEC of 13 June 1983 based on Article 54(3) (g) of the Treaty on consolidated accounts (Official Journal L. 193, 18/07/1983 P. 0001–0017).

such as banking, insurance and anti-trust law, groups of companies have attracted some sort of regulatory efforts.[31]

The European Community has refrained from extensive uniform approaches to particularistic technical changes that can be integrated within the member states.[32] Thus traditionally core areas of company law remain largely untouched by harmonization. Creditors' protection against corporate groups in particular remains a matter of national law. Indeed the EU intervention in some areas, instead of creating a common legal environment, has probably made the law more complicated. The changes that have taken place have often made it more difficult for a resident of a member state to know what the situation is with her own legislation while doing little to inform her about what the law is in other EU countries.[33] Thus implementation of individual legislative and procedural laws on corporate groups is still inadequate in most European countries.[34]

However the EU institutional law at least in theory is more advanced than the English approaches because it can be claimed that, at EU level, there is a wider acceptance of the problems created by groups of companies. Therefore it is not surprising that there have been some ongoing efforts to create better regulations for the corporate groups, even though many of them had failed even before reaching a proposal level. Moreover it is a common practice in the EU to consider groups of companies in the process of preparation of new legislation. For example, the Cross Border Merger Directive[35] would fill an important gap in company law and is the first measure to be presented under the Commission's Action Plan on company law and corporate governance in the EU. In Article 14 of the Merger Directive, which has a title of 'consequences of the merger', it is regulated that the acquiring company will be liable for acquired company's obligations.

The original proposal for a European Company Act (SE)[36] contained provisions similar to those of the German Stock Corporation Act,[37] which would

---

[31] For example, Articles 85 and 86 of the Treaty of Rome refer to undertakings, which are accepted to be a much wider and looser concept than the English concept of separate individual corporate personality under *Salomon*. The provisions apply to parents and subsidiaries – even when not wholly owned.

[32] Sugarman, D., 'Corporate Groups in Europe: Governance, Industrial Organisation, and Efficiency in a Post-Modern World' in Sugarman, D. and Teubner, G. (eds), *Regulating Corporate Groups in Europe* (Baden-Baden, Nomos 1990).

[33] Halbhuber, H., 'National Doctrinal Structures and European Community Law' (2001) 38 C.M.L.Rev. 1385.

[34] Irujo, 'Trends and Realities'.

[35] Directive 2005/56/EC of the European Parliament and of the Council of 26 October 2005 on Cross-Border Mergers of Limited Liability Companies.

[36] European Company Act (SE); Commission for a Council Regulation on the Statute for a European Company: COM (89) 268 final – SYN 218.

[37] See below.

permit management of the group as a single economic unit.[38] It proposed (Article 239/1) that the controlling company of a concern shall be liable for the debts and liabilities of its dependent subsidiary companies. A parent company was presumed to control its subsidiary, and the subsidiary was presumed to be dependent on the parent. The parent could invalidate this presumption if it established a proof that it restricted itself to a mere passive shareholder role.[39] Additionally the Ninth Company Law Directive on the Conduct of Groups Containing a Public Limited Company as a Subsidiary had provisions, as one of its proclaimed goals, to grant adequate protection to a subsidiary's creditors where their primary debtor is dependent on a parent company.[40] However, at present, neither provision has been adopted. The Ninth Directive has not even reached the proposal stage.

The failure of those attempts put new efforts in jeopardy for some time. Only in recent times and in connection with the Forum Europaeum has group regulation again caught the attention of the EU. Following the Winter Report, the recent Company Law Action Plan makes particular reference to the corporate group phenomenon, although from a less ambitious perspective than that of the Ninth Directive.[41] Thus in this chapter I will discuss these recent attempts rather than discussing already failed attempts.

## Action Plan on Modernizing Company Law in the EU

The Action Plan, High Level Group of Company Law Experts and Action Plan on 'Modernising Company Law and Enhancing Corporate Governance in the EU'[42] is the Commission's response to the final report, presented in November 2002, of the High Level Group of Company Law Experts chaired by Japp Winter. The Commission of the European Communities in its Communication and the Action Plan set the principle that the plan for company regulation must be 'flexible in application, but firm in the principles'. The main objectives of the Action Plan are: (1) to strengthen shareholders' rights and protection for employees, creditors and the other parties with which a company deals, while adapting company law and corporate governance rules appropriately for differ-

[38] Commission for a Council Regulation on the Statute for a European Company: COM (89) 268 final – SYN 218 at p. 42 proposal.

[39] Hofstetter, K., 'Parent Responsibility for Subsidiary Corporations: Evaluating European Trends' (1990) 39 ICLQ 576.

[40] Bakst, 'Piercing the Corporate Veil'.

[41] See Irujo, 'Trends and Realities'.

[42] Communication from the Commission to the Council and the European Parliament – Modernizing Company Law and Enhancing Corporate Governance in the European Union – A Plan to Move Forward: COM/2003/0284 final.

ent categories of company; (2) to foster the efficiency and competitiveness of business, with special attention to some cross-border issues.

In relation to corporate groups, the Report states that the existence of risks in the groups of companies challenges neither the legitimacy of groups nor the limited liability principle. Thus the Report supports the view that the enactment of an autonomous body of law, specially dealing with groups, is not recommended at the EU level, but that particular problems should be addressed in three areas: transparency issues; consolidated approach to group policy and bankruptcies; and abusive pyramids. As a result the Report states the need for legislative intervention on corporate groups through three basic issues: (1) the transparency of the group structure and its relations; (2) the tension between the interest of the group and that of the group members; and (3) the special problems of pyramid structures.

Accordingly the Report has made some general recommendations. First, they agree that there is no need to revitalize the dead Ninth Company Law Directive. Secondly, increased disclosure with regard to a group's structure and relations is needed, and the parent company of each group is to be made responsible for disclosing coherent and accurate information. These improvements can be managed by increasing the disclosure requirements in the 7th Directive. Thirdly, the Commission should review the possibility of introducing in member states rules on procedural and substantive consolidation of bankruptcies of group companies. Finally, the EU should require national authorities, responsible for the admission to trading on regulated markets, not to admit holding companies whose sole or main assets are their shareholding in another company, unless the economic value of such admission is clearly demonstrated.

The Commission published its Action Plan based on the evaluation of the Winter Report. Here only issues relating to liability of groups of companies will be discussed. The Commission has agreed with the Winter Report on the view that there is no need to revive the Ninth Directive on affiliated undertakings. The Commission did not want to be in deadlock again and thus created a plan, which is less comprehensive than the Ninth Directive offered.

The Commission acknowledged the fact that groups of companies are a legitimate way of doing business, but they may present risks for shareholders and creditors. Although they apparently accepted the fact that creditors need protection, in terms of offering solutions they have failed to create fundamental principles. They recommended that more transparency could help minimize those risks. Initiatives aimed at improving the financial and non-financial information disclosed by groups are priorities for the short term. Such initiatives would aim to ensure better information on the group's structure and intra-group relations, as well as on the financial situation of the various parts of the group. Moreover the Action Plan supports a framework rule to allow those managing a company belonging to a group to implement a coordinated group policy.

Fortunately, it emphasizes the need for action against abusive pyramids defined by the High Level Group as 'chains of holding companies whose sole or main assets are their shareholding in another listed company'. Accordingly the Commission has concluded its Action Plan for groups of companies dividing it into three phases, short term, medium term and long term.

First, in the short-term, the Commission intends to adopt legislative measures with the intention of improving the group disclosure of financial and non-financial information. Since transparency is felt as the most urgent problem in corporate groups context, whether they are listed or not, the Commission regards these additional initiatives as priorities for the short term.[43] The disclosure requirements have been subjected to many campaigns in recent years and is presented as a tool to make corporations accountable.

Secondly, the Commission aims to come forward in the medium term with a proposal directive providing a framework rule for groups allowing adoption of a coordinated group policy. The Commission also points out that with coordinated group policy the interests of a company's creditors are effectively protected. The Commission does not make any differentiation between voluntary and involuntary creditors under coordinated group policy. The Commission has not followed the recommendation of the Winter Report that proposed rules on procedural and substantive consolidations of bankruptcies of groups of companies in member states. Thus positive approaches taken by the Winter Report have been disregarded by the Commission. Examination of modern structural characteristics of MNEs indicates different realities since most groups already have improved organizational structure with a different nature of control than the Commission suggests.[44] Thus expecting corporate groups to extend their control over their subsidiaries by adopting coordinated group policy, while managerial theory forces them to adopt an organizational structure which gives more independence to subsidiaries, does not reflect the interdisciplinary characteristics of groups of companies. This situation is a result of the Commission's consideration of a group of companies as a simple vertical organization.

Thirdly, the Commission intends in the medium term to give further consideration to the risk inherent in abusive pyramids and, if necessary, make a legislative proposal to prohibit them from Stock Exchange listing. The argument of abusive pyramids is here referring to misuse of corporate form mostly in a technical way. It does not refer to the relationship between the operating subsidiaries and parent companies.

---

[43] Commission suggested that, 'listed companies should be required to include in their annual report and accounts a coherent and descriptive statements covering the key elements of their corporate governance structure and practices': COM/2003/0284 final, p. 12.

[44] See Chapter 2.

As a result the Winter Report and the Action Plan have failed to address the important characteristics of groups of companies. The recommendations in the Action Plan are too shallow to create fundamental changes in the area of corporate groups' liability in Europe.[45] It seems that in the short, medium and even long terms there is no intention to regulate the liability issues arising from the activities of groups of companies. Under those conditions it is impossible to discuss EU law's approach to MNEs since the group of companies law in Europe does not offer anything fundamental. As a result, apart from the aforementioned formulation of basic principles (recognition of the group's interest and protection of external shareholders and creditors), the EU has little room for progress on this subject.

Thus the positive approach taken by the EU in recognizing problems created by groups of companies turned out to be negative when it reached the Action Plan level. The EU has taken a very practical approach to groups of companies' problems and tried to find solutions for practical operational problems of groups. Thus they have ignored the substantive problems of liability. The Action Plan does not touch any problems that might create a huge debate in member countries. As discussed earlier, the issues of MNEs' liability have international characteristics and thus require more coordinated approaches by countries. The EU in this sense has many advantages in terms of creating general laws that binds states and individual in member countries.

The EU should therefore alter the Action Plan in terms of corporate group liability by covering MNEs as well. The new plan should consider the interdisciplinary realities of MNEs. Accordingly the new plan should aim to recognize the fact that MNEs might create problems when operating in their modern structure. Therefore the Plan should disassociate itself from the mistakes made by previous regulations in member states. Rather than bringing different approaches from various member states, the EU should go for innovative solutions and thus create a realistic corporate groups law that considers MNEs as horizontally structured organizations.

---

[45] A Consultation initiative by the Directorate General for Internal Market and Services shows that the issue of groups of companies' problems has not won professional support yet at EU level. The public hearing on future priorities for the Action Plan, organized in Brussels on 3 May 2006, gathered about 300 participants; 29 per cent of the respondents to the consultation addressed the issue of a potential EU initiative on groups, 67.5 per cent of them were opposed to the adoption of EU rules. Even the respondents supporting an EU intervention (31.1 per cent) specified that this should only concern transparency issues, especially for cross-border groups. See more at the Directorate General for Internal Market and Services Consultation and public hearing on future priorities for the Action Plan at http://ec.europa.eu/internal_market/company/consultation/index_en.htm#060706.

## THE FORUM EUROPEAUM: CORPORATE GROUP LAW OF EUROPE

The Forum Europaeum[46] emphasizes that corporate groups are a reality of life. Similar to the Action Plan, the Forum acknowledges the problems and seeks to clearly establish the legitimacy of the corporate group as a legal institution, as well as recognition of its interests and the exercise of management power by the entity controlling the group.[47] The Forum, like the Commission, recognizes that the two most important objectives of corporate group law are the protection of creditors and minority shareholders of subsidiaries. As a way to achieve this, the Forum has taken up the *Rozenblum* doctrine as a main principle,[48] which has been created by the French High Court. According to the doctrine, recognizing the interests of the group requires the practical confirmation of the existence of a solid entrepreneurial structure, a coherent group policy and internal balance between the burdens and advantages.[49]

The Forum claims that there is already a kind of harmonization of corporate groups in the EU under the rules of banking, insurance and the Seventh Directive on Consolidated Annual Accounts and many other individual laws which affect groups of companies.[50] However the Forum aims to limit the proposal just for company law excluding other branches of the law, such as environmental, labour, insolvency and tax.[51] This positive approach to the problem of corporate

---

46 The Forum Europaeum, Konzernrecht, consists of a steering committee. Together with many other European academics, the committee conducts the project 'Konzernrecht fur Europa' (Corporate Group Law for Europe). In an article, the Forum Europaeum makes proposals to the European and national legislatures for addressing the common problem of corporate groups in Europe. See Forum Europaeum Corporate Group Law, Corporate Group Law for Europe (2000) 1 EBOR 165. See for comments Kluver John, 'European and Australian Proposal for Corporate Group Law: A Comparative Analysis' (2000) 1 EBOR 287; Windbichler Christine, 'Corporate Group Law For Europe' Comment on the Forum Europeaum's Principles Proposal for a European Corporate Group Law' (2000) 1 EBOR 265.

47 Forum Europaeum, Corporate Group Law, p. 174.

48 Accordingly, three conditions must be fulfilled in order that the interest of the subsidiary can be legitimately subordinated. First, the group structure must be firmly established and commercial activities of the companies in the group must be interrelated in such a way that they exercise a negative as well as a positive influence on each other. Secondly, a coherent policy for the entire group must be in place; the requirement of group policy presupposes the existence of one inclusive overall group policy for the group as a whole. Thirdly, the advantages and disadvantages for each company must be properly distributed within the group so that a balance is maintained. See Forum Europaeum, Corporate Group Law.

49 Irujo, 'Trends and Realities'.

50 Forum Europaeum, Corporate Group Law, pp. 165–170.

51 *Ibid.* p. 180.

groups is very important. The Forum understands the complexity of scattered regulations under different branches of the law. In other words the Forum suggests that if there is a well-structured law that imposes liability on every member of the group, there will be no need for these complex regulations. Therefore, the most important characteristic of the Forum's proposals is that there is an urgent need to regulate corporate groups at EU level as well as reflecting these regulations in member states. The Forum indicates that harmonization must cover core areas of corporate law in the EU. It must create basic principles of groups of companies' regulations so it must leave some empty space for member states. Aiming a regulation at EU level is a very positive step. Thus the Forum, at least in principle, offers something braver than the Action Plan.

On close examination of the Forum's proposal, the rules proposed by the Forum will be based on the concept of 'control' within the meaning of Article 1(1) and Article 2 of the Seventh Directive. Under the articles, one company controls another company if it has a majority of voting rights; has the power to appoint or remove a majority of the members of the board of directors or the supervisory board; or has the right to exercise a dominant influence pursuant to a contract entered into with the controlled company or pursuant to a provision in the controlled company's constitution. They claim that this concept of control prevents uncertainty, thus should be preferred to dominance.[52] However, this understanding does not reflect the modern management structure of MNEs under which corporations operate as a group even though they do not meet the criteria of control suggested in the Seventh Directive.

The Forum Europaeum proposes that the EU should legitimize in all member states groups which are organized on an EU market-wide basis and thereby ensure that such groups as a whole and their subsidiaries operate on a solid legal basis. The Forum considers the French *Rozenblum* formula as a part of EU law must, in many respects, be merged with the law of each member state, which must regulate the penalties to be imposed in case of non-compliance.[53]

In the issue of the legal recognition of group management, the *Rozenblum* concept makes it possible for the management of subsidiary companies to subordinate the subsidiary to the interest of the group upon the fulfilment of certain conditions. Consequently under this formula, as set out in the Draft Directive of the Forum Europaeum, directors of a group company can act in the interests of the overall corporate group, and subordinate or sacrifice the interest of their own company, if:[54] (1) the corporate group has a balanced and firmly established structure; (2) the company took part in a long-term and coherent group policy;

---

52 *Ibid.* p. 188.
53 *Ibid.* p. 200.
54 Kluver, 'European and Australian'.

and (3) the directors in good faith reasonably assumed that any detriment suffered by their company would in due course be made good by other advantages.

In return for making use of this option of operating as a group, the company is not required to give up the legal independence of its subsidiaries. Rather the parent would be required to presume the liability for the commercial risks of a subsidiary.[55] Approval by the general meeting of the parent is a precondition for a legally effective group declaration. In addition to the entitlement of the parent to direct the management of the subsidiary, the legal consequences of the group declaration include the assumption by the parent of liability for losses incurred by the subsidiary in case of winding-up (creditor protection) and the obligation to compensate the minority shareholders in the subsidiary (minority shareholder protection). The special characteristic of the *Rozenblum* concept is that it does not, compared to the German law, oblige the parent company to provide exact compensation for every disadvantage inflicted on an individual subsidiary.[56] The obligation of the parent does not come into force at the end of the financial year, in opposition to the German Stock Corporation Law, but only: (1) on the opening of insolvency proceedings against the subsidiary; or (2) the effective revocation by the parent of the group declaration.[57] Therefore the liability is not a direct liability but a secondary liability because the parent liability occurs only if a subsidiary goes bankrupt or the parent revokes the group declaration.

The only direct liability of the parent company occurs in favour of the subsidiary's creditors only if the parent is considered as a shadow director.[58] If the criteria for such requirements are not met, then the parent is not required to take any action to rescue the subsidiary, or to accept liability for its debts. In summary, whereas the parent may be motivated to rescue a subsidiary, it has no obligation to do so. This means that the Forum proposes an obligation on a parent company to either rescue or wind up a subsidiary company that has reached 'crisis point', that is, where the subsidiary has 'no reasonable prospect' of avoiding insolvency through its own resources. A holding company which fails to act in these circumstances would be liable for any consequential losses of the subsidiary. An alternative proposal is to impose this liability only where a parent company has exercised actual control over the subsidiary.[59]

Here we can compare the proposed wrongful trading rules to the general idea of the English 'wrongful trading' rules, which regulates that if the directors are able to see that the company cannot continue to pay its debts, they must decide

55 Forum Europaeum, Corporate Group Law, p. 233.
56 *Ibid.* p. 235.
57 *Ibid.* p. 239.
58 *Ibid.* pp. 165–170.
59 Kluver, 'European and Australian', p. 250.

either to rescue the company or to put it into liquidation. Otherwise the directors will be liable fully or in part to creditors for their unpaid claims. The concept of wrongful trading applies both to independent companies and to companies within the groups. The directors of a subsidiary company are subject to the rules, as well as the parent company and its directors if they operate as de facto or 'shadow' directors of the subsidiary.

An extensive study on corporate groups should have produced a more advanced group liability regime. However, the Forum failed to do so. Rather they combine the regimes already proven ineffective due to misunderstandings of the managerial structure of the groups. Even though the Forum's proposal and the *Rozenblum* doctrine require a corporate group to have group structure and operate according to their group policy with balanced distribution of benefits and burdens amongst companies, the liability proposed is still the parent companys' liability. Also, there is no direct liability of the parent but just a secondary liability. Only direct liability is proposed in case of wrongful trading and is based on the excessive control of the parent over its subsidiaries.

Accordingly the Forum failed to absorb contemporary characteristics of MNEs into its proposals. The liability proposed is parent liability and the relationship between the subsidiary and the parent is considered as vertical rather than horizontal. Thus the parent is primarily responsible for subsidiaries' debts in certain conditions of close control. In reality the structures of corporate groups are more complex and control applied by the parent over its subsidiaries is not that simple. There is a complex cultural control in corporate groups that requires more independence for subsidiaries from the parent but more integration as a group by embracing other entities.[60] Under these conditions, it is unrealistic to expect MNEs to undertake the operational structure suggested by the Forum because it is not suitable for the most efficient managerial structure. Moreover the liability based on wrongful trading depends on certain conditions that are very difficult to prove under the modern structure.

As a general idea, the Forum's work is useful to emphasize the extent of importance of corporate groups in the modern business world. It once again points out the differences from the legal model of the single and unattached company. However the Forum entirely lacks innovatory proposals because all the typical missing points discussed in this book appear in the Forum's proposal as well. For example there are no special regulatory provisions for involuntarily creditors. Moreover there is no attempt to create special regulation for MNEs. Under these conditions, the involuntary creditors' protection against MNEs is totally unfilled. Even though the Forum suggests a need of unified regulation in the case of cross-border problems, they just ignore this by not considering the

---

[60] See Chapter 2.

problems that MNEs create. In particular it is not clear what happens if the law governing the subsidiary, the supposedly protected part, does not provide for the group declaration or states different rights and obligations compared to the parent's law. Similarly the substantive law with the possible international private law questions is not addressed.[61]

The overall evaluation of the Forum's proposals suggests that the Forum fails to produce new and evolutionary suggestions. The proposals are rather a mixture of legal principles developed in various jurisdictions in the EU to prevent abuses of corporate law principles by groups of companies. The *Rozenblum* from France, wrongful trading from England and qualified groups from Germany have been mixed. Thus one can easily claim that, after the unsuccessful Ninth Directive, the participants thought it would be more likely to reach agreement if they can manage to bring together principles developed in basic jurisdictions in Europe. However, it should not be forgotten that the legal principles in one jurisdiction are always attractive to the professionals in other jurisdictions; for example, the French doctrine of *Rozenblum* and English doctrine of wrongful trading have been criticized by many academics from these jurisdictions.[62]

Approaching the issues with a more general perspective reveals that the substantive liability in the proposal of the Forum should be read in the light of the concept of 'control'. In the extensive examination of MNE structure it has been proven that the concept of control in corporate groups is different from the way it is perceived in legal studies.[63] The Forum fell into this common misconception of corporate groups since they never mention horizontally structured enterprises. They are unaware of the modern conception of the corporate groups. Moreover case law examination apparently proves that founding liability on the basis of control is unsatisfactory.[64] Thus building the new liability proposal on the control principles is a mistake and the life of the proposal will be short unless the Forum considers the modern managerial structure of MNEs.

[61] Windbichler Christine, 'Corporate Group Law for Europe: Comment on the Forum Europeaum's Principles Proposal for a European Corporate Group Law' (2000) 1 EBOR 265.

[62] *Ibid.*

[63] See Chapter 2.

[64] See Chapter 5.

## EUROPEAN COMPETITION LAW LITIGATION: GROUP AS SINGLE ECONOMIC UNIT

One should expect more fundamental and up-to-date development in competition law because of the multi-disciplinary characteristics of the anti-trust issues. Consequently the emerging EC competition law represents one of the most recent attempts to legislate on groups of companies for anti-competitive behaviours. As a principle, where a subsidiary is wholly owned by its parent company and it is found as a matter of fact that the subsidiary is not able to engage in economic action that is autonomous of its parent company, then in spite of their separate legal identities, the two companies will be regarded as one for the purposes of EC competition law.[65]

In the cases of *Centrafarm v Sterling*[66] and *Viho Europe BV v Commission of European Communities*[67] the ECJ decided that where a company and its subsidiaries are formed as a single economic unit, the subsidiaries cannot enjoy any real autonomy in determining their operations. Consequently the most established basis in EC competition law for asserting jurisdiction and liability over foreign companies is the doctrine of the group as a 'single economic unit'. This doctrine features the foreign parent's responsibility for the anti-competitive activities of a subsidiary that is present and active in Europe and over which they supposedly exert some control. Thus the issue comes to the notion of theory of control, how to determine and how to apply it.[68] Owing to the supposed control that the parent can exert and should have exerted over the subsidiary, the parent, and other relevant members of the group, may be brought within the jurisdiction of European law.[69] The court has emphasized the corporate structural relationship between the parent and the subsidiary and merely considered

---

65 See further Jones, A. and Sufrin, B., *EC Competition Law* (OUP, Oxford 2007), pp. 141–146; Montesa, A. and Givaja, A., 'When Parents Pay for Their Children's Wrongs: Attribution of Liability for EC Antitrust Infringements in Parent-subsidiary Scenarios' (2006) 29 World Competition 555. Similarly, the US Supreme Court in *Copperweld Corp v Independence Tube Corp.* [1984] 467 US 752, has held that a parent and wholly owned subsidiary have a complete unity of interest and because a parent can assert full control at any moment if a subsidiary fails to act in a parent's interest, the parent and subsidiary have a unity of purpose or common design that belies a section 1 Sherman Act of 1890 agreement. See Prell, Owen T. 'Copperweld Corp. v. Independence Tube Corp.: An End to the Intraenterprise Conspiracy Doctrine?' (1986) 71 Cornell Law Review 1151–1180; Gavil, A.I., 'Copperweld 2000: The Vanishing Gap between Sections 1 and 2 of the Sherman Act' (2000) 68 Antitrust L.J. 87.

66 *Centrafarm v Sterling* [1974] ECR 1147.

67 *Viho Europe BV v Commission of European Communities* (Case C-73/95P).

68 Jones and Sufrin, *EC Competition Law*, pp. 141–146.

69 Case 48/69 *ICI v Commission* [1972] ECR 619, CMLR 557, *Viho Europe BV v Commission* [1996] ECR I-5457, C-286/98; *Stora v Comission* [2000] ECR I-9925. See

the parent's ability to control the latter, rather than whether that control was actually exercised.[70]

The court ruled that 'the fact that a subsidiary has separate legal personality is not sufficient to exclude the possibility of imputing its conduct to the parent company… in the circumstances, the formal separation between these companies, resulting from their separate legal personality, cannot outweigh the unity of their conduct on the market for the purposes of applying the rules on competition'.[71] Accordingly the ECJ held that where a subsidiary does not enjoy real autonomy in determining its course of action in the market, the prohibitions set out in Article 81(1) of the EU Treaty might be considered inapplicable in the relationship between it and the parent company with which it forms one economic unit.[72] The application of single economic unit theory in EC competition judgment requires certain conditions. First, the parent and subsidiaries should form an economic unit as explained in *Viho*: 'an economic unit within which the subsidiary has no real freedom to determine its course of action in the market because the parent company permanently supervises the making of decisions by, and the administration of, its subsidiary'. Secondly, the agreements must be solely intended to carry out internal allocation of tasks as between the undertakings.[73]

The examination of the principles indicates that the requirements can only be met by the vertically organized corporate groups because clear control established by a parent over its subsidiaries is apparent only in such groups. The examination of the group subjected to the judgment in *Viho* case indicates that Parker Pen Ltd controls its subsidiaries and is involved in decision making in its subsidiaries in Belgium, Germany, the Netherlands, France and Spain. The key decisions are taken by the parent. For example the parent limits the subsidiaries' area of operations to their own jurisdiction. The examination of other cases indicates similar characteristics that corporate groups brought under the judgment of the ECJ for constituting single economic unit have characteristics similar to vertically organized corporate groups.[74] Accordingly in the cases, there was a control or supposed control by the parent over its subsidiaries and there was a one-way parent liability for this control.

---

Montesa and Givaja, 'When Parents Pay'; Goyder D.G, *EC Competition Law* (OUP, Oxford 2003), p. 499.

[70] Goyder, *EC Competition Law*, p. 500.

[71] *Centrafarm BV v Sterling Drug Inc.* [1974] ECR 1147.

[72] The group economic unit concept was confirmed in the following cases: *Centrafarm BV v Sterling Drug Inc.*; *Instituto Chemioterapico Italiano and Commercial Solvent Corporations v Commission cases* 6-7/73 [1974] ECR 223; *Shell v Commission* [1992] ECR II-884.

[73] *Viho Europe BV.*

[74] See Chapter 2.

Thus the analysis of competition case law demonstrates that the single economic entity theory applied in anti-trust cases by the ECJ has some similarities of veil-piercing doctrine.[75] In the cases, the separate legal personality of the Community subsidiary is ignored in order to reach its corporate shareholders. However, the single economic unit argument in the EU competition law has more advanced features in comparison to the veil-piercing theory in two aspects. First, the required nature of control in the group of companies is less strict than the required level in veil-piercing cases because the court looks for supposed control rather than actual control of the parent. This makes imposing liability on the parent company easier. The second point is the extra-territorial application of the anti-trust ruling on foreign parent companies; the policy in the EU is to extent the applicability of competition rules to companies outside of the jurisdictional barriers of the EU.[76]

However, it seems that this relatively flexible approach is only considered in competition rulings and the single economic unit argument does not ignore the separate personality of the companies under the group. It rather establishes supposed control on the parent because of the difficulty of proving the independent economic decisions by the subsidiary in the common economic policy of the group. However, in the supposed control theory, it is always possible to escape liability by proving that there was no control over a subsidiary by the parent because the nature of supposed control is not clearly defined by the courts. In many cases, the courts still require additional factual examination of the relation between the parent and subsidiary before assuming control.[77] Moreover there are certain difficulties to presume control over partly-owned subsidiaries,[78] and the situation where the parent company is minority shareholder but it is sufficient to exert control is not yet clarified.[79] The presumption of control is rebuttable; in this sense, the courts failed to define clear criteria to determine in which conditions the presumption of control can be rebutted. Accordingly the Commission has to provide evidence to hold a parent liable if the parent provides negative evidence that it did not exert control over the subsidiary.[80] In theory, in competition law cases, there can be attribution of liability if one company controls the others and all the decisions are taken by the control-

---

75 Schenck, Daniel W., 'Jurisdiction over the Foreign Multinational in the EEC: Lifting the Veil on the Economic Entity Theory' (1989–1990) 11 U. Pa. J. Int'l Bus. L. 495.

76 *ICI v Commission*; See Jones and Sufrin, *EC Competition Law*, p. 145.

77 Montesa and Givaja, 'When Parents Pay'.

78 Even the presumption of control is not always invoked by the Commission. See for cases Montesa and Givaja, 'When Parents Pay'.

79 Whish, R. *Competition Law* ( Butterworths, London 2003), p. 88.

80 Montesa and Givaja, 'When Parents Pay'.

ling company, disregarding ownership relationship between companies but all the cases in that argument have been brought against parent companies.[81] For example the Commission does not apply presumption of control theory between the twin companies.[82] Thus liability is imposed only on a parent company for their control over the subsidiaries.

Accordingly the liability regime that is designed according to a belief in a sharp and vertical control theory in corporate groups cannot be applied to complex structure of MNEs under which there is a horizontal organizational structure and cultural control. Thus it is difficult to assume control in every case involving corporate groups; in case of assumption it is easier to rebut the control under modern structure. Accordingly, in some recent cases the Commission refused to apply assumption of control.[83] For example, in the *MCAA* decision, the Commission argued that a 'group of companies and business units that are dependent on a corporate centre for the basic orientation of their commercial strategy and operations, for their investments and finances, for their legal affairs and for their leadership cannot be considered to constitute an economic unit in their own right'.[84]

## EUROPEAN UNION: ADDING MORE COMPLEXITY TO THE PROBLEM OF LIABILITY

Given the urgency of the liability problems in MNEs' activities, the EU, in the interest of involuntary creditors, should recognize corporate groups as a modern organizational form. The regulation of groups of companies in certain areas of practice in order to solve very specific problems does not create a required level of tort liability in corporate groups. Moreover not having inclusive recognition of the groups might cause regulatory competition amongst the member states. The mistake of the EU is that during the period of attempts to regulate, it seemed to prefer a corporate group law based on the formulation of major standards, leaving precise features relating to the formation and operation of corporate groups to the member states or, where applicable, to self-regulation.[85] Exposing the company groups to different legal requirements or differentiated extent of

81 *Ibid.*

82 C-196/99 *Siderursia Aristrain Madrid SL v Commission* [2003] ECR I-1105. See further Montesa and Givaja, 'When Parents Pay'.

83 *Souris-Topps*, Commission Decision of May 2004, Case COMP/37.980, *PO/Yamaha*, Commission Decision of 16 July 2003, Case COMP/37.975.

84 *MCAA*, Commission Decision of 19 July 2005, Case COMP/E-1/37773. See further Montesa and Givaja, 'When Parents Pay'.

85 Irujo, 'Trends and Realities'.

liability according to the laws of the individual member states only complicates and endangers the rights of all creditors at the European level.[86]

Moreover the contents of regulations in the EU are too shallow and exclude many basics. The discussions show that from the beginning, including the Ninth Directive, attempts have failed to provide satisfactory solutions. The Commission's Action Plan and even specific study of the Forum Europeaum have failed to address the problem of MNEs' liability. They even have failed to articulate the problems. This failure to articulate problems has prevented interdisciplinary approaches to groups of companies' problems. Therefore the discussions still concentrate on the control theory.

The deadlock of the control theory, a certain degree of control over the subsidiary imposed by the parent, has not been overcome by any law or proposal at the European level. The Winter Report, the Action Plan and the Forum Europaeum fail to understand that when a regulatory work is based on the idea of control, there is always the possibility of avoiding tort liability because the nature of corporate group structure is not exactly as simple as to be covered by the control theory.[87] There will be huge obstacles to enforcing liability in horizontally organized groups and in regards to MNEs it will be almost impossible to make them accountable for their torts.

The misconception that groups of companies are vertically organized groups, that the parent controls subsidiaries and they operate under the common policy of the parent is still very common. For this reason, in the short term, the possibility of development of groups' notions at the Community level appears to be linked to the adoption of measures of general application containing some specific provisions to be applied to vertically structured enterprises. None of these specific provisions seem to be solving liability problems. As a result because of this common belief of corporate groups as a vertical organization, the legislators, courts and scholars cannot produce better proposals for establishing liability other than liability based on the control theory. However the reality is much more complex in a horizontal organization; the control is completely spread over the subsidiaries and replaced by more common group policy and principles. Companies operate according to policies of the group even in some occasions with no instruction from the centre. In case of a need for direction, the subsidiaries might refer to the parent or sub-parents or other specialized subsidiaries on particular policy creating such as advertisement, information technology, finance and insurance.[88]

---

86 Lombardo, Stefano, 'Conflict of Law Rules in Company Law After *Uberseering*: An Economic and Comparative Analysis of the Allocation of Policy Competence in the European Union' (2003) 4 EBOR 301.

87 See Chapter 2.

88 See Chapter 2.

Therefore it is obvious that being in a group means operating under a complex structure of cultural control and common group policies. Thus there is no particular need to develop a theory that requires many more non-provable conditions in order to make parent companies liable. The European legislators should restart the future efforts from this innovative approach and new proposals should cover national, union-based and transnational enterprises because there is barely another field of law that is better suited for a common European development by jurisprudence than the law of groups of companies. Moreover since groups of companies are operating to a great extent across the barriers of national borders, no national legislation has yet found a complete system but in all of them there seems great public demand for regulation, which can be the trigger to develop a common group of companies' law of Europe.[89] The regulatory concept must cover protection measures against a misuse of subsidiaries established abroad. This issue of protection of people from the hazard of MNEs under the basic principles of the European rules must not be ignored.[90] Tort victims could thus be identified as eligible for general interest status at the EU level from the public policy aspects and thus a form of protection must be built to defend their interests.[91]

## GERMAN STOCK CORPORATIONS ACT 1965

Unlike most other systems, German law has a specific set of rules applicable to groups of companies. These rules are contained in the Stock Corporations Act of 1965. Articles 15–19 define different forms of the enterprise connection and Articles 291–337 contain the substantive provisions. The law on groups of companies deals with the balancing of interests in situations where one enterprise controls the business policies of one or more other enterprises, by directly or indirectly influencing the management of the controlled enterprises.

A group is formed either when a controlling and one or more dependent enterprises are combined under a uniform management of the controlling enterprise or when enterprises which are legally and factually independent of each other come under uniform management. It is presumed that a dependent enterprise forms a group with the controlling enterprise.[92] The concepts of

---

89 Lutter, Marcus, 'The Law of Groups of Companies in Europe' (1983) 1 Forum Internationale, p. 1.

90 Haar, Brigitte, 'Piercing Veil And Shareholder's Product And Environmental Liability in American Law as Remedies for Capital Market Failures – New Developments and Implications for European and German Law After *Centros*' (2000) 1 EBOR 317.

91 Lombardo, Conflict of Law.

92 Avgitidis, *Group of Companies*, p. 189.

controlling influence and uniform management are not defined in the statute. In general it is considered that an enterprise is in a situation to exercise a controlling power if it has authority to make another enterprise comply with its wishes; methods used for this purpose are irrelevant. The controlling influence may be capable of being exercised either by means of major participation in the dependent enterprise or by means of a control contract or by means of the power to control the composition of the management board of the dependent enterprise or by means of the fact that the boards of both enterprises are essentially composed of the same persons.[93] The law divides corporate groups into three classes: integration concerns, contract concerns and de facto concerns.

*Integration concerns*: where a parent holds between 95 and 100 per cent of the stock of a subsidiary, the two companies can agree to integrate officially. The integrated group consists of a parent and wholly owned subsidiaries, which agree to subject themselves formally to the uniform management of the parent that, in exchange, becomes responsible for all their obligations. The chief company is liable to the creditors of the integrated company, jointly and severally, for all its debts and obligations arising before or after the combination. An agreement to the contrary has no effect against third parties. Even though the integration concern has no practical importance, its liability concept has been praised because of its crucial effect that removes the limited liability of the principal enterprise for the obligations of the integrated enterprises. Unlimited liability is the price that the parent has to pay for its unlimited power to direct the operations of the subsidiaries because the parent assumes this liability merely upon integration, without any further requirement.[94]

*Contractual concerns*: the expectation before enactment of the law was that corporate groups linked through control agreements would become the most popular form of corporate groups because control agreements are the only legal way for a parent to acquire broad managing power over its subsidiary corporations.[95] In practice, though, control agreements have been rarely used.[96]

A control contract is usually concluded between a controlling enterprise and one or more enterprises, which are dependent on it. Contractual groups are combined on a basis of a contract of domination whereby a firm subjects itself to management by another. The contract of domination thus changes the organi-

---

93 See *Ibid.* p. 230.

94 *Ibid.* p. 232.

95 Dine, Janet, *The Governance of Corporate Groups* (CUP, Cambridge 2000), p. 59.

96 Assmann, H., 'Microcorporatist Structures in German Law on Groups of Companies' in Sugarman, D. and Teubner, G. (eds) *Regulating Corporate Groups in Europe* (Baden-Baden, Nomos 1990).

zational structure of the now dependent firm.[97] This broad authority of the controlling enterprise in directing the controlled is balanced by the principal enterprise's obligation to compensate the dependent firm for every annual loss, which has occurred during the term of agreement. However, the nature of liability is not a direct liability so the creditors of the dependent enterprise have no right of action against the controlling enterprise but they can enforce the compensation claim against it in accordance with the powers given to them by the civil procedure rules.[98] Because of this complex nature of the contractual concern the contracts were very few, as very well described by the great majority of the courts and commentators, parent corporations have chosen 'cohabitation without marriage certificates'.[99]

*De facto concerns*: as in general practice all over the world, most German parent and subsidiary companies are merely linked through stock ownership so majority stock ownership generates the presumption that subsidiaries are dependent on their parents. Thus Article 311(1) of the Act provides that in the absence of an integration or a control contract, a controlling enterprise may not use its influence to cause a dependent corporation to enter into any transaction, to cause it to take or refrain from taking any measure that may be damaging unless adequate compensation is made to the dependent corporation.[100]

According to Article 317, where the controlling enterprise fails to compensate the dependent firm for any imposed disadvantages by the end of the fiscal year, the controlling enterprise and the responsible legal representatives become jointly and severally liable to the dependent firm for any loss.[101] However, Article 317(2) provides an exemption from liability on the condition that if it is established that an orderly and careful manager of an independent company would also have entered into a similar transaction or taken or omitted to take the same measure.[102] Therefore in order to establish liability under these provisions a plaintiff must prove not only that a controlling enterprise exercised a damaging influence over the management of the dependent corporation, but also the extent of any loss or injury incurred by the dependent corporation as a result of the detrimental influence and the absence of adequate compensation on the part of the controlling enterprise.[103] Consequently as Hofstetter defines, these

---

97 Assmann, 'Microcorporatist Structures'.

98 Avgitidis, *Group of Companies*, p. 234.

99 Hopt, Klaus J., 'Legal Elements and Policy Decisions in Regulating Group of Companies' in Wooldridge, F. and Schmitthoff, C.M. (eds), *Groups of Companies* (Sweet & Maxwell, London 1991).

100 Assmann, 'Microcorporatist Structures', p. 347.

101 Avgitidis, *Group of Companies*, p. 235.

102 Assmann, 'Microcorporatist Structures', p. 348.

103 *Ibid.* p. 349.

provisions are a dead letter since successful actions for damages under them are apparently unknown.[104]

*Qualified de facto group*: since the German Stock Corporations Act turned out to be ineffective in various aspects, most notably as regards the provisions for de facto concerns, in the area of parent liability, the German Federal Court has articulated special rules, 'qualified de facto concerns' which is a corporate group structure in which the parent, as a sole shareholder, applies a long-lasting and persistent control pattern over the relationships of its subsidiary. In a qualified de facto group, a private limited company is subject to continuous and complete influence in management matters by dominating the enterprise which has a continuing disadvantageous influence on the dominated company's own interests. There has to be a fact-specific inquiry to prove the controlling interest.

Consequently the qualified concern is a relatively efficient German corporate-parent liability model because where the boundary between the parent and its subsidiary corporations becomes so intense as to make them inseparable to outsiders, there is an assumption that the subsidiary has no real mind to control itself. Thus in case of damage to subsidiaries' creditors, the burden of proof that there is no damaging influence on the subsidiary by this dominant control shifts to the parent.[105] Thus direct liability applies where a hierarchical relationship has been established between the parent and the subsidiary. Consequently this interpretation, in theory, suggests a sound belief of parent liability for the tort of the subsidiary.[106]

In a specific case examination, in *Autokran*,[107] it was held that where a parent company was permanently and extensively involved in the management of a subsequently bankrupt subsidiary, a rebuttable presumption exists that the parent did not show adequate consideration for the subsidiary. Hence unless the parent is able to defend itself successfully, it is directly liable to creditors for the subsidiary's obligations.[108] Similarly, in *ITT*,[109] the German Federal Court decided that the parent corporation's control of a close corporation by its majority influence had a fiduciary duty to the close corporation.[110] It is now generally thought

---

104 Hofstetter, 'Parent Responsibility'.

105 Stone Alicia, 'Parent Corporate Liability for Hazardous Substance Release from On-Shore Facilities in the International Market: Legal Approaches of the United States, the European Community and Germany' (1992) 12 In. Pub. Interest 57.

106 Assmann, 'Microcorporatist Structures'.

107 BGHZ 95, 330.

108 Hofstetter, 'Parent Responsibility'; Marlow Jennifer 'Germany: Company Law: Lifting the Corporate Veil' (1993) 4 ICCLR 133.

109 BGHZ 1976 JZ 561.

110 Schiessl, M., 'The Liability of Corporations and Shareholders for the Capitalization and Obligations of Subsidiaries Under German Law' (1986) 7 Nw J. Int'l L & Bus. 480.

that it follows from the relevant cases that such an undertaking holding shares in a dependent company has a duty of good faith in all its relationships with the company and its shareholders. The parent is forbidden from exercising any detrimental influence on that company.[111]

The former decisions of the Supreme Court concerning such groups had placed emphasis on the controlling undertaking's lasting and comprehensive involvement in the management of the dependent company, and had made use of definite presumptions in order to impose liability on the controlling company. However the decision in *Video*[112] caused a great deal of argument in the legal profession.[113] In a series of cases leading to the *Video* case, which included *Autokran* and *Tiefbau*[114] the court determined when the single or majority shareholder of a private limited company was to be directly liable if the company failed to fulfil its own obligations and liabilities.[115] In *Video*, the Supreme Court held that a defendant who participated in a private limited company, which were video undertakings, and also carried on a business of his own, was to be regarded as an undertaking.[116] The court went further than previous decisions holding an individual, even though not a corporate enterprise, could be held personally liable for the losses of the subsidiary if he is both the sole managing director and majority shareholder of the subsidiary and he engages in business activities outside the subsidiary as sole owner.[117] The court with this approach held that the controlling shareholder conducting his own business must be responsible for the losses of the controlled company if he could not otherwise prove that such losses had not arisen from actions he had taken for the benefit of his own business. The importance of the *Video* cases lies under the fact that, in making this judgment, the court had successfully transferred the traditional burden of proof away from the plaintiff to the defendant-controlling shareholder.[118]

However, in the *TBB*[119] decision in 1993, the Supreme Court elucidating its earlier judgment held that the shareholder should not be liable simply because it could not invalidate the presumption of control, but rather the plaintiff creditor must establish justifications and prove that the shareholder's act had actually damaged the business of the dependent company. Where the plaintiff is not in a

---

[111] Wooldridge, F., 'The Situation of Dependent Gmbh in a De Facto Group in German law' (1996) Journal of Business Law 627.

[112] 115 BGHZ 187 (1991).

[113] Marlow, 'Germany'.

[114] GBHZ 107, 7.

[115] Marlow, 'Germany'.

[116] Wooldridge, 'The Situation of Dependent'.

[117] Marlow, 'Germany'.

[118] *Ibid.*

[119] Zeitschrift fur Wirtschaftsrecht (1993) 589.

position to know certain matters, the shareholder must make the information available, provided that he is in a position to know such information and the release of such information is reasonable. With this decision, the Supreme Court in effect transferred the burden of proof back to the other side, so that the creditor must first prove that the dependent company has suffered a loss rather than this being an automatic presumption, which must be rebutted by the shareholder.[120]

As a result, whereas the previous decisions based the obligation of the liability on the controlling enterprise on the presumption of detriment to the dependent enterprise where there was comprehensive and lasting control over its affairs, the Supreme Court in *TBB* took a totally different view. The Supreme Court held that the basis of liability in the previous cases was not lasting and comprehensive control over the dependent company but a prejudice caused to its interests. Such prejudice could not, in the opinion of the court, be said to occur on a basis of presumption resulting from such a control. Its existence had to be based on additional factors.[121] However, because of the difficulties in articulating detrimental transactions and measures, the Supreme Court considered that a lesser burden of particularizing and giving evidence of facts should be imposed on a creditor of a subsidiary who lacked insight into the affairs of the group. It was the defendant who, according to the Court's opinion, should bear the burden of giving fuller evidence for facts.[122]

In any event, the qualified de facto group concept constitutes, at least in theory, a significant step towards the issue of the imposition of liability on the controlling enterprise. In spite of the absence of integration and of control contract, liability may be imposed on a parent company merely upon evidence of a continuous and extensive interference with the subsidiary's management (according to the previous approach) or upon some evidence of prejudice of the subsidiary's interest (according to the approach taken in *TBB*).[123] However, changing the burden of proof in its latest decisions (*TBB*) the German Supreme Court made it very difficult to establish liability over parent corporation for its excessive control on the subsidiary company. In highly complex and integrated modern corporate groups with horizontal structures, it can become almost impossible for outsiders to trace and prove past violations of the subsidiary's interests by the parent. Thus shifting the burden of proof to the parent company in a way similar to the previous doctrine might be the only way to rebalance the situation.[124] The decision of *TBB* has had a negative effect on the development process of the group liability in Germany.

---

120 Marlow, 'Germany'.
121 Avgitidis, *Group of Companies,* p. 244.
122 *Ibid.*
123 *Ibid.* p. 246.
124 Hofstetter, 'The Ecological Liability'.

Although being more than four decades old, it is still claimed that German law on corporate groups is the most advanced in the world and seen as an alternative to the traditional piercing the corporate veil law in the corporate group context.[125] It has, more importantly, encouraged the evolution of an advanced German judge-made law outside the scope of the Stock Corporation Act.[126] Thus the qualified concern doctrine of the German Federal Court seems, at least in principle, well differentiated and promising.[127]

However, it should not be thought that, according to the German company law principles, public and private limited liability companies are independent legal entities. The shareholders, including company shareholders, have no personal liability for the commitments of the company. The shareholders of the company can be held personally liable if they have violated their fiduciary duties,[128] because the original legislator of the Act did not want to implement a strict and direct liability over the parent company. This explains why instead of direct liability of the parent company in respect to the subsidiary's creditors, the legislator provided a flexible compensation obligation of the parent company in these particular cases.

As a result the courts have until now only treated the problems of material under-capitalization in connection with the abuse of position. Therefore it is neither required by law nor necessary in itself to interpret the shareholders' liability against the will of the legislators.[129] The legal consequences of the qualified factual group are supposed to be similar to the contractual group of companies; in this case the parent company is likewise obliged to cover the annual losses. Here, again, there is no direct liability of the parent company for the debts of its subsidiaries but an indirect liability for their losses.[130] Therefore under German law, the liability of the parent company for the debts of its subsidiaries clearly remains an exception. Even for wholly owned subsidiaries such a liability does not normally exist; instead indirect forms of protection of the interests of the subsidiary and its creditors have been introduced.

There has also been a considerable amount of controversy about the exact nature of the liability in the qualified de facto group. Lutter argues that this is based upon conduct, namely the breach of the rules governing the proper man-

---

125 Hofstetter, 'Parent Responsibility'.

126 *Ibid.*

127 Hofstetter, 'The Ecological Liability'.

128 Stender, Jens Christopher, 'Company Law (Case Comment) Germany: Company Law – Lifting the Corporate Veil' (1999) 10 ICCLR 71.

129 *Ibid.*

130 Lutter, M., 'The Liability of the Parent Company for the Debts of its Subsidiaries Under German Law (1985) JBL 499.

agement of a group.[131] Hommelhoff[132] challenges that by claiming that liability is based upon results, such as the use of management powers in the dependent company in a way that its interests are subordinated to those of the controlling undertaking.[133] It can be claimed in the comparative examination that the German qualified de facto group liability is a German interpretation of veil-piercing law because it finds its basic principles in existence of the close and extensive control exercised by the parent over its subsidiaries. Whenever liability is imposed on the parent, this is done mainly on the grounds of the parent's managerial control over the subsidiary. Moreover the issue dealt with in the Act is not the problem of liability but the problem of compensation. Therefore in spite of the difference in approach, there are many similarities in language and result between the German law and the rules for such groups under the piercing the corporate veil doctrine.[134] In the German law, the typical problems of unlimited liability are solved by 'piercing the corporate veil in an orderly manner'.[135] In de facto concerns or qualified de facto concerns and after the case of *TBB*, the corporate groups can always avoid liability by proving their control on the company was not reason for the loss or they have no control in the first place.

In a modern MNE, all subsidiaries have independence and ability to make important decisions under the common group policy, but German groups of companies' law just depends on the dependence of the subsidiary to its parent. Thus this law will be applicable to only small-sized companies or better suited to private limited companies rather than huge public limited companies. In a horizontally organized MNEs group, many legally independent companies come under organized management. The German law does not contain any special provisions governing such groups.[136] In such groups there is no apparent control over any subsidiary but there is a common group policy, cultural control and extensive communication so the source of decision-making cannot be traced, which gives subsidiaries the tools to claim to be independent in many cases.[137] The qualified de facto concern is insufficient from this perspective because it considers only simplified vertically structured corporate groups. Moreover,

---

131 *Ibid.*

132 Hommelhoff, P., 'Protection of Minority Shareholders, Investors and Creditors in Corporate Groups: The Strengths and Weakness of German Corporate Group Law' (2001) 2 EBOR 61.

133 Wooldridge, 'The Situation of Dependent'.

134 Schiessl, 'The Liability of Corporations'.

135 Haar, 'Piercing Veil'.

136 Wooldridge, F., 'Connected Undertakings and Groups of Undertakings Under German Law' (1995) 24 Anglo-American Law Review 57.

137 See Chapter 2.

according to German private international law, German Stock Corporation Law is applicable if the controlled company is located in Germany, whether or not the controlling company is located abroad, but is not applicable if only the controlling but not the controlled company is located in Germany.[138]

## GROUPS OF COMPANIES IN ARBITRATION

In international arbitration cases, there is a question with which both arbitrators and the courts are frequently confronted as to whether an arbitration agreement signed by a member of a group of companies can be extended to include another company of the same group, which has not signed the agreement.[139] The question has been responded to in different ways; in most cases arbitrators applied the doctrine of separate legal personality and limited liability. In a situation where justice requires further liability, they have searched solutions on the basic principles of the existing law, which depends on the veil-piercing doctrine, agency arguments or estoppels. In some cases the arbitration tribunals created a new doctrine called 'group of companies doctrine'. The doctrine provides extending the jurisdictional scope of an arbitration clause to the non-signatory parent company or other companies in the group.[140] Consequently the doctrine can in some circumstances expose one side that has a valid arbitration agreement with one member of a group of companies to an award against them in favour of other companies in the same group.[141]

The basic justifications for the 'groups of companies' theory are the single economic unit argument and the development process of the relationship between parties. First, under the doctrine, if a group of companies constitute the same economic reality, one company in the group can bind the other members to an agreement. Secondly, if the result conformed to the mutual intentions of all the parties and reflected the good usage of international commerce, extension of the award is justifiable on the basis of the parties' express or implied intention. The group of companies' doctrine provides that an arbitration agreement

---

[138] Rinze, Jens, 'Konzernrecht: Law on Groups of Companies in Germany' (1993) 14 Comp. Law 143.

[139] See Gaillard, E. and Savage, J (eds), *Fouchard Gaillard Goldman on International Commercial Arbitration* (Kluwer Law International, London 1999) paras 500–506; Gaffney J.P. 'The Group of Companies Doctrine and the Law Applicable to the Arbitration Agreement' (2004) 19 Mealey's International Arbitration Report 6.

[140] Lamm, S.B. and Aqua, J.A., 'Defining the Party – Who is a Proper Party in an International Arbitration Before the American Arbitration Association and Other International Institution' (2002–2003) 34 Geo. Wash. Int'l L. Rev. 711.

[141] Leadley, J. and Williams, L., 'Peterson Farms: There is No Group of Companies Doctrine in English Law' (2004) 7 Int ALR 111.

signed by one company in a group of companies entitles or obligates affiliated non-signatory companies, if the circumstances surrounding negotiation, execution and termination of the agreement show that the mutual intention of all the parties was to bind the non-signatories.

Arbitrators acting under the International Chamber of Commerce (ICC) demonstrate a strong tendency to recognize that an arbitration agreement signed by a company belonging to a group of companies obligates and entitles the other member companies of such a group if that agreement fulfils certain minimum requirements.[142] The tendency is strongest among the supporters of *lex mercatoria*. Following the *Dow Chemical* decision and ICC cases numbered 2375[143] and 5103,[144] the tribunal recognized that since a group of companies constitutes the same economic reality, one company in the group can bind the other members to an agreement if such a result conforms to the mutual intentions of all the parties and reflects the good usage of international commerce.

These rulings of the ICC have found strong support from French jurisprudence so the group of companies' theory has had its consequences on the rulings of French courts, which seem persuaded to follow the new theory as evidenced by the judgment of *Dow Chemical v Isover Saint Gobain*[145] under which the group of companies' doctrine originated.[146] Two Dow Chemical companies entered into contracts with the respondent, a French company, for the distribution of thermal isolation equipment. The agreements contained ICC arbitration clauses and provided that deliveries could be made to the distributor by any Dow company. Two other Dow Chemical companies afterwards faced litigation over one of the products and sought to pass their liability on to the distributor by way of ICC arbitration. The French distributor argued that the tribunal's jurisdiction only allowed it to deliver awards in favour of the two Dow Chemical companies with which it had a direct contract. The tribunal then held that the group of companies represented by Dow Chemicals constituted one and the same economic reality and assumed jurisdiction over the companies that had

---

[142] Sandrock, Otto, 'Arbitration Agreements and Group of Companies' (1993) 27 International Lawyer 941.

[143] ICC award 2375 1985 Rev. Arb. 583, 1976 Journal du Droit International 978; See Hanotiau, B., 'Problems Raised by Complex Arbitrations Involving Multiple Contracts–Parties–Issues–an Analysis' (2001) Journal of International Arbitration 252–360; Hanotiau, B., *Complex Arbitrations* (Kluwer Law International, London 2005) paras 104–110.

[144] ICC Matter No 5103 1988 Journal du Droit International 1206. See Sandrock, 'Arbitration Agreements'.

[145] ICC Interim Award of 23 September 1982 in No 4131, 1984 Rev. Arb. 98. See Born, G.A., *International Commercial Arbitration* (Kluwer Law International, London 2001), p. 654.

[146] For more cases see Sandrock, 'Arbitration Agreements'.

not been named as parties to the contract.[147] Therefore the arbitrators held that the arbitration clause signed by two of the companies was also intended by the parties to be available to other companies in the group, commenting that:[148] 'Irrespective of the distinct juridical identity of each of its members, a group of companies constitutes one and the same economic reality of which the arbitral tribunal should take account when it rules on its own jurisdiction subject to Article 13 (1955 version) or Article 8 (1975 version) of the ICC Rules.'[149]

Since *Dow Chemical*, the group of companies' doctrine has been followed in a number of ICC Tribunal decisions, such as ICC Case No 5103 and the *KIS France SA v SA Société Générale*[150] decision of French Appeal Court settled the application of the theory in France and some others followed the same route.[151] The French courts have generally proved to be in favour of extending the arbitration clause to groups of companies where that extension is justifiable on the basis of the parties' express or implied intention.[152] KIS France had entered into a basic agreement with Société Générale for the sale of miniature photographic laboratories in certain countries. The basic agreement was signed by both parties on their own behalf and on behalf of their subsidiaries. Pursuant to that contract, the subsidiaries themselves dealt with the contractor and its subsidiaries in specific contracts referring to the framework contract. The basic agreement contained an ICC arbitration clause, which was referred to in the contracts that the subsidiaries signed. A dispute arose concerning unpaid lease fees, and Société Générale and two of its subsidiaries commenced an arbitral proceeding against two of the subsidiaries in the KIS group. The arbitrators made an interim award ruling that the claims against the KIS subsidiaries were admissible. The arbitral tribunal held that the co-contractors and their subsidiaries could commence arbitration proceedings based on the framework contract against both the parent company and its subsidiaries.[153] On a challenge by KIS France, the Appeal Court held that 'the notion of group of companies' is rec-

---

147 Woolhouse, S.P., 'Group of Companies Doctrine and English Arbitration Law' (2004) 20 International Arbitration 435.

148 Born, *International Commercial*, p. 656.

149 An American arbitral tribunal reached a similar result, referring to US national court decisions and observing that it is neither rational nor practical to exclude (from arbitral jurisdiction) the claims of companies which have an interest in the venture and which are members of the same corporate family, Partial Final Award No 1510, VII Y.B. Comm. Arb. 151 (Society of Maritime Arbitrators 28 November 1980) cited at Born, *International Commercial*, p. 656.

150 Cour d'Appel, Paris, 31 October 1989, available at www.kluwerarbitration.com.

151 Leadley and Williams, 'Peterson Farms'.

152 Gaillard and Savage, *Fouchard Gaillard Goldman.*

153 *Ibid.*

ognized under French law and, therefore, the arbitrators did not violate the parties' choice of French law by taking it into account.[154]

A similar approach to KIS adopted by the tribunal subsequently rejected by the English courts in *Caparo Group Ltd v Fagor Arrastate Sociedad Cooperative*,[155] even though the principles of 'group of companies' doctrine were assured to be specific to the facts of that case. The Spanish company, Fagor, and an Indian company known as CML had entered into a signed contract for the sale and purchase of printing presses. In a dispute over non-payment, Fagor sought to hold Caparo, which was a 60 per cent shareholder in CML, liable for the alleged default. Clarke J held that:

> Under English law, I can see no basis upon which it could be held that the parties to either the contract or the arbitration agreement were other than Fagor on the one hand and CML on the other. In my judgment, there is no room for a conclusion that Caparo was a party to either the contract or the arbitration agreement.

The position was clarified when Langley J, in the Commercial Court in London, granted the application of Peterson Farms, Inc, an Arkansas company, to set aside parts of an award which had been issued to C&M Farming Limited, an Indian company, in reliance on the group of companies' doctrine. Langley J held that these parts of the award were made without jurisdiction.[156] Under a sales right agreement, Peterson had sold male 'grandparent' chickens to C&M, which mated them to obtain parents, which could be sold on to third parties, including other entities in the same group as C&M. These third parties then mated the parent birds to produce chicks or hatching eggs to produce broilers for the consumer market. The birds supplied by Peterson were found to carry a virus, which reduced the birds' capacity to produce healthy chicks.

The sales right agreement was subject to Arkansas law and contained a provision for disputes to be resolved by ICC arbitration in London. A dispute arose as to whether the ICC Tribunal had power to award damages in respect of losses suffered by other entities in the same group as well as by C&M. The tribunal held, based on the doctrine of separability of the arbitration agreement, that unlike the main body of the sales right agreement, the arbitration provision was not subject to Arkansas law. The tribunal held that the scope of the arbitration agreement is determined autonomously, in accordance with principles of inter-

---

[154] Leadley and Williams, 'Peterson Farms'.

[155] Commercial Court, Queen's Bench Division, 7 August 1998, Lexis.

[156] *Peterson Farms, Inc v C&M Farming Limited* [2004] EWHC 121 (Comm). See Leadley and Williams, 'Peterson Farms'; Woolhouse, 'Group of Companies'; Seeger, Karolos and Friel, Steven 'Challenge Under Section 67 of the Arbitration Act 1996' (2004) 7 Int. A.L.R. 39; Hanotiau, B., *Complex Arbitrations*, paras 461–466; Gaffney, 'The Group of Companies Doctrine'.

national law and arbitral practice rather than application of national law. Thus the tribunal took the view that this entitled it to apply the ICC precedent, including the group of companies' doctrine.

Based on current correspondence, the tribunal in Peterson formed the view that Peterson had intended throughout to deal with the C&M group as a whole and had contracted with one member of the group purely as a matter of convenience, the group not being a legal entity. Accordingly C&M obtained an award of some US$6.7 million, of which some US$5.5 million related to losses suffered by other C&M group entities, which were not named as parties to the Sales Right Agreement. Moreover some of them, at the time the sales right agreement was entered into, were partnerships rather than companies.

Peterson brought a challenge in the Commercial Court in London under s. 67 of the Arbitration Act 1996, arguing that the tribunal had no jurisdiction to award damages to entities which were not parties to the arbitration agreement. Langley J found that the arbitration provision was subject to the same express choice of law clause as the rest of the sales right agreement. Therefore the tribunal's decision was 'seriously flawed' and there was no basis for the tribunal to apply any law other than that chosen by the parties, which was Arkansas law. It was agreed between the parties for the purposes of the s. 67 challenge that Arkansas law was the same as English law in consideration of the 'group of companies' doctrine, and Langley J ruled that 'English law treats the issue as one subject to the chosen proper law of the Agreement and that excludes the doctrine which forms no part of English law'. Accordingly the view of the English court is that an ICC arbitral tribunal has no jurisdiction to apply the 'group of companies' doctrine.[157] However, the decision might have been different if Arkansas law recognized the group of companies' doctrine.[158] Under US law, the ultimate question of whether a party has agreed to arbitrate a dispute is to be decided by the federal courts, not by the arbitral tribunal.[159] Thus the

[157] The group of companies doctrine has been rejected in many jurisdictions. For example, the group of companies doctrine has not been endorsed in the Swiss legal system. Habegger states that an arbitration agreement entered into by a subsidiary will not bind its parent company unless certain circumstances justify that the very independence of the subsidiary as a corporate body be disregarded (piercing of the corporate veil). This will, however, require a finding that the parent company's reliance on its independence is abusive. It is noteworthy that, under Swiss law, the mere fact that the corporate veil is pierced does not mean *per se* that a company will be bound by an arbitration agreement entered into by its shareholders. It is only where the very independence of the company as a self-standing corporate body is denied that the arbitration agreement will be extended to it. See further Habegger P., 'Arbitration and Groups of Companies – the Swiss Practice' (2002) 3 EBOR 517.

[158] Woolhouse, 'Group of Companies'.

[159] Lamm and Aqua, 'Defining the Party'.

basis for binding non-signatories to arbitration agreements under a theory of implied consent derives from the US common law principles pertaining to related parties, veil piercing, alter ago, agency, assumption and estoppels and related agreements.[160]

In consideration of the French Appeal Court's approach in the *KIS* case, it seems that *Peterson* might have been differently decided under French law. The *KIS* case differed from the *Peterson* case in that *KIS* was challenging an award against respondents who were not directly parties to the arbitration agreement, whereas *Peterson* was challenging an award in favour of claimants who were not parties. However, the judgment of the French court is expressed in very general terms, and it appears to provide no immediately obvious reason why the French court would not apply the 'group of companies' doctrine in a case that was closer to the facts of the English decision.

Commentators differ as to whether the 'group of companies' doctrine in arbitration practice is distinct from the existing principles allowing the corporate veil to be pierced. Gaillard and Savage, for instance, consider both together,[161] whereas Born and Honatiau distinguish the group of companies' doctrine from alter ego claims in which a company or individual is deliberately contracting in such a way as to evade legitimate responsibilities.[162] The piercing the veil doctrine based on alter ego characteristically requires an element of fraud to be established but the groups of companies' doctrine can be applied without fraud.

It has been claimed that if a tribunal is justified in allowing entities that were not party to an arbitration agreement to become parties to the arbitration, there are alternative instruments that could be used. For instance it may be possible to argue in appropriate cases that the respondent is estopped by its conduct from denying that the additional entities were parties to the arbitration agreement, or that there has been fraud, which justifies piercing the corporate veil. Consequently a general 'group of companies' doctrine would be unnecessary.[163] The rule created by *lex mercatoria* has little legal certainty and its definite forms are vague and open to discussion.[164] Indeed in the French case of *Orri v Société des Lubrifiants Elf Aquitaine*[165] the Paris Appeal Court relied on both principles, although the *Cour de Cassation* case subsequently upheld the decision based

---

160 Lamm and Aqua, 'Defining the Party'; Hanatiau, 'Problems Raised by Complex'.

161 Gaillard and Savage, *Fouchard Gaillard Goldman.*

162 Born, *International Commercial* pp.653–700; Hanatiau, 'Problems Raised by Complex'.

163 Leadley and Williams, 'Peterson Farms'; Sandrock, 'Arbitration Agreements'.

164 Sandrock, 'Arbitration Agreements'.

165 (1992) Rev. Arb. 90.

on the alter ego ground, while not considering the 'group of companies' argument on the facts.

The examination of the cases indicates that the 'group of companies' doctrine originates from the similar principles that the veil-piercing doctrine originated. The doctrine was created because justice required it. Thus most of the commentators as well as English courts see the doctrine as unnecessary because there is already a valid doctrine that provides sufficient protection under the principles of alter ago or fraud or some principles of estoppels. Moreover it is not so much the existence of a group that results in the various companies of the group being bound by the agreement signed by only one of them, but the true intention of the parties was considered important. Thus the 'group of companies' doctrine originated from the assumption that the involvement of other companies in the group in the negotiation or performance of the contract implicitly proves their agreement to be bound by the clause.[166] Thus the theory has been shadowed most of the time by the phrase 'intended by the parties'.[167] Indeed in the French cases the legitimacy for the application of the theory is established under the principles of justice. The term single economic unit was attached to the extra requirements that the parties to behaviour must have supported the application of the theory. Thus evidence of the managerial facts in each particular case is important. This makes the result of the cases unpredictable and, more importantly, successful awards will be rare.

The argument carried out in this book is that the group of companies must be liable in a way that reflects their ownership and managerial structure in a modern organizational structure. The group of companies' doctrine in arbitration cases has indicated some important points with reference to the single economic enterprise theory. However, requiring extra facts for each case reduces its reliability. Moreover under the horizontal structure of MNEs, the link between companies is not apparently seen in every particular case.[168] Modern organizations have complex horizontal structures and it is almost impossible to trace every transaction or operation. Thus if one searches for extra facts to prove real intention, one will fail to prove clear links between member companies under the group. Thus the group liability introduced by arbitrators has some shortages to be considered as efficient models of imposing liability on corporate groups and it can be claimed that the doctrine is innovative just between the borders of limited liability.

Finally, although the courts in many countries deny the 'group of companies' doctrine, the eagerness of arbitrators to create the 'group of companies' doctrine

166 Gaillard and Savage, *Fouchard Gaillard Goldman.*

167 Hanotiau, *Complex Arbitrations*, para. 466.

168 See Chapter 2.

seems to be enduring. Legal consultants to MNEs will be forced next time to sign agreements that are binding all companies under the group because the arbitrational organizations are more aware of the current economical and organizational structure of the MNEs. Therefore the international law creating the role of international arbitration organizations may bring to MNEs' liability a new perspective.

## THE COMPREHENSIVE ENVIRONMENTAL RESPONSIBILITY AND COMPENSATION ACT (CERCLA)

In 1980, the US Congress enacted the CERCLA[169] to ensure that every party that was potentially responsible for environmental torts would be held responsible for the resulting harm. There are four classes of potentially responsible parties for environmental torts under CERCLA s. 107: (1) the current owners and operators of a facility; (2) persons who formerly owned or operated the facility at the time of disposal or treatment of hazardous substance; (3) persons who arranged for the disposal or treatment of hazardous substance; and (4) transporters of hazardous waste.[170] Accordingly CERCLA liability may attach to a corporate owner in one of two ways: (1) direct liability under the operator language of CERCLA's s. 107(a) and (2) indirect liability as owner through common law veil piercing.[171]

The owner or operator of a facility is defined as any person owning or operating such facility, excluding a person who, without participating in the management of a facility, holds priority of ownership primarily to protect his security interest in the facility. Thus CERCLA failed to express any apparent intention to hold parent corporations or other shareholders individually liable for corporate activities because CERCLA's definitions of person, owner or operators include corporations and other business entities as well as individuals, but no specific reference is made to parent corporations or shareholder liability. Hence there is a dispute about whether owners or operators can be interpreted to include parent companies.

CERCLA's present definition of operator liability has left the courts with no encouragement. In their pursuit for balancing the contradictory liability principles, the courts approached this issue by adopting one of three basic approaches: (1) the most extensive imposition of liability under the 'authority to control' or

---

169 Another US statute, Alien Torts Claims Act, is examined in Chapter 4.

170 Bakst, 'Piercing the Corporate Veil'.

171 Alexander, D.E. and Sawez, S., 'Toward a Uniform Parent Corporation Liability Standard under CERCLA' (1998–1999) 60 U. Pitt. L. Rev. 1235.

'capacity to control' principles; (2) the 'actual control' test; and (3) derivative-only liability, which declines to hold parent corporations directly liable as operators under any conditions, other than when circumstances are adequate to pierce the corporate veil.[172]

First in *State of Idaho v Bunker Hill Co*,[173] a federal district court developed the capacity to control standard, the broadest reaching theory of parent corporation liability under CERCLA. In the case the court concluded that the parent and its subsidiary were 'so intertwined' and that the parent 'so controlled the management and operations' of the subsidiary that the parent constituted an 'owner or operator' for purposes of CERCLA. Parent corporations are supposed to be liable because the CERCLA language points to them as owner and operator. The *Bunker Hill* court relied on *United States v Northeastern Pharmaceutical & Chemical Co*.[174] The court adopted the view that the remedial goal of CERCLA required a more expansive view of liability. Therefore parents have the capacity, if not the totally reserved authority, to make decisions and implement actions and mechanisms to prevent the damage.[175] However, despite the numerous federal district courts recognizing the capacity to control test as the required level of involvement, no federal appellate court has recognized this test in the context of parent-subsidiary liability.[176] They affirm their argument in the belief that this approach seemed to be fully in contradiction to the traditional common law concept of limited liability for owners of corporations, because parents could be liable for simply owning a subsidiary, and not for any actions directly taken by the parent with regard to the contamination.[177]

The second approach, actual control, was created by the District Court of Rhode Island in *United States v Kayser-Roth Corp*.[178] The court stated that a

---

172 See Alexander and Sawez, 'Toward a Uniform'; Hofstetter, 'The Ecological Liability'; Stone, 'Parent Corporate Liability'; Silecchia, Lucia Ann, 'Pinning the Blame and Piercing the Veil in the Mists of Metaphor: The Supreme Court's New Standards for the CERCLA Liability of Parent Companies and a Proposal for Legislative Reform' (1998–1999) 67 Fordham L. Rev. 115.

173 (D. Idaho 1987) 662 F. Supp. 725; See also *Nurad, Inc v William E. Hooper & Sons Co* 966 F2d 837 (4th Cir. 1992).

174 579 F. Supp. 823.

175 Hofstetter, 'The Ecological Liability'; Farmer, Richard S., 'Parent Corporation Responsibility for the Environmental Liabilities of the Subsidiary: A Search for the Appropriate Standard' (1994) 19 J. Corp. L. 769.

176 Alexander and Sawez, 'Toward a Uniform'; Farmer, 'Parent Corporation'.

177 DeMonte, Jessica, 'Impact of United States v. Bestfoods on Parent Liability under CERCLA: When A Door Is Closed, Look for an Open Window' (2000) 61 Ohio St. L.J. 443.

178 910 F. 2d. 24 (1st Cir. 1990) See also other cases; *Jacksonville Electric Authority v Bernuth Corp*. 996 F.2d 1107, *Lansford-Coaldale Joint Water Authority v Tonolli Corp*. 996 F.2d. 1107 (11th Cir. 1993).

parent corporation cannot, as a rule, be believed to be an operator solely on the basis of its status as a shareholder.[179] The court considered the appropriate standard to apply and determined that the *Bunker Hill* court's capacity to control test was too broad. Accordingly the court's ruling was two-sided: it first relied on the basic principle that, under federal law, a corporate entity may be disregarded in the interest of public convenience, fairness and equity. Secondly, direct liability holds the corporate parent liable if it acted as an operator of the site and the parent corporation must have had persistent control over the management of its subsidiary in order to incur direct liability. *Kayser-Roth* was found to merit such liability. Under the case, liability was not imposed on the parent corporation because of its capacity to control but the courts searched for persistent control over the subsidiary.[180]

Thirdly, the Fifth Circuit adopted the traditional alter ego (veil piercing) liability principle for determining the liability of a parent corporation under CERCLA in *Joslyn Manufacturing Co v T.L. James & Co*.[181] The Fifth Circuit refused to apply the expansive reading to CERCLA's liability provisions. The CERCLA does not define 'owners' or 'operators' as including the parent company. The court found that the lack of explicit statutory language addressing the issue of parent corporate liability meant that federal courts lacked the authority to impose liability without piercing the corporate veil.[182] Nor does the legislative history indicate that Congress intended to alter a basic principle of corporation law so significantly. The *Joslyn* court maintained that Congress is quite capable of creating statutes that hold shareholders or controlling entities liable for the acts of corporations.[183] However in *Joslyn* the court was asked to rewrite the language of the Act significantly and hold parents directly liable for their subsidiaries' activities. To do so would dramatically modify traditional concepts of corporation law. The court then returned to the traditional, common law corporate veil-piercing test, and agreed with the district court's findings that the parent's relationship with its subsidiary did not permit imposing liability on the parent. The subsidiary authentically adhered to basic corporate formalities by keeping its own books and records and holding frequent shareholder and directors' meetings. The daily operations of the subsidiary and the

---

179 Hofstetter, 'The Ecological Liability'.

180 Farmer, 'Parent Corporation'.

181 893 F. 2d. 80 (5th Cir. 90). See also *United States v Cordova Chemical Co.* 113 F.3d 572 (6th Cir. 1997).

182 Prebble, Amanda L., 'Corporate Law Confines to Parent Liability under CERCLA: United States v. Bestfoods', 118 S. Ct. 1876 (1998), (1998–1999) 67 U. Cin. L. Rev. 1357.

183 Rolle, Mary Elliott, 'United States v. Bestfoods: Clarifying Parent Corporation Liability under CERCLA' (1999) 6 Wis. Envtl. L.J. 145.

parent were separate. The Supreme Court approved a review of *Joslyn Manufacturing* in *Cordova Chemical Co* that rejected all theories for parent corporation liability except for indirect owner liability under state veil-piercing law.

After these complicated court rulings there was a need for a definitive Supreme Court statement on parent corporation liability under CERCLA. *United States v Bestfoods*[184] provided that statement.[185] This decision reinterpreted the Circuits' stiff reading of parental liability and held that while a parent could still be liable under the restrictive veil-piercing theory employed by the Sixth Circuit, a parent could now also be liable under a direct operator standard if it acted as the operator of a facility owned or operated by its subsidiary. This also diverged from lower court rulings that had previously considered direct liability by looking at the parent's legal relationship to the subsidiary rather than to the facility.[186]

The key question in *Bestfoods* was whether a sole investor, a parent corporation that exercised control over a subsidiary, was safe from liability for damage involving the cleanup of industrial waste when the damage was done by its non-operational subsidiary.[187] The specific issue before the court was whether a parent corporation that actively participated in, and exercised control over, the operations of a subsidiary may, without more, be held liable as an operator of a polluting facility owned or operated by the subsidiary. The court said no; instead concluding that a corporate parent that actively participated in and exercised control over the operations of the facility itself may be held directly liable in its own right as an operator of the facility.[188] The Supreme Court rejected the position that the parent is directly liable as an operator because it actively participated in and exercised significant control over the subsidiary's business and decision-making. The court stated, first, that it is a general principle of corporate law deeply embedded in our economic and legal systems that a parent corporation is not liable for the acts of its subsidiary; secondly, the corporate veil may be pierced and the shareholders held liable for the corporation's conduct when the corporate form would otherwise be misused to accomplish certain wrongful purposes, most notably fraud, on the shareholders' behalf.[189] The court's new, middle ground liability required a parent corporation to actively participate in and exercise control over the subsidiary's

---

184 524 US 51 (1998).
185 Rolle, 'United States v. Bestfoods'.
186 Silecchia, 'Pinning the Blame'.
187 Gelb Harvey, 'CERCLA versus Corporate Limited Liability' (1999–2000) 48 U. Kan. L. Rev. 111.
188 *Ibid.*
189 *Ibid.*

business during a period of disposal of hazardous waste.[190] Instead, according to the court, the question addressed by the district court should have been about the parent's interaction with the facility of the subsidiary. The question is not whether the parent operates the subsidiary, but rather whether it operates the facility, and that operation is evidenced by participation in the activities of the facility, not the subsidiary.[191] As a result the key to direct liability, according to the court, is that the parent must exercise actual control over the facility (without regard for the parent's control of the subsidiary).[192] If any such act of operating a corporate subsidiary's facility is done on behalf of a parent corporation, the existence of the parent-subsidiary relationship under the state corporate law is simply irrelevant to the issue of direct liability.[193] Thus parent corporations can avoid liability by either not participating in the subsidiary's hazardous waste operations, or doing so with cautious oversight.[194] If their interaction with their subsidiaries is not unusual, there is no need to find them liable as owners.[195] The *Bestfoods* decision abolished the capacity to control test and narrowed the actual participation and control test. The decision also preserved indirect liability as a separate means of imposing liability. However while *Bestfoods* did establish that parent corporations could be held directly liable as operators under CERCLA, the determination of which factual scenarios will justify such liability appears to have been left for the lower courts to decide.[196]

As these cases demonstrate, the liability of a parent corporation has stayed untouched despite the consequences of whether liability is based on traditional corporate law or direct statutory liability under the CERCLA. Liability does not occur merely by virtue of their ownership of stock, but rather by direct control over the subsidiary or the facility and for the wrongdoings.[197] In cases in which parent corporations might be held liable under CERCLA, the parents must be in a situation of exercising control over the activities leading to the CERCLA violations. The courts simply hold parties liable that might be held liable under

---

[190] Sutphin, Robert J. Jr., 'Environmental Law – Owners or Operators: Two Distinct Paths to Parent Corporation Liability under CERCLA – United States v. Bestfoods' (2000) 30 N.M. L. Rev. 109.

[191] Gelb, CERCLA.

[192] DeMonte, 'Impact of United States v. Bestfoods'.

[193] Rolle, 'United States v. Bestfoods'.

[194] Yeo, Eric L., 'United States v. Bestfoods: Narrowing Parent Corporation Liability under CERCLA for the Twenty-First Century' (1999) 51 Admin. L. Rev. 1267.

[195] Alexander and Sawez, 'Toward a Uniform'.

[196] Yeo, 'United States v. Bestfoods'.

[197] Dent, George W., 'Limited Liability in Environmental Law' (1991) 26 Wake Forest L. Rev. 151.

traditional corporate law doctrine and veil-piercing doctrine.[198] Analysis of the case law simply does not support a conclusion that the courts are eroding traditional corporate liability rules regarding parent corporations in the CERCLA context.

One of the important reasons of failure of the CERCLA as an efficient example of corporate groups' liability in tort is its misunderstanding of groups' structure by considering them as simple vertically structured organizations rather than horizontally structured organizations. In the original text of the Act, there is no mention of parent liability but owners' and controllers' liability is the source of liability. Accordingly the courts have to search for owner and controller in subsidiaries' environmental damage. This leads courts to look for a particular structure under which a parent applies excessive control over its subsidiaries, which is similar to vertical structure discussed in the second chapter. Thus a regulation based on characteristics of vertical organizations fails to create an extensive liability regime and is thus inefficient. Even though liability claims for corporate groups are brought under CERCLA's provisions, they have failed to offer any better solution than the traditional veil-piercing doctrine offers. In conclusion, CERCLA's provisions are sophisticated, thus they contain many drafting gaps, which might be claimed that Congress intended the federal courts to fill through federal common law.[199] The CERCLA may have developed better liability theories than piercing the corporate veil doctrine because it particularly agrees the issue of the owner's role in the subsidiary. However, it has failed to do so after the courts' traditional interpretation of the rules and their failure to adopt a modern interpretation of operational structure of corporate groups.

## DEVELOPMENTS IN TURKISH LAW

According to the Articles 503/1 and 269/2 of the Turkish Commercial Code, shareholders of the private limited company and public limited company have limited liability. Article 532/1 of the Turkish Commercial Code defines the limit of the liability of the shareholders as the capital promised to be paid into the company. Shareholders can save themselves from further liability by paying this amount if the company's assets are not enough to cover all the debts.

In Turkish law, there are two kinds of companies under which shareholders have unlimited liability. In *kollektif sirket*, every shareholder has unlimited liability disregarding the proportion of capital they promised to pay. In *komandit*

[198] Oswald, Lynda J. and Schipani, Cindy A., 'Cercla and the "Erosion" of Traditional Corporate Law Doctrine' (1992), 86 Nw. U. L. Rev. 259.

[199] Farmer, 'Parent Corporation'.

*sirket*, there are two kinds of shareholders: one has unlimited liability similar to *kollektif sirket* shareholders and the others are liable just for the capital they promised to pay. However, these two kinds of company structure have no importance in commercial practice. Turkish law has two most common company law forms: *limited sirket* (private limited company) and *anonim sirket* (public limited company). Both of them recognize companies as distinct legal personalities and grant limited liability to shareholders of companies. Accordingly the problems that limited liability companies created have occurred under the Turkish system as well.

When there is a claim for misuse of the company structure, there are not many options for the courts except for the general principles of Turkish Commercial and Civil Codes. In cases of breach of good faith rules, Article 2(1) of the Turkish Civil Code states that 'every person is bound to exercise his rights and fulfil his obligations according to the principles of good faith'. Consequently courts might remove the corporate veil and decide according to the facts of the particular case. In this case judges will look at which conditions separate corporate personality and limited liability are used in breach of good faith. Article 2(2) of Civil Code states that 'the law does not sanction the evident abuse of a person's rights'. This regulation might also be used by the courts to ignore the corporate veil in cases where the corporate structure has been misused. In short the courts might use good faith principles to balance the situation of misuse of limited liability.

Even though the Civil Code's good faith principles could have been interpreted wider to develop a theory of veil lifting, there was no mention of a theory of veil lifting in Turkish case law.[200] However, in a recent decision, the Supreme Court based their justification on the good faith principles; while lifting the veil the Court stated that the law does not protect the misuse of limited liability and separate legal personality.[201] And the Court for the first time used the term of lifting the corporate veil (tuzel kisilik perdesinin kaldirilmasi or perdeyi kaldirma teorisi). It is claimed that this usage of lifting the veil theory might open the way to further development of the theory.[202] However, lifting the veil in these decisions was more punishment to misuse of separate legal personality of companies rather than establishing direct liability over shareholders for the debts of companies.

Overall these broad discretion rights have not been used in favour of developing a doctrine similar to piercing the corporate veil. In cases, which are too

---

[200] Seven, V. and Goksoy, C., 'Ticaret Sirketlerinde Tüzel Kisilik Perdesinin Kaldırılması' (2006) 80 Istanbul Barosu Dergisi 1.

[201] Yargitay (Turkish Supreme Court) 19.Hukuk 2005/8774E and 2006/5232 K (15.05.2006).

[202] Seven and Goksoy, 'Ticaret'.

disorganized to classify, the analysis to remove the corporate veil was very similar to the common law fraud doctrine. Similar principles have been applied in the case of corporate groups by courts to remove the corporate veil. In the cases under which shareholders are liable, there must be a connection between the act of misuse and debts. The claimants have to prove that the debts occurred because of the misuse of corporate form. In brief, in Turkish law there is no general concept of lifting the corporate veil similar to the American and English concept so that it is difficult to predict the general terms of the lifting in Turkish application. The recent decision cannot be interpreted as introduction of lifting the veil principles to Turkish law. Rather I interpret this as an indication that Turkish judiciary are following inter-jurisdictional developments and becoming more open to adopt developments in other jurisdictions.

More importantly for this book, there have been some changes in the Law Regarding the Procedure of Collection of the Money Owed to the State (Amme Alacaklarinin Tahsili Usulu Hakkinda Kanun, AATUHK) which introduces an exception to the limited liability principle. The main exception to the limited liability of the shareholders is found in Article 35 (introduced in 1998) of the Law with the phrase 'the shareholders of private limited company are liable in accordance in proportion to their capital shares for the debt owed to the state'. The objective of the law is to prevent misuse of company structures to avoid liabilities.

There are two conditions for the debts: first it must be owed to the state, or local authorities and it must have originated from the performance of public services. The most important sources of debts are taxes, duties, fines and other fees. The second condition is that collecting the money from the company must be impossible. Thus the liability of shareholders is secondary because the shareholders are liable if the company's funds are not enough to pay the debts.[203] The state authorities will try every possible legal avenue to collect money from the company and if they cannot recover the debts they will go to shareholders in proportion to their shares in the company. According to the decisions of the Turkish Council of State, the last owner of the shares must pay the debts. The liability is founded on becoming shareholders of the company. Thus taking legal action against the owner of shareholders at the time that the debt has occurred is wrong.[204] The idea behind this is that if you transfer your shares, you transfer it with the rights and liabilities.

The importance of the law comes from the fact that the law is a fundamental exception to company law and limited liability principles. It removes liability

---

[203] Eyibilir Ihsan, 'Limited Sirket Ortaklarinin Sorumlulugu' (1995) 32 Yak Der 93.

[204] Turkish Council of State (Danistay) D.2/12/1999E.1997/4847 K.1999/4008.

barriers for all shareholders by not requiring any other conditions such as alter ego or misuse of corporate forms. Therefore the application of the law has not brought much confusion in Turkey since it clearly indicated liability on shareholders. More importantly, it neither reduced the number of private limited companies nor deterred people from establishing new companies. However, it only removes the corporate veil in private limited companies. Public limited companies still have their limited liability untouched. Consequently it cannot be claimed this law has changed liability structure of corporate groups in terms of Turkish law.

The most important characteristic of this law is that it has proved that limited liability rules could be abolished for some particular debts of the company. In normal conditions, in any ordinary company, money owed to the state is, in many situations, bigger than debts owed to the involuntary creditors. And the liability to the state will occur for sure since companies have to pay taxes and other fees. If such an important and broad liability can be transferred to shareholders, liability for involuntary creditors can definitely be achievable. This law has also proved that more liability will not destroy the Turkish company structure or Turkish economy. The number of new companies established in Turkey increased fundamentally in recent years even though the application of this law has been settled.[205]

[205] According to the figures of the Ministry of Industry, in 1998 when the law was enacted and later in the year came into force, there were 50,377 new private limited liability companies in Turkey. The number dropped sharply to 23,609 in 1999 and stayed level during 2000–2003 (28 598 in 2000; 27 341 in 2001; 28 178 in 2002 and 29 396 in 2003); the number of new private limited companies increased to 37 809 in 2004 and the number was 37 144 in 2005 and 42 751 in 2006, the first four months of 2007 saw almost 19,000 new limited liability companies, which leads us to predict the figure will exceed the one in 1998. There were two heavy economic crises in Turkey resulting in negative growth in 1999 and 2001. Thus, the drop in the new limited liability companies during 1999–2002 is a result of two heavy economic crises. An interesting point is the connection between the number of new companies and economic growth. I examined the figure of economic growth in Turkey in the last 10 years; there was negative growth in 1999 and 2001; and during this period, the number of new companies established Turkey was the lowest in the last 10 years. In order to prove the connection between new companies and economic stability of Turkey, the changes of new public limited companies support the idea that establishment of new companies in 1998 was highest with 4,048 new companies, and as with limited liability companies there was a sharp drop between 1999–2003 due to economic situations and the current trend indicates the number of new public limited companies established in Turkey is increasing. As a result, considering the changes in AATUHK and unlimited liability of shareholders for the debt owed to the state, this information can be interpreted, by omitting the other economic elements, as that this law has not affected the entrepreneurs' wishes to set up new limited liability companies. These statistics are based on the information provided by the Ministry of Industry of Turkey on my request by using the Freedom of Information Act.

The latest attempt to regulate corporate groups in Turkey is the Draft Commercial Law Reform Bill 2005.[206] Since 2001, a Commission which consists of scholars and practitioners had been preparing the Draft Bill which includes company law regulations. The Commission conducted very detailed comparative work for company law in order to achieve the aim of the new Commercial Code, which is to create the most up-to-date Commercial Code in Europe. In terms of company law provisions, they have been inspired by European, English, German, French and Swiss laws. Moreover the Draft Bill has generated many unique proposals some of which are very innovatory in the world of commercial regulations.

In terms of corporate groups, the Draft Bill provides a section, which is not lengthy, consisting of 20 articles and it aims to create a very broad regulatory system for groups of companies. The Bill mentions the German Stock Corporation Act, developments in French Labour Law, Italian Bankruptcy Law, British Take-Over laws, and 7th and 9th EU Company Law Directives as examples of the developments in groups of companies' laws in comparative perspective. In explaining the regulation, the Draft Bill identifies that groups of companies are in the centre of economic activities both at domestic and international level. Thus the Draft Bill is aiming, by regulating groups of companies, to balance the realities of economic life and the rule of law.

In order to create a new and modern group of companies' regime, the Commission adopted Articles 17–21 of the German Stock Corporation Act related to groups of companies. Some proposed articles relating to subsidiary companies have been inspired by Articles 291–337 of the German Stock Corporation Act. Moreover the Commission has taken into account the suggestions of the Forum Europeaum in creating the organization of the sections on groups of companies. However, the organization of the Draft Bill, especially those related to liability, are unique.

The Draft Bill uses groups of companies as its main description. The Draft uses the term of control in its description of a group of companies rather than domination or applied authority by one company over another.[207] In control, there are certain criteria to determine whether it exists or does not exist, such as holding majority voting rights. In domination criteria, any kinds of established authority over another company will be considered as domination. In many regulations, criteria for the existence of control are determined in advance and, thus, there is no need to search for domination. For example according to the 7th EU Company Law Directive a company cannot omit consolidated ac-

---

206 Turkish Commercial Code Reform, and Draft Commercial Law Reform Bill, 2005 available at http://www2.tbmm.gov.tr/d22/1/1-1138.pdf.

207 The Forum Europeaum takes the control approaches as well. See above.

counts by just proving there is no domination by a parent. Accordingly Article 195(1) of the Draft considers the control theory as its main system, additionally it recognizes supposed control theory in Article 195(2).

The earlier version of the Draft included only limited liability companies, rather than including every enterprise. This was different from the German Stock Corporation Act, which covers not only limited liability companies but also other enterprises recognized by the law. However, later changes made in the Draft include all companies as part of the enterprise. Moreover according to Draft Article 195(6) on top of the group there might be a real person or an unlimited company or any other enterprise.

In determination of parent companies and their subsidiary companies, if there is a control exercised by one company over another, this section (corporate groups) will be applied to those companies and the controlling company is considered to be a parent company while the controlled company is considered to be a subsidiary. According to Draft Article 195(1) there is a control if one company directly or indirectly has: (1) majority voting rights of another company; (2) a right to appoint directors who have the majority of votes in another company; (3) a right to use majority voting rights in another company, together with their votes, based on an agreement with other members. Also, if there is a control agreement between two companies, if a centre of one of the companies in the group is in Turkey, this law will be applied. Moreover in Article 195(2), there is a theoretical (supposed) control if one company holds a majority of shares or shares that might have the effect of a majority over another company. The difference between Article 195(1) and Article 195(2) is that in the first paragraph the control is certain and parties cannot argue the opposite. However, under the second paragraph parties can always avoid being subjected to the groups of companies' regulations by proving there is no exercised control over the subsidiary by the parent company. Moreover Article 195(3) states that there is indirect control if one company controls another company through subsidiary companies or together with them. According to Article 197, titled reciprocal ownership, if two companies own at least a quarter of the shares of each other, there is a mutual group. Also, if one establishes control over the other, the controlled one will be considered a subsidiary company. If both control each other, both will be considered a subsidiary company.

The Draft Bill imposes some duties on parent companies. For example, Article 198 requires a company to register and publicize when it directly or indirectly owns 10, 20, 25, 33, 50, 67, 100 per cent of the shares another company. If a company fails to perform registry and publicity requirements, the punishment will be withholding its voting rights. Article 199 requires parent companies to prepare annual group reports. A parent company has to prepare the report within three months of acquisition of the subsidiary demonstrating the scale of the relationship between parent company and subsidiary company.

The report has to be well prepared and indicate all the facts. Moreover the report has to show any loss of the subsidiary company, which occurred as a result of a parent company's decision. It has to show if the loss is paid back or planned to be paid back.

In liability of groups of companies, the Draft Bill imposes some liabilities for the parent company if it performs its controls over the subsidiary unlawfully. The Commission claims this is a unique regulation as it covers every misuse of control without limiting it to certain types of transaction. The main liability clauses regulated in Draft Article 202 are: (a) unless it is compensated in the operating year or it is clearly stated how it will be compensated before the end of operating year, the parent company cannot use its control in a way to put the subsidiary company at a disadvantage; (b) if the compensation is not performed, every shareholder can demand from the parent company and its directors who have voted in favor of the transaction, reimbursement to the subsidiary company of the amount it lost; (c) creditors of the subsidiary company may also demand, without requirement of the bankruptcy of the company, reimbursement of the loss to the company.[208] Article 202 para. (d) regulates a condition under which compensation cannot be claimed. Accordingly if the decision that caused the disadvantage would have been taken by the independent directors acting in good faith, there will be no compensation liability for the parent company.

In case of a fully owned subsidiary, Article 203 regulates that the directors of the subsidiary have to obey the order of the parent company, which is acting according to pre-determined group policy. This article was inspired from the *Rozenblum* doctrine of the French Supreme Court.[209] However Article 204 prohibits parent companies from giving orders that are exceeding the assets of the subsidiary or endangering its capability to make payments. Consequently the directors of the subsidiary are not liable for the decision they have taken in line with Articles 203 and 204. As a result, creditors of the subsidiary company can demand compensation from the parent company and from its directors if they have not performed their compensation duties for disadvantageous acts which have caused damage to the creditors of the subsidiary (Article 206).

There is an interesting liability imposed on parent companies in Draft Article 209; if a parent company establishes a perception of group image that assures the public and consumers, there will be liability arising from group credibility for losses arising from usage of this image by a subsidiary. The proposal is the

208 The author's translation.

209 The doctrine is examined previously in this chapter. See Tekil Muge (in Turkish) 'Rozenblum Karari ve Grup Cikari Karari' (2006) 10 HPD 213.

first attempt to regulate liability arising from the image of the group, which was first created in Switzerland by the Federal Court's decision in *Wibru v Swissair*.[210]

As a result the Draft Bill could be considered innovative from some perspectives. First of all it brings positive developments by producing a unified proposal including almost every positive development in Europe. The Draft finds its main structure in defining a group of companies in the German Stock Corporation Act and it creates its system inspired by the suggestions from the Forum Europaeum. Moreover it does not refrain from getting some ideas and rules from different jurisdictions such as French *Rozenblum* doctrine or Swiss Federal Courts decision in the *Wibru v Swissair* case. It covers MNEs by establishing that if a centre of one subsidiary or parent is in Turkey, this law will apply.

The liability clauses are much broader. First of all it creates a supposed control theory which was referred to by the German Supreme Court's decisions as well as by CERCLA litigation in the US and European Competition Law litigations. Moreover the enforced liability upon parent companies for any unlawful control over subsidiary companies that cause disadvantageous economic situations is impressive. Imposing liability on groups of companies for a misleading use of a group image is especially interesting and could create a model for future regulatory efforts for groups of companies.

However, there are many weaknesses in the Draft Bill in terms of creating better liability rules for groups of companies and thus for MNEs. First of all neither the Draft Turkish Commercial Bill nor sections related to groups of companies aim to abandon limited liability company principles in corporate groups. Accordingly companies established under Turkish law have limited liability protection for their shareholders and there is no difference between individual shareholders and company shareholders. The liability clauses in the context of groups of companies in the Draft Bill require additional conditions for liability to be established. Thus on those conditions, the draft regulations must be examined from two perspectives: whether they are successful in creditor protection; and whether new understandings of group of companies mirror the modern conception of corporate groups and MNEs.

The liability imposed on the parent company does not necessarily guarantee a payment to a subsidiary's unfulfilled creditors. First of all groups of companies exist only in certain conditions and the supposed control of the parent over a subsidiary is always rebuttable. Although the parent owns the majority

---

[210] Switzerland Federal Court (BGE 120 II 331) See Akkanat, H. and Aydincik, S. (in Turkish) 'Grup Sirketleri Baglaminda Culpa in Contrahendo Sorumlulugu' (2006) 10 HDP 219.

of shares it can escape from liability just by proving it did not perform control over the subsidiary. Moreover there is no liability occurring if the parent companys' control over the subsidiary is not considered unlawful. In this case, on many occasions, especially those related to involuntary creditors, even though a subsidiary committed a tort and it caused mass disruption, the parent company might escape liability by just proving it did not perform unlawful control over the subsidiary corporation. Thus the new regulations will provide better protection for voluntary creditors than it provides for involuntary creditors.

The second argument must be whether the Draft Bill has a perception of modern group of companies and MNEs or whether it makes the same mistake that perceives a group of companies as a vertical organization under which divisions between the units of the group are easily distinguished. It can be claimed that the Draft Bill is based on the idea of vertically integrated groups of companies and comparatively smaller domestic enterprises. It aims to make parent companies liable for the debt of the groups thus there is a requirement of control of the parent over subsidiaries. The whole section of the regulation is dedicated to determine which company is a parent and which company is a subsidiary. The difference between parent and subsidiaries is determined according to the control theory. Accordingly liability is imposed if the parent applies direct control over subsidiaries. Some provisions could be considered, from some aspects, closer to the modern structure of corporate groups, such as mutual ownership or indirect ownership but even these provisions might make its efficiency insignificant under the general liability system created according to the narrow perception of a simple vertical structure. Accordingly the liability proposed in the Draft Bill is the parent companys' liability for its control over its subsidiaries. The difference from the earlier rules and principles discussed above is the comparative reduction of conditions for proving control over subsidiaries. The Draft Bill will not solve the liability problems as horizontally organized groups can still avoid liability because of the difficulties of proving unlawful control applied to subsidiaries. Overall, the Draft Bill is a brave effort as it aims to create the most developed liability regime for group of companies but it cannot be considered innovative enough to solve the tort liability problems of MNEs.

## CONCLUSION: THE DEMISE OF THE CONTROL THEORY

This chapter is devoted to the examination of the existing laws and regulations that impose some forms of liability for corporate groups. It has been discovered that there is no uniform comprehensive modern law and principles that can provide solutions to the liability problems of MNEs. Thus the existent regulations have produced no real challenge to core areas of company law.[211] Indeed even the most compact corporate group law, the German Stock Corporation Act, seeks to preserve the subsidiary as a separate entity in that the parent owes duties of compensation to the creditors of the subsidiary in return for the power of control. In that way German law remains grounded in the logic of the classical theory of corporations. The regulations are insufficient to offer a new, broad and internationally effective system by establishing new theories based on modern social, economic and managerial characteristics of corporate groups and MNEs. Instead some efforts have been put in to find exceptional solutions for the problems under different institutions of law.

The English legislative efforts, in first instance, considered possible economic effects of new regulations on capital markets. In the process towards producing a proposal for the Companies Act 2006, issues related to creditor protection and corporate groups have been removed for basically economic reasons. Accordingly the Act offers no solution to liability problems; even worse it does not accept the existence of any problems regarding tort liability. The main regulatory efforts related to corporate groups concentrated mostly on accountancy, disclosure and auditing issues. On the other hand, creditor protections have been the subject of regulation in insolvency law under fraudulent and wrongful trading principles. However, none of these has challenged the current situation in corporate group law.

The efforts that have been carried on at the EU level have also been undermined by the fear of economic inefficiency. Different approaches to the problems in the member states weakened any chance of possible changes in the EU law. Thus neither of the European efforts creates inclusive proposals that can be a solution to the contemporary liability discussions. Instead they try to walk on a tightrope between the apparent benefits of limited liability and the evident necessity of putting groups of companies under modified liability designs. Some of the proposals (at least in theory) have created better hope and understanding in the area. However, they are still based on existing principles of liability by either requiring proof of some violation of duties to the subsidiary or by giving the parent company a chance to avoid liability by proving non-existence of excessive control over subsidiaries. Even such influential approaches as the former articles of the Draft European Company Statute (SE) would not deliver unconditional liability for the corporate shareholders in corporate groups. Thus there is no group liability for subsidiaries' tort in any situation. Rather there is a plural regulatory approach which makes the situation more complicated.[212]

[211] Prentice, Daniel D., 'Some Aspects of the Law Relating to Corporate Groups in the United Kingdom' (1998–1999) 13 Conn. J. Int'l L. 305.

[212] Irujo, 'Trends and Realities'.

The comparative examination of the laws from various jurisdictions highlights many points of weakness in the area of corporate groups' law since each of these regulations aims to cure a very particular problem of limited liability for corporate groups. For example the CERCLA tries to establish broader liability for environmental hazards. The Turkish AATUHK aims to prevent misuse of private limited company forms for debts owed to the state. However, this plurality of the regulations creates diverse group concepts and various and even conflicting legal policy perceptions towards groups of companies.

This lack of statutory intervention in the problem of groups of companies increases expectations from the courts to fill the gap but they are reluctant to admit the reality of interrelated companies in a complex structure under which they operate as a number of companies affecting each other, at the same time holding each other's shares. This situation leads to the claim that even the statutory laws have offered more developed solutions.[213] Thus in case law, efforts to reach a sound level of liability have been wiped out by the inflexibility of judges because of their rigid devotion to the restrictive characteristics of the doctrine of veil piercing. It can easily be stated that, in the field of general corporate law, the English and American courts are still attached to a traditional piercing the corporate veil doctrine, which requires a situation of the parent company's control over the subsidiary together with some form of unlawful action. In some cases the requirements were relaxed by creating relatively better principles in terms of group liability in order to adjust parent liability concepts to more particular and flexible policies underlying tort and environmental law. However, on the whole, because of the persistent devotion to the separate legal personality principles of the *Salomon* doctrine and the piercing the corporate veil principle, the common law attempts to control the exploitation of the limited liability form has proved unproductive.[214]

The examination of comparative case law from various jurisdictions produces a result not much different to that of English case law. The basic requirements of the parent's control over a subsidiary and the intention to fraud have been interpreted in a similar manner. Accordingly in order to establish liability on a group basis for certain behaviours, one needs to prove the existence of control of the parent over the subsidiary and intent to misuse the relationship between the subsidiary and other companies in the group. Control has been considered as a structural relation similar to property.[215] In practice, control is applied by the powers of decision-making. Accordingly there have been some efforts in

213 Dine, *The Governance*, p.44.

214 Griffin, 'Limited Liability'.

215 Scott, John, 'Corporate Groups and Network Structure' in McCahery, J., Picciotto, S. and Scott, S. (eds) *Corporate Control and Accountability* (OUP, Oxford 1993).

case law in order to ease the requirement of control theory for broader liability of the parent. For example the 'supposed control' theory in EU competition law cases and 'authority to control' or 'supposed control' in German qualified de facto group concern and 'capacity to control' in the CERCLA transfer the burden of proof from plaintiffs to the parent. Moreover a search for the true intention of the parties by applying the group of companies' doctrine in international commercial arbitration cases brings some broad discussion in the area of liability of corporate groups. However, all these efforts have been undermined by the subsequent developments because there has always been a strong resistance to fundamental changes in principles of liability in corporate groups.

As it is already concluded in the previous part of the book, limited liability has never been intended to protect groups of companies or even individual shareholders. Some examinations in this chapter point clearly to this fact. However, the main aim in this chapter, and Chapter 5, has been identifying problems that prevented broader liability within the framework of basic company law principles. There have been efforts to understand how the existing law and principles regarding groups' liability apply to the issue of group liability. The examination reveals that the theory of control is at the centre of existing liability rules. Accordingly this chapter, as a conclusion, states that the theory of control is developed without proper understanding of the interdisciplinary realities of groups of companies and MNEs. The underlying reasons for this failure can be found in the fact of misunderstanding of the structural characteristics of corporate groups and MNEs. Thus many regulations fail to find a solution for subsidiaries' torts as the realities of modern business allow the parent to escape liability. Accordingly the concentration for better liability regimes in MNEs' context must be on bringing the control theory in law together with the control theory in economic and business studies.

This lack of modern and comprehensive understanding of groups of companies, especially from the perspective of MNEs, prevents scholars, practitioners, courts as well as parliaments from developing satisfactory regulations. Even the latest attempts to regulate corporate groups such as the Draft Commercial Law Bill in Turkey and the Companies Act, 2006 in England as well as the EU Action Plan make the same mistake, which is conceptualizing corporate groups as vertical organizations. Thus the main obstacle to reaching broad liability rules is the same in both statutory and case law; the obstacle is a constant and complicated search for control over one company by the other in a group. In Chapter 2, the extensive search to establish the modern structure has indicated different facts than those conceived by the courts or law-makers.[216] The control in a modern horizontal organization is spread over subsidiaries. Each company under

---

[216] See Chapter 2.

the group has broader independence and the control is exercised through group culture and principles rather than apparent involvement on daily decision-making. Therefore management instructions might come not only from centre of the group but also from those who have various specific duties to perform for the group. Consequently the requirements of control that is imposed by the statutes and courts are mostly invisible from outside. This makes all the regulatory efforts based on control theory incompetent in practice.

Another problem of existing regulation is the persistent ignorance of involuntary creditors in MNEs torts. None of the statutory laws aim to solve the problems of tort liability. There is a complete negligence of the issues in contrast to huge public debate. Victims of MNEs' torts are left with no solutions because there is no efficient mechanism to look for comprehensive liability on a group basis.

In conclusion, this broad examination of existing regulations and principles in law can be concluded in a way that there have been many efforts to remove the unjust effects of limited liability in corporate groups but none of them has accomplished the long-awaited breakthrough revolution. In other words, none of the regulations or outcomes principles in existing laws are able to match the economic, managerial and social dynamic of groups of companies and MNEs. Thus the reconsideration of principles of tort liabilities with the aim of creating a better regime of corporate group liability must be conducted. For this purpose, broad examination of existing law must be used as illustrative models to indicate the failures in the area. The final striking outcome of this chapter is the indication of the need for better-structured proposals in the area to offer an adequate framework for assuring MNEs' tort liability.

# 7. Liability options beyond the group liability discussion

## INTRODUCTION

As discussed in the first part of this book, the strict principles of company law have caused problems in the MNEs' tort liability context. Therefore scholars and regulators are searching for relief of the MNEs tort problems outside the narrow sphere of group liability discussions as alternatives to deadlock in company law principles.[1] Here I wish to discuss some examples of alternative solutions suggested, within commercial law, to the MNEs' tort liability problems: mandatory insurance, parent guarantee for subsidiaries' debt, and changes in insolvency laws. Also, I will briefly mention some options within company law: directors' duties and disclosure requirements. As a wider alternative to accountability and liability problems, corporate social responsibility (CSR) movements and voluntary code of conducts will be discussed in more detail.

## OPTIONS WITHIN COMMERCIAL AND COMPANY LAW

The preference in favour of involuntary creditors in insolvency can be considered as a solution to tort liability problems for group of companies. Leebron and Thompson have argued that financial creditors should be deferred to tort claimants in a liquidation procedure.[2] Professor Davies also suggested that, in some jurisdictions, part of a solution to the group problem is to be found in insolvency law, where the court may be given discretion in certain circumstances to bring a solvent company in the group into the insolvency of another company in that group.[3] However, this option is very superficial because changes in in-

1 Easterbrook, Frank H. and Fischel, Daniel R., *The Economic Structure of Corporate Law* (Harvard University Press, London 1991), p. 60.

2 Leebron, David W., 'Limited Liability, Tort Victims, and Creditors' (1991) 91 Colum. L. Rev. 1565; Thompson, Robert B., 'Piercing the Corporate Veil: An Empirical Study' (1990–1991) 76 Cornell L. Rev. 1036.

3 Davies, Paul L., *Gower and Davies' Principles of Modern Company Law* (Sweet & Maxwell, London 2003), p. 205.

solvency law will not fundamentally affect the liability issues discussed in the book; deferring involuntary creditors to voluntary creditors would just improve the conditions of involuntary creditors rather than solving any problems. Moreover this option might work only in small-scale domestic operating corporate groups as the application of insolvency would be much more problematic in big corporate groups and MNEs with complex structures. Thus deferring involuntary creditors in insolvency will have very little influence on the current situation. However, the differentiation of creditors should be made when discussing MNEs' liability; involuntary creditors should be treated differently in application of liability rather than waiting until the insolvency procedure.

Alternatively the business theory might suggest that the key to all liability problems in MNEs' activities lies with insurance. Accordingly laws requiring MNEs to purchase liability insurance against tort claims to the extent that the claims overvalue their assets might be suggested. How it should be done could only be determined after extensive consultation with the insurance industry, carried out by relevant regulatory bodies. On a basic level, small companies can be liable up to a set amount covered by insurance while big companies, which deal with hazardous activities, will make a detailed assessment of the risk.[4] Accordingly, to some extent, insurance can create solutions to compensation problems in MNEs' tort. However, insuring corporate groups who are engaged with extremely hazardous business would be very expensive. Therefore a majority of the companies will refuse to do business in the areas considered dangerous, which might create a monopoly in the hazardous business area. A monopoly in international business and investment would make the current situation worse. Moreover there is another problem that insured companies might conduct their business very carelessly; since the insurance is already very costly, the companies will not be willing to spend more money for safety measures. A possible devastating effect on insurance companies should not be ignored. For example, in an incident like Bhopal, any insurance company could hardly pay for the huge economic damage.

Insurance options must be questioned from the perspective of liability. Even if there were sufficient insurance it will just cover the compensation determined by the courts or agreed by the parties, rather than creating a liability regime for an entire corporate group. However, in this book the aim is to search for a liability regime on a group basis not just a find a way to finance the compensation. Looking back to some tort examples, it can be seen that compensation had already been paid in such cases as the Bhopal tragedy where the company paid the agreed amount. The problems are still not solved in a fair way, thus there is

---

[4] Pettet, B., 'Limited Liability – A Principle for the 21st Century' (1995) CLP 124.

a need for more fundamental changes in liability theories applied to corporate groups.

Another problem with the insurance option would be the question of who will arrange the insurance, the subsidiary or the parent. If a parent corporation has to insure subsidiaries, the problem of insurable interest would arise. Insurance is a business preference for companies and each individual entity should insure their own risks and there is no mechanism to guarantee this worldwide. There are two different persons so the parent company cannot have an insurable interest in the subsidiary according to the principles established under the case of *Macaura*.[5] As a result, for a successful insurance protection of corporate victims, the system must force insurance of corporate groups as whole. However, enforcing insurance on corporate groups as whole will require the same laws and regulations as imposing liability on them; which must be built ignoring the corporate veil and treating corporate groups as a single enterprise. Moreover the existence of limited liability in the corporate group concept and a case like *Adams v Cape industries* supports the idea that corporations are free to split up their enterprises into smaller entities to avoid liability. Under those conditions, groups' purchase of insurance seems inconsistent with the general principle that shareholders are already protected from liability. Thus investors should not be willing to pay insurers to reduce risk as it can be clearly stated 'why buy something you already have for free'.[6]

The deadlock created by strict adherence to limited liability in the corporate group concept switched some attention to corporate directors. The discussion of directors' duties evolved under the movements of better corporate governance, especially after the collapse of Enron.[7] Moreover there has been a huge campaign to change the duties of directors during the preparation of Companies Act 2006.[8] As a result the Companies Act s. 172 sets out for the first time the duties of company directors. In fulfilling their duty to shareholders, the section requires that directors prioritize the interests of shareholders, but that in doing so they 'have regard' to other factors such as the interests of workers and local communities, and the protection of the environment.[9] This has been presented

---

5 *Macaura v Northern Assurance Co Ltd* [1925] AC 619.

6 Easterbrook and Fischel, *The Economic Structure*, p. 54.

7 Muchlinski, P., 'Enron and Beyond: Multinational Corporate Groups and the Internalization of Governance and Disclosure Regimes' (2005) 37 Conn. L. Rev. 725.

8 See for example CORE, 'Companies Act 2006 – Verdict, A Move Towards Making Business Work for People and Planet' available at http://www.corporate-responsibility.org/module_images/CompaniesBill_verdict.doc.

9 The full section states: Section 172: Duty to promote the success of the company: (1) A director of a company must act in the way he considers, in good faith, would be most likely to promote the success of the company for the benefit of its members as a whole, and in doing so have regard (amongst other matters) to (a) the likely consequences

as success by public interest NGOs,[10] but its impact on liabilities of MNEs will be limited due to vague application and standards. Thus it is hard to know until the legislation is implemented what the exact extent of its practical implications will be.

Even though this can be considered a success from a different point of view, diverting our attention to the directors will be eradicated by the principles of limited liability since making them liable outside of their personal misconduct seems unfair while real owners of the companies can avoid liability. Thus from a legal and economic point of view, making directors liable for torts committed in the course of management of the company is inefficient because development of liability of directors for a tort is alien to the concept of efficient balancing of risk that the doctrine of limited resource aims to achieve.[11] Moreover although director's liability provisions have been widely discussed and more generously proposed, neither legislators nor courts have managed any clear articulation of the basis on which they may be explained. There is a contrast in the law, if there is liability imposed on managers of the companies who are working for the benefit of shareholders, there must be liability for shareholders as well.[12] Therefore it can be claimed that liability imposed on directors differs in principle from the liability imposed on corporate groups or shareholders, either company shareholders or individual shareholders, because directors are employed by shareholders to operate companies' daily business and, thus, they must be considered employees of the shareholders. For this reason, making the employees liable rather than employers seem irrational. Moreover it is apparent that, even in the case of full personal liability of directors, the expected level of protection will not be achieved because of the limited funds of directors and easy avoidance of liability by indication that the directors performed their basic legal duties, which is still to fulfil shareholders' expectations by making the company successful with regard to stakeholders.

Requiring companies and groups of companies to disclosure a certain amount of information about the nature of their business and their relationship with an

---

of any decision in the long term, (b) the interests of the company's employees, (c) the need to foster the company's business relationships with suppliers, customers and others, (d) the impact of the company's operations on the community and the environment, (e) the desirability of the company maintaining a reputation for high standards of business conduct, and (f) the need to act fairly as between members of the company.

10 Friends of the Earth, 'Make Business Work for People and Planet Companies Bill Verdict' (November 2006) available at http://www.foe.co.uk/resource/newsletters/companies_act_2006.pdf.

11 Grantham, Ross and Rickett, Charlie, 'The Bootmaker's Legacy to Company Law Doctrine' in Grantham, Ross and Rickett, Charlie (eds), *Corporate Personality in the 20th Century* (Hart, Oxford 1998).

12 *Ibid.*

outside network is considered another important mechanism of accountability in recent years.[13] Already, existing disclosure requirement for groups of companies in the EU under the 7th Company Law Directive is planned to be increased under the European Action Plan, which states that increased disclosure with regard to a group's structure and relations is needed, and the parent company of each group is to be made responsible for disclosing coherent and accurate information.[14] These improvements can be managed by increasing the disclosure requirements in the 7th Directive. The Commission recommended that more transparency could help minimize those risks. Initiatives aimed at improving the financial and non-financial information disclosed by groups are priorities for the short term. Such initiatives would aim to ensure better information on the group's structure and intra-group relations, as well as on the financial situation of the various parts of the group. First, in the short term, the Commission intends to adopt legislative measures with the intention of improving the group disclosure of financial and non-financial information. Since transparency is seen as the most urgent problem in corporate groups' context, whether they are listed or not, the Commission regards these additional initiatives as priorities for the short term.[15] However, disclosure is not a liability mechanism to ensure groups of companies are liable for their tort actions. Thus it should be separated from substantial liability discussions and should be covered under corporate governance principles.

The above-mentioned suggestions are given as examples of wider approaches to liability and accountability problems. These options play around the general principles of company law and do not go to the heart of the problems. Thus they aim to reduce the unjust affect of liability problems rather than solving them. For example it is also suggested that those dealing with an undercapitalized company in a group of companies may obtain a guarantee from the parent company. Or, less securely, the parent company may issue a letter of comfort to the subsidiary's accounts on a going-concern basis, or to a third party considering contracting with the company.[16] As already seen, many of the alternative

---

13 See further Campbell, K. and Vick, D. 'Disclosure Law and the Market for Social Responsibility' in McBarnet, D., Voiculescu, A. and Campbell, T., *The New Corporate Accountability* (CUP, Cambridge 2007), p. 241; Muchlinski, P., *Multinational Enterprises and the Law* (OUP, Oxford 2007), chapter 9; Villiers, C., *Corporate Reporting and Company Law* (CUP, Cambridge 2007).

14 Communication from the Commission to the Council and the European Parliament – Modernizing Company Law and Enhancing Corporate Governance in the European Union – A Plan to Move Forward, COM/2003/0284 final.

15 The Commission suggested that 'listed companies should be required to include in their annual report and accounts a coherent and descriptive statement covering the key elements of their corporate governance structure and practices', COM/2003/0284 final p. 12.

16 Davies, *Gower and Davies' Principles*, p. 185.

suggestions for liability offer solutions that are outside the sphere of group liability discussions. These options have mostly limited applicability or are applicable for voluntary creditors since they require assessments of conditions in advance. Thus it can be stated that these alternative options are useful in practice for conducting business transactions between companies and creditors but they lack comprehensive principles to solve the problem of tort liability. Moreover even the alternatives outside the sphere of group liability discussion have problems with assessing the nature of corporate groups and MNEs as is apparent in the insurance or parent guarantee proposals under which corporate groups are perceived as vertical organizations. Among these alternatives, CSR issue requires broader examination.

## CORPORATE SOCIAL RESPONSIBILITY

Because of the apparent difficulty of creating laws in the area of MNEs' liability, voluntary regulations can be seen as an alternative. The claim is that market and business should be free to consider self-regulation which is a much-discussed topic especially in recent years while attracting very controversial reactions.[17] A strong civil society movement developed around how to make corporations responsible for the uneven distribution of the benefits of globalization. The debate opened by civil society quickly extended through mass media and the Internet,[18] until it assured itself a place in international institutional agendas.[19] This framework of action was based on the premise that economic discourse cannot be separated from the concepts of respect, protection and promotion of human rights. Some examples are the condemnation of child labour and forced labour conditions in the textile industry in South-East Asia[20] or the complicity with such human rights violations as

[17] See further Dine, Janet, *Companies, International Trade and Human Rights* (CUP, Cambridge 2005).

[18] For example the British daily newspaper the *Guardian* has special sections devoted to CSR discussions at http://www.guardian.co.uk/environment/corporatesocial responsibility.

[19] See further McBarnet, D., 'Corporate Social Responsibility Beyond the Law, Through Law, for Law: The New Corporate accountability' in McBarnet, D., Voiculescu, A. and Campbell, T., *The New Corporate Accountability* (CUP, Cambridge 2007), p. 15.

[20] For example important campaigns were lead against Nike for child exploitation in Pakistan in the production of sports wear and shoes. Nike found itself at trial in the United States for making false public commercial statements in relation to the working conditions of its factories and subcontractors worldwide. See the case *Kasky v Nike* 27 Cal. 4th 939 (S.Ct. Cal. 2002).

torture, forced disappearance and extrajudicial killings in the extractive industry, in places like Myanmar or Nigeria.[21] NGOs have not only been critical in their way to approach the matter but also tried a positive contribution, such as the design of fair trade initiatives[22] or putting pressure on states and international institutions to insert human rights clauses in international trade policies and agreements.[23] This means that the campaigns have moved from concentration on single case studies towards a more generally organized policy-creating agenda.[24]

One of the important factors triggered by CSR movements has been the difficulties of imposing liabilities on companies at national or international level.[25] The reason for this can be found on the design of company laws under which shareholders and companies are separate. Therefore it has been difficult to create binding liability on enterprises due to these complexities in national law and international law.[26] On the lack of direct liability on MNEs for the actions of their subsidiaries or suppliers, the broader scheme of CSR is considered as a tool to prevent human rights breaches.[27] Thus the CSR movements cover not

---

21 The energy companies Unocal and Royal Dutch Petroleum and Shell Transport have faced trials in the United States for their complicity in human rights abuses in Myanmar and Nigeria, respectively under the ATCA. See the cases *Doe v Unocal Corp*, 2002 WL 31063976 (9th Cir. Cal.), 18 Sept., 2002 and *Wiwa v Royal Dutch Petroleum Co* No 96 Civ. 8386, 2002, US Dist. LEXIS 3239 (SDNY Feb 22, 2002) 36. See for more examples McBarnet, 'Corporate Social Responsibility', p. 11.

22 More information about the Fair Trade movement can be acquired from the Fair Trade Project at Queen Mary, University of London at http://www.qmul-fairtradeproject.org/.

23 Some of these organizations have been very active in calling for the adaptation of the legal regime to prevent and punish these forms of abuse of human rights and to include MNEs as objects of regulation in international law. Amnesty International, for example, conducts important work on business and human rights and campaigns very strongly for legal accountability. See Amnesty International, *The UN Norms for Business: Towards Legal Accountability* (Amnesty International Publications London 2004). The International Council for Human Rights Policy produced one of the first and most comprehensive works on the international law standards and mechanisms applicable to MNEs, *Beyond Voluntarism: Human Rights and the Developing of International Legal Obligations for Companies* (Versoix 2002).

24 Sabapathy explains the process of developments from a single-issue campaign to more general responsibility campaign for human rights and the environment. See Sabapathy, J., 'In the Dark All Cats are Grey: Corporate Responsibility and Legal Responsibility' in Tully, S., *Research Handbook on Corporate Legal Responsibility* (Edward Elgar, Cheltenham, UK, Northampton, MA, USA 2005) p. 242.

25 Dine, *Companies*, Chapter 5.

26 See Chapters 3, 4, 5 and 6.

27 McBarnett, D. and Kurkchiyan, M., 'Corporate Social Responsibility Through Contractual Control' in McBarnet, D., Voiculescu, A. and Campbell, T., *The New Corporate Accountability* ( CUP, Cambridge 2007), p. 59.

only equity-based MNEs but also networked enterprises.[28] Moreover the CSR movements or reports have always claimed going beyond the legal framework.[29] In this sense, CSR is considered flexible enough to cover enterprises in the widest framework.[30] With this coverage, CSR is presented as a very efficient tool to prevent human rights breaches by MNEs.

Currently, it can be sustained that international law does not provide a satisfactory general framework for the obligations of states or corporations themselves in relation to human rights through international legally binding sources. The reason is that international law norms are mainly addressed to states, which have the capacity to accept and comply with their obligations.[31] States are considered responsible parties in terms of human rights breaches. As a result, it has also been claimed that on the lack of international legal personalities attributed to them, bringing non-state private actors (MNEs) into international regulatory regimes could be possible through creating efficient CSR regimes.[32] The issue of lack of enforcement mechanism against corporate actors in international law is also an important element in emergence of CSR movements because it is considered that jurisdictional problems[33] can be overcome by creating an international concept of socially responsible corporations.[34] The concept of CSR has been created in response to these perceived gaps in the regulatory systems and thus the idea of CSR is considered as one of the big ideas of the century since in theory it offers solutions to problems of corporate crimes.[35] Accordingly corporate responsibility discussion covers many areas, such as direct liability for tort, criminal liability by using international criminal courts,[36] to create an efficient CSR regulation either at international, regional or national level.[37]

---

28 See Chapter 2.

29 For example, BP describes its CSR responsibility as a wider circle that covers legal compliance. See further at http://www.bp.com/productlanding.do?categoryId=6900&contentId=7028276.

30 McBarnet, 'Corporate Social Responsibility', p. 11.

31 Clapham, A., *Human Rights Obligation of Non-State Actors* (OUP, Oxford 2006), Chapter 6.

32 *Ibid.*

33 See Chapter 4.

34 Zerk, J.A., *Multinationals and Corporate Social Responsibility* (CUP, Cambridge 2006), p. 2.

35 *Ibid.*

36 See Chiomenti, C., 'Corporations and the International Criminal Court' in De-Schutter, O. (ed.), *Transnational Corporations and Human Rights* (Hart Publishing, Oxford 2006), p. 287.

37 Steinhardt gives wide range of options and survey of possible regulation of corporate responsibility. See Steinhardt, R., 'Corporate Responsibility and the International

The CSR movement came from various organizations with different social and political agendas in mind. Thus there is a wide range of terminology on the concept of corporate social responsibility such as corporate responsibility, corporate accountability, corporate social responsibility, corporate citizenship, and corporate sustainability.[38] On this base there are fundamental differences in defining the concept of CSR. Therefore it is useful to discuss general approaches to CSRs from institutional points of view.

Public interest NGOs consider CSR as an effective tool to solve the problems of human rights breaches by MNEs. Thus NGOs always aim to reach a wider binding regime. NGOs and corporate accountability have some history. In the last three decades not only ethical consumerism[39] but also a voluntary regulation push have been important to bring the agenda to the notice of the public as well as to prepare the ground for wider and more binding regulations.[40] However, even though the involvement of NGOs in the process of creating efficient CSRs has been important in recent years, it has not gone beyond creating soft-laws. Thus the campaigns have moved towards concentrating on more binding regulations. It is considered that the idea of soft-law could be a great base for binding regulations. For example the CORE Coalition[41] has been developing a proposal for corporate accountability.[42]

On the other hand, business actors mostly emphasize voluntary aspects of CSR movements. The weight in the business and government initiatives of CSR is usually on separation between legal regulation and CSRs.[43] Among the so-

---

Law of Human Rights: The New *Lex Mercatoria*', in Alston, P., *Non-State Actors and Human Rights* (OUP, Oxford 2005), p. 178.

[38] The use of language in CSR meetings by organizations are well presented by Conley, J.M. and Williams, C.A., 'Engage, Embed and Embellish: Theory versus Practice in the Corporate Social Responsibility Movements' (2005–2006) 35 Journal of Corporation Law 1.

[39] See Blecher, M., 'Law in Movement: Paradoxontology, Law and Social Movements' in Dine, J. and Fagan, A. (eds), *Human Rights and Capitalism* (Edward Elgar, Cheltenham, UK, Northampton, MA, USA 2006), p. 80.

[40] Bennett, C. and Burley, H., 'Corporate Accountability: An NGO Perspective' in Tully, S., *Research Handbook on Corporate Legal Responsibility* (Edward Elgar, Cheltenham, UK, Northampton, MA, USA 2005), p. 372.

[41] CORE is an umbrella organization established by respected NGOs to campaign for changes in UK company law to minimize companies' negative impacts on people and the environment and to maximize companies' contribution to sustainable societies. See further at http://www.corporate-responsibility.org/.

[42] Bennett and Burley, 'Corporate Accountability', p. 372; Sullivan, R., 'The Influence of NGOs on the Normative Framework for Business and Human Rights', in Tully, S., *Research Handbook on Corporate Legal Responsibility* ( Edward Elgar, Cheltenham, UK, Northampton, MA, USA 2005), p. 286.

[43] Zerk, *Multinationals*, p. 30.

called corporate social responsibility instruments developed are: corporate codes of conduct;[44] social and environmental reporting initiatives; labelling and certification schemes; partnership of stakeholders with NGOs; intergovernmental organizations or agencies for behaviour monitoring; and social investment indexes. Their content and scope normally vary according to the promoter of the initiative – intergovernmental organizations, public interest NGOs, business associations or a company itself – and the industrial sector in which the company operates. In this sense, those businesses more exposed to the public tend to engage in these initiatives more than those whose activities involve little interface with the general consumer and therefore less reliance on reputation and public relations.[45] Therefore even though a code of conduct can benefit the society their benefits are limited as an accountability mechanism.[46]

International organizations and national states consider CSR options as a voluntary guide for MNEs. Generally, governments of capital-exporting states such as the UK and US are reluctant to take steps which harm international competitiveness.[47] For example in the UK the arguments are shaped on the idea of voluntary and binding regulations, but the government favours voluntary regulations.[48] This situation changes the balance on CSR movements towards soft-laws because those who have the regulatory power favour voluntarily regulation. An important issue for this situation has been the frontal opposition from

---

44 Definition and history can be found in McLeay, F., 'Corporate Code of Conduct and the Human Rights Accountability of Transnational Corporations: A Small Piece of a Larger Puzzle', in DeSchutter, O. (ed.), *Transnational Corporations and Human Rights* (Hart Publishing, Oxford 2006), p. 219.

45 See Martin-Ortega, O. and Wallace, R.M.M., 'The Interaction between Corporate Codes of Conduct and International Law: A Study of Women and Children in the Textile Industry', in Tully, S., (ed.), *Research Handbook on Corporate Legal Responsibility*, (Edward Elgar, Cheltenham, UK, Northampton, MA, USA 2005); McBarnet, 'Corporate Social Responsibility'.

46 McLeay, 'Corporate Code of Conduct', p. 219.

47 Zerk, *Multinationals*, p. 7; Sabapathy, 'In the Dark', p. 239.

48 See the government's official website at www.csr.gov.uk. The UK's Department for International Development (DFID) states 'internationally legally binding frameworks for multinational enterprises may divert attention and energy from encouraging corporate social responsibility and towards legal process'. Business groups and international institutions such as the OECD also support self-regulation. Despite the UK's position that company behaviour is best dealt with through voluntary approaches, past experience has shown that it is not enough See 'DFID and Corporate Social Responsibility, the Government's Role: Legislation and Voluntary Initiatives', (DFID) (September 2003), p. 9. The UK government has appointed Stephen Timms (MP) as the minister for corporate social responsibility within the Department of Trade and Industry (DTI). His view is that the role of governments is to 'work with the corporate sector to facilitate this type of involvement, rather than looking to regulatory measures or new law. Available at http://www.dti.gov.uk/ministers/archived/Timms131202.html#related.

the business community and the lack of embracing by states and international organizations. In this context, the developments in the EU sphere have been closer to this approach rather than to the one advocating a strong normative framework.[49] In short, Addo summarizes different approaches to CSR very well:

> There are practical and doctrinal uncertainties such as the precise scope of the various designations and the basis upon which social or moral responsibility can be imputed to an intangible entity such as a corporation which has no soul of its own to be damned, if necessary. There is a persistently unsatisfactory condition in which the various groups (NGOs, corporations, inter-governmental institutions etc.) attribute different meanings and explanations to designations of their choice. Good governance, good citizenship, or social responsibility can mean anything to anyone.[50]

The supporters of the voluntary regulations in academia claim that CSR as a voluntary basis plays an important role in creating the value of encouraging voluntary virtue before enforcing it; as put by McBarnet, 'The business could best demonstrate a new attitude to corporate social responsibility not so much by surpassing law's requirements, but by meeting those requirements in spirit at least.'[51] Moreover it is claimed that another problem with more binding and legislative approaches is the vagueness of CSR as a general principle based legislation; thus, it can be argued that it is not yet clear enough to produce legislation.[52]

On the other side, supporters of the binding CSR movement have expressed their concern.[53] Academics built their arguments against self-regulation on enforcement and accountability-based concerns.[54] Some raise the issue of lack of accountability and control of business over NGOs because, as partners of business, NGOs lack accountability to anybody, which might cause NGOs to

---

[49] See further Voiculescu, A., 'The Other European Framework For Corporate Social Responsibility: From The Green Paper to New Uses of Human Rights Instruments', in McBarnet, D., Voiculescu, A. and Campbell, T., *The New Corporate Accountability* (CUP, Cambridge 2007), p. 378.

[50] Addo, M. 'Human Rights and Transnational Corporations: an Introduction', in Addo, M. (ed.), *Human Rights, and Transnational Corporations* (Kluwer, The Hague 1999), p. 13.

[51] McBarnet, 'Corporate Social Responsibility', p. 47.

[52] Sabapathy, 'In the Dark', p. 252.

[53] Anti-voluntary approaches are quite wide. In the EU, Socialist and Green Members of the parliament have argued against purely voluntary policy on CSR. See further McBarnet, 'Corporate Social Responsibility', p. 28.

[54] Shamir, R., 'Between Self-Regulation and the Alien Tort Claims Act: On the Contested Concept of Corporate Social Responsibility' (2004) 38 Law and Society Review 4.

lose their influence.[55] As an extensive study indicates, there is reason to be sceptical about business actors because they are using the opportunity to lead the debate and guide it to their way of thinking.[56] Moreover there is a real risk that these voluntarily adopted codes will deceive the consumers, will lack credibility in the absence of any form of independence monitoring, will settle on minimal standards, or will contain important ambiguity in comparison with the internationally agreed standards.[57] But some academics claim that the law is no longer separate from CSR as new legal pressure and new legal mechanisms to enforce CSR policies are brought into play.[58]

As a result, even though there are many sceptics about CSR movements,[59] at least there is almost a common agreement that corporations should be socially responsible. Thus Zerk claims that the first stage of the battle is over, now the question will be how corporations should be made responsible rather than why.[60] This makes the 'voluntary versus mandatory' debate inevitable and more dominating. As parties to this debate between business[61] and public interest, NGOs[62] have already chosen their side, the balance will be determined by the national states and international organizations. Thus CSR should be part of the systems of law that support the efficiency of already existing regulations.[63] Another misconception is that mandatory regulation is not necessarily creating higher standards.[64] As a result, the aim should be what the best regulatory response is. The emphasis should be made on implementation and enforcement because lack

---

55 Conley and Williams examine the changing nature of the linguistic used by NGOs such as 'branding' 'accountability'. See Conley and Williams, 'Engage, Embed and Embellish'.

56 *Ibid.*

57 DeSchutter, O., 'The Accountability of Multinationals for Human Rights Breaches in European Law', in Alston, P., *Non-State Actors and Human Rights* (OUP, Oxford 2005), p. 308.

58 McBarnet, 'Corporate Social Responsibility', p. 31.

59 Christian Aid, 'Behind The Mask: The Real Face of Corporate Social Responsibility' (Christian Aid, January 2004) available at http://www.christianaid.org.uk/indepth/0401csr/csr_behindthemask.pdf accessed 24 June 2006.

60 Zerk, *Multinationals*.

61 For business view in Europe, see CSR Europe at http://www.csreurope.org/. They define CSR Europe as a European business network of CSR professionals based upon the sharing of CSR solutions and shaping the modern day business and political agenda on sustainability and competitiveness. Consists of over 65 leading multinationals; reaches out to a further 2200 companies through 23 national partner organisations; began as an initiative in 1995 by the European Commission President Jacques Delors and senior European business leaders.

62 CORE claims that voluntary approach has failed. See further at http://www.corporate-responsibility.org/.

63 Zerk, *Multinationals*, p. 35.

64 *Ibid.*

of enforcement is an important issue that should be addressed in any CSR movements.[65] The question should be how to ensure consistency between these different initiatives, and whether the time has come for a more ambitious development.[66]

Looking at social responsibility of corporations at the international context, there are some specific international instruments establishing standards directly addressed to companies, as opposed to indirectly through state obligations to protect human rights under their jurisdiction. However, both their legal force and scope are limited as they are no more than soft-law instruments and specifically focused on labour rights rather than more generally related to human rights or liability issues.[67] These instruments are the OECD Guidelines on Multinational Enterprises (1976, reviewed in 2000)[68] and International Labour Organization Tripartite Declaration on Multinational Enterprises and Social Policy (1977, reviewed in 2000).[69] Both documents address enterprises as well as states, and constitute an important guide for the identification of the standards that could be applicable to companies, in particular in relation to labour standards.[70] Even if they are not legally binding and lack mandatory implementation and sanction mechanisms, these instruments have become the point of reference in the regulation of MNEs' social responsibility.[71]

The voluntary-based approach towards business responsibilities has received an important impulse from intergovernmental organizations lately. In particular, within this framework lie instruments such as the Global Compact of the Secretary-General of the United Nations and the European Union's attempts to design its own strategy on CSR. The UN Global Compact was launched by the Secretary General in 1999 at the World Economic Forum, which presented to

---

65 Gelfand, J., 'The Lack of Enforcement in the United Nations Draft Norm: Benefit or Disadvantage?', in DeSchutter, O. (ed.), *Transnational Corporations and Human Rights* (Hart Publishing, Oxford 2006), p. 313.

66 DeSchutter, O., 'The Challenge of Imposing Human Rights Norm on Corporate Actors', in DeSchutter, O. (ed.), *Transnational Corporations and Human Rights* (Hart Publishing, Oxford 2006), p. 2.

67 *Ibid.* p. 6.

68 OECD Doc. DAFFE/IME(2000)20DAF.

69 ILO Doc. GB 277/MNE/3. See further for the ILO Declaration, Kim, K.B., 'A Multilateral Contribution to Corporate Standards of Behaviour: The ILO's Declaration on Multinational Enterprises', in Tully, S., *Research Handbook on Corporate Legal Responsibility* (Edward Elgar, Cheltenham, UK, Northampton, MA, USA 2005) p. 319.

70 Clapham, A. and Martignoni, J.B., 'Are We There Yet? In Search of a Coherent EU Strategy on Labour Rights and External Trade', in Leary, V.A. and Warner, D., *Social Issues, Globalisation and International Institutions* ( Martinus Nijhoff Publishers, Boston 2006), p. 296.

71 See further DeSchutter, 'The Challenge', p. 6.

the world business leaders the challenge, to be assumed by the UN and the private sector, to put a human face to the global marketplace.[72] It was defined as an invitation for business to endorse UN goals and a call for greater corporate responsibility. It started working officially on 26 July 2000. It consists of 10 principles,[73] to which companies adhere, but it is not a normative instrument. It does not try to impose regulations or evaluate particular actions on companies. Therefore it is based on voluntary and responsible action from business sectors or, as the Office for the Global Compact puts it, 'on the search for a contribution to a development which is sustainable and broader than global markets'.[74]

The most ambitious initiative to provide a binding legal framework on human rights for corporations is now being considered as having failed.[75] The UN Norms on the Responsibilities of Transnational Corporations and other Business Enterprises with regard to Human Rights,[76] approved by the Sub-Commission on the Promotion and Protection of Human Rights in August 2003[77] proposed an innovative approach in international law applying standards directly addressed to companies in an attempt to impose internationally binding human rights norms on business.[78] The business community, as could have been antici-

---

72 UN Press Release SG/SM/6881, 1.2.1999.

73 The principles contained in the initiative are divided into four categories: human rights, labour standards, environment and anti-corruption. In relation to human rights, businesses should: (1) support and respect the protection of internationally proclaimed human rights; (2) make sure that they are not complicit in human rights abuses. In relation to labour standards businesses should uphold: (3) the freedom of association and the effective recognition of the right to collective bargaining; (4) the elimination of all forms of forced and compulsory labour; (5) the effective abolition of child labour; and (6) the elimination of discrimination in respect of employment and occupation; support a precautionary approach to environmental challenges. In relation to the environment, businesses should: (7) support a precautionary approach to environmental challenges; (8) undertake initiatives to promote greater environmental responsibility; and (9) encourage the diffusion of environmentally friendly technologies. In relation to anti-corruption practices, businesses should: (10) work against all forms of corruption, including extortion and bribery.

74 Global Compact Office, 'How the Global Compact Works: Mission, Actors and Engagement Mechanisms' (New York, 2003).

75 See further Kinley, D., Nolan, J. and Zerial, N., '"The Norms are dead! Long live the Norms!" The Politics Behind the UN Human Rights Norms for Corporations', in McBarnet, D., Voiculescu, A. and Campbell, T., *The New Corporate Accountability* (CUP, Cambridge, 2007); Gelfand, 'The Lack of Enforcement'.

76 UN Doc. E/CN.4/Sub.2/2003/12/Rev.2, 26 August 2003.

77 Resolution 2003/16.

78 See further Wallace, R.M.M. and Martin-Ortega, O., 'The UN Norms: A First Step to Regulation of Transnational Corporations' Responsibilities for Human Rights" (2004) 26 Dublin University Law Journal 304; Sorell, T. 'The UN Norms', in Dine, J. and Fagan, A. (eds), *Human Rights and Capitalism* (Edward Elgar, Cheltenham, UK, Northampton, MA, USA 2006) p. 284.

pated, has had a rather hostile attitude towards them, considering them as unnecessary and indeed a threat to the current situation. [79]

Looking at the situation in the EU, the legal order of the European Community offers a number of possibilities which are hard to envisage in the circumstance of other multilateral organizations. The regulations can bind both natural and legal persons including states and corporations, so that the rights which are created are actually enforceable before the national courts of the EU member states.[80] However, the EU has opted for a voluntary-based approach towards the private sector's responsibilities for social issues, including human rights and the protection of the environment.[81] The EU has developed this approach through defining its own strategy on CSR, independent of other institutions that had already developed tools in this field. It has, however, constantly manifested support towards initiatives such as those already mentioned: OECD, ILO, the UN Secretary General's Global Compact and, recently, the Kimberley Process[82] certification scheme for the international trade of rough diamonds, by assuming its chairmanship in 2007. The bases of the EU strategy were set out in two documents: the 2001 Green Paper 'Promoting a European Framework for Corporate Social Responsibility'[83] and the 2002 Communication 'Corporate Social Responsibility: A business contribution to sustainable development'.[84]

As a result, as these initiatives were born and developed the discourse on the suitability of a binding versus a voluntary model were central to the debate of the responsibilities of the private sector in relation to human rights and the environment.[85] This discussion should now go beyond the confrontation that double approach creates.

---

79 Wallace and Martin-Ortega, 'The UN Norms'.

80 Clapham and Martignoni, 'Are We There Yet?', p. 296.

81 Clapham and Martignoni, 'Are We There Yet?', p. 296; Voiculescu, 'The Other European Framework', p. 378.

82 More information available at http://www.kimberleyprocess.com/.

83 COM (2001) 366 final, 18.7.2001.

84 COM (2002) 347 final, 2.7.2002.

85 See Martin-Ortega, O., 'International Responses to Multinational Enterprises' Lack of Accountability for Human Rights Abuses in the Context of Globalisation' (2006) 7 Revista de Estudios Juridicos 179.

## CONCLUSION: COUPLING CORPORATE SOCIAL RESPONSIBILITY WITH EFFICIENT TORT LIABILITY REGIMES

The idea of codes of conduct and self-regulation through CSR for companies has no strong legal basis. It leaves many things to the discretion of companies as it does not abandon using company law principles to avoid liability or offer any enforceable duties on them. That might be considered one of the reasons MNEs support CSRs as an alternative to liability rules. However, the level of protection for tort victims cannot be provided by CSR or codes of conduct. Thus states should not risk the safety of their people by supporting policies that suit only business interests.

Even though the topic of voluntary regulations is very popular, the nature of voluntary regulations is not very clear because there is no single guide to CSRs.[86] Therefore the reactions to the issues are very diverse; one argument is that it is just a public relations issue for huge MNEs, ie companies use CSRs as an advertisement tool to increase their profits. On the other side of the argument, CSRs are considered as a result of public pressure that in some cases voluntary codes force MNEs to behave in a lawful manner and thus prevent much misbehaviour of MNEs in host countries. Although being highly promoted, it is a fact that the CSR has not yet been put to a real test.[87] Since there are no binding or powerfully accepted uniform codes for the business, every MNE claims their own codes and of course they report complete compliance with fantastic achievements.[88]

In the voluntary approach, companies are concerned with their own reputations, with the potential damage of public campaigns directed against them and, overwhelmingly, with the desire to secure ever-greater profits. None of this necessarily means that companies do not act responsibly. But it does mean that their attempts to do so are likely to be partial, short term and inconsistent, leaving vulnerable poor communities at risk.[89] For many companies, CSR has become at best an advertisement exercise and at worst a tool for opposing regulation. But both also demonstrate the continued determination of the voluntary sector to make it work properly and their commitment to exposing its misuse.[90]

---

[86] See Zerk, *Multinationals.*

[87] Mazurkiewicz, P, 'Corporate Environmental Responsibility; Is a Common CSR Framework Possible?' http://www.worldbank.org/developmentcommunications/Publications/csrframework.pdf, accessed 13 January 2006.

[88] See for example Shell Nigeria CSR Report at http://www.shell.com/home/content/nigeria/news_and_library/publications/annual_reports_archive.html.

[89] Christian Aid, 'Behind The Mask'.

[90] *The Times* (London 2 February 2004).

Simply many companies have found that CSR has often had a positive impact on corporate profits. Of all the topics related to CSRs, so far, the greatest amount of experimental data links practical companies with positive financial results.[91]

Accordingly self-regulation fails to prevent continued abuses of corporate power, and thus corporate torts, for a number of reasons: (1) they do not provide strong incentives for compliance to balance the financial incentives for non-compliance because sanctions are missing or weak; (2) they rely on the appearance of compliance through self-regulation, without independent confirmation or enforcement; (3) they fail to authorize citizens and stakeholders in the matter; instead, even where a stakeholder discussion approach is used, they present the issue of corporate responsibility as top-down – as defined by the company.[92]

From the standpoint of this book, it can be claimed that arguments of voluntary regulations should not challenge or affect the outcome of the presented arguments of tort liability. Voluntary regulations and legally binding regulations must co-exist. Successful voluntary regulations have a characteristic of preventing mass-misbehaviours by corporations because they establish standards for the industry, workers and directors and so on. Consequently CSRs or codes of conduct might reduce tortious actions of MNEs and tort claims against them. This will make liability regulations much more applicable as the number of claims will be reduced and there will always be the possibility of comparing well-behaving MNEs and tort committing MNEs. However, it should not be forgotten that the existence of CSRs will not eliminate tort actions because they are the reality of life and in some cases it might happen in situations beyond the control of the company or directors. Even if MNEs behave in a very good manner or follow their CSR very closely, there is always the possibility for torts to happen. Nobody can guarantee that, even under very stringent regulations, MNEs behave in a good manner and there will not be another tragedy caused by torts committed by subsidiaries of MNEs.

Therefore voluntary regulation and statutory regulations should not be considered as substitutes to each other; rather they should be evaluated as supporters of each other's applicability and efficiency. The voluntary approach tries to prevent corporate torts or any illegal and moral misbehaviour while the binding liability approach aims to provide a justifiable liability for the torts committed by MNEs and compensate the victims. In this case, principles and tools are

---

91 Mazurkiewicz, 'Corporate Environmental Responsibility'.

92 'Towards Binding Corporate Accountability' (FoEI Position Paper for the WSSD, January 2002) available at http://www.foe.co.uk/resource/briefings/corporate_accountability.pdf accessed 27 June 2006.

fundamentally different; the voluntary approach requires consideration of a number of policy issues and soft-law principles while the binding liability system requires mostly hard law and fundamental changes in statutes and case law.

The legal systems should still develop effective obligatory statutes and soft-law principles to create core principles and regulations to prevent tort actions. However, in order to prevent tort actions of MNEs, there should also be efficient legal regulations that create full legal liability in a deterrent way.[93] Thus the aim of creating efficient liability systems in substantial laws should still be pursued. Using substantive liability rules can be considered as an efficient tool to make corporations responsible because in the absence of other binding regulations, changes in tort liabilities of MNEs can be considered as an alternative to make them liable.[94] This has been tried under the ATCA by bringing MNEs before American courts.[95] Thus this book claims that the best way to achieve justice in MNEs tort cases is to balance profit-maximization theory with liability-expansion through creating efficient liability regimes and thus maximizing the compensation paid for a tort. In other words, a liability regime based on hard law is the most efficient way to hold the balance between the economic theory of profit maximization and requirements of justice in the law. I believe that approaches only based on CSR and other voluntary initiatives will not create the expected level of a justifiable regime to make MNEs liable, even though they would surely have some positive effect. Thus the legal systems should couple CSR initiatives with efficient liability regimes.

On the other hand, the wider coverage of CSR can be used as a tool to bring networked enterprises to regulatory framework either at the national or international level. Accordingly equity-based MNEs must be regulated under binding liability rules introduced by substantial changes in applicable law while the broader relationship of MNEs can be subjected to regulation through the voluntary nature of CSR. The vague coverage of CSR is better suited to networked enterprises under which there is no clear definition of an enterprise as an organization but there are many contractual relationships amongst independent companies.[96] Accordingly the wider limit of enterprises examined in the second chapter as a network of business relationships can be covered, at least in prin-

---

93 DeSchutter, 'The Challenge'.

94 Anderson, Michael, 'Transnational Corporations and Environmental Damage: Is Tort Law the Answer' (2002) 41 Wasburn Law Journal 399.

95 Tully, S., '"Never Say Never Jurisprudence": Comparative Approaches to Corporate Responsibility under the Law of Torts', in Tully, S., *Research Handbook on Corporate Legal Responsibility* ( Edward Elgar, Cheltenham, UK, Northampton, MA, USA 2005), p. 125.

96 See Chapter 2.

ciple, by CSR initiatives. In this way by attaching binding liability regulations to equity-based corporate groups while linking CSR to networked enterprises, two important business challenges of the 21st century can find regulatory responses that suit their organizational and business features.

# PART III

# A way forward

# 8. Future of MNEs' tort liability

## INTRODUCTION

In the previous parts of the book, the torts committed by subsidiaries of MNEs are discussed and gaps in the legal systems are indicated by concluding that MNEs might avoid liability in tort and this problem is urgent and requires attention from academics, parliaments and judges. For this purpose the book has first indicated the distinguishing characteristics of MNEs from other institutions by examining developments in legal, social-economical and managerial-structural characteristics. Accordingly the book claims that an MNE is a distinct institution, which is unique in its characteristics and thus different from other institutions recognized by laws and thus requires different regulatory principles and theories. Accordingly Part II is devoted to the search for laws and regulations on MNEs liability issues, which has demonstrated that the laws and regulations are inefficient to solve the liability problems due to common misunderstandings of interdisciplinary characteristics of MNEs. As a result, even though the time has come to think about real, effective and internationally applicable solutions for MNEs' liability problems, so far no concrete proposal exists for such a solution and governments seem unwilling to commit themselves to a truly legislative solution. From an academic perspective, the suggested solutions have always had weaknesses if they are not totally ineffectual. Accordingly the aim of this chapter is to propose the framework principles on which MNEs' tort liability must be built. The principles will be based on a combination of social, economical and managerial characteristics of MNEs with a particular focus on the problems of MNEs' tort liability.

One of the important aspects of liability issues regarding MNEs is whether liability should aim to protect people against MNEs' torts or should it concentrate on compensating the victims for committed torts. In the first instance, the logical answer seems to be that the aim of any regulation must be preventing corporate torts before they happen but on careful examination it is not that easy. The protective measures already exist and there are many recent developments in environmental, labour or tort laws that aim to prevent MNEs' torts. However, these measures are two sided; in developed countries, preventative measures might work better than they work in less-developed countries. Less-developed countries are systematically prevented from taking more preventative measures since they are scared of losing MNEs' investment in their countries.[1] On the other hand, even though there are very detailed rules to prevent MNEs' misbehaving, there is still a very high likelihood of torts committed by MNEs. To be able to minimize the effect of the MNEs' torts there is a need for a system of liability aiming to compensate victims in a full and justifiable way.

The effects of efficient liability systems will be two sided; first it will create justifiable solutions for victims after torts have been committed which should be the basic aim of every legal system. Secondly, compensation maximization will have an important effect on preventing and deterring MNEs from misbehaving and committing torts. In other words, searching for compensation maximization is not just searching for efficient ways to compensate after a tort; it is, with the same importance, finding effective ways of prevention of MNEs' torts by creating a solid liability regime. It is widely proven in many situations that an efficient liability regime prevents many torts by forcing companies to take necessary measures to avoid it. For example liability imposed on companies for the use of asbestos has made them very careful in their mining operation; a newspaper report states: 'there was a good lesson learnt by companies since nearly 80 companies went bankrupt; the use of deadly asbestos has now completely been abandoned in the USA and many more countries follow this practice'.[2] It is very obvious that one of the reasons for this was high compensation awarded by the American courts. Moreover in the case of purchasing insurance for the risk of companies' operations, insurance companies will require high preventative measures or will sell the insurance at very high prices as the assessment of the risk will be made according to the new liability rules. Accordingly the aim of liability regimes must be creating compensation maximization, under which MNEs will be expected to pay high compensation to tort victims. In short, an efficient tort liability regime offers solutions to problems of MNEs' tort together with other preventative measures.[3]

With this aim, this chapter will be devoted to searching for better liability regimes for groups of companies and thus for MNEs. However, there will not be entirely clear-cut proposals in order to avoid a complex system of proposals

---

1 See Dine, Janet, *Companies, International Trade and Human Rights* (CUP, Cambridge 2005); Dine, Janet, 'Using Companies to Oppress the Poor', in Dine, J. and Fagan, A. (eds) *Human Rights and Capitalism* (Edward Elgar, Cheltenham, UK, Northampton, MA, USA 2006).

2 Hall, Ben and Peel, Michael, 'Law Change to Speed up Asbestos Cases' *Financial Times* (London 21 June 2006). According to the *Financial Times*, asbestos claims cost more than $70 billion and bankrupted nearly 80 companies. *Financial Times* (London, 15 February 2006).

3 Anderson, Michael, 'Transnational Corporations and Environmental Damage: Is Tort Law the Answer' (2002) 41 Washburn Law Journal 399.

that will have little chance of being considered by regulators. Rather the aim will be determination of principles and theories on which MNEs' liability regulations must be built so that the regulatory discussions will be comprehensive enough to solve current and future problems. Principle creating in the first instance will increase the chances of reaching a more global and widespread regime of liability.

Accordingly in this chapter, first, there will be an indication of the basic difficulties and mistakes, which explain why the expected level of protection has not been achieved for MNEs' tort victims. A number of obstacles will be discussed to clear the way for proposing solutions. Acknowledging the difficulties will be very helpful in creating better proposals and help us to avoid mistakes made in the past. Following there will be a search for a number of options by comparing existing laws and principles and solutions offered on the principles discussed in this book; the suggestions will be built on the facts discussed in the first part of the book and will be associated with the findings in the second part. However, there will be no attempt to create precise codes in order not to make contradictions of our claims that MNEs are dynamic institutions and must be regulated according to their contemporary realities. Taking this approach will make the life of the suggestions longer and will give this book a broader base and, more importantly, a guiding mission.

## EXPLORING THE REASONS FOR MISTAKES

At this stage, it is vital to provide a basic explanation why the apparent injustice in current legal order could not be overcome for such a long time. In other words, one should search for what the difficulties are behind this rigid situation since case and statutory laws do not offer solutions to MNEs' torts.

The first difficulty on the way to achieve comprehensive MNEs' liability is the lack of empirical research to assess what would happen if there were no limited liability and separate legal personality since at this stage all forecasts of the economic system of companies without limited liability are subjective and depend on non-empirical prediction. Therefore in the absence of influential experimental research any conclusion has to remain spontaneous and unverified.[4] It is suggested that, from an economic point of view, the abolition of limited liability and separate legal personality for corporate groups would result in a level of damage to the financing of a business enterprise, which would sooner or later be seen to be unacceptable. Accordingly liability rules dependent

[4] Pettet, B., 'Limited Liability – A Principle for the 21st Century' (1995) CLP 124.

on this non-empirical prediction have been inefficient because they either offer some changes under current regime of liabilities or search for alternative options outside the range of company law principles. Thus there has always been a search for solutions that do not touch the core principles of company law.[5]

However not having empirical data must not be an excuse; the legal system should begin to collect empirical data by starting a gradual elimination of limited liability. The discussion carried out previously in this book is not necessarily suggesting that limited liability should be abandoned entirely. This book is devoted to the search for answers to tort liability of MNEs and has indicated that limited liability and separate legal personality principles create unfair distribution of risk. Throughout the book, with interdisciplinary examinations, I have provided evidence that separate legal personality and limited liability principles can be abandoned without damaging efficiency of the market economies. Hence the basic principles of company law should not be considered as inflexible principles which are either entirely applied or totally removed. These principles can easily be applied in flexible ways in certain justified circumstances. I claim that the empirical removal should start with questioning the most urgent and justified cases: abandoning limited liability for the benefit of tort victims in the context of corporate shareholders because there are number of indications mentioned in the first part of the book proving that abandoning limited liability for corporate shareholders might not fundamentally disturb capital market economies. Moreover some case and statutory law examples from comparative jurisdictions have created empirical data. Thus it can be claimed that non-availability of empirical data cannot be an excuse for not solving liability problems in corporate groups' context.

Another important reason for the failure is that a limited liability company is considered as one of the driving forces of modern capital economies putting it at the centre of market-economy regulations. This requires that, in order to solve the problems, the theories in legal and economic studies must be dealt with together by bringing social justice theory into this frame. Thus there is a requirement to create a better background theory and justification not only in legal but also in economic and political and social effects of limited liability. With this aim this book indicates that limited liability in the corporate groups and MNEs context play little role in investment decisions and the functioning of market economies. As a result economic, social and political theories of MNEs have been built to consider options for liability regimes in MNEs context.

This brings the discussion to the conception of shareholders. In academia and in case law, shareholders are considered as innocent participants in the modern capital economies. In need of protection, shareholders are considered

---

5 Pettet, 'Limited Liability'.

almost on the same level as creditors creating a situation that in a sense no solution can be perfect because group responsibility laws will often compensate one group of innocent parties (that is the shareholders and/or creditors of the compensated group member) at the expense of another group of innocent parties (that is the shareholders and/or creditors of the liable group members).[6] In order to avoid this protectionism of shareholders, the conception of corporate shareholders must be differentiated from individual shareholders. Accordingly, in this book there has been a mission to differentiate between corporate shareholders and individual shareholders in the corporate groups' concept by claiming that the law should take a different approach towards individual shareholders and company shareholders in terms of application of limited liability as different treatment and structure of corporate shareholders and individual shareholders is already a common practice in the market economies. The effect of limited liability differs according to types of shareholders; individual shareholders need the protection of limited liability more than company shareholders.

Despite these apparent unjust effects of limited liability and corporate separate legal personality, very little has been done to change the applicability of these principles to either to individual shareholders and corporate shareholders. Thus the book, in Part II, has aimed to explore tort liability principles applied to MNEs' tort. Here I discovered another problem, which is the misconception of business management structure of MNEs in legal practice and academia. The argument carried out through the book is built on the idea that group liability as applied in case and statutory laws is based on a misconception of general characteristics of modern MNEs, particularly the way the control is applied in complex groups. As a result, liability options developed while keeping the core principles of company law have been inefficient due to the creation of the control theory which does not reflect the realities of modern business.

In this situation another difficulty arises which explains that the failure to create a functioning corporate group liability for tort was largely due to the complex structure of corporate groups: the unclear nature of laws applied to groups has caused confusion as to which legal body of the group victims should address their claims. This creates a difficulty for regulators finding a legal person to impose liability on.[7] As a result, liability models have always concentrated on making parent companies liable under various systems and principles. These

---

6 Nolan, A., 'The Position of Unsecured Creditors of Corporate Groups: Towards a Group Responsibility Solution Which Gives Fairness and Equity a Role' (1993) CSLJ 461.

7 Prentice, Dan, 'Corporate Personality, Limited Liability and the Protection of Creditors', in Grantham, Ross and Rickett, Charlie (eds) *Corporate Personality in the 20th Century* (Hart, Oxford 1998).

models to reach the parent as the only logical legal personality to have liability in the group have been at the centre of proposals. The reason for this is that when liability issues for MNEs and group of companies started to be considered in academia, in practice and by law-makers, almost all the proposals, either successful or not, have depended on this simple approach to MNEs structure, under which it is assumed that the parent applies direct control over its subsidiaries.

The extent to which liability of the parent requires specific regulations and the conditions of such a specific group liability are very controversial indeed. There have been attempts to impose three different kinds of liability on the parent.[8] In a simple approach to groups of companies there is a tendency to hold the parent liable for damages inflicted on the subsidiary provided that there was fault, such as in the piercing the corporate veil principles. A second pattern of liability is the assumption of the subsidiary's losses by the parent at the end of the year (approaches taken by German law). Alternatively the law may attach a direct liability on the parent corporation by reason of its failure to exercise proper control over its subsidiary (vicarious liability).

Legal complication in regulation of corporate groups and difficulty of finding legal persons on whom to impose liability has resulted in many variations in legal and academic principles suggested to solve the liability problems. In all these approaches, the basic justification was control of the parent over subsidiaries; that control gives rise to the legal obligation of the parent to the plaintiff.[9] Since there are no critical approaches to group of companies' structure and organizations those principles have fallen into the same models of laws that have already proven inefficient. Interestingly, once alternatives have proved inefficient, the searches have intensified and created more detailed proposals on the same economic and structural symbolization of corporate groups. We have already seen many examples in case and statutory laws.[10] Some examples of variations in proposals made by academics considered alternatives to statutory and case law created veil-piercing doctrine are worth mentioning in order to clear the way for better proposals.

The first alternative proposal would be to impose liability on parent corporations where their subsidiaries have exposed others to knowable risks and are now unable to cover their liabilities for damages caused by these knowable risks. Professor Schwartz's proposed rule would impose unlimited liability for

[8] Hopt, Klaus J., 'Legal Elements and Policy Decisions in Regulating Group of Companies', in Wooldridge, F. and Schmitthoff, C.M. (eds), *Groups of Companies* (Sweet & Maxwell, London 1991), p. 103.

[9] Nygh, Peter, 'The Liability of Multi-National Corporations for Their Subsidiaries' (2002) EBOR 27.

[10] See Chapters 5 and 6.

corporate torts only in the context of knowable, but not remote, risks.[11] The proposal would draw a distinction between the different types of risk, and impose parent corporation liability only for knowable risks. This approach claims to have comparative fairness and efficiency in application, because it encourages the discovery of risks and punishes the parent corporation only when it places a knowable risky activity in a subsidiary corporation without putting sufficient assets into the subsidiary.[12] However, in practice, the liability of the parent only for knowable risk cannot actually create a better solution than the veil-piercing doctrine. Under complex horizontal structures of MNEs, it is unclear and almost impossible to prove to what extent the parent was aware of the activities of subsidiaries. Moreover the evaluation of risk by the parent and by the subsidiary could be totally different as subsidiaries are more independent and self-operated. Under those conditions, to be able to apply liability for knowable risk, the courts have to engage in very fact-specific inquiries of the situation between the parent and the subsidiary similar to one in the veil-piercing doctrine.

Alternatively Professor Dent proposes that liability should be imposed on negligent controlling persons, but not on cautious ones.[13] Dent suggests an alternative to current parent corporation liability standards that would encourage, rather than discourage, active involvement of the parent corporation in the operations of the subsidiary. The firm members can avoid personal liability by showing that the firm implemented reasonable measures and procedures to control the conduct that caused the loss. Therefore firm members can escape personal liability if they can affirmatively show that they acted reasonably in managing the risk.[14] Dent explains that the standard of the cautious parent corporation should not require the monitoring of day-to-day activities of the firm but will require that parent corporations make sure that the subsidiary retains capable officers who install a reasonable programme to prevent

---

[11] Schwartz defines a knowable risk as 'a risk that a product is as dangerous as a firm would predict on the basis of doing the cost-effective amount of research, or less dangerous. Conversely, a remote risk is a risk that a product is more dangerous than a firm would predict if it had done the cost-effective amount of research into safety'. Schwartz, Alan, 'Products Liability, Corporate Structure, and Bankruptcy: Toxic Substances and the Remote Risk Relationship' (1985) 14 Journal of Legal Studies 689.

[12] Farmer, Richard S., 'Parent Corporation Responsibility for the Environmental Liabilities of the Subsidiary: A Search for the Appropriate Standard' (1994) 19 J. Corp. L. 769.

[13] Dent, George W., 'Limited Liability In Environmental Law' (1991) Wake Forest Law Review 151.

[14] Fortney, Susan Saab, 'Seeking Shelter in the Minefield of Unintended Consequences – The Traps of Limited Liability Law Firms' (1997) 54 Wash. & Lee L. Rev. 717.

subsidiaries' tort. This prudence standard or approach would further require that the parent corporation assure financial soundness, the determination of which would be left to the courts where several factors should be relevant.[15] Dent tries to change the traditional parent-subsidiary liability concept by encouraging parental control, not discouraging it. Therefore this new approach to parent corporation liability seems more in tune with the objectives of CERCLA and existing tort law, which were criticized earlier in the book for causing more complexity. Moreover as already tested by many failed statutes and proposals, the encouragement of control has been far from creating solutions and wholly in contradiction to the direction of contemporary changes in MNEs' structures under which the control is decentralized.

Another alternative solution suggested is parent corporation liability for equipping the subsidiary with insufficient assets. Gelb proposes that in cases where creditors are unable to protect themselves, such as tort creditors, the adequacy of the corporation's assets should be the relevant inquiry.[16] The court's focus should be on the adequacy of assets, and the term undercapitalization should be abandoned in favour of this new description because capitalization may overly focus a court's attention on assets provided to a corporation as capital at the time of its organization. Consequently there must be a continuing requirement for the maintenance of an adequate level of assets and not one based solely on the assets situation at the commencement of the business. Gelb concludes his proposal by defending the adequacy of assets approach, stating that consideration of other traditional factors is unnecessary, irrelevant and may lead to error.[17] Courts and commentators often cite inadequate capitalization as an important factor in the corporate veil piercing analysis. However, empirical analysis of the case law suggests that inadequate capitalization in practice is not as persistent an issue as the commentators would suggest.[18] Thus minimum capital requirements arguments also seem not very convincing, since it could be claimed that it has more importance in small-scale private limited companies rather than huge horizontally structured MNEs. Moreover minimum capital has already existed in many jurisdictions but it has not created a solution to the corporate groups' liability. Evaluating the adequacy of asset requires complicated and demanding work before the corporate veil can be disregarded. In this respect, Gelb's proposed standard presents a less dramatic shift from the current veil-piercing doctrine, narrowing the range of factors necessary to pierce the

---

15 *Ibid.*

16 Gelb, Harvey, 'Piercing The Corporate Veil – The Undercapitalization Factor' 1982 Chicago-Kent Law Review 1.

17 *Ibid.*

18 See further Thompson, Robert B 'Piercing the Corporate Veil: An Empirical Study' (1990–1991) 76 Cornell L. Rev. 1036.

corporate veil, but still requiring a fact-specific and specialized inquiry in each individual case.[19]

As a result the examples of proposals on the concept of a parent-subsidiary relationship for the basis of liability cannot provide adequate solutions to the problems of tort liability because they ignore the economic and managerial realities of modern corporate groups. Similar proposals to those mentioned have been tested in different jurisdictions but mostly failed to create dramatic improvements in the MNEs' tort liability situation.[20] The scholars have failed to grasp the common interdisciplinary characteristics of corporate groups and MNEs so the overall outcome of their proposals produced a very complex structure of liability, which requires a number of conditions and are very easy to evade by MNEs. This created a circle in which already tested liability proposals have been reintroduced with different names. Therefore in order to be progressive, the law-makers, courts and scholars should search for liability options by considering interdisciplinary characteristics of MNEs.

Moreover liability options offered by scholars are usually compensatory liability by the parent company rather than direct liability of the parent or group. Liability directed to the parent is not efficient in MNEs' context. The jurisdictional differences between countries and different approaches to liability in a subsidiaries' jurisdiction make it very difficult to create a group-based liability if a parent's liability is considered as compensatory rather than direct liability.

## BUILDING LAWS TO MAKE MULTINATIONAL ENTERPRISES LIABLE FOR THEIR TORTS

In the previous chapters, the background knowledge and discussions have been built to be able to facilitate emergence of principles for the most efficient liability regime for MNEs' torts. The previous discussion suggests the law is inadequate to solve the problems that corporate groups and MNEs create. Thus current legal systems should take action to regulate tort liability of corporate groups and MNEs by elucidating the basic principles for liability regimes for corporate groups. As a result the book next searches for answers to the question of which types of regulations are best suited to corporate groups and MNEs' liability problems. These discussions are made from various perspectives.

---

19 Farmer, 'Parent Corporation'.

20 See Chapters 5 and 6.

## Jurisdictional Concerns

The first regulatory ground to discuss must be the ground for liability under the jurisdictional concerns. The jurisdiction for an effective liability regime which could be at global, international, regional or national level is important as globalization of international economic activities has created new challenges for law-makers. Domestic civil laws have failed to solve the problems or rather have become obstacles to solving some liability problems created by the activities of globalized civil actors. Therefore in order to create efficient tort liability regimes, there must be a search for regulations valid at global level. However this seems very difficult at the moment because of the economic differences and development inequalities amongst countries as well as differentiated roles of MNEs by creating disputes amongst countries according to their interests. This heterogenic structure of countries is an obstacle to reaching a global regime of civil liability, which proposes that consideration of regional or domestic regimes with more global effect will be more realistic.

In regional concerns, the EU might offer some provincial regulatory schemes that guarantee civil liabilities of any parties who are exposed to a tort by a member of a group of companies. Efficient regimes in the EU might have external effect by imposing liability on EU-based MNEs for their tort outside the EU. The regulation at the EU level is more efficient because if an EU member state were to introduce group liability for MNEs' tort, the ECJ's rulings in *Daily Mail*,[21] *Centros*,[22] *Überseering*[23] and *Inspire Art*[24] cases[25] would guarantee that circumvention of this regime by setting up a company in another member state might not be considered an abuse of the freedom of establishment regulated in the EU Treaty.[26] Thus any possible introduction of liability at the EU level will prevent avoidance of the regulatory competition amongst members to attract more companies to establish in their jurisdiction as the regulatory competition is one of the biggest obstacles to introducing an accepted level of liability regimes in any particular country. The ideal regulation must be able to reduce the possible regulatory competition by designing regulations that are widely accepted.

Moreover the complexity of the area of MNEs' liability also favours regulation based on standards to create better applicability. In this case, the EU can

---

21 ECJ Case 81/87 of 27 September 1988, ECR 1988, 5483.

22 ECJ Case C-212/97 of 9 March 1999, ECR 1999, I-1459.

23 ECJ Case C-208/00 of 5 November 2002, ECR 2000, I-9919.

24 ECJ Case C-167/01 of 30 September 2003, in DB 2003, 2219.

25 See Andenas, Mads, 'Free Movement of Companies' (2003) LQR 221.

26 Berkamp, L. and Pak, Wan-Q., 'Piercing the Corporate Veil: Shareholder Liability for Corporate Torts' (2001) 8 Maastricht J. of European and Comparative Law 167.

provide the most efficient regulation for corporate groups, as it focuses on creating standards-based regulation, leaving the role of improvements to member states. Accordingly the EU must start a broader initiative than its current Action Plan on Modernising Company Law to reduce the severe effect of MNEs' torts. Actually the EU should start a new project on this matter either as part of the Action Plan or completely independent from it. It is useful at this stage to mention the discussion of the nature of possible EU action; at the EU level there is a discussion in the case of unitary regulation as to whether it must be obligatory for every state or states to be given a right to opt out from this regulation or some part of the regulation. The self-determination by states under flexible regimes, which might create possible corporate havens similar to Delaware in the US, is always supported by business organizations. However allowing this to happen would result in the emergence of regulatory competition, which any regulation should aim to avoid in the first place. The implementation of possible EU-based laws should be compulsory for member states, at least so far as the basic principles are concerned.

In the absence and failure of the global and regional regulatory efforts, national corporate and tort laws might also create the same effects especially in those countries in which MNEs are originated. The law of a certain nation state might grant jurisdiction rights for victims and might create a regime under which victims pursue their civil liability claims in equal ways to citizens of this particular country. Such law will be at domestic level but the influence will be at a global level as it will have the effect that civil liabilities against MNEs might be pursued in domestic courts as well as implementing liability clauses for other member corporations in the group.

In pursuing the aim of creating the widest possible liability regime either at national or regional level, the basic principles of ATCA can be improved to make it an effective regime of tort liability.[27] The basic nature of ATCA, which is creating civil liability for torts committed by the removal of jurisdiction barriers, must be kept but all the obstacles that restrict application of substantial liability must be removed. First of all, the notion of civil liability must be not just sourced from international law but it must cover any tort liability raised against MNEs. The most remarkable aspects of ATCA, which is bringing the case even if the company has only a minimum connection to the state, must be extended by making domicile of subsidiaries sufficient to establish jurisdiction over the group. In this way victims can start their liability actions in any jurisdiction where a subsidiary of a group is based. Moreover application of *forum non conveniens* must be abandoned and the application of veil-piercing doctrine in corporate groups must be abolished to make the rules more efficient. Accord-

[27] See Chapter 4.

ingly on the lack of global and regional liability regimes for MNEs, the minimum contact to jurisdiction principle introduced in ATCA litigations can be considered sufficient to eliminate the jurisdictional barriers to victims of MNEs' tort. Under this principle, existence of subsidiaries should provide a minimum contact in the forum and therefore create a jurisdiction over parent companies, or other companies in the group. Thus the system of minimum contact would work better if it can be combined with widely accepted group liability. Moreover the system of creating jurisdiction based on minimum contacts is better suited to horizontal structures. On the lack of clear hierarchy in corporate groups, it is better to try to apply liability not only through parent companies but also through other entities in the group.

## Laws for MNEs or Creditors: Economic Concern versus Justice

After determining the jurisdiction to address the problems, it is essential to argue whether there should be protecting regulation for creditors or regulations should aim to facilitate operations of MNEs under the argument of economic concern versus justice. It is a fact that the efforts to create a better liability regime for groups of companies and MNEs have frequently been blocked by the consideration of the economic well-being of society. There is a common belief in international economic studies that MNE operations in home or host countries are necessary for the economic benefit of people at any level of the society.[28] Thus the regulations of MNEs' activities have mainly concentrated on facilitating their operations or opening up borders to these huge economic powers. Consequently regulatory efforts on the basis of tightening liability are kept at a minimum level. Under the belief and policies shaped by modern capital economic theories, the protective regulations for corporate creditors against MNEs' activities are constantly ignored by law-makers in order not to deter MNEs investing in their territory.

The difficulties appear in the understandings and characteristics of these regulatory approaches: the protective regulatory perspective and the organizational approach demonstrate specific features and are based on different standards. While the former is based on a view of the group as a hazardous institution, the latter regards corporate groups as an entrepreneurial reality, trying to provide them with safe guidelines for their operation and for the ongoing relations between the member entities and amongst their organs. Accordingly the complex economic and managerial feature of the activities of MNEs and lack of studies to combine these theories with risky feature of MNEs have caused the current deadlock in MNEs' regulation.

---

[28] See Chapter 1.

The law should come to more comprehensive proposals in order to balance economic need and the need for justice according to social economic analysis discussed in Part I of this book. Both sides of the regulatory arguments have important concerns thus the legal system should not restrain economic or justice concern for the benefit of the other. Some situations might require weighing in on the side of regulation of groups to facilitate their economic activities, while some situations require laws that are protecting creditors and victims. For the better and more contemporary regulation of corporate groups, modern law systems should take both approaches in equal measure and try to integrate them into the modern regulatory regime.

Accordingly the regulatory approach should consider this imbalanced situation while introducing new laws by imposing liabilities on MNEs. Moreover the book has indicated that imposing liability for subsidiaries' torts on MNEs would not result in the collapse of company groups or collapse of any national economy. In the area of MNEs' liability, it has already been indicated that the prospective liability imposed on MNEs for their tort in home or host countries is not really unbalancing the economic developments of any nation. In other words, being liable for their subsidiaries' tort will not substantially affect the economic existence of MNEs.

## With or Without Limited Liability

At this stage the discussion of differentiation amongst shareholders must be made. In a situation where many solutions to MNEs' tort liability problems have been somehow blocked by the limited liability principles, one should think that limited liability should be abandoned entirely. Accordingly the most extreme departure from current legal systems towards liability would be abandoning limited liability and introducing pro-rata shareholders' liability for corporate torts by creating unlimited shareholders' liability. It is claimed that a rule of unlimited pro rata liability would protect the marketability of corporate shares without permitting shareholders to externalize the cost of corporate torts.[29] Some historical evaluation of limited liability principles reveals that the limited liability was not an essential element to the emerging of the joint stock company.[30] Thus the limited liability could easily be abolished if sufficient political support is attracted. However, this proposal aims to abolish limited liability not only for

[29] Hansmann, H. and Kraakman, R., 'The Essential Role of Organisational Law' (2000) Yale L.J. 387.

[30] Ireland, Paddy, 'Rentier Investment and Corporate Irresponsibility: A Brief History of Limited Liability' (Forthcoming in Cambridge Journal of Economics, 2008).

corporate shareholders but also for individual shareholders, thus it could not attract many supporters.[31]

However abandoning limited liability entirely might have very diverse effects on capital market economies. Even though there is not sufficient empirical data to evaluate capital market economies without limited liability, it is obvious that drastically changing a core of the company laws might affect the structures of modern enterprises negatively. I believe that the time has not yet come for discussing complete abolition of limited liability. Even abolishing limited liability for tort victims would have many procedural and practical problems and seems very unlikely to be possible in the near future because it requires much more preparation and empirical testing. Since, in this book, I discuss the tort liabilities of MNEs it is not necessary to discuss the option of total abandonment of limited liability very deeply at this stage. I believe the concentration must be on eliminating limited liability in corporate groups, which could provide more empirical analysis to discuss further elimination of limited liability.

In this argument the book claims in Part I that limited liability and separate legal personality in corporate groups' context are not necessary elements of economic efficiency of market economies. Numbers of investment theories discussed in Chapter 1 and business structure of modern MNEs discussed in Chapter 2 suggest that limited liability in corporate groups' context can easily be removed. Moreover Chapter 3 shows that economic efficiency of limited liability for corporate groups is somehow an overworked claim and has no legal and economic basis. Accordingly limited liability in corporate groups is the source of liability problems and can be tackled if we are able to change these core principles of company law. However, as discussed in Part II, liability problems have not been solved not only because of core principles of company law but also a misconception of the real nature of corporate groups, and the theory of control built on this misunderstanding. Accordingly even though these issues overlap, the problems can be addressed properly by taking different regulatory approaches to them. In the first one there is a need to change core principles of company law while in the latter one changing the understanding of the theory of control might produce solutions to tort liability problems. In brief, even though abolishment of limited liability and separate legal personality principles in the context of corporate groups would create solutions to the liability prob-

[31] See Hansmann, Henry and Kraakman, Reiner, 'Do the Capital Markets Compel Limited Liability: A Response to Professor Grundfest' (1992–1993) 102 Yale L.J. 427; Hansmann, Henry and Kraakman, Reiner 'Toward Unlimited Shareholder Liability for Corporate Torts' (1990–1991) 100 Yale L.J. 1879; Hansmann, Henry and Kraakman, Reiner 'Procedural Focus on Unlimited Shareholder Liability' (1992–1993) 106 Harv. L. Rev. 446; Grundfest, Joseph A., 'Limited Future of Unlimited Liability: A Capital Markets Perspective' (1992–1993) 102 Yale L.J. 387.

lems, the liability problems can also be tackled by introducing new principles of liability which are based on modern characteristics of MNEs.

**Case Law or Statutory Law**

In the process of liability discussions, given basic principles of common law, the discussion of the role of the courts in any regulatory approach will be unavoidable. There should be the question whether the regulation should be statutory or case law. Professor Lowry claims that any shortcomings in limited liability problems can be addressed by the courts being prepared to adopt a bolder and more principled approach to the issue of piercing the corporate veil, which would at least provide a necessary counter-balance against the abuse, which it is claimed *Salomon* has given rise to.[32] Apparently the claim is that if the universal availability of limited liability does produce abuse, the appropriate solution may well lie with the courts rather than the creation of a new principle of liability. The principle that should guide the courts in determining whether or not to pierce the corporate veil should be firmly based upon notions of justice or more general equitable considerations. Only thus will the judges be able to strike the best possible balance between devotion to *Salomon* principles and the doctrine of limited liability.[33]

However, previous examination of the case law in England and comparative examination prove that leaving liability problems to the courts will not create better results than veil-piercing principles. This fact has already been stated in many incidents by courts by addressing the parliaments for fundamental changes. The problem in the case law is the lack of principles and a difficulty in changing their stand on limited liability and *Salomon* principles. In these conditions, it is difficult for courts to develop a fundamental departure from old and settled practice without statutory interference from parliaments. The parliamentary effort would create the basics of regulations to make MNEs liable since it is relatively easier to change the current situation by a statute than changing it by case law. The requirement of statutory interference does not mean the courts would be inactive in creating and developing liability regimes for MNEs. The creative role of the courts is required at every stage of the practice and for further application of the rules to new and changing situations in the practical world. Therefore any forthcoming reconsideration of a liability regime should consider both statutes and case law.

---

32 Lowry, John, 'In Defence of Salomon: Promoting The Corporate Veil', in Rider, Barry A.K. and Andenas, Mads (eds) *Developments in European Company Law, Vol 2/1997: The Quest for an Ideal Legal Form for Small Businesses* (Kluwer Law International, London 1999).

33 *Ibid.*

## Single or Plural Regulation

Deciding requirements of statutory intervention triggers another question as to whether there should be single or plural regulation. In strict terms whether to have a single exclusive regulation or different ways of legally ordering corporate groups within the same legal system is indeed a question that needs to be addressed before the features of group regulation are dealt with.[34] The discussion was conducted earlier in this book that the regulation of corporate groups has been made under different branches of law and this creates some problems for those who expect some kind of harmony and predictability in law of a particular matter. On the other hand, there is a discussion that corporate groups are of interest not only to company law but a very broad range of laws spread through other branches of law such as competition, tort, labour or insolvency. Therefore it is claimed that it will be necessary for other branches of law to have provisions and principles related to corporate groups from their own perspective.

For the purpose and the aim of this book, giving some credit to opposite ideas, groups of companies must be regulated under a single law, but it should consider the dynamics of the other branches of law. There is a need for a group of companies' regulation covering MNEs but this law should not be initiated just from the basics of company law; rather it should possibly consider and take into account experience and principles that have been created under other branches of law examined in the previous chapters. Corporate groups' law must be comprehensive enough not to require other branches of law to search for further liability clauses. For example it must cover and thus offer solutions to the jurisdictional problems so that there will not be a time-consuming battle to establish jurisdiction on MNEs. The law-makers should examine how different characteristics of tort, labour, competition, environments and human rights laws might impact on MNEs and group of companies and company laws. Doing so will enrich the basics of MNEs' liability laws so that the law will be long-lasting and well-equipped in creating more justifiable solutions.

## Company Law, Corporate Groups Law or Multinational Enterprises Law

In order to achieve the aim of the most comprehensive regulatory law, we should look for an answer to the question of whether there should be company law or corporate groups' law or MNEs law. For practical purposes or, more importantly, for the life of durable regulations of MNEs, the legal regimes should decide

[34] Irujo, José Miguel Embid, 'Trends and Realities in the Law of Corporate Groups' (2005) 6 EBOR 65.

whether there should be a new corporate groups law covering MNEs or the law-makers should still regulate group of companies' law under company law. One side of the argument is that there is no need to regulate corporate groups under different principles since they consist of independent companies operating together, but on the other hand the examination of groups of companies and MNEs as social and economic institutions in this book indicates some different institutional characteristics for MNEs. Under those conditions, the law should create its own applicable principles to MNEs because the basic principles of company law have failed to regulate MNEs and thus failed to prevent the unjustifiable situation in tort claims. Accordingly the best way to regulate corporate groups must be generating regulation that determines the basic requirements and principles of corporate groups as new institutions. This law must create basic principles of corporate groups including liability issues. This new regulation must be innovative relying on its own theories rather than borrowing theories from company law.

## General or Detailed Regulation

After determination of the requirement for a single regulation, there should be a discussion whether the law should be standards-based or detailed regulation.[35] The issue is simply whether regulation must be expressed through a number of general standards or a detailed set of legal rules. Actually case law based characteristics of the common law support regulation on principles. In other words, if there is a necessity for regulation it will support standard-based regulation rather than rule-based regulation. However, from the perspective of the discussion in the previous chapters of the book, the standard-based regulation seems more logical and efficient. It would not be advisable to undertake a detailed regulation aimed at forecasting problems caused by diverse corporate entities in a group.[36] The need to encompass all general situations requires supporting standard-based regulatory approaches.

The principal discussion carried out in this book regarding managerial structure of MNEs also points out more general and standard-based regulations. The dynamic characteristics of modern enterprises with a complex horizontal structure might make detailed regulations inefficient. The laws that have very rigid detailed regulations and principles might create unexpected results such as the *Salomon* ruling did in the corporate groups' context. Rather than trying to regulate any details based on a rigid single understanding of corporate groups, the focus should be on creating a regime that is suited to the complexity of groups and thus flexible in application.

---

[35] Irujo, 'Trends and Realities'.

[36] *Ibid.*

It can be claimed that the Forum Europaeum proposal and the recent EU Action Plan are in favour of standards-based regulation.[37] According to the general policy of the EU, during the period of attempts at regulation, the EU seemed to prefer a corporate group law based on the formulation of major standards, leaving specific aspects relating to the formation and operation of corporate groups to the member states or, where applicable, to self-regulation.[38] The other side of the argument claims that exposing groups of companies to different legal requirements or a differentiated extent of liability according to the laws of the individual member states only complicates and endangers the rights of all creditors at the European level. The fear always exists that regulation based on just standards for corporate groups might put regulations in jeopardy and there would be complex and differentiated regulatory systems for MNEs in every member state.

However, at a regional level, the lack of international aspects in company law and sovereign and local characteristics of the law support standard-based regulations while leaving the details of rules to nation states. On the other hand, one can claim that since MNEs and institutions have very similar characteristics and structures, the regulations should support detailed liability rules being applicable in all jurisdictions. In conclusion the issue must be considered in accordance with the level of the regulation; there must be standard-based regulations if regulations are at regional or international level. There must be more detailed regulations if regulatory effort is at national level. In other words, standard and rule-based regulations might exist jointly; the efforts to regulate corporate groups must be built considering the different characteristics of legal systems. There must be principle-creating regulations at global level, standard-based regulation at regional level and rule-based regulation at national level so that the conflict of principles of liability will be avoided.

## Static or Dynamic Regulation

The discussion of standard or rule-based regulation reflects another challenge establishing regulation as situation or process. The discussion carried out on this book is that the corporate groups are in constant changing process and thus they must be regulated with specific concern to this reality. MNEs are under a changing process resulting from basic structural principles of capitalist economies and pressure of maximizing profits.[39] Regulatory efforts should consider those processes and it should have impact on the future of corporate

---

[37] See Chapter 6.
[38] Irujo, Trends and Realities.
[39] See Chapters 1 and 2.

group law. If law-makers regulate MNEs as static institutions, the new legal regime would be struggling to solve problems the next generation of MNEs will create.

The legal systems have already made a mistake by considering companies as standstill institutions and kept the same structure and principles of company law for decades. The laws and principles have been established considering corporate groups as simple structured institutions with quite clear separation between parent and subsidiaries and amongst subsidiaries. This mistake of considering corporate groups as simple organizations has resulted in a very complex and inefficient legal regime of liability for group of companies. Considering groups as static institutions is one of the reasons that prevents possible developments because it is very difficult to change legal rules once the rules have been settled. For example the mistake made while applying limited liability to corporate groups prevents changes of limited liability rules in modern company laws; even in very specific circumstances it requires very detailed discussions and burdensome efforts. Moreover concentrating on a static situation in law-making demolishes the possibility to produce empirical data for alternative regulations. Regulations of corporate groups should thus not focus totally on the principles considering the group as a mere static situation since formation of corporate groups require that all references to different approaches must not be ruled out. Understanding groups as a process allows us to have necessary flexibility. The difference with the static standards is therefore that the economic and legal processes that lead to such a situation are also included in regulation thus giving it better chance of adoption in economic and legal life.[40] The regulatory efforts should focus on the basics of MNEs' characteristics and should try to cover many situations including the current structure of the MNEs. It also should consider future developments by aiming to have influence in shaping the future of the structure of MNEs.

## How to Personalize MNEs

The next step in discussions of the future of MNEs' tort liability must be to search for an answer to how MNEs should be personalized in law. There should be discussion of regulations from the perspective of whether regulations should be based on the concept of groups of companies or a concept of MNE. One of the interesting aspects of the recent attempts in regulatory efforts of corporate groups' liability is concentration on the concept of corporate groups. This situation creates the problem of separation between group of companies and MNEs. Right from its most basic principles, corporate group law certainly reveals an

40 Irujo, 'Trends and Realities'.

institutional concern despite the group's lack of a corporate personality.[41] Accordingly groups of companies have attracted some regulatory efforts in national jurisdiction but when attempts are made to extend these regulatory efforts to MNEs, more problems arise because of the jurisdictional limits of the regulations or reluctance of law-makers to apply the same laws to groups of companies outside of national borders. There are a number of characteristics and institutional differences between groups of companies and MNEs. As a result these differences between groups of companies and MNEs might affect the outcomes of any legal regulation aiming to create justifiable liability for MNEs since any effort has to consider special characteristic differences of MNEs.

For these reasons, the problem of MNEs' personality must be clarified. One of the most important arguments in this area is whether MNEs are recognized as international legal personalities or they are considered a group of independent companies operating together under common management. To be able to discuss the possibility of attributing legal personality to MNEs, one should begin with clarifying the legal situation of groups of companies. No legal system grants legal personality to groups of companies, rather the national laws impose some liabilities and responsibilities on parent companies while maintaining the separate legal personality of member companies. In an application of the situation of a group of companies' law to MNEs, it is indisputable that MNEs are not recognized as international legal personalities; international law does not grant them a privileged international legal personality status. Public international law is only implemented in their regard through state action, so that they continue to be subject only to domestic law of states.

In this discussion, logically, it is not appropriate to change the situation of MNEs' personality by attributing an international legal personality status to MNEs, because their direct participation in the process of creating legal norms applicable to them and their access to mechanism for the application of international law could be at the expense of certain values and essential principles of international law, in view of their discretional function in the economic sphere.[42] In other words, the legal world has to consider their huge economic and political influence on the governance of nation states and the world economy since granting MNEs with legal personality is like equipping them with most powerful weapons in a war.

Accordingly under no situation should international law be applied when contracting with MNEs and it is unacceptable that a contract should provide for

41 *Ibid.*

42 The Activities of Transnational Corporations: The Need for a Legal Framework (Geneva, July 2001) available at http://attac.org.uk/attac/document/transnationals-legal-framework.pdf?documentID=41.

the application of such law, because it would mean that national law is being disregarded and it accepts the ambition of MNEs to evade state control. In order for MNEs to be held accountable for their actions, it is not necessary to give them an international legal status, because national legislation might contain provisions which are applicable to all companies under the group, and there are treaties between states to deal with conflicts of laws and enforcement issues. Any means of liability can be imposed on MNEs without considering them as legal persons in international law. In conclusion either regional law, such as EU law, or domestic laws are capable of imposing liability without further recognition of groups of companies and MNEs as legal persons. The enforcement of laws on groups has already been common practice for tax and group accounting purposes. It is also possible to manage similar enforcement in terms of tort liability.

**Parent, Subsidiary or Group Liability**

Clarifying legal personality, the next stage of discussion must be models of liability imposed on different personalities under the discussions of group liability, parent liability and subsidiary liability. In other words, the question is whether liability should be either entity or enterprise liability. There have always been some discussions about liability models of liability on corporate groups. Models for regulations have varied, some pointed to parent companies to be held liable for the subsidiary's tort and some support the subsidiary liability together with some obligations on the parent. The recent attempts usually concentrate on aggregation of assets in corporate groups since the corporations' law already requires this to be done for accounting purposes. This would seem to provide creditors and other interested parties with information that would allow such persons to make an informed assessment of the creditworthiness of a related group of companies.[43]

Liability for parent companies, finding its justification for allowing creditors to reach the assets of parent corporations, does not create unlimited liability for any MNE. Thus the benefits of diversification, liquidity and monitoring by the capital market are unaffected. Moreover the moral-hazard problem is probably greater in parent-subsidiary situations because subsidiaries have less incentive to insure creditor protection.[44] However, liability aimed at parent companies has many weak points. The parents can escape liability by proving their non-

---

[43] See Fridman, S., 'Removal of the Corporate Veil: Suggestions for Law Reform in *Quintex Australia Finance Ltd. v Schroders Australia Ltd.*' (1991) 19 ABLR 211.

[44] Easterbrook, Frank H. and Fischel, Daniel R., '*The Economic Structure Of Corporate Law*' (Harvard University Press, London 1991), p. 57.

involvement in control of the subsidiary. Thus the concentration on parent company for liability does not create solutions under the current organizational structure, which is always more complicated than the one described or presumed by the court or law-makers.

In the case of group liability concept, this perception is not very different from parent corporation liability as in cases or statutes the liability is mostly directed to the parent. The parent mostly has mere duties imposed on the limit of separation between subsidiary and the parent. Interestingly any term of group liability used in statutes or case law or even by scholars do not exactly mean group liability but rather they refer to parent liability.

This lack of group liability concept or failure to distinguish differences between parent liability and group liability has affected the emergence of the concept of enterprise entity doctrine.[45] The doctrine is different from the existing understanding of group liability in that it replaces an approach based on exceptions to the otherwise unbreakable corporate separation between the parent and subsidiary (whether through the lifting of the corporate veil or through specialized group liability laws) with one that assumes parent corporation liability from the fact of economic unity between itself and the subsidiary.[46] This recognizes the corporate group as a distinctive form of business association, so opening the way for the evaluation of a specialized legal regime going beyond the model of the single unit limited liability company.[47] Thus the concepts of enterprise liability may offer a solution, especially in the case of mass torts, but its extent and limitations remain to be explored.[48] The closest example to enterprise theory can be found in the *Amoco Cadiz* case but, as already mentioned, that case was exceptional and never created a better doctrine in the common law case law.[49] Therefore a broader conception of groups as an enterprise has not prevented criticism of the enterprise theory. For example an enterprise entity approach has been criticized for being too hierarchical as it aims again basically at parents for imposing liability ignoring the current developments in corporate group structure.[50] In this sense the enterprise theory does not offer a practical radical solution to corporate group liability but it offers a better ground for veil lifting.

---

45 Strasser, K.A. and Blumberg, P.I. 'Replacing Misused Limited Liability with Enterprise Analysis in Corporate Groups' (Conference on Corporate Accountability, Limited Liability, and the Future of Globalization, School of Oriental and African Studies, London, UK, 20–21 July 2007).

46 Muchlinski, P, *Multinational Enterprises and the Law* (OUP, Oxford 2007), p. 317; Strasser and Blumberg, 'Replacing Misused'.

47 Blumberg P.I., *The Multinational Challenge to Corporation Law* (OUP, Oxford 1993), p. 92.

48 Nygh, 'The Liability'.

49 See Chapter 5.

50 Muchlinski, *Multinational*, p. 320.

The examination of enterprise theory also proves that corporate groups have been considered vertical organizations and thus the corporate veil is always considered as clearly existing and thus should be lifted since separation amongst the entities is still the basis of the theory. Liability could be avoided by proving there is no jeopardizing corporate veil between entities. Enterprise liability on those conditions turn to be veil-piercing law in corporate groups with a more appealing name.

The major problem underlying the evaluation of an enterprise entity approach to group liability rests in identifying the existence of such a business association. This requires the use of economic theories of corporate integration so as to develop a clearer concept of the group under which the parent can be said to control its subsidiaries for the purpose of liability. The outcome of any claim based on the enterprise theory depends on an interpretation of evidence that reveals a more complex structure than the theory suggests. Therefore the enterprise theory has not developed in connection with reality but developed on the same belief of the parent and subsidiary divisions and belief of the parent's control over subsidiaries. It still contains many obstacles because it requires examination of structure of the enterprise to prove that the enterprise is operating in integrated ways.[51] On the issue of comparison of entity and enterprise theories in group liability concept, one will see that the developments of enterprise approach or parent liability approach through veil-piercing judgment is not really a huge departure from *Salomon*'s entity law principles. The separation between entities and the liability is based not on ownership nor derived from the economic realities but is developed from tort law under which control and involvement of the parent is searched for to impose liability for their acts.

## Liability Based on Ownership or Business Organization or Control

In order to break the deadlock created by these theories, the discussion must concentrate on why corporate groups must be liable. On this stand the discussion must be whether liability must be based on ownership and business organization or control. It is inevitable that in any case of liability regime there must be a basic justification; in order to create the theory for the future of liability issues relating to MNEs, the legal systems should base their justification on certain theories. Thus principles for liability are very important questions to consider on the aim to achieve justifiable regulation for MNEs' torts. On the earlier and existing regulations and application of liability in corporate groups,

[51] Teubner, G., 'Unitas Multiplex: Corporate Governance In Group Enterprises', in Sugarman, D. and Teubner, G. (eds) *Regulating Corporate Groups in Europe* (Nomos, Baden-Baden 1990).

the emphasis has been on the control theory, under which there is a search for excessive control of one entity over another in order to impose liability on the controller. In the absence of this excessive control, the controller entity might escape liability even though it owns all the shares in the connected entity. In these circumstances, there is an unfair situation that the owner of the shares might escape liability even though they collect all the benefits of subsidiary's success.

The level of required control or practical approaches to prove the control has been varied in the past in regulation and case law. In the introduction of the control theory, there was liability only in clear fraudulent use of control over a subsidiary. When this was insufficient, the required level of control was reduced or burden of proof was shifted from claimants to the company itself (supposed control) but there has been no shift from the requirements of control in corporate groups to make one entity liable for others' acts. However, as it was already mentioned in qualified de facto groups in German law or assumed control in EU competition cases, even the presumption of control is always rebuttable.[52] Under the complex horizontal structure of MNEs, it is not difficult for a parent company to submit conclusive evidence of proof that the subsidiary was independent and was making its own decision since the modern structure of MNEs suggests that subsidiaries are not only becoming more independent in their own decision-making but also becoming more dependant on principles of decision-making. There is a situation under which a day-to-day involvement in subsidiaries' decision-making is not common practice but there is a consistent application of cultural control in MNEs.[53] Establishing liability on the basis of control is very difficult and more likely to be effective in single member companies and small-scale domestic corporate groups.

These changing characteristics of decision-making and control with horizontal structure should force law-makers to think of better functioning theories for liability in MNEs' torts. With the failure of the control theory, we should divert our attention to liability based on principles of ownership and business organization. These principles should be considered together with social, economic and managerial structure of MNEs.

Of course broad examination of ownership theory might lead us to a complete removal of limited liability. However, bringing these theories with the justification theories for the existence of limited liability and differentiation between individual shareholders and company shareholders, a reinterpretation of limited liability in corporate groups' context might be justified. As a result it will be more efficient to create liability on corporate groups not by their control over

---

52 See Chapter 6.
53 See Chapter 2.

their subsidiaries but common ownership of the enterprise as a group through separate legal entities. By doing this, the burden of proof in control theory will be removed so that strict requirements of factual examination of the relationship between the parent and the subsidiary will be eliminated. Together with this positive development, the law should consider every company under the group as part of business organization and thus liable for any tort other entities of the business organization has committed. The system of liability based on ownership and business organization will be built on removal of limited liability for the purpose of creating effective liability for tort victims similar to allowing corporate groups to apply group relief for the losses made by subsidiaries.[54] Applying the same logic to tort creditors, parent companies or other subsidiary companies under a group should be held liable for the tort actions of any subsidiary.

Accordingly any country that a subsidiary of MNEs is established in will have jurisdiction over all components of MNEs through the subsidiary established in that country. This can in a sense create a subsidiary-to-subsidiary liability, which means liability for subsidiaries tort not only on parent but also on other subsidiaries in a group. Basically there will be group liability for the torts committed by subsidiaries but since the group has no legal personality, this liability is imposed on legal personalities in the groups. Accordingly the liability can be imposed on parent or other subsidiaries.

As a result, efforts must concentrate on a comprehensive liability regime that is built by taking into consideration the problems in historical developments in the area and taking modern interdisciplinary realities of MNEs into account. Therefore, in principle, imposing liability on business organization principles together with ownership theory while considering managerial structure of the modern enterprise, in other words, liability on entities without necessarily involving the parent, is attractive.[55]

The new liability regimes must be based on creative theories that are wide enough to solve current and future problems. Therefore considering MNEs as non-veil enterprises in tort liability is very appealing. For the better and most efficient liability regimes, the corporate groups should be considered as an enterprise with no veil amongst entities for the issues relating to liability and the corporate veil might be kept in the extent of necessity for practical economical functions. In this way there will be a balance between economic requirements of modern global capitalism and requirements of justice. The victims of MNEs' torts must be able choose the entity against which they want to bring their cases.

---

[54] The ECJ allowed Marks & Spencer Plc as parent company to reduce the loss made by its European subsidiaries from its profits. See ECJ Grand Chamber: *Marks & Spencer* plc *v David Halsey* (Her Majesty's Inspector of Taxes) (C-446/03).

[55] Muchlinski, *Multinational*, p. 324.

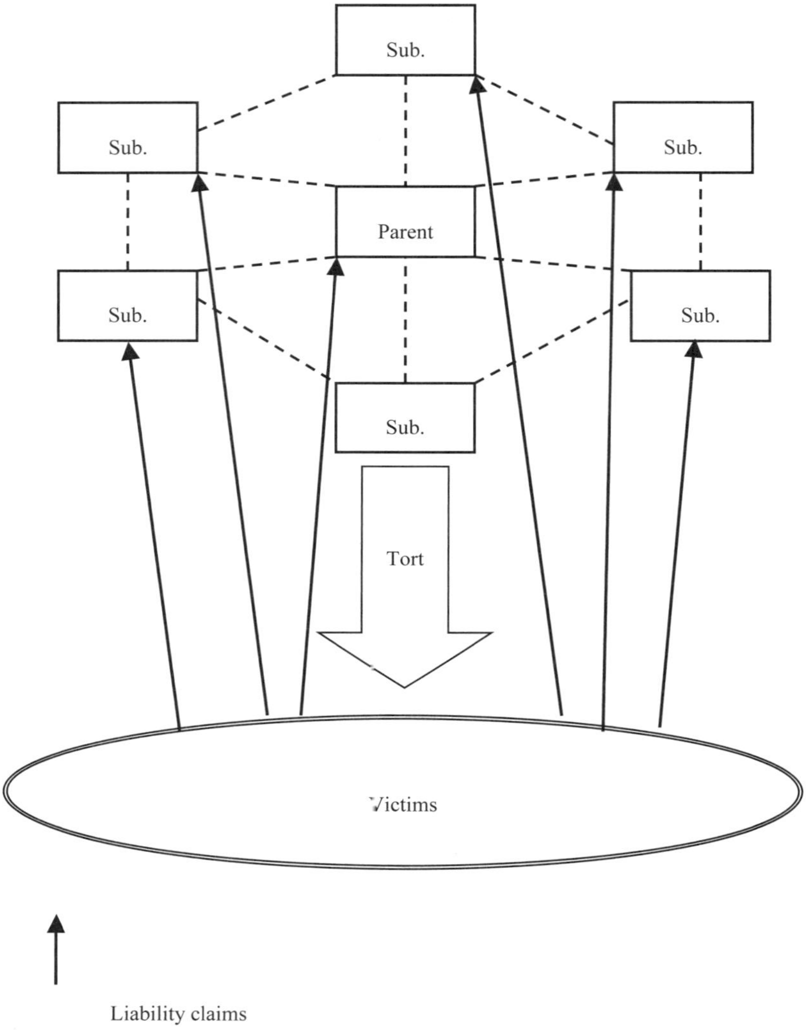


*Figure 8.1 Liability based on organizational structure*

The judgment of the tort actions must be made on behalf of the business organization so the organization must be held liable through the personality of the entity that the case has been brought against. In this system the liability of parent or other entities will not just cover compensation but there will be direct liability for the tort action. Attributing direct liability to enterprise itself by making entities under an enterprise face civil liability action will also remove jurisdictional barriers. The proposed liability regime is indicated by figure 8.1.

## FINAL CONCLUSIONS

Finding solutions to MNEs' tort liability problems will start by questioning social-economic roles of MNEs in modern capital industries and will lead to the question of how ready modern law regimes are to change some basics of modern capital economic principles. In other words, the fundamental issue in the regulation of corporate groups and MNEs is to which level market economies are willing and able to move beyond the traditional models of the company to one contemporary justified model of MNEs. Implementation of broader liability is a problem of political choice as a legal problem.

Consequently political obstacles must be overcome by creating alternative movements to current standings. In this sense, the book has made two points. The first is that key elements of the existing law on MNE group structures are based upon a specific understanding of the characteristics of those structures. In particular, the method in which central control is exercised within the modern enterprises is based on the idea of vertical structures. This understanding is increasingly in conflict with their actual nature under which control is increasingly being exercised in a different, horizontal way. Therefore there is a need for law to take these modern features of MNEs. Legal understandings of the nature of control based on the idea of vertical structure are simplistic and outdated. The second point is a broader point about the divergence between the legal structures of MNEs and their business nature. In legal theory, there is the idea of groups as made up of lots of formally separate entities. However, the economic business structure of MNEs reflects different and more single enterprise structure for MNEs. Therefore this point reveals a wider problem which goes to the heart of company law, the theory of separate corporate personality. Accordingly, throughout the book, there have been suggested solutions to these problems.

This book has dealt with legal issues by illustrating the injustice created by the current system of liability even though none of them have yet been able to create a notable influence on a political stance on liability issues. The author believes that the issues will come to the political agenda eventually. It is predicted that public pressure on politicians will reach a level to force them to introduce a fair liability regime for MNEs. The proposed solutions to the problem of MNEs' tort liability should be comprehensive enough to overcome not only today's practical challenges but also create a future for the regulation of MNEs' tort liability. The book indicates that the problems are not impossible to solve and alternative regimes are readily available with some compromise.

The current groups of companies' regimes ignore the most important characteristics of MNEs, for this reason they mostly fail to satisfy requirements of justice in social justice theory. However, there is no such a thing as creating a new legal system from nothing. The new legal structure must be created by examining past efforts, either successful or unsuccessful, with the aim of improving the ideas or developing better principles. In this sense, this book has indicated suggestions for solutions to the problem of multinational enterprises and tort liabilities.

# Bibliography

## BOOKS


Addo, M.K. (ed.), *Human Rights Standards and the Responsibility of Transnational Corporations* (Kluwer Law International, The Hague 1999).

Addo, M.K., 'Human Rights and Transnational Corporations – An Introduction' in Addo, M.K. (ed.), *Human Rights Standards and the Responsibility of Transnational Corporations* (Kluwer Law International, The Hague 1999).

Adinolfi, A., 'The Legal Notion of the Group Enterprise: The EC Approach' in Sugarman, D. and Teubner, G. (eds), *Regulating Corporate Groups in Europe* (Baden-Baden, Nomos 1990).

Aldrich, H., *Organisations Evolving* (Sage Publications, London 1999).

Alston, P. (ed.), *Non-State Actors and Human Rights* (OUP, Oxford 2005).

Amnesty International, *The UN Norms for Business: Towards Legal Accountability* (Amnesty International Publications, London 2004).

Andenas, M. and Sugarman, D. (eds), *Developments in European Company Law* (Volume 3, Kluwer, London 2000).

Anderson, Sarah and Cavanagh, John, *The Rise of Corporate Global Power* (Institute for Policy Studies, Dec. 2000).

Andersson, U. and Johanson, J., 'International Business Enterprise' in Bjorkman, I. and Forsgren, M., *The Nature of the Transnational Firm* (Copenhagen Business Scholl Press, Copenhagen 1997).

Antunes, J.A., *Liability of Corporate Groups Autonomy and Control in Parent Subsidiary Relationship in US, German, and EU Law* (Kluwer Law and Taxation Publisher, Deventer 1994).

Asheghian, P., *The Multinational Corporation: Environments and Operations* (Nova Science Publishers, Commack NY 1998).

Assmann, H., 'Microcorporatist Structures in German Law on Groups of Companies' in Sugarman, D. and Teubner, G. (eds), *Regulating Corporate Groups in Europe* (Baden-Baden, Nomos 1990).

Austin, Robert P., 'Corporate Groups' in Grantham, Ross and Rickett, Charlie (eds), *Corporate Personality in the 20th Century* (Hart, Oxford 1998).

Avgitidis, Dimitris K., *Group of Companies; The Liability of Parent Company for the Depths of its Subsidiary* (Sakkoulas, Athens-Komotini 1996).

Ayhan, Riza, (in Turkish) *Limited Sirketlerde Ortaklarin Sorumlulugu* (Istanbul, 1992).

Barnet, R.J. and Muller, R.E., *Global Reach: The Power of Multinational Corporations* (Simon & Schuster, New York 1974).

Bartlett, C.A. and Ghoshal, S., 'Managing in a Transnational Network' in McKern, B. (ed.), *Managing the Global Network Corporation* (Routledge, London 2003).

Bartlett, C.A. and Ghoshal, S., 'The Evaluation of Transnational' in Islam, I. and Shepherd, W. (eds), *Current Issues in International Business* (Edward Elgar, Cheltenham, UK, Northampton, MA, USA 1997).

Bartlett, C.A. and Ghoshal, S., *Managing Across Borders – the Transnational Solution* (Harvard Business School Press, Boston 1989).

Bartlett, C.A., 'Building and Managing Transnational: The New Organizational Challenge in Competition' in Porter, M.E. (ed.), *Global Industries* (Harvard Business School Press, 1986).

Bartlett, C.A., Doz, Y. and Hedlund, G. (eds), *Managing the Global Firm* (Routledge, London 1990).

Baughen, Simon, *Corporate Accountability and the Law of Tort: The Inclusive Verdict of Bhopal* (University of Manchester, 1993).

Bell, J. and Young, S., 'Towards an Integrative Framework of the Internalisation of the Firm' in Hooley, G. and Loveridge, Wilson D. (eds), *Internationalisation: Process, Context and Markets* (St Martins Press, London 1998).

Bennett, C. and Burley, H., 'Corporate Accountability: An NGO Perspective' in Tully, S., *Research Handbook on Corporate Legal Responsibility* (Edward Elgar, Cheltenham, UK, Northampton, MA, USA 2005).

Bercusson, B., 'The Significance Of The Legal Form of the Group Enterprise in the United Kingdom' in Sugarman, D. and Teubner, G. (eds), *Regulating Corporate Groups in Europe* (Baden-Baden, Nomos 1990).

Betlem, Gerrit, 'Transnational Litigation against Multinational Corporations Before Dutch Civil Courts' in Kamminga, Menno T. and Zia-Zarifi, Saman (eds), *Liability of Multinational Corporations under International Law* (Kluwer Law International, The Hague 2000).

Birkinshaw, J. (ed.), *The Future of Multinational Company* (John Wiley, London 2004).

Birkinshaw, J., 'Strategy and Management in MNE Subsidiaries' in Rugman, Alan M. and Brewer, T.L. (eds), *Oxford Handbook of International Business* (OUP, Oxford 2001).

Birkinshaw, Julian and Hood, Neil (eds), *Multinational Corporate Evolution and Subsidiary Development* (Palgrave Macmillan, London 1998).

Bjorkman, I. and Forsgren, M. (eds), *The Nature of the Transnational Firm* (Mumkgaard, Copenhagen 1997).

Blecher, M., 'Law in Movement: Paradoxontology, Law and Social Movements' in Dine, J. and Fagan, A. (eds), *Human Rights and Capitalism* (Edward Elgar, Cheltenham, UK, Northampton, MA, USA 2006).

Blumberg, P.I., 'The American Law of Corporate Groups' in McCahery, J., Picciotto, S. and Scott, S. (eds), *Corporate Control and Accountability* (OUP, Oxford 1993).

Blumberg, P.I., Strasser, K.A., Georgakopoulos, N.L. and Gouvin, E.J., *Blumberg On Corporate Groups* (Aspen Publishers, New York 2005).

Blumberg, P.I., *The Law of Corporate Groups: Problems of Parent and Subsidiary Corporations Under State Statutory Law of General Application* (Little Brown, Boston 1989).

Blumberg, P.I., *The Law of Corporate Groups: Procedural Problems in the Law of Parent and Subsidiary Corporations* (Little Brown, Boston 1983).

Blumberg, P.I., *The Law of Corporate Groups: Tort, Contract, and Other Common Law Problems in the Substantive Law of Parent and Subsidiary Corporations* (Little Brown, Boston 1987).

Blumberg, P.I., *The Multinational Challenge to Corporation Law* (OUP, Oxford 1993).

Born, G.A., *International Commercial Arbitration* (Kluwer Law International, London 2001).

Borrowdale, Andrew, 'Commentary on Austin' in Grantham, Ross and Rickett, Charlie (eds), *Corporate Personality in the 20th Century* (Hart, Oxford 1998).

Braithwaite, J. and Drahos, P., *Global Business Regulation* (CUP, Cambridge 2000).

Brewer, T. and Young, S., *The Multilateral Investment System and Multinational Enterprises* (OUP, Oxford 1998).

Briggs, A., *Civil Jurisdiction and Judgments* (LLP, London 2002).

Briggs, Adrian, *The Conflict of Laws* (OUP, Oxford 2002).

Buckley, P.J. and Casson, M., *The Economic Theory of Multinational Enterprise* (Macmillan, London 1985).

Buckley, P.J. and Casson, M., *The Future of Multinational Enterprise* (Macmillan, London 1976).

Buckley, P.J., *Cooperative Forms of the TNC Activity* (Routledge, London 1993).

Burton, F., Chapman, M. and Cross, M. (eds), *International Business Organization: Subsidiary Management* (Palgrave Macmillan, London 1999).

Campbell, K. and Vick, D., 'Disclosure Law and the Market for Social Responsibility' in McBarnet, D., Voiculescu, A. and Campbell, T., *The New Corporate Accountability* (CUP, Cambridge 2007).

Cashel, T.W., 'Groups of Companies – Some US Aspects' in Wooldridge, F. and Schmitthoff, C.M. (eds), *Groups of Companies* (Sweet & Maxwell, London 1991).

Casson, M., 'General Theories of Multinational Enterprise: Their Relevance to Business History' in Hertner, Peter and Jones, Geoffrey (eds), *Multinationals: Theory and History* (Gower, Aldershot 1986).
Casson, M., *The Growth of International Business* (George Allen & Unwin, London 1983).
Casson, Mark, *The Economic Analyses of Multinational Trading Companies* (University of Reading, Department of Economics, Reading 1997).
Caves, R.E., *Multinational Enterprises and Economic Analyses* (CUP, Cambridge 2007).
Chandler, A.D., *Scale and Scope: The Dynamics of Industrial Capitalism* (Harvard University Press, Cambridge 1990).
Chandler, A.D., *Strategy and Structure* (MIT Press, Cambridge 1998).
Charlton, A., 'Incentive Bidding for Mobile Investment: Economic Consequences and Potential Responses' (OECD Development Centre, Working Paper No 203, Paris 2003).
Cheffins, Brian R., *Company Law: Theory, Structure and Operation* (Clarendon Press, Oxford 1997).
Chesnais, F., Letto-Gillies, G. and Simonetti, R., *European Integration and Global Corporate Strategies* (Routledge, London 2000).
Chiomenti, C., 'Corporations and the International Criminal Court' in DeSchutter, O. (ed.), *Transnational Corporations and Human Rights* (Hart Publishing, Oxford 2006).
Christos, M., Pitelis, N. and Sugden, R. (eds), *The Nature of the Transnational Firm* (Routledge, London 2000).
Clapham, A. and Martignoni, J.B., 'Are We There Yet? In Search of a Coherent EU Strategy on Labour Rights and External Trade' in Leary, V.A. and Warner, D., *Social Issues, Globalisation and International Institutions* (Martinus Nijhoff, Boston 2006).
Clapham, A., *Human Rights Obligation of Non-State Actors* (OUP, Oxford 2006).
Clarkson, C.M.V. and Hill, J., *Jaffey on the Conflicts of Laws* (Butterworths, London 2002).
Cohen, R.B., *Strategy and Structure of Multinational Corporations* (Mimeo 1977).
Collier, J.G., *Conflict of Law* (OUP, Oxford 2001).
Collins, L., *Dicey and Morris on the Conflicts of Laws* (Sweet & Maxwell, London 2000).
Darcy, L.C. and Murray, B., *Cleave Schmitt Hoff's Export Trade* (Sweet & Maxwell, London 2000).
Davies, Paul L., *Gower and Davies' Principles of Modern Company Law* (Sweet & Maxwell, London 2003).
DeSchutter, O., 'The Accountability of Multinationals for Human Rights Viola-

tions in European Law' in Alston, P. (ed.), *Non-State Actors and Human Rights* (OUP, Oxford 2005).

DeSchutter, O., 'The Challenge of Imposing Human Rights Norms on Corporate Actors' in DeSchutter, O. (ed.), *Transnational Corporations and Human Rights* (Hart Publishing, Oxford 2006).

DeSchutter, O. (ed.), *Transnational Corporations and Human Rights* (Hart Publishing, Oxford 2006).

Dine, J. and Fagan, A. (eds), *Human Rights and Capitalism* (Edward Elgar, Cheltenham, UK, Northampton, MA, USA 2006).

Dine, J., 'Using Companies to Oppress the Poor' in Dine, J. and Fagan, A. (eds), *Human Rights and Capitalism* (Edward Elgar, Cheltenham, UK, Northampton, MA, USA 2006).

Dine, Janet, 'The Law Commission Report: Sweeping the Issues under the Carpet in Andenas, M. and Sugarman, D. (eds), *Developments in European Company Law* (Volume 3, Kluwer, London 2000).

Dine, Janet, *Companies, International Trade and Human Rights* (CUP, Cambridge 2005).

Dine, Janet, *The Governance of Corporate Groups* (CUP, Cambridge 2000).

Dosi, G. (ed.), *Organization and Strategy in the Evaluation of Enterprise* (Macmillan, London 1996).

Doz, Y., Santos, J. and Williamson, P., 'The Metanational: The Next Step in the Evolution of Multinationals' in Birkinshaw, J. (ed.), *The Future of Multinational Company* (Wiley, London 2004).

Dunning, J.H., *The Multinational Enterprise* (Allen & Unwin, London 1971).

Dunning, J.H., *Economic Analysis and the Multinational Enterprises* (Allen & Unwin, London 1974).

Dunning, J.H., *The Theory of Transnational Corporations* (Routledge, London 1992).

Dunning, J.H., *Multinational Enterprises and the Global Economy* (Addison-Wesley, Wokingham 1993).

Dunning, J.H., *Governments, Globalisation, and International Business* (OUP, Oxford 1997).

Dunning, J.H., *Globalisation and the Theory of MNE Activity* (University of Reading, Department of Economics, Reading 1999).

Dunning, J.H., *Multinational Firms: The Global-local Dilemma* (Routledge, London 2001).

Dunning, J.H., 'The Key Literature on IB Activities: 1960–2000' in Rugman, A.M. and Brewer, T.L. (eds), *Oxford Handbook of International Business* (OUP, Oxford 2001).

Dunning, J.H. and Robson, P., *Multinationals and the European Community* (Basil Blackwell, Oxford 1988).

Dunning, J.H., Cantwell, J.A. and Corley, T.A.B. 'The Theory of International

Production: Some Historical Antecedents' in Hertner, Peter and Jones, Geoffrey (eds), *Multinationals: Theory and History* (Gower, Aldershot 1986).

Easterbrook, Frank H. and Fischel, Daniel R., *The Economic Structure of Corporate Law* (Harvard University Press, London 1991).

Edelstein, M., *Overseas Investment in the Age of High Imperialism: The United Kingdom, 1850–1914* (Colombia University Press, New York 1982).

Faouros, A.A. (ed.), *Transnational Corporations: The International Legal Framework* (Routledge, London 1994).

Farrar, John H., *Company Law* (Butterworths, London 1998).

Fawcett, J.J. (ed.), *Reform and Development of Private International Law* (OUP, Oxford 2002).

Fawcett, J.J., *Declining Jurisdiction in Private International Law* (OUP, Oxford 1995).

Fieldhouse, D.K., 'The Multinational: a Critique of a Concept' in Teichova, Alice, Lévy-Leboyer, Maurice and Nussbaum, Helga (eds), *Multinational Enterprise in Historical Perspective* (CUP, Cambridge 1986).

Fletcher, I., *The Law of Insolvency* (Sweet & Maxwell, London 2002).

Folsom, M.W., Gordon, J. and Spanogle, A., *International Business Transaction* (West Group, St. Paul. Minn. 2001).

Forsgren, M., Holm, U. and Johanson, J., *Managing the Embedded Multinational* (Edward Elgar, Cheltenham, UK, Northampton, MA, USA 2005).

Forsgren, M., Holm, U. and Thilenius, P., 'Network Infusion in the Multinational Corporation' in Bjorkman, I. and Forsgren, M. (eds), *The Nature of the Transnational Firm* (Mumkgaard, Copenhagen 1997).

Fortun, K., *Advocacy After Bhopal: Environmentalism, Disaster, New Global Orders* (Chicago University Press, Chicago 2001).

Francioni, F. and Scovazzi, T. (eds), *International Responsibility for Environmental Harm* (Graham & Trotman, London 1991).

Franko, L., *The European Multinationals* (London 1976).

Fridenson, P., 'The Growth of Multinational Activities in the French Motor Industry, 1890–1979' in Hertner, Peter and Jones, Geoffrey (eds), *Multinationals: Theory and History* (Gower, Aldershot 1986).

Gaillard, E. and Savage, J. (eds), *Fouchard Gaillard Goldman on International Commercial Arbitration* (Kluwer Law International, London 1999).

Gelfand, Jacop, 'The Lack of Enforcement in the United Nations Draft Norms: Benefit or Disadvantage?' in De Schutter, O. (ed.), *Transnational Corporations and Human Rights* (Hart Publishing, Oxford 2006).

Ghoshal, S. and Barlett, C.A., *The Individualized Corporation* (Harper Collins Publishers, New York 1997).

Ghoshal, S. and Westney, D.E., *Organization Theory and the Multinational Corporation* (Macmillan St Martins Press, London 1992).

Gillooly, M., *The Law Relating to Corporate Groups* (Butterworths, Sydney 1993).

Griffiths, Andrew, *Corporate Governance and the Uses of Company* (University of Manchester, 1993).

Gleichmann, K., 'The Law of Corporate Groups in the European Community' in Sugarman, D. and Teubner, G. (eds), *Regulating Corporate Groups in Europe* (Baden-Baden, Nomos 1990).

Global Compact Office, *How the Global Compact Works: Mission, Actors and Engagement Mechanisms* (New York, 2003).

Goddard, David, 'Corporate Personality – Limited Sources and Its Limits' in Grantham, R. and Rickett, C. (eds), *Corporate Personality in the 20th Century* (Hart, Oxford 1998).

Goode, R., *Principles of Corporate Insolvency Law* (Sweet & Maxwell, London 2005).

Gooderham, Paul N. and Ulset, Svein, 'Is the Governance of Transnational Really "Beyond the M-Form?" A Critical Review of Barlett and Ghoshal's New Organizational Model' in Taggart, H., Berry, M. and McDermott, M. (eds), *Multinationals in a New Era* (Palgrave, London 2001).

Goyder, D.G., *EC Competition Law* (OUP, Oxford 2003).

Grantham, Ross and Rickett, C., 'The Bootmaker's Legacy to Company Law Doctrine' in Grantham, Ross and Rickett, C. (eds), *Corporate Personality in the 20th Century* (Hart, Oxford 1998).

Grantham, Ross and Rickett, C., *Company and Securities Law* (Brookers, Wellington 2002).

Grantham, Ross and Rickett, Charlie (eds), *Corporate Personality in the 20th Century* (Hart, Oxford 1998).

Hadden, T., 'Regulating Corporate Groups: International Perspective' in McCahery, J., Picciotto, S. and Scott, S. (eds), *Corporate Control and Accountability* (OUP, Oxford 1993).

Hadden, T., *Company Law and Capitalism* (Weidenfeld and Nicolson, London 1977).

Hadden, T., *The Control of Corporate Groups* (Institute of Advanced Legal Studies, London 1983).

Hagstrom, P., 'The "Wired" Multinational Corporation: The Role of Information Systems for Structural Change in Complex Organizations' (PhD, Stockholm School of Economics, 1991).

Hanotiau, B., *Complex Arbitrations* (Kluwer Law International, London 2005).

Hawke, Neil, *Corporate Liability* (Sweet & Maxwell, London 2000).

Hedlund, G. and Ridderstrahle, J., 'Towards a Theory of the Self-Renewing MNC' in Toyre, B. and Night, D. (eds), *International Business: An Emerging Vision* (South Coralline Press, Columbia SC University 1997).

Hellmann, R., *Transnational Control of Multinational Corporations* (Praeger, New York 1977).

Heng, L.L. (ed.), *Current Legal Issues in the Internalisation of Business Enterprise* (Butterworths, London 1996).

Hertner, P., 'German Multinational Enterprise Before 1914: Some Case Studies' in Hertner, Peter and Jones, Geoffrey (eds), *Multinationals: Theory and History* (Aldershot, Gower 1986).

Hertner, Peter and Jones, Geoffrey (eds), *Multinationals: Theory and History* (Aldershot, Gower 1986).

Hertz, Noreena, *The Silent Take-Over* (William Heineman, London 2001).

Hill, Jennifer, 'Changes in the Role of the Shareholder' in Grantham, Ross and Rickett, Charlie (eds), *Corporate Personality in the 20th Century* (Hart, Oxford 1998).

Hobbes, Thomas, *Leviathan* (1651).

Hofstetter, Karl, 'The Ecological Liability of Corporate Groups: Comparing US and European Trends' in Teubner, G., Farmer, L. and Murphy, D. (eds), *Environmental Law and Ecological Responsibility: The Concept and Practice of Ecological Self-Organization* (Wiley, Chichester 1994).

Hood, N. and Young, S., *The Economics of Multinational Enterprises* (Longman, London 1984).

Hopt, Klaus J., 'Legal Elements and Policy Decisions in Regulating Groups of Companies' in Wooldridge, F. and Schmitthoff, C.M. (eds), *Groups of Companies* (Sweet & Maxwell, London 1991).

Horn, N. and Kocka, J., *Law and the Formation of Big Enterprises in the 19th and Early 20th Centuries* (Gottingen, 1979).

Humes, S., *Managing the Multinational Confronting the Global-Local Dilemma* (Prentice Hall, New York 1993).

Huner, Jan, 'The Multilateral Agreement on Investment and the Review of the OECD Guidelines for Multinational Enterprises' in Kamminga, Menno T. and, Zia-Zarifi, Saman (eds), *Liability of Multinational Corporations under International Law* (Kluwer Law International, The Hague 2000).

ICC, *Commercial Agency: Guide for the Drawing up of Contracts* (International Chamber of Commerce, Paris 1983).

Immenga, U., 'The Law of Groups in the Federal Republic of Germany' in Wymeersch, E. (ed.), *Groups of Companies in EEC* (De Gtuyter, Berlin 1993).

Inkpen, A.C., 'Strategic Alliances' in Rugman, A. and Brewer, T.L. (eds), *Oxford Handbook of International Business* (OUP, Oxford 2001).

Ireland, Paddy, 'Enlightening the Value of Shareholders: To Whom should Directors Owe Duties?' in Andenas, Mads and Sugarman, David (eds), *Developments in European Company Law* (Volume 3, Kluwer, London 2000).

Islam, I. and Shepherd, W. (eds), *Current Issues in International Business* (Edward Elgar, Cheltenham, UK, Northampton, MA, USA 1997).
Jagers, Nicola, 'The Legal Status of the Multinational Corporation Under International Law' in Addo, M.K. (ed.), *Human Rights Standards and the Responsibility of Transnational Corporations* (Kluwer Law International, The Hague 1999).
Jagers, Nicola, *Corporate Human Rights Obligations: In Search of Accountability* (Intersentia, New York 2002).
Johanson, J. and Mattson, L.G., 'Internationalization in Industrial Systems – Network Approach' in Hood, H. and Vahlne, J.E. (eds), *Strategies in Global Competition* (John Wiley, Chichester 1987).
Jones, A. and Sufrin, B., *EC Competition Law* (OUP, Oxford 2007).
Jones, C. and Hesterly, W.S., *A Network Organization: Alternative Governance Form or a Glorified Market?* (Academy of Management Meetings, Atlanta, Georgia 1993).
Jones, G., 'The Performance of British Multinational Enterprise, 1890–1945' in Hertner, Peter and Jones, Geoffrey (eds), *Multinationals: Theory and History* (Gower, Aldershot 1986).
Jones, G., *Transnational Corporations: A Historical Perspective* (Routledge, London 1992).
Jones, G., *The Evaluation of International Business: An Introduction* (Routledge, London 1996).
Jones, G. and Schroter, H.G., *The Rise of Multinationals in Continental Europe* (Edward Elgar, Aldershot, UK and Brookfield, US 1993).
Joseph, Sarah, 'An Overview of the Human rights Accountability of Multinational Enterprises' in Kamminga, Menno T. and Zia-Zarifi, Saman (eds), *Liability of Multinational Corporations under International Law* (Kluwer Law International, The Hague 2000).
Joseph, Sarah, *Corporations and Transnational Human Rights Litigation* (Hart Publishing, Oxford 2004).
Kamminga, M.T., 'Holding Multinational Corporations Accountable for Human Right Abuses: A Challenge for the EC' in Alston, Philip (ed.), *The EU and Human Rights*, (OUP, Oxford 2000).
Kamminga, M.T. and Zia-Zarifi, Saman (eds), *Liability of Multinational Corporations under International Law* (Kluwer Law International, The Hague 2000).
Kamminga, M.T. and Zia-Zarifi, Saman, 'Liability of Multinational Corporations Under International Law: An Introduction' in Kamminga, Menno T. and Zia-Zarifi, Saman (eds), *Liability of Multinational Corporations under International Law* (Kluwer Law International, The Hague 2000).
Karahasan, M.R., (in Turkish) *Sorumluluk Hukuku* (Ankara, 1995).
Keay, Malcolm, 'Towards Global Corporate Social Responsibility' (Briefing

Paper of the Royal Institute of International Affairs, Energy and Environment Programme, 3 April 2002).

Kim, K.B. 'A Multilateral Contribution to Corporate Standards of Behaviour: The ILO's Declaration on Multinational Enterprises' in Tully, S., *Research Handbook on Corporate Legal Responsibility* ( Edward Elgar, Cheltenham, UK, Northampton, MA, USA 2005).

Kinley, D., Nolan, J. and Zerial, N., '"The Norms are dead! Long live the Norms!" The Politics behind the UN Human Rights Norms for Corporations' in McBarnet, D., Voiculescu, A. and Campbell, T., *The New Corporate Accountability* (CUP, Cambridge 2007).

Kobrin, S.J., 'The Architecture of Globalisation: State Sovereignty in a Networked Global Economy' in Dunning, J.H. (ed.), *Governments, Globalization, and International Business* (OUP, Oxford 1997).

Kwan, E.C. and Harrigan, J. (eds), *Handbook of International Trade* (Blackwell, London 2003).

Lall, Sanjaya, *The Multinational Corporation* (Macmillan, London 1980).

Lall, Sanjaya, *The New Multinationals: The Spread of Third World Enterprises* (Wiley, Chichester 1983).

Lawson-Remer, T.E., 'A Role for the International Finance Corporation in Integrating Environmental and Human Rights Standards into Core Project Covenants: Case Study of the Baku-Tbilisi-Ceyhan Oil Pipeline Project' in DeSchutter, O. (ed.), *Transnational Corporations and Human Rights* (Hart Publishing, Oxford 2006).

Lew, J.D.M., Mistelis, L.A. and Kroll, S.M., *Comparative International Commercial Arbitration* (Kluwer Law International, London 2003).

Likosky, M. (ed.), *Transnational Legal Processes: Globalisation and Power Disparities* (Butterworths, London 2002).

Lipsey, Robert E., *Foreign Direct Investment and the Operations of Multinational Firms: Concepts, History and Data* (National Bureau of Economic Research, Cambridge 2001).

Loomis, Worth, 'The Responsibility of Parent Corporations for the Human Rights Via Lotions of their Subsidiaries' in Addo, M.K. (ed.), *Human Rights Standards and the Responsibility of Transnational Corporations* (Kluwer Law International, The Hague 1999).

Lowenfeld, A., 'National Jurisdiction and the Multinational Enterprise' in Lowenfeld, A. (ed.), *International Litigation and the Quest for Reasonableness* (Clarendon, Oxford 1996).

Lowry, John and Digman, Alan, *Company Law* (LexisNexis UK, London 2003).

Lowry, John, 'In Defence of Salomon: Promoting The Corporate Veil' in Rider, B.A.K. and Andenas, Mads (eds), *Developments in European Company Law,*

*Vol 2/1997: The Quest for an Ideal Legal Form for Small Businesses* (Kluwer Law International, London 1999).

Manev, Ivan, *The Managerial Network in a Multinational Enterprise* (Edwin Mellen Press, New York 2001).

Mares, R., *Business and Human Rights, A Compilation of Documents* (Martinus Nijhoff Publishers, Boston 2004).

Markusen, J.R. and Maskus, K.E., *Discriminating Among Alternative Theories of the Multinational Enterprise* (NEBR Working Paper, No 7164).

Marschan, Rebecca, *New Structural Forms and Inter-Unit Communication in Multinationals* (HSEBA Publications, Helsinki 1996).

Marschan, Rebecca, 'Dimensions of Less-Hierarchical Structures in Multinationals' in Bjorkman, I. and Forsgren, M. (eds), *The Nature of the Transnational Firm* (Mumkgaard, Copenhagen 1997).

Martin-Ortega, O. and Wallace, R.M.M., 'The Interaction between Corporate Codes of Conduct and International Law: A Study of Women and Children in the Textile Industry', in Tully, S., (ed.), *Research Handbook on Corporate Legal Responsibility*, (Edward Elgar, Cheltenham, UK, Northampton, MA, USA 2005).

Mathews, J.A., *Dragon Multinational: A New Model for Global Growth* (OUP, Oxford 2002).

McBarnet, D., 'Corporate Social Responsibility Beyond the Law, Through Law, For Law: The New Corporate Accountability' in McBarnet, D., Voiculescu, A. and Campbell, T., *The New Corporate Accountability* (CUP, Cambridge 2007).

McBarnett, D. and Kurkchiyan, M., 'Corporate Social Responsibility Through Contractual Control' in McBarnet, D., Voiculescu, A. and Campbell, T., *The New Corporate Accountability* (CUP, Cambridge 2007).

McCahery, J., Picciotto, S. and Scott, S. (eds), *Corporate Control and Accountability* (OUP, Oxford 1993).

McKern, B. (ed.), *Managing Global Network Corporation* (Routledge, London 2003).

McLeay, F., 'Corporate Code of Conduct and the Human Rights Accountability of Transnational Corporations: A Small Piece of a Larger Puzzle' in DeSchutter, O. (ed.), *Transnational Corporations and Human Rights* (Hart Publishing, Oxford 2006).

Meeran, R., 'The Unveiling of Transnational Corporations: A Direct Approach' in Addo, M.K. (ed.), *Human Rights Standards and the Responsibility of Transnational Corporations* (Kluwer Law International, The Hague 1999).

Meeran, Richard, 'Liability of Multinational Corporations: A Critical Stage in the UK' in Kamminga, Menno T. and Zia-Zarifi, Saman (eds), *Liability of Multinational Corporations under International Law* (Kluwer Law International, The Hague 2000).

Miles, R.E. and Snow, C.C., 'Internal Market and Network Organisations' in Halal, W.E., Geranmayeh, A. and Pourdehnad, J. (eds), *Internal Market, Bringing the Power of Free Enterprise Inside Your Organization* (John Wiley & Sons Inc. London 1993).

Mockler, R.J., *Multinational Strategic Alliances* (Wiley, Chichester, New York 1999).

Moore, Karl, *Birth of the Multinational: 2000 Years of Ancient Business History, from Ashur to Augustus* (Zed Books, London 1999).

Moore, M., *World Without Walls* (OUP, Cambridge 2002).

Morgan, G., Kristensen, P.H. and Whitley, R., *The Multinational Firm: Organising Across Institutional and National Divides* (OUP, Oxford 2001).

Morris, J.H.C., *The Conflict of Laws* (Sweet & Maxwell, London 2000).

Muchlinski P., 'Attempts to Extend the Accountability of Transnational Corporations: The Role of UNCTAD' in Kamminga, Menno T. and Zia-Zarifi, Saman (eds), *Liability of Multinational Corporations under International Law* (Kluwer Law International, The Hague 2000).

Muchlinski, P., 'The Company Law Review and Multinational Corporate Groups' in DeLacy, John (ed.), *Reform of United Kingdom Company Law* (Cavendish, London 2002).

Muchlinski, P., *Multinational Enterprises and the Law* (OUP, Oxford 2007).

Muscat, Andrew, *The Liability of the Holding Company for the Debts of Its Subsidiaries* (Dartmouth, Aldershot 1996).

Nam, C.Y.J., 'Competing for Foreign Direct Investment through the Creation of Export Processing Zones' in DeSchutter, O. (ed.), *Transnational Corporations and Human Rights* (Hart Publishing, Oxford 2006).

Nicholas, S.J. and Casson, M., 'The Economics of Trust: Explaining Differences in Corporate Structures Between the U.S. and Japan', in Casson, M. (ed.), *Enterprise and Competitiveness* (Clarendon Press, 1990).

Nicholas, S.J., 'The Expansion of Multinational Firms: New Evidence from British Foreign Direct Investment' in Foreman-Peck, J. (ed.), *Reinterpreting the Nineteenth Century British Economy: Essays in Quantitative Economic History* (OUP, Cambridge 1990).

Nicholas, S.J., 'The Theory of Multinational Enterprise as a Transactional Mode' in Hertner, Peter and Jones, Geoffrey (eds), *Multinationals: Theory and History* (Gower, Aldershot 1986).

Nohria, N. and Eccles, R.C., *Networks and Organisations: Structure Form and Action* (Harvard Business School Press, Boston 1992).

Nohria, N., *The Differentiated Network: Organising Multinational Corporations for Value Creation* (Jossey-Bass Publishers, San Francisco 1997).

North, P.M. and Fawcett, J.J., *Cheshire and North's Private International Law* (Butterworths, London 1999).

North, P.M. and Fawcett, J.J., *Private International Law* (Butterworths, London 1987).

North, P.M., *Private International Law Problems in Common Law Jurisdiction* (Martinus Nishoff, London 1993).

Nygh, P., 'Declining Jurisdiction Under the Brussels Regulations 2001 and the Preliminary Draft Hague Judgments Convention A Comparison' in Fawcett, J.J. (ed.), *Reform and Development of Private International Law* (OUP, Oxford 2002).

O'Brien, J., *Conflict of Law* (OUP, Cambridge 2001).

Ocaktan, Hasan, (in Turkish) *Anonim Sirketlerde Sinirli sorumluluk Ilkesi Karsisinda Sirket Alacaklarinin Korunmasi* (Gazi University, 2000).

OECD, *Guideline For Multinational Enterprises: Focus: Global Instruments For Corporate Responsibility* (OECD 2001).

OECD, *Guidelines for Multinational Enterprises* (OECD, 27 June 2000).

Österle, H., Fleisch, E. and Alt, R., *Business Networking: Shaping Collaboration between Enterprises* (Springer, Berlin 2001).

Ostroff, F., *The Horizontal Organization* (OUP, Oxford 1999).

Oxfam, *Global Finance, Hurts the Poor* (Oxfam America, 2002).

Ozbalci, Yilmaz, (in Turkish) *Amme Alacaklarinin Tahsili Usulu Hakkinda Kanun Yorum ve Aciklamalari* (Ankara, 2002).

Pekguclu, M.K., (in Turkish) *Turk Hukukunda Anonim Sirket Alacaklilarinin Korunmasi* (Ankara University, 1996).

Pettigrew, A.M. and Fenton, E.M., (eds) *The Innovating Organisation* (Sage Publications, London 2000).

Pettigrew, A.M. and Fenton, E.M., 'Integrating A Global Professional Services Organisation: The Case Of Ove Arup Partnership' in Pettigrew, A.M. and Fenton, E.M. (eds), *The Innovating Organisation* (Sage Publications, London 2000).

Pettigrew, A.M. and Fenton, E.M., 'Theoretical Perspectives on New Forms of Organizing' in Pettigrew, A.M. and Fenton, E.M. (eds) *The Innovating Organisation* (Sage Publications, London 2000).

Png, Cheong-Ann, *Corporate Liability in Principles of Attribution* (Kluwer Law International, London 2001).

Porter, M.E., *Global Industries* (Harvard Business School Press, 1986).

Prentice, D.D., 'Corporate Personality, Limited Liability and the Protection of Creditors' in Grantham, Ross and Rickett, Charlie (eds), *Corporate Personality in the 20th Century* (Hart, Oxford 1998).

Prentice, D.D., 'Group Indebtedness' in Wooldridge, F. and Schmitthoff, C.M. (eds), *Groups of Companies* (Sweet & Maxwell, London 1991).

Prentice, D.D., 'Some Comments on the Law relating to Corporate Groups' in McCahery, J., Picciotto, S. and Scott, S. (eds), *Corporate Control and Accountability* (OUP, Oxford 1993).

Price, L.R., 'International Framework Agreements: A Collaborative Paradigm for Labour Relations' in DeSchutter, O. (ed.), *Transnational Corporations and Human Rights* (Hart Publishing, Oxford 2006).

Pulasli, Hasan (in Turkish), *Sirketler Hukuku* (Ankara, 2001).

Rammeloo, S., *Corporations in Private International Law* (OUP, Oxford 2001).

Ramsay, I.M., 'Models of Corporate Regulation: The Mandatory Enabling Debate' in Grantham, Ross and Rickett, Charlie (eds), *Corporate Personality in the 20th Century* (Hart, Oxford 1998).

Randoy, Turquand Rule, 'Towards a Firm-based Model of Foreign Direct Investment' in Bjorkman, I. and Forsgren, M. (eds), *The Nature of the Transnational Firm* (Mumkgaard, Copenhagen 1997).

Richter, Judith, *Holding Corporations Accountable: Corporate Conduct, International Codes, and Citizen Action* (Zed Books, New York 2001).

Rider, B.A.K. and Andenas, M. (eds), *Developments in European Company Law, Vol 2/1997: The Quest for an Ideal Legal Form for Small Businesses* (Kluwer Law International, London 1999).

Rugman, A.M. and Brewer, T.L. (eds), *Oxford Handbook of International Business* (OUP, Oxford 2001).

Rugman, A.M. and Verbeke, A., 'Environmental Policy and International Business' in Rugman, A.M. and Brewer, T.L. (eds), *Oxford Handbook of International Business* (OUP, Oxford 2001).

Rugman, A.M., *Inside The Multinationals: The Economics of Internal Markets* (Colombia University Press, New York 1981).

Ruttley, P., Mac Vay, I. and Carol, G., *The WTO and International Trade Regulation* (Cameron May, London 1998).

Sabapathy, J., 'In the Dark all Cats are Grey; Corporate Responsibility and Legal Responsibility' in Tully, S. (ed.), *Research Handbook on Corporate Legal Responsibility* (Edward Elgar, Cheltenham, UK, Northampton, MA, USA 2005).

Sahni, B.P., *Transnational Corporate Liability: Accountability for Human Injury* (Cameron May, London 2006).

Salerno, F., 'The Brussels Jurisdiction and Enforcement Convention' in Hoffmann, B. (ed.), *European Private International Law* (Ars Aequi Libri, Nijmegen 1998).

Sapelli, G.A., 'Historical Typology of Group Enterprises: The Debate on the Decline of Popular Sovereignty' in Sugarman, D. and Teubner, G. (eds), *Regulating Corporate Groups in Europe* (Baden-Baden, Nomos 1990).

Schmitthoff, C.M. and Wooldridge, F. (eds), *Groups of Companies* (Sweet & Maxwell, London 1991).

Scott, John, 'Corporate Groups and Network Structure' in McCahery, J., Picciotto, S. and Scott, S. (eds), *Corporate Control and Accountability* (OUP, Oxford 1993).

Scovazzi, T., 'Industrial Accidents and the Veil of Transnational Corporations' in Francioni, F. and Scovazzi, T. (eds), *International Responsibility for Environmental Harm* (Graham & Trotman, London 1991).

Servan, Schreiber J., *The American Challenge* (Hamish Hamilton, London 1968).

Shrivastava, Paul, *Bhopal: Anatomy of a Crisis* (P. Chapman Publishing, London 1992).

Sorell, T., 'The UN Norms' in Dine, J. and Fagan, A. (eds), *Human Rights and Capitalism* (Edward Elgar, Cheltenham, UK, Northampton, MA, USA 2006).

Steinhardt, R., 'Corporate Responsibility and the International Law of Human Rights: The New Lex Mercatoria' in Alston, P. (ed.), *Non-State Actors and Human Rights* (OUP, Oxford 2005).

Stephens, Beth, 'Corporate Accountability: International Human Rights Litigation Against Corporations in US Courts' in Kamminga, Menno T. and Zia-Zarifi, Saman (eds), *Liability of Multinational Corporations under International Law* (Kluwer Law International, The Hague 2000).

Stiglitz, J., *Globalization and its Discontents* (Allen Lane, London 2002).

Stopford, J.M. and Dunning, J.H., *Multinationals: Company Performance and Global Trends* (Macmillan, London 1983).

Stopford, J.M. and Wells, L.T., *Managing the Multinational Enterprise: Organization of the Firm and the Ownership of the Subsidiaries* (Basic Books, New York 1972).

Suda, R., 'The Effect of Bilateral Investment Treaties on Human Rights Enforcement and Realization' in DeSchutter, O. (ed.), *Transnational Corporations and Human Rights* (Hart Publishing, Oxford 2006).

Sugarman, D. and Teubner, G. (eds), *Regulating Corporate Groups in Europe* (Baden-Baden, Nomos 1990).

Sugarman, D., 'Corporate Groups In Europe: Governance, Industrial Organization, and Efficiency in a Post-Modern World' in Sugarman, D. and Teubner, G. (eds), *Regulating Corporate Groups in Europe* (Baden-Baden, Nomos 1990).

Sullivan, R., 'The Influence of NGOs on the Normative Framework for Business and Human Rights' in Tully, S., *Research Handbook on Corporate Legal Responsibility* (Edward Elgar, Cheltenham, UK, Northampton, MA, USA 2005).

Taggart H., Berry, M. and McDermott, M. (eds), *Multinationals in a New Era* (Palgrave, London 2001).

Teichova, A., 'Multinationals in Perspective' in Teichova, Alice, Lévy-Leboyer,

Maurice and Nussbaum, Helga (eds), *Multinational Enterprise in Historical Perspective* (CUP, Cambridge 1986).

Teichova, A., Levy-Leboyer, M. and Nussbaum, H. (eds), *Multinational Enterprise in Historical Perspective* (CUP, Cambridge 1986).

Teichova, A., Levy-Leboyer, M. and Nussbaum, H., *The Historical Studies in International Corporate Business* (CUP, Cambridge 1989).

Tekkotun, M., (in Turkish) *Limited Sirketlerde Pay Sahibinin Sinirli Sorumlulugu ve Istisnalari* (Ankara University, 2002).

Telfer, Thomas G.W., 'Commentary on Prentice' in Grantham, Ross and Rickett, Charlie (eds), *Corporate Personality in the 20th Century* (Hart, Oxford 1998).

Teubner, G., 'The Many-headed Hydra: Networks as Higher-Order Collective Actors' in McCahery, J., Picciotto, S. and Scott, S. (eds), *Corporate Control and Accountability* (OUP, Oxford 1993).

Teubner, G., 'Unitas Multiplex: Corporate Governance In Group Enterprises' in Sugarman, D. and Teubner, G. (eds), *Regulating Corporate Groups in Europe* (Baden-Baden, Nomos 1990).

Teubner, G., Farmer, L. and Murphy, D. (eds), *Environmental Law and Ecological Responsibility: The Concept and Practice of Ecological Self-Organization* (Wiley, Chichester 1994).

Thomas, J.S. and Meyer, M.A., *The New Rules of Global Trade* (Carswell, Ontario 1997).

Tindall, Robert Emmett and Dobbs, Ferry, *Multinational Enterprises: Legal and Management Structures and Interrelationship With Ownership, Control, Antitrust, Labor, Taxation, and Disclosure* (Oceana Publications, New York 1975).

Tofalo, J., 'Overt and Hidden Accomplices, Transnational Corporations' Range of Complicity for Human Rights Violations' in DeSchutter, O. (ed.), *Transnational Corporations and Human Rights* (Hart Publishing, Oxford 2006).

Tolentino, P.E.E., *Multinational Corporations: Emergence and Evaluation* (Routledge, London 2000).

Toyre, B. and Night, D. (eds), *International Business: An Emerging Vision* (South Coralline Press, Columbia SC University 1997).

Tugendhat, Christopher, *The Multinationals* (Penguin, Harmondsworth 1973).

Tully, S. (ed.), *Research Handbook on Corporate Legal Responsibility* (Edward Elgar, Cheltenham, UK, Northampton, MA, USA 2005).

Tully, S., 'Never say Never Jurisprudence; Comparative Approaches to Corporate Responsibility under the Law of Torts' in Tully, S. (ed.), *Research Handbook on Corporate Legal Responsibility* (Edward Elgar, Cheltenham, UK, Northampton, MA, USA 2005).

Turner, L. and Stopford, J.M., *Britain and the Multinationals* (John Wiley & Sons, London 1983).

UNCTAD World Investment Report 2002.

UNCTAD World Investment Report 2003.

UNCTAD World Investment Report 2004.

UNCTAD World Investment Report 2005.

UNCTAD World Investment Report 2006.

UNCTAD World Investment Reports, 1993–2003.

UNCTAD, *Companies Without Borders: Transnational Corporations in the 1990s* (International Thomson Business Press, London 1996).

Villiers, C., *Corporate Reporting and Company Law* (CUP, Cambridge 2007).

Voiculescu, A., 'The Other European Framework For Corporate Social Responsibility: From The Green Paper to New Uses of Human Rights Instruments' in McBarnet, D., Voiculescu, A. and Campbell, T., *The New Corporate Accountability* (CUP, Cambridge 2007).

Wallace, C.D., *The Multinational Enterprises and Legal Control Host State Sovereignty in an Era of Economic Globalisation* (Martinus Nijhoff, London 2002).

Ward, Halina, 'Corporate Accountability in Search of a Treaty? Some Insight From Foreign Direct Liability' (Briefing Paper of the Royal Institute of International Affairs, 4 May 2002).

Ward, Halina, 'Governing Multinationals: The Role of Foreign Direct Liability' (Briefing Paper of the Royal Institute of International Affairs, Energy and Environment Programme, 18 February 2001).

Weiler, J.H.H., *The EU, the WTO and the NAFTA; Towards a Common Law of International Trade Regulation* (OUP, Oxford 2000).

Weisbrodt, D. and Kruger, M., 'Human Rights Responsibilities of Businesses as Non-State Actors' in Alston, P. (ed.), *Non-State Actors and Human Rights* (OUP, Oxford 2005).

Wellman, B. and Berkowitz, S.D., *Social Structures: A Network Approach* (CUP, Cambridge 1988).

Wells, C. and Elias, J., 'Catching the Conscience of the King: Corporate Players on the International Stage' in Alston, P. (ed.), *Non-State Actors and Human Rights* (OUP, Oxford 2005).

Westney, D.E., 'The Multinational Enterprise as an Organization' in Rugman, A.M. and Brewer, T.L. (eds), *Oxford Handbook of International Business* (OUP, Oxford 2001).

Whish, R., *Competition Law* ( Butterworths, London, 2003).

White, R. and Poynter, T.A., 'Organising for World-Wide Advantages' in Bartlett, C., Doz, Y. and Hedlund, G. (eds), *Managing the Global Firm* (Routledge, London 1990).

Whittington, R. and Mayer, M., *The European Corporation Strategy, Structure and Social Science* (OUP, London 2000).

Wilkins, M., 'The History of Multinational Enterprise' in Rugman, A.M. and Brewer, T.L. (eds), *Oxford Handbook of International Business* (OUP, Oxford 2001).

Wilkins, M., *Emergence of Multinational Enterprise* (Cambridge, Mass 1970).

Wilkins, M., *The Growth of Multinationals* (Edward Elgar, Aldershot, UK and Brookfield, US 1991).

Wilkins, M., *The Maturing of Multinational Enterprise* (Cambridge, Mass 1974).

Williamson, O.E., *Markets and Hierarchies: Analysis and Antitrust Implications* (Free Press, New York 1975).

Wilson, A.J., 'Beyond Unocal: Conceptual Problems in Using International Norms to Hold Transnational Corporations Liable under the Alien Tort Claims Act' in DeSchutter, O. (ed.), *Transnational Corporations and Human Rights* (Hart Publishing, Oxford 2006).

Wooldridge, F. and Schmitthoff, C.M. (eds), *Groups of Companies* (Sweet & Maxwell, London 1991).

Wouters, J. and Schneider, H., *Current Issues of Cross-Border Establishment of Companies in the European Union* (Antwerb, Maklu 1995).

WTO Secretariat, *From GATT to WTO: The Multilateral Trading System in the New Millennium* (Kluwer Law International, London 2000).

Wymeersch, E. (ed.), *Groups of Companies in EEC* (De Gtuyter, Berlin 1993).

Yamin, Mo, 'Subsidiary Entrepreneurship and the Advantage of Multinationality' in Virpi, Havila, Forsgren, Mats and Hakansson, Hakan (eds), *Critical Research on Multinational Corporations* (Pergamon Press, Oxford 2002).

Zerk, J.A., *Multinationals and Corporate Social Responsibility* (CUP, Cambridge 2006).

## ARTICLES

Abadie, Pauline A., 'New Story of David and Goliath: The Alien Tort Claims Act Gives Victims of Environmental Injustice in the Developing World a Viable Claim Against Multinational Corporations' (2004) 34 Golden Gate U.L. Rev. 745.

Abraham, C.M. and Abraham, S., 'The Bhopal Case and the Development of Environmental Law In India' (1991) 40 ICLQ 334.

Abraham, Kennet S., 'The Relation Between Civil Liability and Environmental

Regulation: An Analytical Overview' (2002) 41 Washburn Law Review 379.

Agarwal, S. and Ramaswami, S.N., 'Choice of Foreign Market Entry Mode, Impact of Ownership, Location and Internalisation Factors' (1992) 23 Journal International Business Studies 1.

Akkanat, H. and Aydincik, S., (in Turkish) 'Grup Sirketleri Baglaminda Culpa in Contrahendo Sorumlulugu' (2006) 10 HDP 219.

Alderman, Hila J., 'Ghost of Progress Past: A Comparison of Approaches to Hazardous Waste Liability in the European Community and the United States' (1993–1994) 16 Hous. J. Int'l L. 311.

Alexander, D.E. and Sawez, S., 'Toward a Uniform Parent Corporation Liability Standard under CERCLA' (1998–1999) 60 U. Pitt. L. Rev. 1235.

Alexander, Janet Cooper, 'Unlimited Shareholder Liability through a Procedural Lens' (1992–1993) 106 Harv. L. Rev. 387.

Allen, Gary, 'Refining the Scope of CERCLA's Corporate Veil-Piercing Remedy' (1986–1987) 6 Stan. Envtl. L. J. 43.

Andenas, Mads, 'Free Movement of Companies' (2003) LQR 221.

Anderson, J.C., Hakansson, H. and Johanson, J.A., 'Dyadic Business Relationships within a Business Network Context' (1994) 58 Issue 4 Journal of Marketing 1.

Anderson, Michael, 'Transnational Corporations and Environmental Damage: Is Tort Law the Answer' (2002) 41 Washburn Law Journal 399.

Arlow, Joanna E., 'Utility of ATCA and the Law of Nations in Environmental Torts Litigation: Jota v. Texaco, Inc. and Large Scale Environmental Destruction' (2000) 7 Wis. Envtl. L. J. 93.

Aronovsky, R.C. and Fuller, L.D., 'Liability of Parent Corporations for Hazardous Substance Releases Under CERCLA' (1990) 24 U.S.F.L. Rev. 421.

Bahls, S.C., 'Application of Corporate Law Doctrines to Limited Liability Companies' (1994) 55 Mont. L. Rev. 43.

Bainbridge, Stephen M., 'Abolishing Veil Piercing' (2000–2001) 26 J. Corp. L. 479.

Bakst, David S., 'Piercing the Corporate Veil for Environmental Torts in the United States and the European Union: The Case for the Proposed Civil Liability Directive' (1996) 19 B. C. Int'l & Comp. L. Rev. 323.

Barnard, C., 'Social Dumping and Race to the Bottom: Some Lessons for the European Union from Delaware?' (2000) 25 E.L.Rev. 57.

Bartlett, C.A. and Ghoshal, S., 'Beyond the M-form: Toward a Managerial Theory of the Firm' (1993) 14 Strategic Management Journal 23.

Bartlett, C.A. and Ghoshal, S., 'The Multinational Corporation as an Interorganizational Network' (1990) 15 Ac Man Rev. 603.

Baughen, S., 'Multinationals and the Export of Hazard' (1995) 58 MLR 54.

Baums, T., European Company Law Beyond the 2003 Action Plan (2007) 8 EBOR 143.

Baxt, R., 'The Need to Review the Rule in Salomon's Case as it Applies to Groups of Companies' (1991) Jun. CSLJ 185.

Behrens, Peter, 'International Company Law in View of the Centros Decision of the ECJ' (2000) EBOR 125.

Behrens, Peter, 'Reactions of Member State Courts to the Centros Ruling by the ECJ' (2001) EBOR 159.

Berkamp, L. and Pak, Wan-Q, 'Piercing the Corporate Veil: Shareholder Liability for Corporate Torts' (2001) 8 Maastricht J. of European and Comparative Law 167.

Berzek, Ayse Nur, (in Turkish) 'Limited Sirketlerde Ortaklarin Sorumlulugu' (1996) 47 Yak. Der 32.

Betz, D., 'Holding Multinational Corporations Responsible for Human Rights Abuses Committed by Security Forces in Conflict-Ridden Nations: An Argument Against Exporting Federal Jurisdiction for the Purposes of Regulating Corporate Behaviour Abroad' (2001) 14 DePaul Business Law Journal 163.

Birchall, Jonathan, 'The Questions Over Aiding and Abetting: Alien Tort Statute an Oil Company's Fight With The Human Rights Lobby Tests an 18th Century Law' The *Financial Times* (London, 5 August 2004).

Birkinshaw, J., 'How Multinational Subsidiary Mandates are Gained and Lost' (1996) 27 Journal of International Business Studies 467.

Birnbaum, S.L. and Dunham, D.W., 'Foreign Plaintiff and Forum Non Conveniens' (1990) 16 Brook. J. Int'l. L. 241.

Bishop, R.D., Dimitroff, S.D. and Miles, G.S., 'Strategic Options Available When Catastrophe Strike the Major International Energy Project' (2001) Tex Int'l L.J 635.

Blankenship, Scott, 'Unveiled-Corporate Officer, Parent, and Successor Liability under CERCLA' (1990) 4 Tul. Envtl. L.J. 213.

Blanquet, F., 'European Company Statute (SE)' (2002) 15 Australian Journal of Corporate Law 61.

Blumberg, P.I., 'Limited Liability and Corporate Groups' (1986) 11 Journal of Corporation Law 573.

Blumberg, P.I., 'Corporate Entity in an Era of Multinational Corporations' (1990) 15 Del. J. Corp. L. 283.

Blumberg, P.I., 'Increasing Recognition of Enterprise Principles in Determining Parent and Subsidiary Corporation Liabilities' (1995–1996) 28 Conn. L. Rev. 295.

Blumberg, P.I., 'Accountability of Multinational Corporations: The Barriers Presented by Concepts of the Corporate Juridical Entity' (2000–2001) 24 Hastings Int'l & Comp. L. Rev. 297.

Blumberg, P.I., 'Asserting Human Rights against Multinational Corporations under United States Law: Conceptual and Procedural Problems' (2002) 50 American Journal of Comparative Law 493.

Booth, Richard A., 'Limited Liability and the Efficient Allocation of Resources' (1994–1995) 89 Nw. U.L. Rev. 140.

Bornstein, H.R. 'The Alien Tort Claims Act in 2007: Revolving the Delicate Balance Between Judicial and Legislative Authority' (2007) 82 Ind. L. J. 1077.

Bosko, Marybeth, 'Best of Both Worlds: The Limited Liability Company' (1993) 54 Ohio St. L.J. 175.

Bowmer, Simon, 'Company Law to Pierce or Not to Pierce the Corporate Veil – Why Substantive Consolidation is Not an Issue Under English Law' (2000) 15 JIBL 193.

Boyd, Kathryn Lee, 'Inconvenience of Victims: Abolishing Forum Non Conveniens in U.S. Human Rights Litigation' (1998–1999) 39 Va. J. Int'l L. 41.

Boyle, T., 'The Company Law, Review and Group Reform' (2002) 23 Company Lawyer 35.

Bradley, M., Schipani, C.A., Sundaram, A.K. and Walsh, J.P., 'The Purposes and Accountability of the Corporation in Contemporary Society: Corporate Governance at a Crossroads' (1999) 62 Law&Contemp. Probs. 9.

Bratton, William W., 'Inquiry into the Efficiency of the Limited Liability Company: of Theory of the Firm and Regulatory Competition' (1997) 54 Wash. & Lee L. Rev. 629.

Breed, L.M., 'Regulating Our 21st Century Ambassadors: A New Approach to Corporate Liability for Human Rights Violations Abroad' (2002) 42 Virginia Journal of International Law 1005.

Bridgeford, T.A., 'Imputing Human Rights Obligations on Multinational Corporations: The Ninth Circuit Strikes Again in Judicial Activism' (2003) 18 American University International Law Review 1009.

Brown, John M., 'Parent Corporation's Liability under CERCLA Section 107 for the Environmental Violations of Their Subsidiaries' (1995–1996) 31 Tulsa L.J. 819.

Brown, Kamie Frischknecht, 'Parent Corporation Liability for Subsidiary Violations under 107 of CERCLA: Responding to United States v. Cordova Chemical Co' (1998) BYU L. Rev. 265.

Bruno, K., 'De-Globalisation Justice, The Corporate Campaign to Foreign Victims of Corporate-Induced Human Rights Violations of the Right to Sue in US Courts' 24 (2003) Multinational Monitor n. 3.

Buckley, P.J. and Casson, M., 'Models of the Multinational Enterprise' (1998) 29 Journal of International Business Studies 21.

Cabral, P. and Cunha, P. 'Presumed Innocent: Companies and the Exercise of the Right of Establishment under Community Law' (2000) 25 E.L.Rev. 157.

Callison, J.W., 'Rationalizing Limited Liability and Veil Piercing' (2002–2003) 58 Bus. Law. 1063.

Campbell, Rutherford B., 'Limited Liability for Corporate Shareholders: Myth or Matter-of-Fact' (1974–1975) 63 Ky. L.J. 23.

Cantwell, J.A. and Piscitello, L., 'The Emergence of Corporate International Networks for the Accumulation of Dispersed Technological Competencies' (1999) 39 Management International Review 123.

Carlos, A. and Nicholas, S.J., 'Theory and History of the Early Trading Companies' (1996, December) Journal of Economic History 56.

Cashel, Thomas W., 'Multinational Challenge to Corporation Law: The Search for a New Corporate Personality (Publication Review)' (1994) 9 JIBL 249.

Cassels, Jamie, 'Uncertain Promise of Law: Lessons from Bhopal' (1991) 29 Osgoode Hall L.J. 1.

Chandler, A.D., 'The Growth of Transnational Industrial Firms in the UK and US: A Comparative Analysis' (1980) 33 Economic History Review 396.

Chapman, S., 'British Based Investment Group Before 1914' (1985) Economic History Review 230.

Chinen, M.A., 'Jurisdiction: Foreign Plaintiffs, Forum Non Conveniens and Litigation Against Multinational Corporations' (1987) 28 Harvard International Law Journal 209.

Chopra, Sudhir K., 'Multinational Corporations in the Aftermath of Bhopal: The Need for a New Comprehensive Global Regime for Transnational Corporate Activity' (1994) 24 Valparaiso University Law Review 256.

Cleveland, S.H., 'Global Labor Rights and Alien Tort Claim Act' (1998) 76 Tex L. Rev. 1533.

Coase, R.H., 'The Nature of the Firm' (1937) 4 Economia 386.

Coffey, Michael P., 'In Defense of Limited Liability – A Reply to Hansmann and Kraakman' (1994) 1 Geo. Mason L. Rev. 59.

Cohen, David L., 'Theories of the Corporation and the Limited Liability Company: How Should Courts and Legislatures Articulate Rules for Piercing the Veil, Fiduciary Responsibility and Securities Regulation for the Limited Liability Company' (1998) 51 Okla. L. Rev. 427.

Collins, Hugh, 'Ascription of Legal Responsibility to Groups in Complex Patterns of Economic Integration' (1990) 53 Modern Law Review 731.

Conley, J.M. and Williams, C.A. 'Engage, Embed and Embellish: Theory versus Practice in the Corporate Social Responsibility Movements' (2005–2006) 35 Journal of Corporation Law 1.

Cooter, Robert D., 'Defective Warnings, Remote Causes, and Bankruptcy: Comment On Schwartz' (1985) 14 Journal of Legal Studies 737.

Coye-Huhn, Scott, 'No More Hiding behind Forms, Factors, and Flying Hats:

A Proposal for a Per Se Piercing of the Corporate Veil for Corporations That Violate the Law of Nations under the Alien Tort Claims Statute' (2003–2004) 72 U. Cin. L. Rev. 743.

Delaney, L., 'Flores v. Southern Peru Copper Corporation the Second Circuit Fails to Set a Threshold for Corporate Alien Tort Claims Act Liability' (2004–2005) 25 Nw. J. Int'l L. & Bus. 205.

DeMonte, Jessica, 'Impact of United States v. Bestfoods on Parent Liability under CERCLA: When A Door Is Closed, Look for an Open Window' (2000) 61 Ohio St. L.J. 443.

Dent, George W., 'Limited Liability In Environmental Law' (1991) 26 Wake Forest Law Review 151.

Deye, K., 'Can Corporations be Held Liable under the Alien Tort Claims Act?' (2005–2006) 94 KY. L.J. 649.

Dobson, J.M., 'Lifting the Veil in Four Countries: The Law of Argentina, England, France and the US' (1986) 35 ICLQ 839.

Dodge, William S., 'Historical Origins of the Alien Tort Statute: A Response to the Originalists' (1995–1996) 19 Hastings Int'l & Comp. L. Rev. 221.

Dodge, William S., 'Which Torts in Violation of the Law of Nations' (2000–2001) 24 Hastings Int'l & Comp. L. Rev. 351.

Dorward, Daniel J., 'Forum Non Conveniens Doctrine and the Judicial Protection of Multinational Corporations from Forum Shopping Plaintiffs' (1998) 19 U. Pa. J. Int'l Econ. L. 141.

Doz, Y.L. and Prahalad, C.K., 'Managing Diversified MNCs: A Search for a New Paradigm' (1991) 12 Strategic Management Journal 145.

Drury, R.R., 'The Regulation and the Recognition of Foreign Corporations: Responses to Delaware Syndrome' (1998) 57 Cambridge Law Journal 165.

Dunham, D.F. and Gladbach, E.F., 'Forum Non Conveniens and the Foreign Plaintiffs in the 1990s' (1998–1999) 24 Brook J Int'l L 665.

Duval-Major, J., 'One-Way Ticket Home: The Federal Doctrine of Forum Non Conveniens and the International Plaintiff' (1991–1992) 77 Cornell Law Review 650.

Dyrberg, P., 'Free Movement of Companies in the European Community at Last' (2003) ELR 528.

Easterbrook, F.H. and Fischel, D.R., 'Limited Liability and the Corporation' (1985) 52 U. Chi. L. Rev. 89.

Ebke, W.F., 'Centros – Some Realities and some Mysteries' (2001) 48 A.J. Comp. Law 623.

Edwards, Vanessa, 'Case-Law of the European Court of Justice on Freedom of Establishment After Centros' (2000) EBOR 147.

Erkan, Fikret, (in Turkish) 'Limited Sirket Kanuni Temsilci ve Ortaklarin Amme Borclarindan Dolayi Takibi' (2001) 108 Yak Der 221.

Eskenazi, Nancy J., 'Forum Non Conveniens and Choice of Law in Re: The Amoco Cadiz Oil Spill' (1993) 24 J. Mar. L. & Com. 371.

Ethier, W.J., 'The Multinational Firm' (1986) 101 Quarterly Journal of Economics 806.

Everett, Danielle, 'New Concern for Transnational Corporations: Potential Liability for Tortious Acts Committed by Foreign Partners' (1998) 35 San Diego L. Rev. 1123.

Eyibilir, Ihsan, (in Turkish) 'Limited Sirket Ortaklarinin Sorumlulugu' (1995) 32 Yak Der 93.

Farha, A.S., 'Corporate Conscience and Environmental Issues: Responsibility of the Multinational Corporation' (1989–1990) 10 Nw. J. Int'l L. & Bus. 379.

Farmer, Richard S., 'Parent Corporation Responsibility for the Environmental Liabilities of the Subsidiary: A Search for the Appropriate Standard' (1994) 19 J. Corp. L. 769.

Farrar, J.H., 'Fraud, Fairness and the Piercing the Corporate Veil' (1990) 16 Canadian Business Law Journal 474.

Farrar, J.H., 'Legal Issues Involving Corporate Groups' (1998) 16 CSLJ 184.

Fawcett, J.J., 'Jurisdiction and Subsidiaries' (1985) Journal of Business Law 16.

Fleur, Johns, 'The Invisibility of the Transnational Corporation: An Analysis of International Law and Legal Theory' (1994) 19 Melb. U.L. Rev. 893.

Fliegstein, N., 'The Spread of the Multinational Form Among Large Firms 1919–1979' (1985) 50 American Sociological Review 377.

Fortney, Susan Saab, 'Seeking Shelter in the Minefield of Unintended Consequences – The Traps of Limited Liability Law Firms' (1997) 54 Wash. & Lee L. Rev. 717.

Forum Europaeum, 'Corporate Group Law, Corporate Group Law For Europe' (2000) EBOR 165.

Fox, Eric, 'Piercing the Veil of Limited Liability Companies' (1993–1994) 62 Geo. Wash. L. Rev. 1143.

Freckmann, Anke, 'The Incorporation of a German Limited Liability Company' (2000) International Company and Commercial Law Review 210.

Freedman, Judith, 'Limited Liability: Large Company Theory and Small Firms' (2000) 63 Modern Law Review 317.

Freedman, Judith, 'Small Businesses and the Corporate Form: Burden and Privilege?' (1994) 57 MLR 555.

Freeman, B., Pica, M. and Camponovo, C., 'New Approach to Corporate Responsibility: The Voluntary Principles on Security and Human Rights' (2000–2001) 24 Hastings Int'l & Comp. L. Rev. 423.

French, Peter, 'Parent Corporation Liability: An Evaluation of the Corporate

Veil Piercing Doctrine and Its Application to the Toxic Tort Arena' (1991–1992) 5 Tul. Envtl. L.J. 605.

Fridman, S., 'Removal of the Corporate Veil: Suggestions for Law Reform in Quintex Australia Finance Ltd. v Schroders Australia Ltd.' (1991) 19 ABLR 211.

Gabaldon, Theresa A., 'Lemonade Stand: Feminist and Other Reflections on the Limited Liability of Corporate Shareholders' (1992) 45 Vand. L. Rev. 1387.

Gaffney, J.P. 'The Group of Companies Doctrine and the Law Applicable to the Arbitration Agreement' (2004) 19 MEALEY'S International Arbitration Report 6.

Gallagher, Lynn and Peter Ziegler, 'Lifting The Corporate Veil in the Pursuit of Justice' (1990) Jul J.B.L. 292.

Gates, Games L., 'Bhopal Chemical Gas Leak Incident: A Research Guide and Bibliography' (1991) 19 Int'l. J. Legal Info. 11.

Gatinghon, H. and Anderson, E., 'The Multinational Corporation's Degree of Control Over Foreign Subsidiaries: An Empirical Test of Transaction Cost Explanations' (1988) (2) Journal of Law, Economics and Organisations 305.

Gavil, A.I. 'Copperweld 2000: The Vanishing Gap between Sections 1 and 2 of the Sherman Act' (2000) 68 Antitrust L.J. 87.

Gelb, Harvey, 'Piercing The Corporate Veil – The Undercapitalization Factor' (1982) Chicago-Kent Law Review 1.

Gelb, Harvey, 'CERCLA versus Corporate Limited Liability' (1999–2000) 48 U. Kan. L. Rev. 111.

Gevurtz, F.A., 'An Attempt to Lift the Veil of Confusion Surrounding the Doctrine of Piercing the Corporate Veil' (1997) 76 Oregon Law Review 853.

Ghoshal, S. and Barlett, C.A., 'The Multinational Corporations as an Inter Organizational Network' (1990) 15 Academy of Management Review 603.

Goerzen, A. and Beamish, P.W., 'The Effect of Alliance Network Diversity on Multinational Enterprise Performance' (2005) 26 Strategic Management Journal 333.

Goforth, Carol R., 'Rise of the Limited Liability Company: Evidence of a Race between the States, but Heading Where' (1994) 45 Syracuse L. Rev. 1193.

Gomes-Gasseres, B., 'Ownership Structures of Foreign Subsidiaries' (1989) 2 Journal of Economic Behaviour and Organization 1.

Gooderham, Paul N. and Ulset, Svein, 'Beyond the M-form: Towards a Critical Test of the New Form' (2002) 9 International Journal of the Economics of Business 117.

Graham, Boyce L., 'Navigating the Mists of Metaphor: An Examination of the Doctrine of Piercing the Corporate Veil' (1990–1991) 56 J. Air L. & Com. 1135.

Greathead, S., 'The Multinational and the "New Stakeholder": Examining the Business Case for Human Rights' (2002) 35 Vanderbilt Journal of Transnational Law 719.

Griffin, S., '(Case Comment) Holding Companies and Subsidiaries – The Corporate Veil' (1991) 12 Comp Law 16.

Griffin, S., 'Limited Liability: A Necessary Revolution' (2004) 25(4) Comp. Law 99.

Griggs, L. and Lowry, J., 'Minority Shareholders Remedies: A Comparative View' (1994) JBL 463.

Grossman, Peter Z., 'The Market for Shares of Companies with Unlimited Liability: The Case of American Express' (1995) 24 J. of. Legal St 63.

Grundfest, Joseph A., 'Limited Future of Unlimited Liability: A Capital Markets Perspective, (1992–1993) 102 Yale L.J. 387.

Guest Editorial, 'First Steps for a European Law on Corporate Groups' (1999) 36 CMLR 1.

Gupta, A.K. and Govindarajan, V., 'Knowledge Flows and the Structure of Control Within Multinational Corporations' (1991) 16 The Academy of Management Review 768.

Haar, Brigitte, 'Piercing Veil and Shareholder's Product and Environmental Liability in American Law as Remedies for Capital Market Failures – New Developments and Implications for European and German Law After Centros' (2000) EBOR 317.

Habegger, P., 'Arbitration and Groups of Companies – the Swiss Practice' (2002) 3 EBOR 517.

Hadden, T., 'Inside Corporate Groups' (1984) 12 Int'l. J. Soc L. 271.

Halbhuber, H., 'National Doctrinal Structures and European Community Law' (2001) 38 C.M.L.Rev. 1385.

Hall, Ben and Peel, Michael, 'Law Change to Speed up Asbestos Cases' *Financial Times* (London 21 June 2006).

Halpern, P., Trebilcock, M. and Turnbull, M. 'An Economic Analysis of Limited Liability in Corporation Law' (1980) 30 University of Toronto Law Journal 117.

Hamblett, M., 'Environmental Suit Disallowed under U.S. Statute. Court Sees Limits to Alien Tort Claims Act' (2003) 26 National Law Journal 3.

Hamill, Susan, 'Pace Origins behind the Limited Liability Company' (1998) 59 Ohio St. L.J. 1459.

Hamilton, Robert W., 'Limited Liability and the Real World' (1997) 54 Wash. & Lee L. Rev. 687.

Hanatiau, B., 'Complex-Multicontract, Multiparty-Arbitrations' (1998) 14 Arb. Int.l 369.

Hanatiau, B., 'Problems Raised by Complex Arbitrations Involving Multiple

Contracts – Parties – Issues – an Analysis' (2001) Journal of International Arbitration 252.

Hansen, S.F., 'From C 212 to L 212 – Centros Revisited' (2001) EBOR 141.

Hansmann, Henry and Kraakman, Reiner 'Procedural Focus on Unlimited Shareholder Liability' (1992–1993) 106 Harv. L. Rev. 446.

Hansmann, Henry and Kraakman, Reiner, 'Do the Capital Markets Compel Limited Liability: A Response to Professor Grundfest' (1992–1993) 102 Yale L.J. 427.

Hansmann, Henry and Kraakman, Reiner, 'Toward Unlimited Shareholder Liability for Corporate Torts' (1990–1991) 100 Yale L.J. 1879.

Hansmann, Henry and Kraakman, Reiner, 'The Essential Role of Organizational Law' (2000) 110 Yale L.J. 387.

Hedlund, G., 'The Hypermodern MNC – A Heterarchy?' (1986) 25 International Studies of Management 9.

Heidelberg, Evelyn F., 'Parent Corporation Liability under CERCLA: Toward a Uniform Federal Rule of Decision' (1990–1991) 22 Pac. L.J. 854.

Herz, R., 'Litigating Environmental Abuses Under The Alien Tort Claims Act: A Practical Assessment' (2000) 40 Virginia Journal of International Law 545.

Herz, R., 'Text of Remarks on Panel: Indigenous Peoples, Environmental Torts and Cultural Genocide' (2000–2001) 24 Hastings Int'l & Comp. L. Rev. 503.

Hilbert, Catherine Ann, 'United States v. Bestfoods: Parent Corporation Liability under CERCLA' (1999) 24 Del. J. Corp. L. 919.

Hill, J., 'Cross Guarantees in Corporate Groups' (1992) 10 CSLJ 312.

Hofstetter, K., 'Parent Responsibility for Subsidiary Corporations: Evaluating European Trends' (1990) 39 ICLQ 576.

Holm, U., Johanson, J. and Thilenius, P., 'Headquarters' Knowledge of Subsidiary Network Contexts in Multinational Corporation' (1995) 25 International Studies of Management & Organisations 97.

Hommelhoff, P., 'Protection of Minority Shareholders, Investors and Creditors in Corporate Groups: The Strengths and Weakness of German Corporate Group Law' (2001) 2 EBOR 61.

Hopkins, G.C., 'United States v Bestfoods: the U.S. Supreme Court Sets New Limits on the direct liability of Parent Corporations for Polluting Acts of Subsidiaries' (1999) 29 Envtl. L. Rep. 10545.

Hopt, K.J. and Pistor, K., 'Company Groups in Transition Economies: A Case for Regulatory Intervention?' (2001) EBOR 1.

Hosking, J.M., 'The Third Party Non-Signatory's Ability to Compel International Commercial Arbitration: Doing Justice without Destroying Consent' (2003–2004) 4 Pepp. Disp. Resol. L.J. 469.

Hottel, D.A. and Jeffcoat, M.R., 'Caught in the Web: CERCLA Owner or

Operator Liability of Lenders, Shareholders, Parent Corporations, and Attorneys' (1997) 6 S.C. Envtl. L J. 161.

Howell, Claire 'The Company White Paper: A Descriptive Overview' (2005) 26 Comp. Law 203.

Huss, Rebecca J., 'Revamping Veil Piercing for All Limited Liability Entities: Forcing the Common Law Doctrine into the Statutory Age' (2001–2002) 70 U. Cin. L. Rev. 95.

Irby, S.M., 'United States v. Bestfoods: CERCLA's Effect on Climbing the Corporate Ladder of Liability' (1999) 52 Ark. L. Rev. 613.

Ireland, P., 'Company Law and the Myth of Shareholder Ownership' (1999) 62 Modern Law Review 32.

Irujo, José Miguel Embid, 'Trends and Realities in the Law of Corporate Groups' (2005) 6 EBOR 65.

Ismail, Hilmy, 'Forum Non Conveniens, United States Multinational Corporations, and Personal Injuries in the Third World: Your Place or Mine' (1991) 11 B. C. Third World L.J. 249.

Jarillo, J.C., 'On Strategic Networks' (1993) 9 Strategic Management Journal 31.

Jeffrey, M.B. and Steinhardt R.G., 'Federal Jurisdiction Over International Human Rights Claim: the Alien Tort Claim Act after Flartiga v. Pena-Irala' (1981) 22 Harv. Int'l L.J. 53.

Jessel-Holst, Christa, 'Regulatory Approaches to Groups of Companies in States in Transition in Central and Eastern Europe' (2001) EBOR 45.

Johanson, J. and Mattson, L.G., 'Internationalisation in Industrial Systems: A Network Approach Compared with a Transaction Cost Approach' (1987) 17 International Studies of Management and Organization 34.

Joseph, S., 'Taming the Leviathans: Multinational Enterprises and Human Rights' (1999) 46 Netherlands International Law Review 171.

Juric, 'A review of Liability Issues Arising from the Grounding of the Oil Tanker Amoco Cadiz' (1987) 31 Trial Law Guide 297.

Kahn-Freund, O., 'Some Reflection on Company Law Reform' (1943–1944) 7 Modern Law Review 54.

Karjala Dennis, S., 'Planning Problems in the Limited Liability Company' (1995) 73 Wash. U. L.Q. 455.

Khalil, S.A., 'The Alien Tort Claims Act and Section 1983: The Improper Use of Domestic Laws To "Create" and "Define" International Liability For Multinational Corporations' (2002) 31 Hofstra Law Review 207.

Khokhryakova, A., 'Beanal v. Freeport-McMoran Inc.: Liability of a private actor for international environmental tort under the Alien Tort Claims Act' (1998) 9 Colorado Journal of International Environmental Law 463.

Kieserman, B.J., 'Profits and Principles: Promoting Multinational Corporate

Responsibility by Amending the Alien Tort Claims Act' (1998–1999) 48 Catholic U.L. Rev. 881.

King, J.A., 'Kayser-Roth, Joslyn, and the Problem of Parent Corporation Liability under CERCLA' (1991–1992) 25 Akron L. Rev. 123.

Kinley, D. and Joseph, S., 'Multinational Corporations and Human Rights: Questions about their Relationship' (2002) 27 Alternative Law Journal 7.

Kipp, Matthew, 'Piercing the Veil of the Amoco Cadiz Decision: Judge Posner's Jurisdictional Analysis Runs Aground' (1988–1989) 38 DePaul Law Rev. 703.

Klass, A.B., 'From Reservoirs to Remediation: The Impact of CERCLA on Common Law Strict Liability Environmental Claims' (2004) 39 Wake Forest L. Rev. 903.

Kluver, John, 'European And Australian Proposal For Corporate Group Law: A Comparative Analysis' (2000) EBOR 287.

Kochan, D.J., 'Note, Constitutional Structure as a Limitation on the Scope of the "Law of Nations" in the Alien Tort Claims Act' (1998) 31 Cornell Int'l L. J. 153.

Kornhauser, Lewis A., 'Economic Analysis of the Choice between Enterprise and Personal Liability for Accidents' (1982) 70 Cal. L. Rev. 1345.

Lamm, S.B. and Aqua, J.A., 'Defining the Party – Who is a Proper Party in an International Arbitration Before the American Arbitration Association and Other International Institution' (2002–2003) 34 Geo. Wash. Int'l L. Rev. 711.

Leadley, J. and Williams, L., 'Peterson Farms: There is No Group of Companies Doctrine in English Law' (2004) 7 Int. ALR 111.

Leebron, David W., 'Limited Liability, Tort Victims, and Creditors' (1991) 91 Colum L. Rev. 1565.

Livermore, S., 'Unlimited Liability in Early American Corporations' (1935) 43 J. Pol. Econ. 674.

Lombardo, Stefano, 'Conflict of Law Rules in Company Law After Uberseering: An Economic and Comparative Analysis of the Allocation of Policy Competence in the European Union' (2003) 4 EBOR 301.

Londis, L., 'The Corporate Face of the Alien Tort Claims Act: How an Old Statute Mandates a New Understanding of Global Interdependence' (2005) 57 Me. L. Rev. 141.

Looijestijn, Clearie, 'Centros Ltd – A Complete U-Turn in the Right of Establishment for Companies' (2000) 49 ICLQ 621.

Lowry, J., 'Lifting the Corporate Veil' (1993) JBL 41.

Lutter, M., 'The Liability of the Parent Company for the Debts of its Subsidiaries Under German Law' (1985) JBL 499.

Lutter, M., 'The Law of Groups of Companies in Europe' (1983) 1 Forum Internationale 1.

Lutter, M., 'Enterprise Law Corp. vs. Entity Law Inc. Philip Blumberg's Book from the Point of View of an European Lawyer' (1990) 38 American Journal of Comparative Law 949.

Lynn, M.L., 'The Death of Liability' (1996) 106 Yale L.J. 1.

Macey, Jonathan R., 'Limited Liability Company: Lessons for Corporate Law' (1995) 73 Wash. U.L. Q. 433.

Magaisa, A.T., 'Suing Multinational Corporate Groups for Torts in Wake of the Lubbe Case' (2001) 2 Law, Social Justice and Global Development 1.

Magaisa, A.T., 'Corporate Groups and Victims of Corporate Torts – Towards a New Architecture of Corporate Law in a Dynamic Marketplace Law (2002) 1 Law, Social Justice and Global Development 1.

Malnight, T.W., 'The Transition from Decentralised to Network Based MNC Structures: An Evolutionary Perspective' (1996, first quarter) Journal of International Business Studies 43.

Manchester, K.A., 'Their Subsidiaries' Keepers: Should Parent Corporations Be Vicariously or Directly Liable for the Environmental Violations of Their Subsidiary Corporations under CERCLA' (1991) 1 U. Balt. J. Envtl. L. 68.

Marlow, Jennifer, 'Germany: Company Law: Lifting the Corporate Veil' (1993) 4 ICCLR 133.

Marlowe, C.M., 'International Forum Non Conveniens' (2001) 32 Inter-American LR 295.

Martin, Jennifer S., 'Consistency in Judicial Interpretation – A Look at CERCLA Parent Company and Shareholder Liability after United States v. Bestfoods' (2000–2001) 17 Ga. St. U. L. Rev. 409.

Martin-Ortega, O., 'International Responses to Multinational Enterprises' Lack of Accountability for Human Rights Abuses in the Context of Globalisation' (2006) 7 Revista de Estudios Juridicos 179.

Matheson, John H., 'Doctrine of Piercing the Veil in an Era of Multiple Limited Liability Entities: An Opportunity to Codify the Test for Waiving Owners' Limited-Liability Protection' (2000) 75 Wash. L. Rev. 147.

Mattei, Ugo and Jeffrey, L., 'U.S. Jurisdiction over Conflicts Arising Outside of the United States: Some Hegemonic Implications' (2000–2001) 24 Hastings Int'l & Comp. L. Rev. 381.

McKane, M.E., 'Operator Liability for Parent Corporations under CERCLA: A Return to Basics' (1996–1997) 91 Nw. U.L. Rev. 1642.

McPhail, Mark R., 'Environmental Law: CERCLA Liability of Corporate Parents for Their Dissolved or Undercapitalised Subsidiaries' (1991) 44 Okla. L. Rev. 345.

Meeran, Richard, 'Process Liability of Multinationals: Overcoming the Forum Hurdle' (1995) (Nov) JPIL 170.

Meiners, Roger E., 'Piercing the Veil of Limited Liability' (1978–1979) 4 Del. J. Corp. L. 351.

Menell, Peter S., 'Legal Advising on Corporate Structure in the New Era of Environmental Liability' (1990) Colum. Bus. L. Rev. 399.
Micheler, E., 'The Impact of Centros Case on Europe's Company Laws' (2000) Comp. Law. 179.
Miles, R.E. and Snow, C.C., 'Designing Strategic Human Resources Systems' (1984) 13 Organizational Dynamics 36.
Miles, R.E. and Snow, C.C., 'The Functioning of Network Organisations' (1992) (summer) California Management Review 34.
Miller, Laurel E., 'Forum Non Conveniens and State Control of Foreign Plaintiff Access to U.S. Courts in International Tort Actions' (1991) 58 U. Chi. L. Rev. 1369.
Miller, S.K., 'Piercing The Corporate Veil Among Affiliated Companies in the European Community and in the US: A Comparative Analysis of US, German and UK Veil Piercing Approaches' (1998) 36 Am. Bus. L.J. 73.
Mitchell, Charles, 'Lifting the Corporate Veil in the English Courts: An Empirical Study' (1999) Company, Financial and Insolvency Law Review 15.
Montesa, A. and Givaja, A., 'When Parents Pay for their Children's Wrongs: Attribution of Liability for EC Antitrust Infringements in Parent-subsidiary Scenarios' (2006) 29 World Competition 555.
Muchlinski, P., 'Corporations in International Litigation Problems of Jurisdiction and the United Kingdom Asbestos Cases' (2001) 50 ICLQ 1.
Muchlinski, P., 'Holding Multinationals to Account: Recent Developments in English Litigation and the Company Law Review' (2002) 23 Company Lawyer 168.
Muchlinski, P., 'The Bhopal Case Controlling Ultra-hazardous Industrial Activities Undertaken By Foreign Investors' (1987) 50 Modern Law Review 545.
Muchlinski, P., 'Enron and Beyond: Multinational Corporate Groups and the Internalization of Governance and Disclosure Regimes' (2005) 37 Conn. L. Rev. 725.
Myers, R.L., 'Parent Corporate Liability for the CERCLA Debt of Its Insolvent Subsidiary' (1991–1992) 69 U. Det. Mercy L. Rev. 93.
Nakajima, Chizu, 'Lifting the Veil' (1996) 17 Comp. Law. 187.
Nashenveng, Silvia, 'Company Law (Legislation Comment) Companies' Liabilities Under The First EC Directive' (2001) 12 EBL Rev. 89.
Newman, L. and Zaslowsky, D., 'The Alien Tort Claims Act: How far Will It Go?' (2003) 2 New York Law Journal 39.
Neyers, Jason W., 'Canadian Corporate Law, Veil-Piercing, and the Private Law Model Corporation' (2000) 50 U. Toronto L.J. 173.
Nicholas, S.J., 'British Multinational Investment before 1939' (1982) Journal of European Economic History 605.
Nicholas, S.J., 'The Motivation and Direction of UK Direct Investment 1870–1939' (1982) Journal of European Economic History 605.

Nicholas, S.J., 'Total Factor Productivity Growth and the Performance of the British Economy, 1870–1914' (1985) (November) Economic History Review 83.

Nicholas, S.J., 'The Growth of the Multinational Corporation' (1986 May) Corporate History Bulletin 396.

Nicholas, S.J. and Hutchinson, D., 'Theory in Business History: New Approaches to Institutional Change' (1988) Journal of European Economic History 17.

Nicklish, F., 'Multi-party Arbitration and Dispute Resolution in Major Industrial Projects' (1994) 11 J. Int'l Arb. 57.

Nobel, Peter, 'Social Responsibility of Corporations' (1998–1999) 84 Cornell L. Rev. 1255.

Nolan, A., 'The Position of Unsecured Creditors of Corporate Groups; Towards a Group Responsibility Solution Which Gives Fairness And Equity A Role' (1993) 11 CSLJ 461.

Noonan, E.A., 'To Pierce Or Not to Pierce – When Is the Question – Developing a Federal Rule of Decision for Piercing the Corporate Veil under CERCLA' (1990) 68 Wash. U.L.Q. 733.

Note, 'Should Shareholders be Personally Liable for the Torts of Their Corporations' (1966–1967) 76 Yale L.J. 1190.

Note, 'Liability of Parent Corporations for Hazardous Waste Cleanup and Damages' (1985–1986) 99 Harv. L. Rev. 986.

Nygh, Peter, 'The Liability of Multi-National Corporations for Their Subsidiaries' (2002) 3 EBOR 27.

O'Donnell, S.W., 'Managing Foreign Subsidiaries: Agent of Headquarters, or an Independent Network?' (2000) 21 Strategic Management Journal 525.

O'Donnell, Sharon Watson, 'Managing Foreign Subsidiaries: Agents of Headquarters, or an Interdependent Network?' (2000) 21 Strategic Management Journal 525.

O'Keeffe, J., 'Environmental Issues in Corporate Transactions in the United Kingdom' (1999) ICCLR 344.

Ochoa, C., 'Access to US Federal Courts as a Forum for Human Rights Disputes Pluralism and the Alien Tort claims Act' (2005) 12 Ind. J. Global Legal Stud. 631.

Olah, F.C., 'MNC Liability for International Human Rights Violations under the Alien Tort Claims Act: A Review and Analysis of the Fundamental Jurisprudence and a Look at Aiding and Abetting Liability Under the Act' (2006–2007) 25 QLR 751.

Osofsky, H.M., 'Environmental Human Rights Under the Alien Tort Statute: Redress for Indigenous Victims of Multinational Corporations' (1997) 20 Suffolk Transnat'l L. Rev. 335.

Oswald, Lynda J. and Schipani Cindy A., 'Cercla and the "Erosion" of Traditional Corporate Law Doctrine' (1992) 86 Nw. U.L. Rev. 259.

Ottolenghi, S., 'From Peeping Behind The Corporate Veil to Ignoring it Completely' (1990) 53 MLR 338.

Palmisano, S.J., 'The Globally Integrated Enterprise' (2006) 85 Foreign Affairs 127.

Patterson, Mark R., 'Is Unlimited Liability Really Unattainable: Of Long Arms and Short Sales' (1995) 56 Ohio St. L.J. 815.

Paul, Joel R., 'Holding Multinational Corporations Responsible under International Law' (2000–2001) 24 Hastings Int'l & Comp. L. Rev. 285.

Payne, J., 'Lifting the Corporate Veil: A Reassessment of the Fraud Exception' (1997) 56 CLJ 284.

Perlmutter, H.V., 'The Tortuous Evolution of the Multinational Corporation' (1969 Jan–Feb) Columbia Journal of World Business 9.

Pettit, B., 'Limited Liability – A Principle for the 21st Century' (1995) CLP 124.

Picciotto, S., 'Rights, Responsibilities and Regulation of International Business' (2003) 42 Columbia Journal of Transnational Law 131.

Png, Cheong Ann, 'Lifting the Veil of Incorporation: Creasey v Breachwood Motors: A Right Decision With The Wrong Reasons' (1999) Co. Law 122.

Poli, S., 'Shaping the EC Regime on Liability for Environmental Damages: Progress or Disillusionment?' (1999) 8 European Environmental Law Review 299.

Powell, W.W., 'Neither Market Nor Hierarchy: Network Forms of Organization' (1990) 12 Research in Organization Behaviour 295.

Prebble, Amanda L., 'Corporate Law Confines to Parent Liability under CERCLA: United States v. Bestfoods, 118 S. Ct. 1876 (1998)' (1998–1999) 67 U. Cin. L. Rev. 1357.

Prell, Owen T. 'Copperweld Corp. v. Independence Tube Corp.: An End to the Intraenterprise Conspiracy Doctrine?' (1986) 71 Cornell Law Review 1151–1180.

Prentice, D.D., 'Some Aspects of the Law Relating to Corporate Groups in the United Kingdom' (1998–1999) 13 Conn. J. Int'l L. 305.

Prentice, D.D., 'Veil Piercing and Successor Liability in the United Kingdom' (1995–1996) 10 Fla. J. Int'l L. 469.

Presser, Stephen B., 'Thwarting the Killing of the Corporation: Limited Liability, Democracy, and Economics' (1992–1993) 87 Nw. U. L. Rev. 148.

Prince, Peter, 'Bhopal, Bougainville and OK Tedi: Why Australia's Approach to Forum Non Conveniens is Better' (1998) 47 International and Comparative Law Quarterly 573.

Priskich, V., 'Corporate Groups: Current proposals for Reform in Australia and the United Kingdom and a Comparative Analysis of the Regime in Germany' (2002) ICCLJ 37.

Racquet, B.E. and Romsdahl, R.J., 'Piercing the Corporate Veil under the Oil Pollution Act of 1990' (1992–1993) 5 U. S. F. Mar. L. J. 369.

Ramsay, I.M. and Noakes, D.B., 'Piercing the Corporate Veil in Australia' (2001) 19 Company and Securities Law Journal 250.

Ramsey, Michael D., 'Multinational Corporate Liability under the Alien Tort Claims Act: Some Structural Concerns' (2000–2001) 24 Hastings Int'l & Comp. L. Rev. 361.

Randall, K., 'Federal Jurisdiction Over International Law Claims: Inquiries Into the Alien Tort Statute' (1985) 18 New York University Journal of International Law and Politics 11.

Ratner, S., 'Corporations and Human Rights: A Theory of Legal Responsibility' (2001) (December) Yale Law Journal 443.

Ribstein, Larry E., 'The Deregulation of Limited Liability and the Death of Partnership' (1992) 70 Wash. U.L.Q 417.

Ribstein, Larry E., 'Limited Liability Unlimited' (1999) 24 Del. J. Corp. L. 407.

Rinze, Jens, 'Konzernrecht: Law on Groups of Companies in Germany' (1993) 14 Comp. Law. 143.

Rivera, F., 'A Response to the Corporate Campaign Against the Alien Tort Claims Act' (2003–2004) 14 Ind. Int'l & Comp. L. Rev. 251.

Rixon, F.G., 'Lifting The Veil Between Holding and Subsidiary Companies' (1986) 102 L.Q.R. 415.

Robertson, D.E., 'Uberseering: the Nailing the Coffin on Sitztheorine' (2003) Comp. Law 184.

Robertson, D.W., 'Forum Non Conveniens in America and England: A Rather Fantastic Fiction' (1987) 103 Law Quarterly Review 398.

Robertson, D.W., 'The Federal Doctrine of Forum Non Conveniens' (1994) 29 Texas ILJ 353.

Rocencrantz, N., 'The Parent Trap: Using The Good Samaritan Doctrine to Hold Parent Corporations Directly Liable for Their Negligence' (1996) 37 Boston collage L.R. 1061.

Rogers, S., 'Corporate Law: Looking to Federal Common Law to Determine Parent Corporation Liability under Cercla – United States v. Kayser-Roth Corp' (1991) 4 U. Fla. J.L. & Pub. Pol'y 123.

Rolle, Mary Elliott, 'United States v. Bestfoods: Clarifying Parent Corporation Liability under CERCLA' (1999) 6 Wis. Envtl. L.J. 145.

Rosencranz, Armin, 'Foreign Environmental and Human Rights Suits Against U.S. Corporations in U.S. Courts' (1999) 18 Stan. Envtl. L.J. 145.

Rosenthal, Linda and Raper, Carol, 'Amoco Cadiz and Limitation of Liability for Oil Spill Pollution: Domestic and International Solutions' (1985–1986) 5 Va. J. Nat. Resources L. 259.

Roth, Wulf-Henning, 'From Centros to Uberseering: Free Movement of Companies, Private International Law and Community Law' (2003) ICLQ 178.

Sacharoff, Ariadne K, 'Multinationals in Host Countries: Can They Be Held Liable under the Alien Tort Claims Act for Human Rights Violations' (1997–1998) 23 Brook. J. Int'l L. 927.

Salazar, C.T., 'Applying International Human Rights Norms in the United States; Holding Multinational Corporations Accountable in the Unites States for International Human Rights Violations Under the Alien Tort Claims Act' (2004–2005) 19 St. John's Legal Comment 111.

Sandrock, Otto, 'Arbitration Agreements and Group of Companies' (1993) 27 International Lawyer 941.

Sargent, N.C., 'Beyond the Legal Entity Doctrine: Parent Subsidiary Under the West-German Konzernrecht' (1985) 10 Canadian Business Law Journal 327.

Schenck, Daniel W., 'Jurisdiction over the Foreign Multinational in the EEC: Lifting the Veil on the Economic Entity Theory' (1989–1990) 11 U. Pa. J. Int'l Bus. L. 495.

Schiessl, M., 'The Liability of Corporations and Shareholders for the Capitalization and Obligations of Subsidiaries Under German Law' (1986) 7 Nw J. Int'l L & Bus. 480.

Schipani, Cindy A., 'Integrating Corporate Law Principles with Cercla Liability for Environmental Hazards' (1993) 18 Del. J. Corp. L. 1.

Schwartz, Alan, 'Products Liability, Corporate Structure, and Bankruptcy: Toxic Substances and the Remote Risk Relationship' (1985) 14 Journal of Legal Studies 689.

Seeger, Karolos and Friel, Steven, 'Challenge Under Section 67 of the Arbitration Act 1996' (2004) 7 Int. A.L.R. 39.

Sen, J., 'Can Defects of Natural Justice be cured by Appeal? Union Carbide v. Union of India' (1993) 42 ICLQ 369.

Seven, V. and Goksoy, C., Ticaret Sirketlerinde Tüzel Kisilik Perdesinin Kaldrılması, 2006, (80 (6)) Istanbul Barosu Dergisi 1.

Shamir, R., 'Between Self-Regulation and the Alien Tort Claims Act: On the Contested Concept of Corporate Social Responsibility' (2004) 38 Law and Society Review 4.

Shaw, Courtney, 'Uncertain Justice: Liability of Multinationals Under the Alien Tort Claims Act' (2001–2002) 54 Stan. L. Rev. 1359.

Shew, Dianna Baker, 'United States-Based Multinational Corporations Should Be Tried in the United States for Their Extraterritorial Toxic Torts' (1986) 19 Vand. J. Transnat'l L. 651.

Sigvard, Jarvin, 'The Group of Companies Doctrine and the Law Applicable to the Arbitration Agreement' (2004) 19(6) Int'l Arb. Rep. 47.

Siig, K.M. 'Multi-Party Arbitration in International Trade: Problems and Solutions', (2007) 1 Int. J. Liability and Scientific Enquiry, 72–84.

Silecchia, Lucia Ann, 'Pinning the Blame and Piercing the Veil in the Mists of Metaphor: The Supreme Court's New Standards for the CERCLA Liability of Parent Companies and a Proposal for Legislative Reform' (1998–1999) 67 Fordham L. Rev. 115.

Slawotsku, J., 'Doing Business around the World: Corporate Liability under the Alien Tort Claims Act' (2005) Mich. St. L. Rev. 1065.

Snow, C.C., Miles R.E. and Coleman H.J., 'Managing 21st Century Network Organisations' (1992) (Winter) Organizational Dynamics 5.

Sorensen, K.E., 'Prospects for European Company Law after the Judgement of the European Court of Justice in Centros Ltd' (1999) Cambridge Yearbook of European Legal Studies 203.

Stallworthy, Mark, 'Environmental Liability and the Impact of Statutory Authority' (2003) 15 J. Env. L. 3.

Stender, Jens Christopher, 'Company Law (Case Comment) Germany: Company Law – Lifting the Corporate Veil' (1999) 10 ICCLR 71.

Stephens, Beth, 'Corporate Liability: Enforcing Human Rights through Domestic Litigation' (2000–2001) 24 Hastings Int'l & Comp. L. Rev. 401.

Stohlmeir, Thomas, 'German Limited Liability Company – Unlimited Liability of Parent Company?' (1993) 21 Int'l Bus. Law. 135.

Stone, Alicia, 'Parent Corporate Liability for Hazardous Substance Release from On-Shore Facilities in the International Market: Legal Approaches of the United States, the European Community and Germany' (1992) 12 In Pub. Interest 57.

Stovall, A.C., 'Limiting Operator Liability for Parent Corporations under CERCLA: United States v. Cordova Chemical Co.' (1998) 43 Vill. L. Rev. 219.

Strasser, K.A. and Blumberg, P.I. 'Replacing Misused Limited Liability with Enterprise Analysis in Corporate Groups' (Conference on Corporate Accountability, Limited Liability, and the Future of Globalization, School of Oriental and African Studies, London, UK, 20–21 July 2007).

Suen, Wing, 'Risk Avoidance under Limited Liability' (1995) 65 Journal of Economic Theory 627.

Sutphin, Robert J. Jr., 'Environmental Law – Owners or Operators: Two Distinct Paths to Parent Corporation Liability under CERCLA – United States v. Bestfoods' (2000) 30 N.M. L. Rev. 109.

Swain, J.A. and Aguilar E.E., 'Piercing the Veil to Assert Personal Jurisdiction over Corporate Affiliates: An Empirical Study of the Cannon Doctrine' (2004) 84 B.U. L. Rev. 445.

Tekil, Muge, (in Turkish) 'Rozenblum Karari ve Grup Cikari Karari' (2006) 10 HPD 213.

Thompson, R.B., 'Piercing the Corporate Veil: An Empirical Study' (1990–1991) 76 Cornell L. Rev. 1036.

Thompson, R.B., 'Unpacking Limited Liability: Direct and Vicarious Liability of Corporate Participants for Torts of the Enterprise (1994) 47 Vand. L. Rev. 1.

Thompson, R.B., 'Limits of Liability in the New Limited Liability Entities' (1997) 32 Wake Forest L. Rev. 1.

Thompson, R.B., 'Piercing the Veil within Corporate Groups: Corporate Shareholders as Mere Investors' (1999) 13 Connecticut Journal of International Law 379.

Tolentino, P.E., 'Hierarchical Pyramids and Heterarchical Networks: Organizational Structures of Multinational Corporations and Its Impact on World Development' (2002) 21 Contrib. Pol. Economy 69.

Townsend, J., 'Signatories and Arbitration' (1998) 3 ADR Currents 19.

Tully, Stephen, 'Company Law: The 2000 Review of the OECD Guidelines for Multinational Enterprises' (2001) 50(2) ICLQ 394.

Tung, Frederick, 'Limited Liability and Creditors' Rights: The Limits of Risk Shifting to Creditors' (1999–2000) 34 Ga. L. Rev. 547.

Udwadia, S., 'Corporate Responsibility for International Human Rights Violations'(2003–2004) 13 Cal. Interdisc. L.J. 359.

Voets, Henk J.L. and Biggiero Lucio, 'Globalization and Self-organization: The Consequences of Decentralization for Industrial Organ' (2000) 10 International Review of Sociology 73.

Wallace, R.M.M. and Martin-Ortega Olga, 'The UN Norms: A First Step to Universal Regulation of Transnational Corporations' Responsibilities for Human Rights?' (2004) 26 Dublin U.L.J. 304.

Ward, Halina, 'Securing Transnational Corporate Accountability through National Courts: Implications and Policy Options' (2000–2001) 24 Hastings Int'l & Comp. L. Rev. 451.

Warsh, Kevin M., 'Corporate Spinoffs and Mass Tort Liability' (1995) Colum. Bus. L. Rev. 675.

Weber-Rey, Daniela, 'Germany: Company Law: Piercing Corporate Veil' (1996) 11 JIBL 73.

Wedderburn, L., 'Multinationals and the Antiquities of Company Law' (1984) 47 MLR 87.

Weinstein, Mark I., 'Limited liability in California' (2005) 7 American Law and Economics Review 439.

Weisbrodt, D. and Kruger, M., 'Current Developments: Norms on the Responsibilities of Transnational Corporations and Other Business Enterprises with Regard to Human Rights' (2003) 97 American Journal of International Law 901.

Weissberg, M., 'Piercing The Corporate Veil In France' (1987) Int. Fin. L. Rev. 33.

Werlauff, E., 'EC Company Law' (1998) EBLR 169.

Werlauff, E., 'Using a Foreign Company for Domestic Activities' (1999) 10 EBLR 306.

Werlauff, E., 'The SE Company – A New Common European Company' (2003) EBLR 85.

Westbrook, Jay Lawrence, 'Theories of Parent Company Liability and the Prospects for an International Settlement' (1985) 20 Tex. Int'l L. J. 321.

Westbrook, Jay Lawrence, 'Global Solution to Multinational Default' (1999–2000) 98 Mich. L. Rev. 2276.

Whincup, Michael, 'Inequitable Incorporation – the Abuse of a Privilege' (1981) 2 Company Lawyer 158.

Williamson, O.E., 'The Modern Corporation: Origins, Evaluation and Attributes' (1981) Journal of Economic Literature 1537.

Williamson, O.E., 'Comparative Economic Organization: The Analysis of Discrete Structural Alternatives' (1991) 36 Administrative Science Quarterly 269.

Williamson, O.E., 'Strategizing, Economizing, and Economic Organization' (1991) 12 Strategic Management Journal 75.

Windbichler, Christine, '"Corporate Group Law For Europe": Comment on the Forum Europeaum's Principles Proposal for a European Corporate Group Law' (2000) 1 EBOR 265.

Woodward, Susan E., 'Limited Liability in the Theory of the Firm' (1985) 14 J. Institutional & Theoretical Econ. 601.

Wooldridge, F., 'The Position of Minority Shareholders and Creditors in French Companies Belonging to a Group of Companies' (1988) 9 Comp. Law 225.

Wooldridge, F., 'Closely Integrated De Facto Groups under German Law' (1992) 3 EBLR 67.

Wooldridge, F., 'Connected Undertakings and Groups of Undertakings Under German Law' (1995) 24 Anglo-American Law Review 57.

Wooldridge, F., 'The Situation of Dependent GmbH in a de facto Group in German Law' (1996) Journal of Business Law 627.

Wooldridge, F., 'Uberseering: Freedom of Establishment of Companies Affirmed' (2003) EBLR 227.

Woolhouse, S.P., 'Group of Companies Doctrine and English Arbitration Law' (2004) 20 International Arbitration 435.

Worden, J.S.G., 'CERCLA Liability of Parent Corporations for the Acts of Their Subsidiaries' (1993–1994) 30 Idaho L. Rev. 73.

Wouters, J., 'European Company Law: Quo Vadis?' (2000) 37 CML Rev. 257.

Wouters, J., 'Private International Law and Companies' Freedom of Establishment' (2001) EBOR 101.

Wymeersch, E., 'The Transfer of the Company's Seat in European Community Law' (2003) 40 CMLR 690.

Wymeersch, Eddy, 'Financial Institutions as a Member of Company Groups in the Law of the European Union' (2001) EBOR 81.

Xanthaki, H., 'Centros: Is This Really the End for the Theory of the Siege Real' (2001) Comp. Law. 2.

Yavasi, Mahmut, 'Limited Liability Companies in Turkish Company Law' (1997) International Company and Commercial Law Review 392.

Yeo, Eric L., 'United States v. Bestfoods: Narrowing Parent Corporation Liability under CERCLA for the Twenty-First Century' (1999) 51 Admin. L. Rev. 1267.

Zia-Zarifi, Saman, 'Suing Multinational Corporations in the U.S. for Violating International Law' (1999–2000) 4 UCLA J. Int'l L. & Foreign Aff. 81.

## INTERNET SOURCES

ABB, http://www.abb.com.

Alarik, B., 'From M-form to N-form: The Structure of Multinational Enterprises' (FE-rapport 2000-378) http://swoba.hhs.se/gunwba/papers/gunwba2000_378.pdf accessed 22 June 2006.

Amnesty International, 'Human Rights on the Line', http://www.amnestyusa.org/business/humanrightsontheline.pdf accessed 22 June 2006..

Andersson, U., Bjorkman, I. and Forsgren, M., 'Explaining Subsidiary Network Embeddedness: The Impact of Headquarters Control Mechanisms' (Uppsala University Working Paper, 2002), available at http://www.aueb.gr/deos/EIBA2002.files/PAPERS/W24.pdf accessed at 13 January 2005.

Barters, F.L., 'Multinationals in International Equity Joint Ventures' (Nanyang Business School, 10 November 1999, S3-B1C-94), available at http://www.ntu.edu.sg/nbs/sabre/working_papers/08-99.pdf.

Bayer, www.bayer.com.

Bhopal Tragedy, http://news.bbc.co.uk/1/hi/programmes/bhopal/default.stm,.

Bhopal, www.bhopal.net.

BP http://www.bp.com/productlanding.do?categoryId=6900&contentId=7028276.

Burma Report at www.guardian.co.u/burma, and the *Guardian*, 15 December 2004.

Business and Human Rights, http://www.business-humanrights.org/Categories/Lawlawsuits/Lawsuitsregulatoryaction/AlienTortClaimsActUSA?&&batch_start=21.

Christian Aid International, www.christianaid.org.
Christian Aid, 'Behind the Mask: the Real Face of Corporate Social Responsibility' (Christian Aid, January 2004), http://www.christianaid.org.uk/indepth/0401csr/csr_behindthemask.pdf accessed 24 June 2006.
Collingsworth, T., 'Recent ILRF, Cases to Enforce Human Rights Under the ATCA' (International Civil Liberties Report 2001), available at http://sdshh.com/ICLR/ICLR_2003/16_Collingsworth.pdf).
Commentary by the ICC Chairmanship, Extra-territorial Application of National Laws (Department of Policy and Business Practices, December, 2002), at http://www.iccwbo.org/id506/index.html?cookies=no accessed 27 June 2006.
Controlling Corporate Wrongs: The Liability of Multinational Corporations (IRENE, 20 March 2000) available at http://www.irene-network.nl/download/wrongs.pdf.
CORE http://www.corporate-responsibility.org/.
CORE, 'Companies Act 2006 – Verdict, A Move Towards Making Business Work for People and Planet' available at http://www.corporate-responsibility.org/module_images/CompaniesBill_verdict.doc.
CSR Europe at http://www.csreurope.org/.
Fair Trade Project at Queen Mary, University of London at http://www.qmul-fairtradeproject.org/.
Ferran, Eilis, 'Company Law Reform in the UK: A Progress Report' (ECGI – Law Working Paper No 27, March 2005) http://ssrn.com/abstract=644203.
Friends of Earth, 'Behind the Shine: The Other Shell Report 2003' available at http://www.foei.org/publications/pdfs/shell_shine.pdf.
Friends of Earth, Make Business Work for People and Planet Companies Bill Verdict (November 2006) at http://www.foe.co.uk/resource/newsletters/companies_act_2006.pdf.
Griswold, Daniel T, 'Abuse of 18th Century Law Threatens U.S. Economic and Security Interests' (Cato Institute, 25 January 2003), at http://www.cato.org/dailys/01-25-03.html accessed 27 June 2006,.
Gurak, H., 'Multinational Enterprises and Foreign Direct Investments', available at http://129.3.20.41/eps/get/papers/0404/0404004.pdf.
http://www.kimberleyprocess.com/.
http://www.shell.com/home/Framework?siteId=in-en&FC2=&FC3=/in-en/html/iwgen/about_shell/who_we_are/structure_of_shell_ga_1011.html.
http://www.texacorainforest.com.
Human Rights Watch, 'The Price of Oil: Corporate Responsibility and Human Rights Violations in Nigeria's Oil Producing Communities, http://www.hrw.org/reports/1999/nigeria/ accessed 25 June 2006.
Hurriyet, (Istanbul, 04. September, 2005), http://www.hurriyetim.com.tr/haber/0,,sid~4@nvid~626118,00.asp accessed 27 June 2006.

International Council on Human Rights and Policy, Beyond Voluntarism: Human rights and the developing of international legal obligations for companies, at http://www.ichrp.org/paper_files/107_p_02.pdf.

IRENE, 'Controlling Corporate Wrongs: The Liability of Multinational Corporations' (IRENE, 21 March 2000), http://www.indianet.nl/irene.html.

James, A.P. and Jason, G., 'Making Corporations Accountable, A Background Paper for the United Nations Financing for Development Process' (Global Policy Forum, December, 2000), http://www.globalpolicy.org/socecon/ffd/2000papr.htm accessed 25 June 2006.

Jurisdiction Over Corporations (Committee on International Civil and Commercial Litigation), available at http://www.ila-hq.org/pdf/Civil%20&%20Commercial%20Litigation/Civil%20&%20Commercial%20Litigation%20Resolution%202002%20English.pdf.

Kleinert, J., The Role of Multinationals in Globalisation (Kiel Working Papers No 1069), at http://www.uni-kiel.de/ifw/pub/kap/2001/kap1069.pdf.

Lipsey, Robert E., 'Foreign Direct Investment and the Operations of Multinational Firms: Concepts, History, and Data' Cambridge, MA, National Bureau of Economic Research, 2001), available at http://papers.nber.org/papers/w8665.pdf.

Mazurkiewicz, P., 'Corporate Environmental Responsibility; Is a Common CSR Framework Possible?', http://www.worldbank.org/developmentcommunications/Publications/csrframework.pdf, accessed 13 January 2006.

Multinational Enterprises and Foreign Direct Investments at http://econwpa.wustl.edu:8089/eps/get/papers/0404/0404004.pdf accessed 20 February 2005.

Oxfam America, 'Global Finance Hurts the Poor' (Oxfam America, 2002), http://www.oxfamamerica.org/newsandpublications/publications/research_reports/art2613.html/OA-Global_Finance_Hurts_Poor.pdf.

Parmer, Alice, 'Community Redress and Multinational Enterprises' FIELD, November 2003) at http://www.christian-aid.org.uk/indepth/311field/field.pdf.

Phil, Hakan, 'A New Organizational Form in Multinational Enterprises', available at http://www.aueb.gr/deos/EIBA2002.files/PAPERS/W21.pdf.

Phil, Hakan, 'On the Idealised Institutional Evaluation Of Organizational Forms', available at http://www.hkr.se/avdld/2/doc/wp2003_8.pdf.

Ross, J.P., 'Sempra: Exporting Pollution, U.S.-Mexico Border Region to Pay the Price for California's Power', http://www.corpwatch.org/article.php?id=2588.

Shell Nigeria CSR Report at http://www.shell.com/home/content/nigeria/news_and_library/publications/annual_reports_archive.html.

Shell, www.shell.com.

Stephen, Timms (MP) as the Minister for Corporate Social Responsibility within the Department of Trade and Industry (DTI) Corporate Social Responsibility, http://www.dti.gov.uk/ministers/archived/Timms131202.html#related.

Tavares, A.T., 'Strategic Management of Multinational Networks: A Subsidiary Evaluation Perspective' (University of Porto) at http://www.ifm.eng.cam.ac.uk/cim/imnet/symposium2001/papers/tavares.pdf accessed 25 June 2006.

The Activities of Transnational Corporations: The Need for a Legal Framework (Geneva, July 2001), http://attac.org.uk/attac/document/transnationals-legal-framework.pdf?documentID=41.

The Center for Constitutional Rights Historic Advance for Universal Human Rights: Unocal to Compensate Burmese Villagers at http://ccrjustice.org/newsroom/press-releases/historic-advance-universal-human-rights:-unocal-compensate-burmese-villagers.

The Directorate General for Internal Market and Services Consultation and public hearing on future priorities for the Action Plan at http://ec.europa.eu/internal_market/company/consultation/index_en.htm#060706.

The *Guardian* http://www.guardian.co.uk/environment/corporatesocialresponsibility.

Towards Binding Corporate Accountability (FoEI position paper for the WSSD January 2002), http://www.foe.co.uk/resource/briefings/corporate_accountability.pdf accessed 27 June 2006.

UN Global Compact, www.unglobalcompact.org.

Weinstein, Mark Ira, 'Limited Liability in California: 1928–1931' (September 2000, USC Law School, Olin Research Paper No 00-17; and USC Finance and Business Econ. Working Paper No 01-13. Available at SSRN: http://ssrn.com/abstract=244333).

Wouters, Jan, de Smet Leen and Ryngaert Cedric, 'Tort Claims Against Multinational Companies for Foreign Human Rights Violations Committed Abroad: Lessons from the Alien Torts Claim Act' (Institute for International Law, Working Paper No 46, November, 2003) at http://www.law.kuleuven.ac.be/iir/nl/wp/WP/WP46e.pdf.

www.csr.gov.uk.

# Index